THE
FRENCH
DEFENCE

Svetozar Gligoric

with the collaboration of **Wolfgang Uhlmann**

introduction by **Mikhail Botvinnik**

and a contribution by **Anatoly Karpov**

RHM PRESS
a division of RHM Associates of Delaware, Inc.
220 Fifth Avenue, New York, N.Y. 10001

Library of Congress Catalog Card No: 75-8368

ISBN 0-89058-010-3

Photosetting by Quickset, 89-97, St. John Street, London, EC1M 4AS.
Printed in the United States of America

SPECIAL ANNOUNCEMENT

The reader's attention is directed to the back of this book where we describe in full the whole concept of THE RHM SURVEY OF CURRENT CHESS OPENINGS.

With a world-renowned Editorial Board which includes Anatoly Karpov, Viktor Korchnoy, Boris Spassky, Tigran Petrosian, Svetozar Gligoric, Bent Larsen, Lubosh Kavalek and other top Grandmasters, we are presenting an important new approach to the Openings in chess, which we are sure you will find of great interest.

Please refer to the back of this book for full details.

RHM Press

Symbols

! A good move.

!! An excellent, beautiful or hard-to-find move.

? A poor move.

?? A very poor move or a blunder.

!? An interesting move, possible involving some risk.

?! A dubious move.

Acknowledgements

There are many people whom R.H.M. wish to thank for their help in the editing of this book. The original typescript by Gligoric and Uhlmann was translated from the German by **John Littlewood.** Botvinnik's introduction was translated from the Russian by **Katya Young** who also translated 22 of the illustrative games from Russian and games 7 and 21 from Hungarian. These two Hungarian games appear by kind permission of *Magyar Sakkelet.* Two other games also stem from Russian sources. The notes to part of the main game in chapter 4 are by Mikhail Tal from his excellent book of the 1960 World Championship match and the translation appears by kind permission of **Hanon Russell** who published his own translation of Tal's book. Game 39 was translated by **Dr. Ken Neat.** Games 4 and 34 originally appeared in Serbo-Croat and the translations are by **Alan Ferguson.** Game 1 is taken from *Larsen's Selected Games of Chess* by Bent Larsen and appears here by kind permission of **G. Bell and Sons.** The contribution by World Champion Anatoly Karpov was translated from the Russian by **Bernard Cafferty.**

The English manuscript was typed by **Margaret Fitzjames.** The final typescript was checked by **Svetozar Gligoric** for accuracy of content and by **Kevin O'Connell** for accuracy of typing. Kevin O'Connell also prepared most of the diagrams and read the proofs.

Publisher's Foreword

R.H.M. Press is proud to present the first volume in our series *The R.H.M. Survey of Current Chess Openings*. All the books in this series will be written by leading International Grandmasters and the material will be presented in a way that makes the books invaluable to players at all levels.

The French Defence has long been known as one of Black's most solid replies to 1 P-K4, but it was not until **Mikhail Botvinnik** successfully adopted the defence in the 1930s, and made it his principle reply to 1 P-K4, that the defence achieved the mark of respectability. Botvinnik's excellent results with the black pieces throughout his long reign as World Champion did much to popularize the French Defence, and it is therefore with particular pleasure that R.H.M. welcomes Botvinnik's introduction to this book. Botvinnik's article, "Understanding the French Defence", explains the basic ideas of the defence for all to understand, and he traces its development in order to show how and why certain variations have become popular whilst others are considered dubious.

After reading Botvinnik's introduction the reader will understand the principles of the French Defence and he will be ready to digest the main body of this book. Each chapter deals with a different main line and the authors have taken care to explain the point behind the key moves. There is sufficient in-depth analysis to give the reader a thorough understanding of each variation without swamping him with an indigestible mass of material. And in order to make the ideas behind the variations even more clearly understood, the authors have augmented the text with 72 complete, annotated games.

Svetozar Gligoric and **Wolfgang Uhlmann** rank amongst the leading International Grandmasters of today. Gligoric was an expert in the use of the French Defence during the early part of his career and at the same time he often faced it with the white pieces. Uhlmann's experience on the black side of the French Defence stretches back over twenty years and since the end of the Botvinnik era he has been its leading practitioner in the international arena, playing nothing else in reply to 1 P-K4.

Between them, our two authors possess an unrivalled understanding of the French Defence, and their expertise is clearly shown in the pages that follow. As an added and most valuable bonus to their work, R.H.M. is delighted to present a contribution by World Champion **Anatoly Karpov,** who analyses the most critical variation in current French Defence theory — the one employed in seven of the games from his match with Korchnoy at the end of 1974.

Please be sure that you read the description of THE R.H.M. SURVEY OF CURRENT CHESS OPENINGS which follows the indexes at the end of this book. As well as announcing our forthcoming titles in the series, this description will acquaint you with our new loose-leaf updating service which will, we feel certain, prove of immeasurable help to all chess players in attaining rapid forward progress in the quality of their play.

We take this opportunity to thank you for your interest in R.H.M. Press publications.

Sidney Fried
Publisher

As a **free bonus** to all readers of "The French Defence", we would like to send you, with our compliments, an additional current booklet containing twenty recent French Defence games. These games are all annotated and they have been chosen from recent tournaments to bring you up to date with the latest ideas in the French Defence that have appeared since our book went to press.

To receive this free booklet you need send only a postcard with your name and full address, specifying FRENCH DEFENCE BOOKLET, to R.H.M. Press, 840 Willis Avenue, Albertson, N.Y. 11507. European readers should send their postcards to R.H.M. Press Ltd., P.O. Box 55, London N13, England 5BE.

There is absolutely no charge. This free booklet is our way of expressing our appreciation for your support.

Contents

Understanding the French Defence
By Mikhail Botvinnik

The defence **1 P-K4 P-K3** was known long ago, but it used to be less popular than the open games arising from 1 P-K4 P-K4. La Bourdonnais introduced the move 1...P-K3 into master practice at the beginning of the last century and it was used by the Parisians to win a correspondence game London-Paris (1834-36), since when it has been called the French Defence.

For a long time no strong continuation was found for White. First of all the disadvantage of the French Defence was thought to be Black's cramped position, and attempts were made to constrict Black still further by playing **2 P-K5** and, of course, **2 P-Q4 P-Q4 3 P-K5.** Some masters interpreted the French Defence in open style and played 2 P-Q4 P-Q4 3 P×P P×P, trying to exploit the advantage of the move in the resulting symmetrical open position. From these attempts only the variation 2 P-Q4 P-Q4 3 P-K5 has stood up to the severe test of time (the exchange variation 3 P×P P×P is now only played as a drawing line).

In time it was concluded that White's QN should be developed, and the MacCutcheon variàtion appeared **(2 P-Q4 P-Q4 3 N-QB3 N-KB3 4 B-KN5 B-QN5),** along with its "blood-brother" **4...B-K2.** Capablanca himself played the MacCutcheon variation with White. The Tarrasch variation **3 N-Q2** also saw the light of day. Chigorin's innovation **2 Q-K2** (which leads to a closed game of similar character to the King's Indian Reversed) stood apart from other systems. It is curious that Chigorin, who was such a conoisseur of open games (the Giuoco Piano, Evans' Gambit, King's Gambit, etc.), interpreted the French Defence as a closed opening when playing White.

Rubinstein tried to create a drawing weapon for Black from the French Defence, and after **2 P-Q4 P-Q4 3 N-QB3** he played **3...P×P,** avoiding all complications. This continuation has never been especially popular, as it offers Black few ways of obtaining any counterplay.

To be quite frank, the real history of the French Defence starts with Nimzovich. Along with Reti, Grunfeld and Alekhine he was the author of many new ideas in the opening, in which his basic concept was the control of the centre by pieces in conjunction with an attack on the centre by pawns. Nimzovich applied these ideas, which originated at the beginning of this century, to the theory and practice of the French Defence. He breathed new life into the old variation **1 P-K4 P-K3 2 P-Q4 P-Q4 3 P-K5 P-QB4;** before his time White automatically responded **4 P-QB3** in order to keep a pawn on the central square Q4, whereas Nimzovich's reply was **4 N-KB3,** using the Q4 square for piece play. The variation **4...P×QP 5 Q×P! N-QB3 6 Q-KB4** was considered to be good for White for a long time. It was only in the games Levenfish-Botvinnik (USSR 1937), where there followed: **4...N-QB3 5 B-Q3** or 5 P×P B×P **5...P×P 6 O-O B-B4!!**

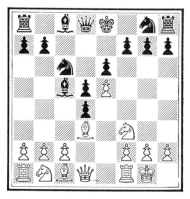

7 QN-Q2 KN-K2 8 N-N3 B-N3 9 B-KB4 N-N3, and Bondarevsky-Botvinnik (USSR 1941), which continued **7 P-QR3 KN-K2 8 QN-Q2 N-N3 9 N-N3 B-N3,** that the Nimzovich Variation suffered a blow. It transpires that if Black plays ...B-QB4 then it is he, and not White, who gets control of the centre, so that White's main idea cannot be effected.

Even though Nimzovich did not manage to improve White's play radically in the French Defence, he achieved astonishing results for Black in the variation **1 P-K4 P-K3 2 P-Q4 P-Q4 3 N-QB3 B-N5.** At first this variation was viewed as a sort of eccentricity. At the beginning of my chess career, when I blindly trusted authority, under the influence of games from the New York tournament of 1924 I played this variation as White with great pleasure, for example, against Ragozin in 1927: **4 P-K5 P-KB3** At that time players were influenced by the game Lasker-Maroczy, New York 1924, in which White obtained the better game after 4...P-QB4. Nowadays it is well known that 4...P-QB4 is stronger. **5 N-B3 P-QB4 6 P-QR3 B-R4 7 P-QN4 P×NP 8 N-QN5 N-B3 9 RP×P** with advantage to White. Botvinnik-Ragozin, Leningrad 1937. However, a mere two months after that game I started playing the variation 3...B-N5 as Black. In this the decisive influence was that of Master A.Model, who was a great believer in this variation for Black. It is true that my first attempt was rather unhappy: I fell prey to a non-chess trick, though I did at least gain some essential experience thereby. The variation was still viewed with suspicion for a few more years, and it was only at Hastings (1934/35) in my game against Milner-Barry that I "mastered" it: **1 P-K4 P-K3 2 P-Q4 P-Q4 3 N-QB3 B-N5 4 P-K5 P-QB4 5 P-QR3 B×Nch 6 P×B N-K2 7 N-B3 QN-B3 8 B-K2 B-Q2 9 O-O Q-B2 10 R-N1 P-B5 11 N-K1 O-O-O 12 P-B4 P-B3**

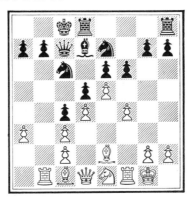

⌜How many inaccuracies can a contemporary master detect in White's play! White has omitted, for example, to play P-QR4 followed by B-R3; also, the move 12 P-B4 is a mistake on principle: it limits the sphere of action of the white pieces and weakens the light squares. The above position is commonplace and stereotyped for the contemporary master, but it was quite a rare sight in those days and it is not surprising that Milner-Barry started sinking. The pawns which block the position bisect the board into two parts. White can only transfer his strength from one flank to the other through the square QB1, while it is much easier for Black to manoeuvre. Besides, the weakness of White's Q-side pawns is quite obvious. White does not have any real compensation for these disadvantages.

If White does not make the above-mentioned mistakes then his position is not too bad. One can, for example, follow Antoshin (Antoshin-Botvinnik, USSR 1955): **6 P×B Q-B2 7 N-B3 N-K2 8 B-Q3 N-Q2 9 O-O P-B5 10 B-K2 N-QN3 11 N-K1!** This is the heart of the matter: the knight is preparing the journey N-K1-N2-B4. **11...N-R5 12 B-Q2 B-Q2 13 P-N3 O-O-O 14 N-N2**

Fischer also prefers this variation for White. It requires a subtle positional struggle and the person who has prepared the better middle-game plan (before the game!) usually wins. In the thirties and forties, when very few people understood these positions, the variation worked wonderfully. How many games I managed to win at the most decisive moments in those years!

It should be noted that deviation from the strongest continuation **4 P-K5** does not bring White any particular advantage. White has played **4 B-Q3** as well as **4 P-QR3 B×Nch 5 P×B P×P 6 Q-N4** and lastly **4 N-K2**. **4 B-Q3** looks quite harmless, but **4 P-QR3** has been played by quite a few great players (suffice it to mention Alekhine, Smyslov, Keres and Fischer); nevertheless, by giving up his KNP Black can come out of the opening quite satisfactorily. The quiet continuation **4 N-K2** was fruitful for a time until Alatortsev, in the thirties, found the strong move **8...N-B3** in the variation **4...P×P 5 P-QR3 B-K2 6 N×P N-KB3 7 N(K2)-B3 O-O 8 B-K2**.

If now **9 B-K3** then **9...N×N 10 N×N P-B4** followed by ...P-B5 and ...N×P. Thus, in the variation 4 N-K2 Black gets an equal game.

Smyslov has often played **4 P-QR3** against me (as in the Alekhine-Euwe match in 1935): after **4...B×Nch 5 P×B P×P 6 Q-N4 N-KB3 7 Q×NP R-N1 8 Q-R6 P-B4 9 N-K2 R-N3**

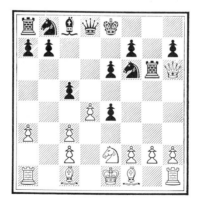

White does not achieve any significant advantage. This conclusion also applies to another method of defence by Black, which was played in the more recent game Fischer-Kovacevic, Rovinj/Zagreb 1970: **8...P-N3 9 N-K2 QN-Q2 10 B-N5 Q-K2 11 Q-R4 B-N2 12 N-N3 P-KR3** (see game 4, page 46).

Thus, taking everything into account, the continuation **4 P-K5** is the strongest.

For a long time the following was the main variation: **1 P-K4 P-K3 2 P-Q4 P-Q4 3 N-QB3 B-N5 4 P-K5 P-QB4 5 P-QR3 B×Nch 6 P×B N-K2 7 Q-N4 P×P.** Fine had shown that 7...N-B4 8 B-Q3 P-KR4 9 Q-B4 was to White's advantage. **8 Q×NP R-N1 9 Q×RP**

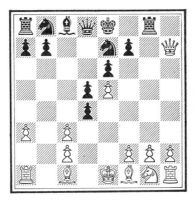

Players of the white pieces used to avoid this continuation while I, playing Black, was aiming for it. This continued up to the radio-match USSR-Great Britain (1946), when I was badly defeated by Alexander. It was foolish on my part, of course, to play such a system in a radio-match. All these systems are for practical play, where one has to make forty moves in two and a half hours and the depth of the game corresponds to that speed. In a radio game everything happens at least twice as slowly and so in the first half of the game (before the participants become too tired) a deeper game is possible. Alexander's play was very subtle and I did not manage to overcome my difficulties. The greatest blow was that everybody, at last, perceived the inadequacies of the system and became braver. It is true that since then Uhlmann has analyzed this variation in great detail and played it as Black not without sucess, but that is credit to him alone! This system can no longer meet the demands of the arsenal of the contemporary tournament soldier. It has become bound up with sophisticated research which is hardly accessible to the practical chessplayer.

The need, therefore, arose for a new system, and one was found based on the variation **4...P-QB4 5 P-QR3 B-R4** (which was rejected by Alekhine in the tournament book of New York 1924). This variation lived a few years until Smyslov, in the ninth game of our 1954 World Championship match, played **6 P-QN4 P×QP 7 Q-N4!** and proved that White has plentiful opportunities.

So I had to stop playing that variation.

But here was another idea! To try to defend the KNP with the queen by means of **4...P-QB4 5 P-QR3 B×Nch 6 P×B Q-B2 7 Q-N4 P-B4** (as in my game against Reshevsky back in 1948). In 1957, in the fourteenth game of our match, Smyslov did not take the KNP after **8 Q-N3 N-K2** and he did not achieve anything; in 1960 and 1961, however, in the first and twelfth games of my match and return match respectively against Tal, he played **9 Q×NP!** and won both times. So this variation had to go into the archives as well, but even so it had done its duty. Thus the variation **4...P-QB4 5 P-QR3 B×Nch 6 P×B N-K2 7 Q-N4 P×P** (which Uhlmann has played several times) has proved to have the best chance of survival after all.

The system without the move ...P-QB4 also deserves attention: Black plays **4...Q-Q2** followed by ...N-QB3 and if 5 Q-N4 (or 5 P-QR3) then he can play 5...B-B1. This defence has not, however, achieved wide popularity.

While the Nimzovich Variation (3...B-N5) was in its infancy, the MacCutcheon Variation gradually disappeared from practice, apparently because after **3 N-QB3 N-KB3 4 B-KN5 B-N5 5 P-K5 P-KR3 6 B-Q2**, Black has few opportunities for counterplay.

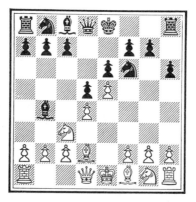

The other sub-division of this line, **4...B-K2**, has shown greater signs of life, thanks largely to the efforts of the Swedish Grandmaster Stahlberg who championed Black's defence in this line for many years. However, Alekhine successfully played **5 P-K5 KN-Q2 6 P-KR4,** when it is risky for Black to accept the pawn. Also quite good for White is **6 B×B Q×B 7 P-B4** because here too Black's counterplay is very limited.

TARRASCH VARIATION

Now let us consider the Tarrasch variation, which is still popular. When White thinks of safety first the move **3 N-Q2** suggests itself. If **3...P-QB4 4 KP×P KP×P 5 KN-B3 N-QB3 6 B-N5 B-Q3 7 P×P B×BP 8 O-O N-K2 9 N-N3** and the weakness of the QP and of Q5 makes White's chances preferable.

White's task is now to exchange the minor pieces (and first of all, the dark-squared bishops), which will facilitate the attack on the pawn at Q5 and the conquest of the Q4 square. A classical example of White's play is found in the eighteenth game of the Karpov-Korchnoy match, 1974 (see page 242).

If Black refrains from playing **3...P-QB4,** then the battle has more to it, but White still keeps the advantage. The move **3...N-QB3** suffered a serious blow in the game Botvinnik-Boleslavsky, USSR 1945 (and by the way Keres achieved a quick victory against me with this variation in 1955). More attention should be paid to the continuation **3...N-KB3 4 P-K5 N(B3)-Q2.** In the game Abramian-Botvinnik, USSR 1938, after **5 B-Q3 P-QN3 6 Q-K2** Otherwise 6...B-R3 **6...P-QB4 7 P-QB3 P×P 8 P×P N-QB3 9 KN-B3 N-N5** Black solved all his opening problems by exchanging White's light-squared bishop.

In the sixth game of our match in 1940, Ragozin played **4 P-K5 N(B3)-Q2 5 B-Q3 P-QB4 6 P-QB3** against me, and after **6...P-QN3,** instead of 7 Q-K2 transposing to the Abramian game, he played **7 N-K2,** which for a time was thought to be stronger. Against Ragozin I played **7...B-R3 8 B×B N×B 9 O-O P-N3,** and White continued strongly with **10 N-B3 B-N2 11 B-N5 Q-B1 12 Q-Q2 P-KR3 13 B-K3 Q-N2,** whereupon **14 P-KR4!** would have given him the advantage. In

1952 I improved on 9...P-N3, playing **9...N-B2!** against Tolush who was unable to achieve anything. Subsequently a strong move was found for White: **5 P-KB4!** and after **5...P-QB4 6 P-B3 N-QB3 7 N(Q2)-B3** White's outlook is quite favourable (for instance, 7...B-K2 8 B-Q3 Q-R4 9 K-B1). Uhlmann, however, has his own opinion on the matter and stubbornly (and not without success) continues to play this variation. Uhlmann's courage and conviction in playing the French Defence deserve full credit and the French Chess Federation should somehow have recognized it long ago!

Lastly I want to mention two deviations from the move 2 P-Q4. The first is the move **2 Q-K2** which was introduced to tournament practice by Chigorin (who has quite a few original ideas to his credit in opening theory) at the end of the last century. Fifty years elapsed before one of the shortcomings of this move became clear: in the game Stoltz-Botvinnik, Groningen 1946, the queen's position proved to be awkward after: **2...P-QB4 3 P-KN3** 3 P-QN3 is somewhat stronger. **3...N-QB3 4 B-N2 KN-K2 5 N-QB3 P-KN3 6 P-Q3 B-N2 7 B-K3 P-Q4! 8 P×P N-Q5!**

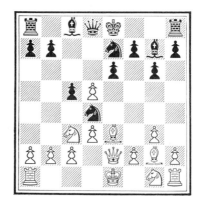

The move **2 P-Q3** sets Black a more complex task. The idea is to play the King's Indian Defence with colours reversed (and so with an extra tempo) with the addition of the inappropriate move P-K3 by Black. In 1955 Reshevsky played this move against me; and a year later I played it against Uhlmann. In the latter game the continuation was quite original for that time: **2...P-Q4 3 N-Q2 N-KB3 4 KN-B3 P-B4 5 P-KN3 N-B3 6 B-N2 B-K2 7 O-O O-O 8 R-K1 R-N1 9 P-K5 N-Q2 10 N-B1 P-QN4!**

In the past twenty years this variation has been repeated an enormous number of times and it is safe to judge that Black has adequate counterplay.

Towards the end of my competitive career I started losing with the French Defence against players of the very first rank and I had to give up the opening with which I had waged so many successful battles over the chessboard. What is there to be done? Everything progresses and everything changes. In the period 1941-48 I was significantly stronger than my opponents and I could permit myself to play complex and dangerous positions with Black. Then, during 1951-63, when I was *primus inter pares,* I found it necessary to choose a more solid, but less promising defence, the Caro-Kann.

Does this mean that the French Defence is fading away and that it will have no renaissance? That is unlikely. Time will pass by and a new generation will appear which is unacquainted with its subtleties; a new strong practical player will appear who will have an equally strong talent for research. His imagination and intuition will open up new ideas in the French Defence; he will try it against the ordinary masters, he will grow to like it and once again the French Defence will become a strong weapon as it was in the thirties and forties of our century. Anyway, what else is there to play? The Ruy Lopez? It has been studied even more thoroughly. The Sicilian? It is so "worn out" that in the near future it will turn into rags. The Caro-Kann? It is so difficult to tempt one's opponent into a risky attack with it.

We must, however, remember that not everybody is suited to the French Defence. The person who does not have a real chess character, who does not have the talent of a researcher or who is not prepared to work hard had better play something else! The French Defence is a difficult and dangerous opening!

M.Botvinnik
July 1975

Part One

The Nimzovich (Winawer) Variation

1	P-K4	P-K3
2	P-Q4	P-Q4
3	N-QB3	B-N5

Chapter 1

The Nimzovich (Winawer) Variation with 6...N-K2 7 Q-N4

White: Ivkov ~ *J-6/7/81*
Black: Sofrevsky

Yugoslav Championship 1962

1	P-K4	P-K3
2	P-Q4	P-Q4
3	N-QB3	B-N5

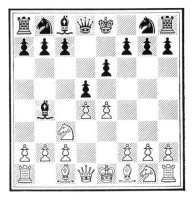

One of the main variations of the French Defence. Nimzovich achieved good results with this system, the main idea of which is to apply indirect pressure on White's K4 square without allowing White to gain time as he does after 3...N-KB3 4 P-K5 (or 4 B-KN5). This variation usually leads to the sharpest lines of the French Defence, because the frequent exchange of bishop for knight results in an unbalanced position with points of attack on both sides of the board. Whilst White normally conducts operations on the K-side, Black tries to exploit the weakened pawn position brought about by the exchange of bishop for knight on White's QB3 square. Before we examine in detail the main continuation 4 P-K5, let us consider other possibilities open to White on his fourth move.

(a)   4   B-Q3

A quiet move which in practice usually leads to equalizing exchanges.

(a1)   4...P×P   This is the simplest way of achieving full equality. **5 B×P P-QB4** Usually the alternative 5...N-KB3 simply transposes if White replies 6 B-B3 when Black can immediately try to solve his opening problems by playing 6...N-B3. After 7 N-K2 P-K4! (8 P-Q5 P-K5!) Black has already equalized. However, White should not answer 5...N-KB3 with 6 B-N5 because of 6...P-B4! giving him an unfavourable line of the MacCutcheon Variation, e.g. 7 P×P (7 N-K2 P×P 8 B×N Q×B 9 Q×P Q×Q 10 N×Q N-Q2 with equality) 7...Q×Qch 8 R×Q QN-Q2 9 B×N N×B 10 B-B3 B×P 11 KN-K2 K-K2 and Black's two bishops give him a slight edge. Lasker-Tarrasch, 1908. **6 KN-K2** Black has no problems after 6 P-QR3 B×Nch 7 P×B N-KB3 8 B-Q3 (or 8 B-B3 N-B3 with equality) 8...QN-Q2 9 N-B3 Q-B2! (or the equally good 9...P-QN3 10 O-O B-N2 11 Q-K2 O-O 12 N-K5 R-B1 13 B-KN5 N×N 14 P×N Q-Q4 15 P-KB4 P-B5, as in Tartakower-Przepiorka, Debrecen 1925) 10 O-O P-B5 11 B-K2 N-Q4 and Black's centrally posted knight on Q4 gives him slightly the better game. **6...N-KB3 7 B-B3 N-B3!** It is bad to liquidate in the centre at once, as 7...P×P 8 Q×P Q×Q 9 N×Q P-QR3 10 O-O QN-Q2 11 R-K1 O-O 12 B-Q2 R-Q1 13 P-QR3 B-Q3 14 QR-Q1 gave White a positional advantage in Gligoric-Stahlberg, Zurich 1953. **8 P-QR3** After 8 B-K3 P×P 9 N×P (better is 9 B×Nch! P×B 10 Q×P with equality) 9...N-

12

K4! 10 B-K2 N-Q4! 11 B-Q2 N×N 12 P×N B-K2! (not 12...B-R4!? 13 O-O
O-O 14 P-KB4 with attacking chances) 13 O-O O-O 14 P-KB4 N-Q2 15 B-Q3 N-
B4 16 Q-B3 B-Q2 17 QR-K1 N×B 18 P×N Q-B2 19 R-K3 B-KB3 20 Q-R5 P-KN3
21 Q-R6 B-N2 22 Q-R4 Q-Q1! Black has the better ending. Fichtl-Uhlmann,
Zinnowitz 1966. **8...B×Nch 9 P×B P-K4!** 10 B-N5 KP×P! This is more exact than
10...BP×P 11 B(B3)×Nch P×B 12 P×P P×P 13 Q×P Q-R4ch 14 Q-Q2 Q-Q4 with
a level game as in Hort-Pietzsch, Kecskemet 1964. **11 B(B3)×Nch** After 11 P×P
P-KR3 12 B(N5)×N Q×B 13 P-B3 O-O 14 O-O R-Q1 15 Q-R4 B-Q2 16 Q-B4 N-
R4! 17 Q-R2 B-N4 Black is a little better. Ortega-Uhlmann, Polanica Zdroj
1967. **11...P×B 12 P×P B-R3! 13 O-O O-O 14 R-K1 R-K1!?** Better is 14...P-R3
with a slight edge for Black. **15 N-N3!** Q×P **16 Q-B3** with an even game. Grottke-
Uhlmann, East Germany 1973.

(a2)   4...P-QB4 5 P×QP The best try for achieving a small advantage. **5...Q×P**
5...KP×P is more solid. After 6 P×P N-QB3 7 B-Q2 B×P 8 N-B3 KN-K2 9 O-O
O-O 10 B-KB4 B-KN5 Black has equalized. (After 10...N-N5 11 N-QR4 White
stands a little better). **6 B-Q2!** A dangerous pawn sacrifice suggested by
Kondratiev. Alternatives are:

(1)   6 B-QN5ch N-B3 7 N-B3 P×P 8 B×Nch Q×B 9 Q×P B×Nch with good play
for Black;
(2)   6 K-B1 (Alekhine's move) 6...B×N 7 P×B N-KB3 8 N-K2 Q-B3 9 N-B4 QN-
Q2 10 R-QN1 P-QR3 11 Q-K2 with a slight edge to White. Szily-Rethy,
Budapest 1950;
(3)   6 N-B3 P×P 7 P-QR3 B×Nch 8 P×B P×P and White has insufficient compensation for the sacrificed pawns.

6...B×N After 6...Q×QP 7 N-B3 Q-Q1 8 O-O N-KB3 9 P-QR3 B-R4 10 Q-K2 N-B3 11 QR-Q1, White's lead in development is well worth the sacrificed pawn. **7 B×B P×P** White has a strong initiative after the premature 7...Q×NP 8 Q-B3 Q×Q 9 N×Q P×P 10 N×P K-B1 (if 10...P-B3 White plays 11 R-KN1 or 11 N-N5) 11 R-KN1 P-B3 12 B-N4ch K-B2 13 N-N5. Michel-Guimard, Mar del Plata 1948. **8 B×QP Q×NP 9 Q-B3** 9 Q-Q2?! has not been tested in practical play. **9...Q×Q 10 N×Q P-B3** This is the critical position arising from the pawn sacrifice. Results so far confirm that White has good attacking chances. **11 R-KN1 K-B2 12 O-O-O N-B3 13 B-QB5 N-R3 14 N-Q2** With his two bishops, open files for the rooks and the ability to exploit Black's weak Q3 square, White is guaranteed a good game.

(b)   4 P×P A move which renounces all claims of maintaining the initiative.

4...P×P 5 Q-B3 In order to avoid symmetry Larsen experimented with this move against Portisch at the Amsterdam Interzonal, 1964 (illustrative game 1). For the less risky alternative, 5 B-Q3, see Eley-Uhlmann, Hastings 1972/3 (illustrative game 2) in which White played in too desultory a fashion.

(c)   4 B-Q2

This leads to great complications but examples from practice show that Black can accept the pawn sacrifice.

4...P×P The logical continuation, attacking the QP at once. Other lines favour White:

(1) 4...P-QB4 5 P-QR3! B×N 6 B×B N-KB3 (essential, as 6...P×QP 7 Q×P or 6...P×KP 7 P×P are clearly better for White) 7 P×BP N×P 8 B×P R-N1 9 B-Q4 N-QB3 10 N-B3 with advantage to White;

(2) 4...B×N 5 B×B P×P 6 Q-N4 N-KB3 7 Q×NP R-N1 8 Q-R6 again with the advantage;
(3) 4...N-KB3 after this move we reach a kind of MacCutcheon variation with 5 P-K5 B×N 6 P×B N-K5, the only difference being that Black's KRP is not on R3;
(4) 4...N-QB3 5 P-QR3 (the only way to keep the initiative, since 5 Q-N4 N-B3 6 Q×NP R-KN1 7 Q-R6 N×QP 8 O-O-O R-N3 9 Q-K3 P-B4 gives an equal game) 5...B×N 6 B×B N-B3 (not 6...P×P 7 P-Q5!) 7 P-K5 N-K5 8 B-Q3 with attacking chances on the K-side.

5 Q-N4 Now there are two main lines:

(c1) 5...Q×P 6 N-B3 The strongest continuation, albeit leading to speedy equality. The two main alternatives do not seem adequate:

(1) 6 O-O-O P-KR4! (6...P-KB4 7 Q-N3 [or 7 B-KN5 P×Q 8 R×Q B-K2] 7...B-Q3 8 B-KB4 B×Bch 9 Q×B Q-B4 10 P-B3 N-K2 11 P×P O-O 12 N-B3 N-Q2 13 P×P N×P 14 Q-B4! with good play, according to Keres) 7 Q-N3 (7 Q-N5 B-K2 gives the same position, and 7 Q-R4 B-K2 8 B-KN5 Q-B4 9 N×P B×B 10 N×B N-QB3 is equal. The retreat 7 Q-K2 is probably White's best chance) 7...B-Q3 8 B-KB4 P-R5! 9 Q-N4 (after 9 Q-N5 Q-B3 10 Q×Q N×Q 11 B×B P×B 12 N-N5 N-R3 13 N×QPch K-K2 Black had the better ending in Lundquist-Uhlmann, Marianske Lazne 1961) 9...N-KB3 10 Q-N5 (not 10 Q×NP?? B×Bch 11 K-N1 R-R2!) 10...B×Bch 11 Q×B Q-B4 12 N×P N×N 13 Q×N N-B3 with advantage to Black.
(2) 6 KN-K2 Q-B3! (6...Q-K4 is also possible) 7 O-O-O (or 7 Q×KP N-B3 8 O-O-O B-Q2 etc.) 7...Q-N3 8 Q-R3 N-KB3 9 P-B3 O-O and Black maintains his extra pawn.

6...N-KR3 The simplest way of equalizing. Other possibilities are:

(1) 6...P-KB4? 7 Q-R5ch P-N3 8 N×Q P×Q 9 N(B3)×P B×Bch 10 N×B and White stands better;
(2) 6...P-KR4 7 Q×P(K6)ch (7 Q-B4 comes strongly into consideration, when 7...Q-N3 would give White a clear advantage after 8 Q×KP N-QB3 9 B-QN5) 7...B×Q 8 N×Q B-Q2 9 N×P B×Bch 10 K×B N-QB3 with equality.

7 Q×P(K6)ch No final judgement has yet been made about 7 Q-B4 P-K4 8 Q×P(K5)ch (interesting is 8 Q×N P×Q 9 N×Q P×N 10 N×P B×Bch 11 K×B with good play for the pawn) 8...Q×Q 9 N×Q N-N5 (it is worth considering 9...B×N 10 B×B N-B4 or 10...O-O keeping the extra pawn) 10 N×N B(B1)×N 11 N×P with an even game. **7...B×Q 8 N×Q B-Q2 9 N×P** The chances are even.

15

(c2) **5...N-KB3** Theory has not yet made a final decision about this important variation, giving back the pawn for speedy development. **6 Q×NP R-N1 7 Q-R6 Q×P** Equally playable is 7...N-B3 8 O-O-O R-N3 (not 8...N×P 9 N-N5!) 9 Q-R4 B×N 10 B×B Q-Q4 11 P-QN3 N-K2 12 P-B3 B-Q2 with chances for both sides. Keres-Botvinnik, World Championship Match Tournament 1948. **8 O-O-O B-B1** Bronstein's idea. **9 Q-R4** The best. If 9 Q-R3 Q×P 10 B-K3 Q-B4 or 9 Q-K3 Q×Q 10 B×Q N-N5. Black stands well in both cases. If 9 Q-B4 B-Q3 10 Q-R6 B-B1 there is a draw by repetition. **9...R-N5 10 Q-R3 Q×P** So far we are following the game Boleslavsky-Bronstein, 14th Match Game 1950, in which White now continued weakly with 11 N-N5 N-R3 12 K-N1 B-Q2 13 B-K3 Q-B4 with great advantage to Black. The correct method of play is **11 B-K2 Q×P.** Alternatives to this exchange sacrifice are:

(1)   11...R-N3 12 P-KN4 Q-QB4 13 B-K3 Q-K4 14 B-Q4 Q-B5ch 15 B-K3;
(2)   11...R-R5 12 Q×R! Q×Q 13 P-KN3 Q-R3 14 B×Q B×Bch 15 K-N1 B-Q2;
with equality in both cases.

12 B×R Q×B(N5) 13 Q×Q N×Q 14 N×P N-Q2 15 N-KB3 and White has the better of it, since he can answer 15...P-KB4 with 16 N(K4)-N5.

(d)   4 N-K2

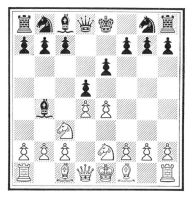

The popularity of this move declined as soon as Black refused to accept the pawn sacrifice. **4...P×P 5 P-QR3 B-K2** The best defence. It is risky to try to hold on to the pawn by 5...B×Nch?! 6 N×B N-QB3 (see 4); even riskier is the line 6...P-KB4 and now:

(1) 7 B-QB4 N-KB3 8 B-KN5 O-O 9 Q-Q2 N-B3 10 O-O-O with an attack. Maroczy-Seitz, Györ 1924;

(2) 7 B-KB4 N-KB3 8 Q-Q2 O-O 9 O-O-O N-R4 10 B-B4 N-QB3 11 P-B3! P×P (if 11...N×B 12 Q×N N×P 13 N-N5 P-B4 14 P-B3!) 12 P×P N×B 13 Q×N Q-Q3 14 Q-K3 with good attacking chances;

(3) 7 P-B3 P×P 8 Q×P Q×P (8...Q-R5ch is no improvement, since after 9 P-KN3 Q×QP 10 N-N5 Black can no longer play ...Q-KR5ch followed by ...Q-K2) 9 Q-N3 N-KB3 (after 9...N-K2 10 B-K3 Q-B3 11 O-O-O White has an equally strong attack, according to Alekhine) 10 Q×NP Q-K4ch (a little better is 10...R-N1 11 Q×BP N-B3 12 B-KB4!) 11 B-K2 R-N1 12 Q-R6 R-N3 13 Q-R4 B-Q2 14 B-KN5 B-B3 15 O-O-O with a winning attack. Alekhine-Nimzovich, Bled 1931.

(4) (after 6...N-QB3) 7 B-QN5 KN-K2 8 B-N5! P-B3 9 B-K3 O-O 10 Q-Q2 (if 10 N×P P-B4 followed by 11...P-B5 winning t e QP) 10...P-B4 (after 10...P-K4 11 P-Q5 N-Q5 12 B-QB4 K-R1 13 O-O-O Wh e has the advantage) 11 P-B3 N-Q4 (11...P-B5 gives better chances, with complications after 12 B×P P×P) 12 B×N N×N 13 Q×N P×B and despite Black's extra pawn White has the better prospects.

6 N×P N-QB3 There is an acceptable alternative in 6...N-KB3 7 N(K2)-N3 N-B3 8 P-QB3 P-K4! 9 N×Nch B×N 10 P-Q5 N-K2 11 B-QB4 O-O 12 O-O N-N3 13 N-K4 B-K2 14 Q-R5 K-R1! 15 N-N5 B×N 16 B×B Q-Q3! Gheorghiu-Uhlmann, Skopje Olympiad 1972; or here 7 N(K2)-B3 N-B3 transposing into our main variation. **7 B-K3** Sharp situations arise after 7 P-QB3 P-K4 e.g. 8 P-Q5 N-N1 9 P-QB4 P-KB4 10 N(K4)-N3 N-KB3 11 P-B4 P-K5 12 N-Q4 O-O 13 B-K2 P-B3 14 B-K3 K-R1 15 Q-N3 P-B4 16 N-B2 P-QN3 17 O-O Drawn. Minev-Balanel, 1954. Alekhine's suggestion of 7 P-KN4 does not seem adequate after 7...N-B3 8 N×Nch B×N 9 B-K3 P-KR4! 10 P×P Q-Q4 with a positional advantage to Black. **7...N-B3 8 N(K2)-B3** Or 8 N×Nch B×N 9 Q-Q2 P-K4 10 O-O-O O-O 11 P-Q5 N-K2 12 N-N3 N-N3 with equality. Lilienthal-Botvinnik, Moscow 1936. **8...N×N.** For 8...O-O? see Dvoretsky-Vaganian, 42nd USSR Championship, Leningrad 1974 (illustrative game 3). **9 N×N P-K4! 10 P×P** If 10 P-Q5? then 10...N-Q5 11 B×N Q×P gives Black the advantage. **10...Q×Qch** with an even game.

(e)   4 P-QR3 A move originally championed by Alekhine and occasionally adopted by ex-World Champion Fischer. The idea is to crystallize the Q-side situation at once so that White can begin action on the K-side before Black has time to create counterplay with ...P-QB4. **4...B×Nch 5 P×B P×P 6 Q-N4 N-KB3 7 Q×NP R-N1 8 Q-R6**

This is the critical position in which Black has four continuations which we shall examine in turn:

(e1) **8...R-N3**

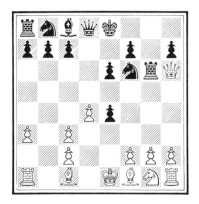

9 Q-K3 N-B3 10 B-N2 Q-Q3 Perhaps 10...N-K2 is better here, e.g. 11 P-QB4 P-N3 12 N-K2 B-N2 13 N-B4 N-B4 with good play for Black. Or if 11 O-O-O P-N4, an interesting pawn sacrifice the consequences of which are unclear. Lebedev-Golovko, 1951. **11 P-B3!** The correct idea, eliminating the KP and thus increasing the scope of his bishops. **11...P×P?** The critical variation is 11...P-K4 12 BP×P P×P 13 P×P N×KP 14 O-O-O. Now 14...R-K3 is met by 15 P-Q5 and 14...B-B4 by 15 B-K2 followed by P-N4. So Black must play 14...P-B4 with an unclear position. After the text move White has too much control of the centre. **12 N×P B-Q2 13 O-O-O O-O-O 14 P-B4 N-KN5 15 Q-Q2 P-B4 16 P-Q5!** N-N1 A necessary evil, since Black loses at least the exchange after 16...P×P 17 P×P N-K2 18 P-R3 N-KB3 19 N-K5! **17 P-R3 N-KB3 18 N-K5!** N-K5 19 Q-Q4 R-N6? It was better to defend the back rank with 19...R(N3)-N1. After 20 Q×P (20 N-B7 is no longer effective, as after 20...Q-B5ch 21 K-N1 QR-B1 there is no need to fear 22 P×P because the mate on Q8 is covered) 20...P-N3 with a playable position. **20 N-B7!** Q-B5ch 21 K-N1 P-B4 Black cannot play 21...R-B1 22 P×P as mate in two follows any move of the bishop. **22 Q-K5!** After this move Black has no defence. **22...Q×Q 23 B×Q R(Q1)-N1 24 B-Q3!** The most exact winning method. **24...R×NP 25 B×N P×B 26 N-Q6ch K-B2 27 N×KPch K-N3 28 N-B6!** **B-R5 29 N×R B×Pch 30 K-B1 N-Q2 31 QR-N1 Resigns.** Fischer-Uhlmann, Zagreb 1970.

(e2) **8...P-B4** This logical looking move, striking at White's QP, has usually favoured White in practice, but according to Botvinnik Black can equalize.

9 N-K2 R-N3 If 9...B-Q2 10 P×P B-B3 11 R-QN1 QN-Q2 12 N-Q4 Q-R4 13 N-N5 and White stands better. Ignatiev-Khasin, Moscow 1959; or 9...QN-Q2 10 N-N3 Q-B2 (after 10...Q-R4 11 B-Q2 P-N3 12 P-QR4 P×P 13 P×P Q-Q4 14 Q-K3 followed by 15 P-QB4 we prefer White's position) 11 Q-K3 Q-B3 12 P-QR4! P-QR3 13 P×P Q×BP 14 Q×Q N×Q, and White stood a little better in Fischer-R. Byrne, US Championship 1966/67; or finally 9...N-B3 10 P×P R-N3 11 Q-Q2 B-Q2 12 R-QN1 Q-B2 13 Q-Q6! O-O-O 14 Q×Qch K×Q and in Smyslov-Botvinnik, 19th Match Game 1954, White could have retained some advantage with 15 N-N3. **10 Q-Q2!** 10 Q-K3 is not so good in view of 10...N-B3 11 P×P Q-R4 12 B-Q2 B-Q2 13 P-QB4 N-KN5! 14 Q-QB3 Q×BP 15 P-R3 Q×KBPch 16 K-Q1 N(N5)-K4 with advantage to Black. Boleslavsky-Uhlmann, Krynica 1956. **10...QN-Q2** 10...N-B3 11 P×P transposes to the Smyslov-Botvinnik game mentioned above. **11 B-N2 Q-B2** followed by **12...P-N3** and **13...B-N2** is given by Botvinnik as equalizing.

(e3)   8...P-N3

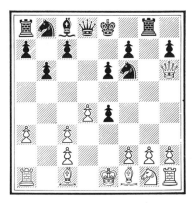

9 B-KN5 R-N3 10 Q-R4 B-N2 11 P-B3 Black has nothing to fear from 11 B-N5ch QN-Q2 12 B×QNch K×B 13 N-K2 P-KR3! If 11 N-K2 Black must play 11...P-KR3, as 11...QN-Q2 12 N-B4 R-KN1 13 N-R5 R-N3 14 B-N5 P-B3 15 B-K2 is better for White in view of the pin. After 11...P-KR3 12 B×P R-N5 13 Q-R3 QN-Q2 Black has excellent play for the pawn. **11...QN-Q2 12 P×P P-KR3 13 B×N Q×B** 13...N×B is also possible. **14 Q×Q N×Q 15 P-K5 N-Q4** with an unclear position. Bronstein-Hort, Moscow 1971. Simpler would have been 15...R×P 16 B×R B×B 17 P×N B×R 18 K-B2 with equality.

(e4) 8...QN-Q2 This move led to Fischer's sensational defeat at the hands of the unknown Yugoslav Master Kovacevic at Zagreb 1970 (see illustrative game 4).

√ **(f) 4 Q-N4?!** 6/7/81

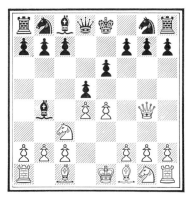

√ The weakest of the replies to 3...B-N5. Black obtains the advantage as follows: **4...N-KB3! 5 Q×NP R-N1 6 Q-R6 P-B4** Also possible is 6...P×P. See Planinc-Ivkov, Yugoslav Team Championship 1971 (illustrative game 5). **7 P-QR3 R-N3 8 Q-K3 B-R4** Or 8...B×Nch 9 P×B P×QP 10 BP×P N×P with a good game for Black. **9 B-Q2 P×QP 10 Q×P N-B3** and Black stands better after **11 Q-Q3 N-K4 12 Q-Q4 N(K4)-N5.**

4 P-K5

The most common move, leading in almost all lines to situations full of tension. After the coming exchange of bishop for knight on his QB3, White strengthens his pawn chain on QB3, Q4 and K5 and usually attacks Black's weakened K-side. Black's chances lie in a counter-attack against the weakness of White's doubled QBPs. In spite of a wealth of games with this line, along with theoretical analyses, it is still impossible to pass a final judgement on this whole variation.

4   ...   P-QB4

The most flexible reply. Black tends to undermine White's exposed pawn centre and also to develop positional pressure along the QB-file and the QR4-K8 diagonal.

(a) 4...N-K2 usually transposes to one of the main lines by 5 P-QR3 B×Nch 6 P×B P-QB4, but the move can take on an independent character if, after **5 P-QR3 B×Nch 6 P×B,** Black plays **6...P-QN3.**
This variation was made popular for a brief period during the mid-1960s by Robert Byrne and Ivkov, but it soon fell out of favour. **7 Q-N4 N-N3** The natural way to defend the KNP. 7...P-QB4 8 B-Q3 is even better for White than the obsolete variation 6...P-QB4 7 Q-N4 N-B4 8 B-Q3 (page 30) because the delay in playing ...P-QB4 retards Black's Q-side counterplay. 7...O-O allows White to build up a quick attack: 8 B-KN5 Q-Q2 9 P-KR4 N-B4 10 N-B3 P-B4? 11 B-B6! K-R1 12 N-N5! P×B 13 KP×P P-KR3 14 Q-R5 P×P 15 B-Q3 with tremendous pressure against Black's king. Klovski-Nei, Riga 1968. Lastly, 7...N-B4? is met by 8 B-Q3 P-KR4 9 Q-R3 with a difficult game for Black. e.g. 9...P-KN4 10 P-N4 N-R5 11 P×P P-KB4 12 P×Pe.p. Q×P 13 Q-N4 R-N1 14 P-KB4. **8 P-KR4 P-KR4 9 Q-B3** Also possible is 9 Q-Q1. See Levy-Birnboim, Netanya 1973 (illustrative game 6). 9 Q-N3, on the other hand, puts the queen on a less effective square. **9...N×RP** Even worse for Black is 9...B-R3 10 B×B N×B 11 B-N5 Q-Q2

(or 11...Q-B1 12 N-K2 P-QB4 13 R-R3 N-N1 14 P-B4! — Keres) 12 P-R4 Q-B3 13 N-K2 Q-B5 14 O-O P-QB4 15 KR-Q1 (15 N-N3 P×P 16 N×P is also crushing) 15...P×P 16 P×P Q×BP? 17 QR-B1 Q-K5 18 Q-QR3! P-B3 (if 18...Q×N 19 Q-Q6 followed by 20 Q-B6ch) 19 P-B3 Q×N 20 R-Q2 Resigns. Ivkov-R. Byrne, Havana Olympiad 1966. **10 Q-R3 N-B4** Inferior is 10...N-N3? 11 B-Q3 Q-Q2 12 Q-N3 N-B3 13 B×N P×B 14 Q×Pch Q-B2 15 Q×Qch K×Q 16 P-N4 B-R3 17 P×P with a clear plus for White. Parma-Ivkov, Bled 1961. **11 P-N4 N-K2 12 B-KN5!** Now Black cannot reply ...P-KB3 and for this reason 9 Q-B3 is possibly stronger than 9 Q-Q1 (compare the note to move 11 in the Levy-Birnboim game, page 50). **12...Q-Q2** Also very good for White is 12...B-R3 13 B×B N×B 14 Q-Q3 N-QN1 15 R×P R×R 16 P×R K-Q2 17 P-QB4! P×P 18 Q×P QN-B3 19 O-O-O and Black is in serious trouble. Matulovic-Antoshin, Yugoslavia-USSR Match 1964. **13 N-K2 B-R3 14 N-B4 B×B 15 K×B Q-N4ch 16 K-N2 QN-B3 17 N×RP R-KN1 18 Q-B3 K-Q2 19 P-R4 Q-B5 20 B-B6!** with an overwhelming position. Lukin-Rizkov, USSR 1972.

After 4...N-K2, White can take advantage of the omission of 4...P-QB4 to launch an immediate attack on the K-side: 5 Q-N4 N-B4 (if 5...O-O? 6 B-Q3 P-QB4 7 B-KN5, or 5...P-QB4 6 P×P with some advantage to White in both cases) 6 N-B3 N-B3 7 B-Q3 P-KR4 8 Q-B4 N(B3)-K2 9 O-O N-N3 10 Q-Q2 and Black has a passive position.

Yet another alternative for White is 5 N-B3!? aiming to support the KP so that ...P-QB4 can be met by QP×P. See Honfi-Farago, Hungarian Team Championship 1973 (illustrative game 7).

Apart from the (usual) text move and 4...N-K2, Black has two other moves that should be mentioned.

(b) 4...P-QN3

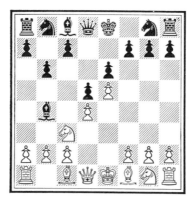

The idea of this move is to exchange white-squared bishops. White has two good continuations:

(b1) **5 Q-N4 B-B1** If 5...K-B1 6 B-Q2 and 7 O-O-O, and if 5...P-N3 6 P-KR4 with good play. **6 N-B3** The attempt 6 P-QR4 proved successful in the game Ljubojevic-Andersson, Hilversum 1973, after 6...B-R3 7 N-N5! Q-Q2 8 B-Q3 N-K2 9 Q-K2 B-N2, as Black has not managed to exchange bishops. However, Black has better with 6...N-QB3 7 P-R4 B-N2 8 N-N1 Q-Q2 9 P-QB3 N-R4 10 N-Q2 P-QB4 11 PxP PxP 12 KN-B3 O-O-O 13 B-Q3 P-B4 with good play. Kurajica-Planinc, Yugoslav Championship 1972. Also possible is 6 B-KN5. **6...Q-Q2 7 B-QN5** For 7 P-QR4 see Ljubojevic-Andersson, Amsterdam, 1972 (illustrative game 8.) **7...P-QB3 8 B-K2 B-R3 9 O-O N-K2 10 B-KN5 N-B4 11 N-KR4 P-R3 12 NxN PxN 13 Q-R3** and White stands a little better. Cherepkov-Mokacjan, USSR 1955.

(b2) **5 P-QR3 BxNch** Again 5...B-B1 is possible, e.g. 6 P-KB4 N-K2 7 B-K3 P-KR4 8 N-B3 Q-Q2 (more exact is the immediate 8...B-R3 9 BxB NxB 10 Q-Q3 Q-B1) 9 B-B2 N-B4 10 B-Q3 B-R3 11 BxB (there is nothing in 11 BxN PxB 12 Q-Q2 N-B3 13 O-O-O B-K2 14 KR-K1 O-O-O!) 11...NxB 12 Q-Q3 N-N1 13 N-K2 P-B4!? and now instead of the 14 P-QN3 of Zuidema-Andersson, Wijk aan Zee 1973, White stands better after 14 P-B4! **6 PxB Q-Q2 7 N-R3** Another important line is 7 Q-N4 P-KB4 8 Q-N3 B-R3 9 BxB NxB 10 N-K2 O-O-O (if 10...N-K2 11 Q-Q3 N-QN1 12 P-QB4; or 10...K-B2 11 P-QR4 P-B4 12 Q-Q3 Q-B1 13 B-R3 with the better chances for White) 11 P-QR4 K-N2? (he should play 11...N-N1 12 P-R5 N-QB3 with equality) 12 O-O Q-B2 13 P-QB4 with advantage to White. Fischer-Bisguier, USA Championship 1958. **7...B-R3 8 BxB NxB 9 Q-N4 P-KB4 10 Q-R5ch P-N3** Not 10...Q-B2 11 Q-K2 N-N1 12 P-QB4. Now the chances are about even. Ciocaltea-Hecht, Budapest 1973 (illustrative game 9).

(c) **4...Q-Q2** A refinement of the 4...P-QN3 system designed to avoid the disadvantages of variation b1. Now, after 5 Q-N4, Black does not need to retreat his KB, as he can play ...P-KB4. **5 P-QR3** The usual continuation. If 5 Q-N4 P-KB4 (even now Black can play 5...B-B1 if he wishes, e.g. 6 B-K3 P-QN3 7 P-B4 P-KB4 8 Q-R5ch P-N3 9 Q-R4 B-N5 10 N-K2 B-R3 11 O-O-O N-QB3 with equal chances. Vasyukov-Gulko, Moscow 1972. White can, however, improve on this with 6 B-Q2 P-QN3 7 P-QR4! B-R3 8 N-N5, e.g. 8...P-KB4 9 Q-B4 N-R3 10 Q-B3 N-B2 11 P-B4 P-B3 12 PxP KPxP 13 B-Q3! PxN 14 BxBP with a winning attack. Muchej-Muratov, USSR 1972) 6 Q-N3 (no practical test of 6 Q-R5ch has yet been made) 6...P-QN3 with three lines:

(1) 7 B-Q2 B-R3 8 B×B N×B 9 KN-K2 B-B1 10 P-KR4 N-N5! 11 O-O-O O-O-O
12 Q-R3 P-B4 13 P-KN4 P×NP 14 Q×P N-QB3 15 P×P B×P 16 N-B4 N-Q5! with
good play for Black. Tringov-Bronstein, Amsterdam Interzonal 1964;
(2) 7 N-B3 B-R3 8 B×B N×B 9 O-O B-B1 (better is 9...B×N 10 P×B N-N1 and it
is not easy for White to find a plan against Black's intended ...N-QB3 and ...O-
O-O) 10 N-K2 O-O-O 11 P-QR4 N-N5 12 P-B3 N-QB3 13 P-N4 and White
stands better. Cherepkov-Stoljar, Leningrad 1964;
(3) 7 P-QR3 B-B1 (for 7...B×Nch see the main variation) 8 N-B3 (better is 8
N-R3 B-R3 9 B×B N×B 10 O-O with a slight plus for White) 8...B-R3 9 B×B N×B
10 P-KR4 P-B4 11 B-N5 N-R3 12 P-R5 N-KB2 13 O-O-O N×B 14 Q×N N-B2 15
P-KN4 P×NP 16 Q×P(N4) O-O-O with equality. Boleslavsky-Bannik, USSR
1957.

5...B×Nch 6 P×B P-QN3 7 P-QR4 For 7 N-R3 see variation b2, page 23. **7...B-
R3 8 B×B N×B 9 Q-N4** If 9 Q-Q3 N-N1 10 P-R4 N-QB3 11 N-B3 (11 P-KR5 P-
B3!) 11...N-R4 gives Black a good game. Diez del Corral-Hort, Las Palmas
1973. **9...P-KB4** The chances are roughly equal. Tringov-Spiridonov, Varna
1973 (illustrative game 10).

5   P-QR3

The most usual reply, though two other moves deserve a mention:

(a)   5 B-Q2 A less aggressive continuation, but nevertheless a sound developing
move which avoids the weakening of White's Q-side pawn structure.

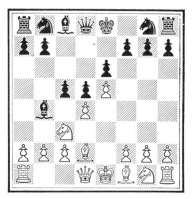

5...N-K2 The best reply. After 5...N-QB3 or 5...P×P, 6 N-N5 gives White the
edge, e.g. 5...P×P 6 N-N5 B×Bch 7 Q×B N-QB3 8 N-KB3 (also possible is 8 P-

KB4) 8...P-B3 9 Q-B4 N-R3 10 N-Q6ch! K-B1 11 B-N5 N-B2 12 N×N K×N 13 B×N P×B 14 P×P P×P 15 N-K5ch with a clear advantage to White. Fine-Capablanca, AVRO 1938. **6 N-N5** There are two important alternatives.

(1) 6 P×P O-O (6...B×P 7 Q-N4 N-N3 is more exact, with an even game) 7 Q-N4 QN-B3 8 O-O-O B×P (and here 8... N-B4 is better, with equality) 9 N-B3 N-N3 10 Q-R5 P-B3 11 P×P P×P 12 B-Q3 R-B2 13 B×N P×B 14 Q×NPch R-N2 15 Q-R5 R-R2 16 B-R6 B-Q2 17 P-KR4 B×P 18 R-Q2 and White stood a little better in Ivkov-Uhlmann, 1957;
(2) 6 P-QR3 is weaker. See Pachman-Uhlmann, Dresden 1957 (illustrative game 11).

6...B×Bch 7 Q×B O-O 8 N-KB3 Other possibilities are:

(1) 8 P-QB3 (Black has good play after both 8 N-Q6 P×P 9 N-B3 QN-B3, and 8 P×P N-Q2 9 Q-B3 P-QR3 10 N-Q6 Q-B2) 8...QN-B3 (after 8...N-B4 9 B-Q3 B-Q2 10 N-B3 B×N 11 B×B Q-N3 12 B-Q3 N-B3 White stood slightly better in Stoltz-Nimzovich, 1934) 9 P-KB4 P×P 10 P×P N-B4 11 N-KB3 P-B3 12 B-Q3 P-QR3 13 B×N P×N 14 B-Q3 Q-R4 with good play for Black. Lilienthal-Mikenas, Moscow 1940;
(2) 8 P-KB4 Q-N3 9 P×P Q×P 10 N-KB3 B-Q2 11 N(N5)-Q4 QN-B3 12 B-Q3 N×N 13 N×N N-B3 14 N-B3 (better is 14 N-N3 Q-N3 15 Q-B2 with equal chances) 14...N-N5 15 P-B3 N×Bch 16 Q×N B-N4 17 Q-Q4 Q-K2 and Black has the initiative. Dubinin-Bondarevsky, Leningrad 1947.

8...P×P 9 B-Q3 QN-B3 The chances are equal.

(b) 5 Q-N4 A very ambitious, double-edged attempt at a direct attack on Black's sensitive K-side. The idea temporarily disregards the necessity of taking protective measures on behalf of White's threatened Q-side. **5...N-K2 6 P×P** 6 Q×NP is too risky after 6...R-N1 7 Q-R6 (not 7 Q×RP? P×P 8 P-QR3 Q-R4 with a clear advantage to Black) 7...P×P 8 P-QR3 B-R4 (or 8...B×Nch 9 P×B Q-B2) 9 P-QN4 B-B2 10 N-N5 P-R3 11 N×Bch Q×N and Black stands better. 6 P-QR3 seems even more suspect, as is shown in Jansa-Korchnoy, Luhacovice 1969 (illustrative game 12). **6...QN-B3** Also possible is 6...B×Nch 7 P×B N-Q2 8 N-B3 (Black stands well after 8 Q×NP R-KN1 9 Q×RP N×KP 10 B-K2 Q-R4 as in Reshevsky-Botvinnik, 1946) 8...Q-B2 9 Q×NP R-KN1 10 Q×RP N×KP 11 Q-R5 N×Nch 12 Q×N B-Q2 13 B-KB4 Q×P with even chances. **7 B-Q2** 7 N-B3 is bad after 7...P-Q5! 8 B-QN5 (8 P-QR3 Q-R4!) 8...Q-R4! 9 B×Nch P×B and now Black wins after both 10 Q×NP R-KN1 11 Q×RP B-R3!, and 10 Q×QP N-B4! 11 Q-K4 B×Nch 12 P×B Q×P(B6)ch 13 K-Q1 R-QN1! or here 11 Q-QB4 B-R3 12 Q-N3 Q-N4! etc. **7...O-O 8 N-B3 P-B4 9 P×Pe.p.** After 9 Q-N3 P-Q5 10 N-QN1 Q-

Q4! Black is better. **9...R×P 10 O-O-O P-K4 11 Q-R5 R-B4 12 Q-R4 B×N! 13 P×B** If 13 B×B R-B5! **13...Q-R4 14 K-N2 N-N3 15 Q-N3 Q×P(B4)** and Black had the advantage in Pietzsch-Uhlmann, East Germany 1963.

Now let us return to the normal move, 5 P-QR3.

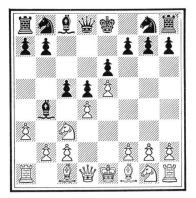

5   ...   B×Nch

Both 5...P×P and 5...B-R4 have almost disappeared from tournament practice. For example: 5...P×P 6 P×B P×N 7 N-B3 (7 Q-N4 is equally promising, e.g. 7...P×P 8 B×P P-KN3 9 P-KR4 P-KR4 10 Q-KB4 N-QB3 11 N-B3 B-Q2 12 N-N5 N-R3 13 P-N5! N-K2 14 P-N4 P×P 15 Q-B6 R-KN1 16 N-R7 N(K2)-B4 17 Q-N5! R-R1 18 N-B6ch K-B1 19 B-Q3 P-R3 20 P-R5!, and White had a decisive attack in Batik-Skoda, 1961) 7...Q-B2 (after 7...P×P 8 B×P N-QB3 9 P-N5 QN-K2 10 B-Q3 N-R3 11 Q-Q2 B-Q2 12 P-KR4 N-B1 13 R-KR3 N-N3 14 R-N3 N-B5 15 B×N P×B 16 N-Q4 Q×P 17 O-O-O, White had the advantage in Bannik-Tolush, USSR 1963) 8 Q-Q4 N-K2 9 B-Q3 N-Q2 10 O-O, and White's lead in development guarantees him an advantage.

5...B-R4 was for a long time an important variation. The move became well known during the early 1950's, but after Smyslov's powerful play in the 9th game of his 1954 World Championship match against Botvinnik, 5...B-R4 suffered a decline in popularity. Nevertheless, it is still seen in occasional master games, in particular those of Duckstein, Enklaar and Hug.

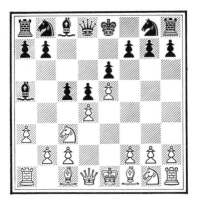

6 P-QN4 A dynamic move, offering a pawn in return for a big lead in development. Apart from this main reply, White may also try 6 B-Q2, e.g. 6...P×P (or 6...N-QB3 7 N-N5 B×Bch 8 Q×B N×QP 9 N×N P×N 10 N-B3 N-K2 11 Q×P O-O 12 B-Q3 N-B3 13 Q-K3 P-B4 14 O-O B-Q2 15 P-B4 with a slight plus to White) 7 N-N5 N-QB3 (After the retreat 7...B-B2 8 P-KB4 N-QB3 9 Q-N4 P-KN3 10 N-KB3 White is better, as in Janosevic-Matanovic, Yugoslav Championship 1955) 8 N-KB3 KN-K2 9 B-Q3 N-N3 10 B×N RP×B 11 O-O B-B2 12 B-N5 Q-Q2 13 N×Bch Q×N 14 R-K1 B-Q2 15 N×P N×N 16 Q×N P-B3 17 B-Q2 P-KN4 18 P-KB4 P×BP 19 B×P and White has the edge. Kurajica-Enklaar, Amsterdam 1971. **6...P×QP** 6...P×NP is much too risky, as White's strong centre allows him to use all his forces for the attack, e.g. 7 N-N5! N-QB3 (if 7...P-N6ch 8 P-QB3! or 7...P×Pch 8 P-QB3 N-Q2 9 N-Q6ch K-B1 10 Q-B3 P-B4 11 B×P N-K2 12 N-R3 with a clear advantage) 8 P×P B×Pch 9 P-QB3 B-K2 10 B-Q3 P-QR3 11 Q-N4 K-B1 12 B-R3, and White has more than enough compensation for the pawn. Now White has two strong continuations:

(a) **7 N-N5 B-B2** Not 7...B-N3 8 N-Q6ch K-B1 9 Q-R5! **8 P-KB4 N-K2 9 N-KB3** 9 Q-N4 N-B4 10 B-Q3 P-KR4 is unclear. **9...QN-B3** After 9...O-O 10 B-Q3 P-B3 11 O-O B-N3 12 B-N2 P-QR3 13 N(N5)×P QN-B3 14 K-R1 P-B4 15 P-B4 White had good play in Zuidema-Enklaar, Dutch Championship 1972. **10 B-Q3 B-N1** Or 10...P-QR3 11 N×Bch Q×N 12 O-O B-Q2 13 B-N2 Q-N3 14 K-R1 O-O-O 15 P-QR4!? N×NP 16 P-R5 Q-B2 17 B×QP QR-N1 18 B-QN6 Q-B6 19 Q-N1 N(N5)-B3 20 R-R4 with a clear advantage. Ibrahimoglu-Capello, Lugano Olympiad 1968. If here 15...Q×P then 16 B-R3 Q-R4 17 Q-K2 with good play for White down the QN-file after 18 KR-QN1. **11 N(N5)×QP P-QR3** Or 11...N×N 12 N×N P-QR3 13 B-K3 B-R2 14 Q-K2 B-Q2 15 O-O O-O 16 R-B3 with advantage to White. Westerinen-Dückstein, Lugano Olympiad 1968. **12 B-**

K3 B-R2 13 P-B3! P-R3 14 O-O B-Q2 15 Q-K1 N×N 16 B×N B×B 17 N×B P-KN3 18 K-R1 P-KR4 19 P-B4 with excellent play for White. Tal-Koblenz, Riga Championship 1954.

(b) 7 Q-N4 N-K2 Not 7...Q-B2 8 Q×NP Q×Nch 9 K-Q1 with advantage to White. Nor 7...K-B1 8 P×B P×N 9 N-B3 (also good is 9 Q-N4ch N-K2 10 Q×BP QN-B3 11 B-Q2) 9...N-K2 10 B-Q3 N-Q2 (after 10...QN-B3 11 O-O Q×P 12 R-K1 White has the initiative) 11 Q-N4! Q-B2 12 O-O! with an excellent game for White. Unzicker-Botvinnik, Amsterdam Olympiad 1954. **8 P×B** Also playable is 8 N-N5 B-B2 9 Q×NP R-N1 10 Q×RP. See Timman-Hug, Nice Olympiad 1974 (illustrative game 13). **8...P×N 9 Q×NP R-N1 10 Q×RP QN-B3** In the game Gligoric-Duckstein, Zagreb 1955, White had the better game after 10...N-Q2 11 P-B4 Q×P 12 N-B3 N-B1 13 Q-Q3 B-Q2 14 N-N5 R-B1 15 R-QN1 P-N3 16 P-KR4!; or 10...N-Q2 11 N-B3 Q-B2 (if 11...N-B1 12 Q-Q3 Q×P 13 P-KR4 B-Q2 14 B-N5 R-B1?! 15 N-Q4 with advantage to White. Smyslov-Botvinnik, 9th Match Game 1954, but better here is 14...N-B3) 12 B-QN5 P-QR3 (or 12...R×P 13 K-B1 R-KN1 14 R-KN1!) 13 B×Nch B×B 14 O-O P-Q5! 15 B-N5! (if 15 N-N5 O-O-O 16 N×BP B-B3 17 B-N5 N-B4!) 15...B-B3 16 B×N K×B 17 Q-R4ch! (not 17 N-N5? R×N 18 Q-R4 Q×KP 19 P-B4 Q-K6ch 20 R-B2 R-KN1 21 P×R R×P with advantage to Black in view of his well posted bishop) 17...K-K1 18 N-N5 Q×KP 19 P-B4 with unclear play. **11 N-B3** Weak is 11 P-B4? Q×P 12 N-B3 B-Q2 13 N-N5 R-KB1 (After the exchange sacrifice 13...R×N 14 P×R O-O-O 15 B-Q3 Q-B4 16 Q-R4! N×P 17 Q-QN4! White stands better.) 14 R-QN1 (After 14 B-K2 O-O-O 15 N×BP R×N! 16 Q×R N-Q5! 17 B-Q3 Q-B4 18 P-QR4 N(K2)-B4! Black had the better game in Jesso-Harzer, 1961.) 14...O-O-O 15 N×BP R×N 16 Q×R B-K1! 17 Q×Pch B-Q2 18 Q-B6 B-B4 19 B-K2 (If 19 B-N5 B×P 20 B×N N×B 21 R-R1 Q-B4 and Black has the advantage.) 19...Q-B4! 20 R-N5 Q-Q5 21 Q-R4 Q-K5! 22 Q-B2 Q×QBP 23 O-O P-Q5 and Black's passed pawns proved a decisive factor in Fichtl-Blatny, Czechoslovakia 1964. **11...Q-B2 12 B-QN5** 12 B-KB4 B-Q2 13 B-Q3 O-O-O 14 B-N3 N-N3 offers approximately equal chances. **12...B-Q2 13 O-O** White has a clear advantage. Fischer-Tal, Leipzig Olympiad 1960 (illustrative game 14).

6 P×B

In this position Black must make his first serious decision. His choice lies between 6...N-K2 and 6...Q-B2. There are many transpositional possibilities from one variation to the other, particularly if White chooses the quieter of the two plans at his disposal.

We first examine the more flexible move.

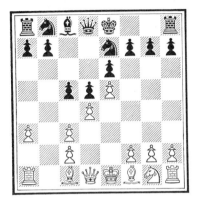

A useful developing move that Black will have to play sooner or later. By playing it at once he preserves the option of where to put his queen (QR4 or QB2). For 6...Q-B2 see Chapter 4.

7   Q-N4

The sharpest and most interesting move at White's disposal. The more positional continuations 7 P-QR4! and 7 N-B3 are examined in chapters 2 and 3.

With the text move White threatens to decimate Black's K-side by 8 Q×NP R-N1 9 Q×RP. Black can either try to hold his K-side together (somewhat passive) or seek immediate counterplay on the opposite wing.

7 ...   Q-B2!

The most active move and the best. Other lines are:

(a)   7...P×P   This usually transposes to the main line, by 8 Q×NP R-N1 9 Q×RP Q-B2 but White can avoid this:

(1) 8 P×P Q-B2 9 R-R2 (Against Lutikov in 1960 Spassky played 9 K-Q1 N-B4 10 N-B3 N-B3 11 B-Q3 N(B3)-K2 12 B-Q2 B-Q2 13 P-QR4 with a very good game, but Black has better with 9...O-O 10 B-Q3 P-B4. After 9 N-K2 Black can equalize by 9...N-B4 10 B-Q2 N-B3, whilst after 9 B-Q2 Q×BP 10 Q×NP R-N1 11 Q-R6 Q-N7 12 R-B1 Q×QP 13 B-B3 Q-K5ch White has insufficient play for the sacrificed pawn.) 9...N-B4 10 N-B3 N-B3 11 B-Q3 (Interesting is 11 K-Q1!?)

11...P-KR4! 12 Q-N5 N(B3)×QP 13 N×N Q-B6ch 14 K-B1 Q×N 15 B-N2 Q-KN5 16 Q-Q2 Q-QR5 and is doubtful if White has enough for the pawn;
(2) 8 B-Q3 (This move of Geller's was first played by him against Sokolsky in the 18th USSR Championship, 1950. The idea is to develop as quickly as possible.) 8...Q-R4 (8...Q-B2 transposes to the note on 8 B-Q3, page 31) 9 N-K2 O-O (also possible is 9...N-N3 10 O-O P×P 11 P-KR4 B-B3 12 P-B4 P-R4 13 Q-N3 N(B3)-K2 14 N-Q4 when White has some compensation for the pawn) 10 O-O (10 R-QN1 is a suggestion of Keres) 10...P×P 11 N-N3, and White has some compensation for the pawn — Keres.

It should also be mentioned that after 7...P×P 8 Q×NP R-N1 9 Q×RP, 9...Q-R4 is over optimistic. Alexander-Botvinnik, Great Britain-USSR Radio Match 1946 continued 10 R-N1! Q×BPch 11 B-Q2 Q-B2 (if 11...Q×RP 12 B-N4, or 12 P-KB4 QN-B3 13 N-B3 as in the game, when 13...B-Q2 would have been impossible) 12 P-KB4 QN-B3 13 N-B3 B-Q2 14 N-N5 R×N! 15 P×R O-O-O 16 Q×P Q×Pch 17 K-Q1 N-B4, and now White's strongest continuation is probably Botvinnik's suggestion 18 B-Q3 N-K6ch 19 B×N Q×B (if 19...P×B 20 Q-B6 is still strong) 20 Q-B6! P-K4 21 R-K1 B-N5ch 22 B-K2 B×Bch 23 R×B Q-N8ch 24 R-K1 "with good chances for a win".

(b) **7...N-B4** A common variation at one time, but discredited by the games Gligoric-Pachman and Yanofsky-Uhlmann, e.g.: **8 B-Q3 P-KR4 9 Q-B4!** The best move; after 9 Q-R3 P×P 10 N-B3 Q-B2 11 R-QN1 P×P 12 P-N4 N-K2 13 P×P QN-B3 14 B-KB4 N-N3! 15 B-N3 N(N3)×P 16 N×N N×N 17 K-B1 B-Q2 Black stood very well in Tal-Korchnoy, Riga 1958; and after 9 Q-B3 N-B3 10 B×N P×B 11 Q-N3 P-KN3 12 B-N5 Q-R4 13 B-B6 N×QP Black has nothing to fear. **9...Q-R5** The attempted improvement 9...P×P gave White the better ending in Yanofsky-Uhlmann, Stockholm Interzonal 1962, after 10 P×P Q-R5 11 Q×Q N×Q 12 B-KN5! N-B4 13 N-K2 N-B3 14 P-QB3 N-R4 15 N-B4! N-K2 16 B-K2 P-KN3 17 B-B6 R-R2 18 B-QN5ch B-Q2 19 B×Bch K×B 20 N-R3 P-R5 21 K-K2. **10 N-K2 Q×Q 11 N×Q N-K2** This retreat is essential, as White wins a pawn after both 11...P×P 12 B×N P×B 13 N×QP and 11...P-KN3 12 P×P N-Q2 13 B×N NP×B 14 N-Q3. **12 B-K2!** White has a slight advantage. Gligoric-Pachman, Munich Olympiad 1958 (illustrative game 15).

(c) **7...O-O** Although this move is seldom played it is perfectly acceptable. 8 N-B3 (after 8 B-KN5 Q-R4! 9 Q-R3 [not 9 B×N Q×BPch 10 K-K2 N-B3 winning] 9...N-N3 10 B-Q2 Q-R5 11 N-B3 P-B4 12 P×Pe.p. R×P 13 B-Q3 N-B3 the chances are equal. Gligoric-Pietzsch, 1962) 8...QN-B3 9 B-Q3 P-B4 10 P×Pe.p. (in the game Klovan-Vaganian, USSR 1970, the game was even after 10 Q-N3 Q-R4 11 B-Q2 P×P 12 P×P Q-R5 13 Q-R4 B-Q2 14 O-O N-N3 15 Q-R5 B-K1 16

N-N5 P-KR3 17 N×P N-B5! 18 N-B5 B×Q 19 N×Q N×B 20 P×N N×QP) 10...R×P
11 B-KN5 R-B2 (White has the advantage after 11...P-K4 12 B×Pch! K×B 13 Q-
R5ch K-N1 14 B×R P×B 15 P×KP) 12 B×N (after 12 Q-R3 P-KR3 13 B-N6 R-B1
14 N-K5 N×N 15 P×N Q-B2! Black stood well in Levy-Farago, 1973. Or 12 N-K5
N×N 13 P×N Q-B2 14 B×N Q×Pch 15 K-Q2 P-B5 with equality. Fichtl-Fuchs,
1960. Or 12 Q-R5 P-KN3 13 Q-R6 Q-R4 14 B-Q2 P-B5. Or 12 Q-R4 P-KR3 13
O-O P-B5 14 B-N6 N×B 15 B×Q N×Q 16 B×N B-Q2 with equality. Parma-Fichtl,
1962) 12...R×B 13 Q-R4 P-KN3 14 O-O P-B5 15 B-K2 B-Q2 16 KR-K1 Q-R4 17
N-K5 QR-K1 18 N-N4 Q×BP! 19 Q-B6 with an even game (Korchnoy-Bronstein,
USSR 1958). Black would have the better chances here after 19 N-B6ch K-N2 20
N×Rch R×N 21 R(K1)-Q1 Q×BP.

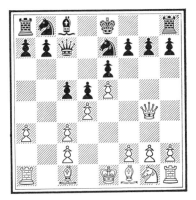

8   Q×NP

The sharpest and most interesting variation of the French Defence. The move
8 B-Q3 is worth noting, contributing much more by developing White's K-side
than the somewhat premature, time-consuming destruction of Black's K-side
pawn formation in the main line. The idea originated with Geller and has
frequently been used of late by Velimirovic, e.g. **8...P×P** If 8...P-B5 9 B-K2 N-
B4 10 Q-R3! **9 N-K2 P×P** Not 9...Q×KP 10 B-KB4 Q-B3 11 P×P P-KR4 12 Q-
N3 QN-B3 13 B-KN5 N-B4 14 B×Q N×Q 15 B×P R-KN1 16 RP×N R×B 17 R×P
with the better ending for White. **10 Q×NP R-N1 11 Q×RP** Velimirovic's idea of
11 Q-R6 is more risky, e.g. 11...N-Q2 12 B-KB4 (not 12 B×P R-R1 13 Q-N7
Q×P) 12...N-B1 13 N-N3 B-Q2 14 N-R5 O-O-O with unclear play. Or here 12 O-
O N×P 13 B-KB4 (or 13 B×P N-N5!) 13...N-N5! 14 B×Q N×Q, or 12 P-B4 N-QB4
13 B×P R×P 14 K-B1 R×N 15 K×R B-Q2 with good play for Black in both cases.
11...QN-B3 12 B-KB4?! Keres recommends 12 P-B4 but after 12...Q-N3 Black

is no worse. **12...B-Q2 13 O-O O-O-O** Black already has a clear initiative. Unzicker-Uhlmann, Varna Olympiad 1962 (illustrative game 16).

8	...	**R-N1**
9	**Q×RP**	**P×P**
10	**N-K2**	

The usual continuation. White has a chain of sensitive spots on QB3, Q4 and K5, and this move protects against Black's main threats to White's Q-side (which has been deserted by White's queen) and to White's unstable pawn centre.

The alternative, Dr. Euwe's recommendation of **10 K-Q1,** deprives White of his right to castle in order to obtain the more natural developing square KB3 for White's knight, from where it does not obstruct the action of the KB. After 10 K-Q1, if Black captures White's QB6 pawn or the KP with his queen, it will not be with check. Euwe's move has fluctuated in popularity, with the latest results favouring Black.

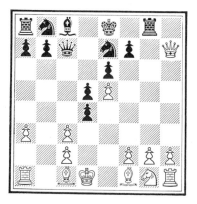

10...QN-B3! Not 10...Q×KP 11 N-B3 Q-B3 12 P×P and White stands better. For a long time 10...N-Q2 was thought to be playable, but the game Bronstein-Uhlmann, Zagreb 1965, changed this opinion (illustrative game 17). **11 N-B3** White has no time to play 11 P-KB4 B-Q2 12 N-B3 P×P 13 N-N5 R×N! 14 P×R O-O-O with good play for Black. **11...P×P 12 N-N5** After 12 B-KB4 B-Q2 13 B-N3 O-O-O 14 B-Q3 Q-N3 15 K-K2 N-B4! Black had good play in Kuijpers-Padevsky, 1963. **12...N×P** This is the critical position in this variation. In the game Matulovic-Uhlmann, Budapest 1967, play continued 13 B-KB4 Q-N3! 14 B×N R×N 15 P-KR4! (not 15 B×P Q×P) 15...R-KN1 16 K-K1 B-Q2 17 R-R3 R-N5 18 R-B3 O-O-O 19 B-B6 (it would be risky to play 19 R×QBPch because of

19...N-B3 or 19...B-B3) 19...R-K1 20 B×N? (20 B-Q3 was essential) 20... R×B? (Black could obtain a decisive advantage by the zwischenzug 20...R-K5ch 21 B-K2 [if 21 K-Q1 Q-N7 22 R-B1 Q×Rch 23 K×Q R-K8 mate] 21...B-N4 22 R×QBPch K-N1 23 B-B5 [or 23 K-B1 R×B 24 B-B5 Q-R4 25 B-N4 R-K5ch and 26...R×B winning, or 23 R-K3 R×R 24 P×R Q×P 25 B-Q6ch K-R1 26 Q-R5 B×B 27 Q×B Q-QB6ch wins] 23...Q-R4 24 B-N4 R×B(N5) 25 P×R Q×Rch 26 K-Q2 B×B winning for Black) 21 Q-R8ch R-K1 22 Q×Pch B-B3 23 R×P R×RP and Black stood a little better. This line needs further practical tests.

We shall examine the alternative 13 P-B4 by following a game.

13 P-B4 R×N 14 P×R N(K4)-N3.

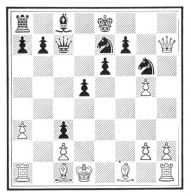

A highly interesting position which theory has not yet fully explored. **15 B-K2** If 15 B-Q3 P-K4 16 R-B1 B-N5ch 17 K-K1 O-O-O 18 R×P P-K5 and Black had an excellent game in Adorjan-F. Portisch. 15 P-KR4 may be an improvement. See Hansen-Wirth, Correspondence Game 1973 (illustrative game 18). **15...P-K4 16 R-B1 B-K3 17 B-N5ch** Once again 17 P-KR4 is worth considering. **17...K-Q1! 18 B-K3?** 18 P-KR4 still offered the best chances, though Black can play 18...Q-B4!, whilst in reply to 18 R×P he has the powerful zwischenzug 18...Q-N3! **18...P-Q5 19 B-N1 Q-B4! 20 B-K2 Q-Q4** Black's strong pawn centre and mobile minor pieces clearly give him a winning game. **21 R-B3 K-B2 22 Q-N7 R-Q1 23 K-K1 Q-K5 24 K-B1 Q×P 25 B-Q3 Q-N7 26 R-K1** 26 R-N1 fails to 26...P-B7. **26...P-B7** The pawns cannot be stopped. **27 B×BP Q×B 28 B-B2 R-KN1 29 Q-R7 P-Q6! 30 B-N3 P-Q7 31 R×KP P-Q8=Qch 32 R-K1ch K-Q2 33 R×Q Q×Rch** and Black won. Matulovic-Tatai, Venice 1969.

10	...	QN-B3
11	P-KB4	B-Q2
12	Q-Q3	

This is the normal move here, but Robert Byrne produced the interesting innovation 12 P-R3 in his game with Uhlmann at Monte Carlo, 1968 (illustrative game 19).

12 ...   P×P

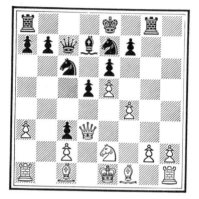

White now has six possibilities open to him, of which 13 N-N3 is the most solid. First, however, we shall look at the alternatives:

(a) 13 Q×BP N-B4 14 R-QN1! Preventing ...Q-N3. Weaker is 14 B-Q2, for which see Bogdanovic-Uhlmann, Sarajevo 1963 (illustrative game 20). **14...P-Q5** Another possibility is 14...R-QB1. **15 Q-B4 Q-R4ch 16 B-Q2 Q×RP 17 R×P Q-R8ch?** White now had the advantage in Portisch-Uhlmann, Monte Carlo 1968. The correct idea is 17...N-K6 18 B×N P×B 19 Q-B3 Q×Qch 20 N×Q N-Q5 21 N-K4 B-B3! 22 N-Q6ch K-Q1 when White has nothing better than perpetual check.

(b) 13 N×P?! It is wrong to expose himself in this way. White should first develop. **13...P-QR3** The best reply, since 13...N-B4 14 N-N5 Q-Q1 is unclear. **14 R-QN1 N-R4!** Better than 14...R-QB1 15 P-KR4! N-R2 16 R-R3 N-N4 17 R-QN3 N-B4 with an edge to White, Bednarski-Uhlmann, Marianske Lazne 1965; or here 15...N×P 16 P×N Q×Nch 17 Q×Q R×Q 18 R×P R×BP 19 B-KN5 is better for White; or 15...N-B4 16 R-R3 N(B3)-Q5 17 P-R5 N-N4 18 N-Q1 N(N4)-Q5 19 P-B3! B-N4 20 R×B and White has the better prospects. An instructive illustration of this idea went as follows: **15 P-KR4 N-B4 16 R-R3 O-O-O 17 P-R5** White has insufficient after 17 Q×N P×Q 18 N×P Q×BP 19 R-QB3ch Q×Rch 20 N×Q B-K3, as occurred in Fuchs-Uhlmann, 1967. **17...R-N5!** This is more exact than 17...N-B5 18 R-N4 B-B3 19 N-K2 with complicationns, Hort-Uhlmann, Hastings 1970/71. **18 P-R6 R-R1 19 P-R7 R-N2 20 R-N4 N-B5**

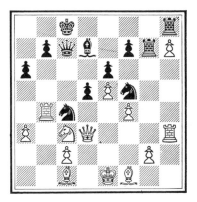

21 Q×N(KB5)? An interesting but incorrect queen sacrifice. But in any case it is almost impossible to find a satisfactory move for White. Black's forces are extremely well co-ordinated and he has full compensation for the sacrificed pawn. 21 N×P is also bad in view of 21...P×N 22 Q×P N-R4! 23 B×P N-K2 winning. **21...P×Q 22 N×P Q-R4! 23 B×N R(R1)×P! 24 R-QB3** If 24 N-N6ch K-B2 25 R-Q3 B-B3 wins for Black. **24...R-R8ch 25 B-B1ch K-Q1!** 25...K-N1 is more complex, but still better for Black after 26 N-N6 B-N4 27 R-B8ch K-R2 28 N-B4 B×N 29 B-K3ch P-N3 30 R(N4)×B R-N3, etc. **26 N-N6 B-N4 27 N-B4** Forced, since 27 R-B8ch K-K2 28 R-B7ch K-K3 loses at once. **27...B×N 28 R(B3)×B** If 28 R(N4)×B R-N6! **28...R×P 29 B-K3 Q×RP 30 B-N6ch K-K2 31 Resigns.** Dueball-Uhlmann, Raach 1969.

(c) 13 R-QN1 O-O-O After 13...N-B4 14 P-N3 P-Q5 15 B-KN2 O-O-O the situation is unclear. Shamkovich-Uhlmann, Sarajevo 1963. However, the refutation may lie in 14 P-N4! as 14...R×P 15 B-R3 followed by 16 B×N seems very good for White. **14 N×P** Black has the advantage after 14 B-K3 N-B4 15 N-Q4 (or 15 B-B2 P-Q5 16 P-R3 P-B3 17 P×P P-K4 18 P-N4 P-K5! 19 Q×KP R(N1)-K1 20 Q-Q3 Q×P, etc.) 15...N(B4)×N 16 B×N P-B3! 17 R-N3 P×P 18 P×P R-N5! **14...N-R4 15 N-N5 B×N 16 R×B** Or 16 Q×B N-B5. **16...K-N1** and Black has excellent play for the pawn.

(d) 13 B-K3?! N-B4 14 N-Q4 If 14 B-Q4 O-O-O 15 B×P P-Q5 16 B-Q2 P-B3! 17 P×P P-K4! Fichtl-Golz, Dresden 1959; or 14 B-B2 O-O-O 15 N×P P-Q5 16 N-K4 N×P 17 P×N Q×KP 18 O-O-O B-B3 19 N-N3 N-K6 20 R-K1 B-R5 and Black has a strong attack. Walther-Diaconescu. **14...N(B4)×N 15 B×N O-O-O 16 P-N3 P-**

B3! **17 P×P P-K4 18 P×P R-N5** with advantage to Black. Padevsky-Berthold, Dresden 1959.

(e) 13 P-KR4 N-B4 14 P-R5 O-O-O 15 P-R6 R-N3 16 P-R7 R-R1 17 R-QN1 P-B3 Or 17...P-Q5 followed by 18...B-K1. **18 P×P B-K1 19 Q×BP R×RP 20 R×R Q×R 21 R-N3** (Vasyukov-Doroshkevich, Moscow 1967), and now, with Ivkov's suggestion 21...P-Q5!, Black has a good game.

13   N-N3

The most reliable continuation. Creating some cover on the KN-file, this move enables White to complete the development of his K-side and keep the position on the other wing more closed so that Black's counterplay and initiative will have fewer prospects of success.

	13	**...**	**O-O-O**
	14	**B-K2**	**N-B4**

The normal move here, but a good alternative is 14...Q-N3 to make castling difficult and to prevent R-QN1.

	15	**N×N**	**P×N**
	16	**O-O**	

After 16 B-B3 the game Ree-Darga, Amsterdam 1969, continued 16...Q-N3!? 17 Q×QBP K-N1 18 Q-N3 (or 18 Q-N2 Q-B4 19 R-QN1 P-N3 20 P-B3 P-Q5 21 B-Q2 with unclear complications) 18...Q×Q 19 P×Q N-Q5 20 K-B2 N×P 21 R-QN1 B-R5 with an unclear position.

16	...	P-Q5
17	R-QN1	

If 17 B-B3 P-B3 with equality, though Pachman suggests 18 B-Q5 as giving White a slight advantage.

17	...	P-B3

Black must not allow White time for B-R3-Q6.

18	P×P	KR-B1

Why not the QR?

19	B-B3	R×P
20	R-K1	R-K3
21	R×R	B×R
22	P-QR4	

Otherwise the situation would be tragic for White. The text move is the only way to create a square for the underdeveloped QB and to connect White's heavy pieces.

22	...	P-R3
23	B-R3	Q-Q2
24	B-K2	B-Q4
25	Q×RP	P×Q
26	B×Pch	K-B2
27	R-N7ch	K-B1
28	R-N1ch	K-B2
29	R-N7ch	K-B1
30	R-N1ch	Drawn

GAME 1

White: Larsen
Black: Portisch

Amsterdam Interzonal 1964

Notes by Larsen

1	**P-K4**	**P-K3**
2	**P-Q4**	**P-Q4**
3	**N-QB3**	**B-N5**
4	**P×P**	**P×P**
5	**Q-B3!?**	

This set Portisch thinking! The exchange variation has had a reputation as a dull drawish line for many years; for instance, 5 B-Q3 N-QB3 (also see the next game) 6 N-K2 KN-K2 followed by ...B-KB4, and there are no problems for Black.

The text move, which I had played in some blitz games against my friend Palle Ravn (Danish champion, 1957), is directed against the very manoeuvre ...KN-K2 and ...B-KB4; after 5...N-K2 6 B-Q3 QN-B3 7 N-

K2 White's position is quite attractive.

Because of this game 5 Q-B3 became almost popular for a short while, but is disappeared again because of the reply 5...Q-K2ch!, for instance 6 N-K2 N-QB3 7 Q×QP N-B3 with more than enough for the pawn.

During the game I thought of the possibility 5...Q-K2ch and toyed with the idea 6 B-K3 B×Nch 7 P×B Q-R6 8 K-Q2, which may look strange but is very good for White. However, a Yugoslav game Mestrovic-Maric, Kraljevo, 1967, seems to prove that 6 B-K3 is of dubious value because of 6...N-KB3 7 B-Q3 P-B4! After this I tend to believe that 5...Q-K2ch is Black's strongest move.

Immediately after the game O'Kelly stated that the easiest solution for Black was 5...B-K3, but I don't agree; after 6 B-Q3 Q-B3 White ought to play 7 B-KB4!

Also 5...P-QB4 has been recommended, but 6 P×P P-Q5 7 P-QR3 Q-R4 8 R-N1 looks very good for White.

Portisch had enough to think about!

5	**...**	**N-QB3**
6	**B-QN5**	**N-K2**
7	**B-KB4**	**O-O**

Konstantinopolsky, Bronstein's second during this tournament, later recommended 7...B-KB4. The idea must be 8 O-O-O Q-Q2 followed by ...O-O-O. This is probably a satisfactory development for Black, but can 7...O-O be a mistake? As Portisch's next move clearly demonstrates, he is now in a fighting mood and doesn't mind that the two kings do not seek shelter on the same side.

8 O-O-O   N-R4?

A premature attack, as far as I can see. But afterwards we are all so very wise. 8...B-KB4 has been recommended, but it is not obvious to me why Black should let White's P-KN4, part of a broad advance on the K-side, gain a tempo by attacking the bishop. To me 8...B-K3 looks like the right move.

9 KN-K2   P-QB3
10 B-Q3   P-QN4
11 P-KR4!

The right prelude to the attack, because it very quickly creates a threat, gaining an important tempo.

11 ...   N-B5
12 P-R5   P-B3

There it is. Why does Black not play 12...Q-R4 or 12...P-R4.? Because of the threat 13 P-R6 P-N3 14 B-B7! Q×B 15 Q-B6 and wins.

That Black does not like 12...P-KR3 is understandable: the advance of the white KNP would create powerful threats.

13 P-KN4   Q-R4?

Here Portisch probably overlooked an important defensive resource for White. Afterwards 13...P-R4 was recommended, but after, for instance, 14 Q-N3 P-R5 15 P-N5 P-KB4 16 B×N QP×B 17 P-R3, Black is faced with almost the same problems as in the game.

14 B×N   QP×B

After 14...NP×B it would be difficult for Black to make use of the QN-file. And he would give up all hopes of a pawn storm.

15 P-R3!   B×N

The resource mentioned earlier was a trap for the queen: 15...B×RP 16 P×B Q×Pch 17 K-Q2 P-N5 18 R-R1 P×Nch 19 N×P Q-N5 20 KR-QN1!

But after this exchange White's advantage is clear. Black is very weak on the black squares, and White occupies the K-file first.

16 N×B   Q-Q1

A sensible decision. After 16...P-N5 17 P×P Q×P 18 KR-K1 Black has a wretched game. Now White might play 17 N×P, but Black gets good counter-chances: his very best reply is 17...Q-Q4!

17 KR-K1   P-R4?

It is easy for the commentators to write that Portisch ought to play 17...N-Q4. The ending after 18 N×N

Q×N 19 Q×Q P×Q 20 P-KB3 is very unpleasant for Black in spite of the bishops of opposite colours. The black bishop is very passive, and White controls the only open file. In some variations the white king goes to QB3, threatening to march right into the black position. This must be prevented with ...P-QR4, but then this pawn becomes vulnerable.

| 18 | Q-N3 | R-R2 |

To 18...P-N5 19 B-Q6! was a nasty reply.

19   P-R6!

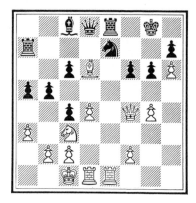

It is not necessary for White to open any lines on this side, the K-file being there to be used. But a further weakening of the black squares in Black's position is welcome.

| 19 | ... | P-N3 |
| 20 | B-Q6 | R-K1 |

Weakens KB3. But also after 20...R-KB2 21 R-K2 Black is lost.

21   Q-B4!

White has a clearly won position. Would that have happened just as quickly with a theoretical line? (I have only played 5 Q-B3 in a tournament game on this one occasion: since then it is no longer a surprise weapon.)

| 21 | ... | K-B2 |

Or 21...N-Q4 22 N×N P×N 23 Q×BP! Q×Q 24 R×Rch K-B2 25 R-B8ch K-K3 26 R-K1ch! or 23...R-KB2 24 Q-R4!

| 22 | B-K5 | P-KB4 |

A draught is blowing through the black squares now! But 22...N-N1 23 N-K4 and 22...N-Q4 23 N×N P×N 24 B×P! are no better.

| 23 | B-N8 | R-N2 |
| 24 | Q-K5! | |

The most elegant solution. But naturally 24 N-K4 N-Q4 25 N-Q6ch K-B1 26 N×R(N7) was also good enough.

| 24 | ... | R-KN1 |
| 25 | P-N5 | P-N5 |

After 25...N-Q4 26 N×N P×N 27 P-B4 Black is completely paralysed and White wins by doubling rooks on the

K-file. That was my plan, I believe, and it is very pretty. But 27 B-Q6! is a quicker method.

26	Q-B6ch	K-K1
27	Q×QBPch	K-B2

Or 27...Q-Q2 28 R×Nch K×R 29 Q-B6ch or 27...R-Q2 28 N-Q5 or 27...K-B1 28 B-Q6 P×N 29 R×N R×R 30 R-K1.

White has more than one winning continuation. Good enough, for instance, is 28 Q×BPch K-B1 29 R×N R×R 30 P×P. But I found something that looks more energetic.

28	Q-B6ch	K-K1
29	P-Q5	

Another idea was 29 N-Q5 Q×N 30 B-Q6 Q-B2 31 B×N R×B 32 Q-B6ch K-Q1 33 R×R K×R 34 Q-B7ch B-Q2 35 R-K1ch or 33...Q×R 34 Q-Q5ch. But Black may prolong the game with 31...Q×Q.

29	...	R-B1

After 29...P×N 30 P-Q6 Black has no reasonable move.

30	Q-B6ch	Q-Q2

Or 30...K-B2 31 Q×BP.

31	B-Q6	R-KB2

Or 31...Q×Q 32 P×Q R-R2 33 N-Q5 R-KB2 34 P-B7.

32	B×N	P×N

Or 32...Q×Q 33 B-B5ch. Or 32...R×B 33 R×Rch.

33	B-N4ch	Resigns

GAME 2

White: Eley
Black: Uhlmann

Hastings 1972/3

1	P-K4	P-K3
2	P-Q4	P-Q4
3	N-QB3	B-N5
4	P×P	P×P
5	B-Q3	N-QB3
6	N-K2	KN-K2
7	O-O	O-O

Or 7...B-KB4 8 N-N3 B-N3 9 QN-K2 Q-Q2 10 P-KB4 P-B4 with equality.

8	N-N3?	

This move already hands over the initiative to Black. White had to play 8 B-KB4 or 8 P-QR3. After 8 B-KN5 P-KR3 9 B-R4 B-K3 10 P-QR3 B×N 11 P×B Q-Q2 Black has a good game as in Hennings-Uhlmann.

| 8 | ... | **P-B4!** |

Also satisfactory is 8...B-K3 9 QN-K2 B-Q3 10 P-QB3 N-N3 11 N-B5 B×N 12 B×B N(B3)-K2 with an equal game.

| 9 | QN-K2 | B-Q3 |
| 10 | N-R5 | |

It was essential to play 10 P-KB4.

10	...	Q-K1
11	N(R5)-B4	P-KR3
12	B-QN5?	

This pointless move brings White into serious trouble. He should try 12 P-B4. After 12 P-KN3 P-KN4 13 N-N2 P-B5! 14 P×P Q-R4! Black has a winning K-side attack.

12	...	P-N4
13	B×N	Q×B
14	N-Q3	P-B5!
15	P-KB3	N-B4
16	N-K5	Q-N3!
17	N-N4	-	B-Q2
18	P-QR4	QR-K1
19	Q-Q3!	K-N2

Countering the threat of 20 N×RP ch N×N 21 Q-N6ch.

20	B-Q2	N-R5
21	P-R5	Q-N4
22	N-B3	Q×Q

This weakening of White's pawn structure ensures Black the better endgame.

23	P×Q	P-B3
24	N-R4	B-KB4
25	N-B5	R-B2!
26	QR-K1	R×R
27	B×R	

The best defence, as White loses at least a pawn after 27 R×R QB×N 28 P×B P-B6! etc.

27	...	N-N3
28	B-B3	P-R4
29	N-B2	P-N5

Obtaining a greater advantage in space.

30	P×P	P×P
31	R-K1	P-N6!
32	P×P	P×P
33	N-R1	

A sad retreat for the knight, but the only way to avoid loss of material. After 33 N-R3 QB×N 34 P×B N-R5! 35 R-KB1 (not 35 N-K6ch? K-B3!) 35...R-K2 the black rook penetrates to the seventh rank, with a win.

| 33 | ... | P-N3! |
| 34 | N-K6ch | |

If 34 P×P P×P 35 N-R4 B×P 36

N×QNP B-KB5 followed by 37...B-K6ch and 38...R-B8 mate.

34	...	K-B3
35	N-Q8	R-B2
36	P-R6	B-B5
37	R-Q1	B-N5
38	R-K1	R-B1

This rook now penetrates decisively into White's K-side, at the same time decentralizing the white knight.

39	N-N7	R-KR1!
40	B-N4	R-R7!
41	N-Q8	

There is no defence as 41 B-Q6 fails to 41...B×B 42 N×B N-B5!

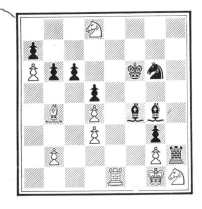

| 41 | ... | P-B4! |

A fine move, cutting off the bishop, so that White cannot answer ...N-R5 with B-K7ch.

| 42 | P×P | N-R5 |

43	P×P	R×Pch
44	K-B1	R-R7
45	Resigns	

GAME 3

White: Dvoretsky
Black: Vaganian

USSR Championship 1974

Notes by Dvoretsky

1	P-K4	P-K3
2	P-Q4	P-Q4
3	N-QB3	B-N5
4	N-K2	P×P
5	P-QR3	B-K2
6	N×P	N-QB3
7	B-K3	N-B3
8	N(2)-B3	O-O?

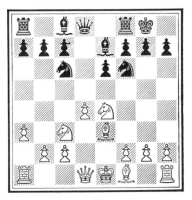

A definite inaccuracy. Black can equalize at once by 8...N×N 9 N×N P-K4 10 P×P Q×Qch 11 R×Q N×P since 10 P-Q5 doesn't work for White — 10...N-Q5 11 B×N Q×P!

Apart from 9...P-K4 Black could

43

also consider 9...O-O creating the characteristic threat in this line of ...P-B4-B5.

| 9 | N-N3! | N-Q4 |

Against Alekhine in his 1935 world title match Euwe got an approximately level game by 9...P-QN3 10 B-K2 B-N2 11 O-O Q-Q2.

| 10 | N×N | P×N |
| 11 | B-Q3 | P-B4 |

A move that is interesting and characteristic of Vaganian's style, but insufficiently thought out. However, Black already stands slightly worse.

| 12 | N-K2 |

In Fyodorov-Gulko, Moscow Championship 1974, White played the weaker 12 Q-R5 P-KN3 13 Q-R6 R-B2 when Black has adequate counter-play. The text prepares to fix the enemy KBP.

| 12 | ... | B-N4 |

While Black prepares to advance the said pawn. At this point I thought a long time to see which line was better — 13 Q-Q2 B×B 14 P×B followed by 15 O-O-O with a clear advantage, or 13 B×B Q×B 14 P-KB4 preparing to transfer my knight to K5. After a lot of hesitation I chose the latter line.

| 13 | B×B? | Q×B |

Then, straight away I realized that 14 P-KB4 would leave the KNP en prise, and otherwise Black gets in ...P-B5 with an excellent game. Thus my gross miscalculation at move 13 robbed me of all my advantage.

14	P-KN3	P-B5!
15	Q-Q2	B-N5
16	O-O-O	Q-B3

Black has seized the initiative, but White's position is quite sound.

17	P-QB3	N-R4
18	Q-B2	Q-KR3
19	K-N1	B-B6
20	KR-N1	P×P

If 20...Q×P then the simple 21 QR-K1 is good, since Black can then easily find himself under attack.

| 21 | RP×P | N-B5 |
| 22 | QR-K1 | B-K5 |

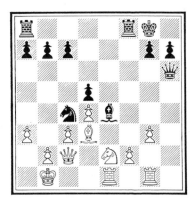

| 23 | N-B4? |

44

I saw that after 23 B×B P×B (not 23...N-Q7ch 24 K-R1 P×B? 25 R-R1 Q-N4 26 N-B4 or 24...N×B 25 N-B4 with the better game for White) 24 N-B4 QR-K1 25 K-R1 White stands no worse, but I decided to see if I could achieve more. I calculated that after 23 N-B4 Black cannot play 23...QR-K1 because of 24 R×B! R×R 25 B×N, and then I started analysing 23...B×B 24 Q×B Q-QN3 25 R-K2.

I established that after 25...N×RPch (25...QR-K1 26 K-R2 Q-N4 27 R(1)-K1) 26 K-B1 N-B5 27 N×P Q-QR3 28 N-K7ch K-R1 29 R-R1 Q-R8ch 30 Q-N1 Q×Qch 31 K×Q KR-K1 32 P-B4 (threat 33 R×Pch!) 32...P-KR3 33 R(1)-K1, White has the advantage. So I confidently played 23 N-B4 and immediately realized that Black can play ...Q-QN3 at once without exchanging bishops first. Without much thought my opponent chose this line.

23   ...   Q-QN3

With two fearsome threats: 24...N×RPch and 24...R×N 25 P×R B×B.

For a moment it seemed to me that White could save himself by the queen sacrifice 24 B×B N×RPch 25 K-B1 N×Q 26 B×QPch K-R1 27 R-K6, threatening 28 N-N6ch. However, after 27...R×N! 28 R×Q RP×R 29 P×R Black wins by 29...R-R8ch 30 K×N R×R. Still, White does have a defence.

24   K-R2!   R×N

Could Black not have taken advantage of White's oversight at move 23? Yes! He should have reversed the order of his moves: 23...R×N! 24 P×R Q-QN3 25 B×B N×RPch 26 K-B1 N×Q 27 B×QPch K-R1, or 24 R×B R×R 25 B×N Q-K3 26 B-Q3 R-K8ch 27 R×R Q×Rch 28 K-R2. In both variations White still has some chances but there is no doubt about Black's advantage. (Note that in the second variation White has the threats 29 B×Pch and 29 Q-N3.)

| 25 | R×B! | R×R |
| 26 | B×N | Q-K3 |

Or 26...R-K2 27 B×Pch and White is all right.

27	B-Q3	R-K8
28	B×Pch	K-R1
29	B-B5	Q-K2

Or 29...Q-K7? 30 R-R1ch! K-N1 31 B-R7ch etc.

30   P-KB4!

Forcing the draw. After 30 R-N2 R-KR8 it would be a hard fight with some advantage to Black.

30	...	R×R
31	Q-R2ch	K-N1
32	Q-R7ch	K-B1
33	Q-R8ch	K-B2
34	Q-R5ch	**Drawn**

If 34...P-KN3 35 Q-R7ch! etc.

GAME 4

White: Fischer
Black: Kovacevic

Rovinj/Zagreb 1970

Notes by Kovacevic

1	P-K4	P-K3
2	P-Q4	P-Q4
3	N-QB3	B-N5
4	P-QR3	B×Nch
5	P×B	P×P
6	Q-N4	N-KB3
7	Q×NP	R-N1
8	Q-R6	QN-Q2

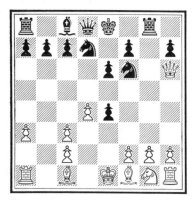

The opening move to Alatortsev's plan wherein Black saves time by omitting the move ...P-QB4. The game Foguelman-R.Byrne, Buenos Aires 1964, went 9 B-N2 N-N3 10 P-QB4 N-R5 11 O-O-O B-Q2 12 P-KB3 Q-K2 with advantage to Black.

9 N-K2

After 9 P-B3 P-B4 a sharp situation arises, not yet tested in practice — Uhlmann.

9	...	P-N3
10	B-N5	Q-K2

The key move! White must meet the threat of 11...N-N5, forcing 12 B×Q N×Q 13 B-R4 B-N2 14 B-N3 O-O-O with better play for Black.

11 Q-R4

This creates a very similar position to that in the game Watson-Whiteley (8...P-N3 9 B-KN5 R-N3 10 Q-R4) but with the basic difference that the black rook is not on KN3 so that White cannot play N-B4 with tempo. Apart from that, with 10...Q-K2! Black is preparing to castle, while at the same time preventing White from doing so. Finally, by employing the correct sequence of moves (...N-Q2, ...P-N3, ...Q-K2, ...B-N2) according to Alatortsev's plan, Black has even saved two tempi in the opening. This is decisive, since after the text move Black is in a rather more favourable position.

11	...	B-N2
12	N-N3	

12 N-B4 would have led to 12...P-KR3! and if 13 B×P R-R1 or if 13 Q×RP O-O-O! with dangerous threats.

12	...	P-KR3!

A logical move which relieves White's pressure on the KR4-Q8 diagonal and effectively demolishes his strategical plan. White does not dare to accept the gift with 13 Q×RP, since he loses a piece after 13...N-N5 14 B×Q N×Q 15 B-R4 R-N5, nor with 13 B×P on account of 13...R-N5! 14 Q-R3 O-O-O 15 B-K2 (if 15 B-Q2 R(1)-N1 16 B-K2 R(5)-N2 with a dangerous attack) 15...R(5)-N1 16 Q-R4 R-R1 17 Q-B4 N-Q4 18 Q-Q2 R(Q1)-N1 19 P-QB4 P-K6! 20 B×P N×B 21 Q×N B×P 22 R-KN1 R×P with advantage to Black.

13 B-Q2?

He should have played 13 B-B1 to leave open the possibility of withdrawing the queen, now standing quite passively on KR4.

13	...	O-O-O
14	B-K2	N-B1

Suddenly Black's finely positioned pieces threaten the white queen. Not 14...P-K6?? 15 P×P B×P 16 R-KN1 B-N2 17 P-K4! with a great advantage to White.

15 O-O

This is simply suicidal. Better is 15 N-R5 N-Q4 16 Q×Q N×Q 17 N-N3 with equal chances, but not here 17 B×P R×NP 18 N-N3 P-K6! 19 B×P? R×N winning. — Uhlmann.

| 15 | ... | N-N3 |

16 Q×RP

16 Q-R3 is no better because of 16...N-Q4 17 Q×RP N-R5! 18 P-QB4 R-R1 19 Q-N5 P-KB3 20 Q-N4 R(Q1)-N1 21 Q×KP(4) N-QB6 22 Q-K3 N×Bch 23 Q×N B×P, and Black's attack penetrates.

16	...	R-R1
17	Q-N5	R(Q1)-N1
18	P-B3	

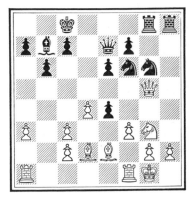

White offers his queen for a rook and a knight — e.g. 18...N-R5? 19 P×P R×Q 20 B×Q followed by B×N and White would gain a clear advantage.

| 18 | ... | P-K6 |

An effective response to the trap.

19 B×P

After 19 Q×P comes 19...N-Q4 and ...Q-R5 with irresistible threats.

19	...	N-B1
20	Q-N5	N-Q4
21	K-B2	

This reply is forced. After the retreat of the bishop comes ...P-R3 and ...Q-R5.

21	...	P-R3
22	Q-Q3	R×P
23	R-R1	Q-R5
24	R×R	Q×R
25	N-B1	

25 N-K4 would allow 25...R×Pch 26 K-K1 P-KB4 27 N-B2 N×B 28 Q×N P-B5.

25	...	R×Pch
26	K-K1	Q-R5ch
27	K-Q2	N-N3!
28	R-K1	N(3)-B5
29	B×N	N×B
30	Q-K3	R-B7!

Because of the threat of ...B×P and ...N-N7 White loses at least a piece.

31 Resigns

√-2/27/84   GAME 5

White: Planinc
Black: Ivkov

Yugoslav Team Championship 1971

Notes by Isayev

1	P-K4	P-K3
2	P-Q4	P-Q4

3	N-QB3	B-N5
4	Q-N4?!	N-KB3
5	Q×NP	R-N1
6	Q-R6	

Here 6...P-B4 is accepted as the most energetic move. Ivkov, however, prefers another, quieter path: he takes a pawn and then hastens to develop his Q-side.

6	...	P×P
7	N-K2	P-N3
8	B-N5	QN-Q2
9	O-O-O	B-N2
10	P-Q5	

This looks strong. 10...P×P can be advantageously met by 11 N×QP, but Black has a refutation which Planinc did not reckon with.

10	...	B-KB1
11	Q-R4	P×P
12	R×P	

1-2-900

This is forced, since 12 N×QP now fails against 12...R×B 13 Q×R N×N

48

14 R×N Q×Q 15 R×Q B-KR3, (this is why 10...B-KB1! was necessary) 16 P-KR4 P-KB3.

12	...	B×R
13	N×B	B-K2
14	N×Nch	N×N
15	N-B3	N-N5

This forces exchanges, after which Black has not only the advantage of the exchange, but also the initiative.

16	Q×N	B×Bch
17	K-N1	K-B1
18	B-B4	

18 Q×P is of course met by 18...Q-K1.

18	...	Q-Q5
19	B-Q5	R-Q1
20	Q-B5	B-B3
21	B×KP	R-N4
22	Q-B3	R-N4!
23	R-Q1	R×Pch
24	K-B1	

If 24 K×R then 24...Q-N5ch 25 K-B1 B-N4ch.

| 24 | ... | R-N8ch |

If 25 K×R then follows 25...Q-N5ch 26 K-B1 B-N4ch 27 Q-K3 B×Qch 28 P×B R×Rch.

25 Resigns

White: Levy
Black: Birnboim

Netanya 1973

Notes by Levy

1	P-K4	P-K3
2	P-Q4	P-Q4
3	N-QB3	B-N5
4	P-K5	N-K2
5	P-QR3	B×Nch
6	P×B	P-QN3
7	Q-N4	N-N3
8	P-KR4	P-KR4
9	Q-Q1	

| 9 | ... | B-R3 |

Naturally 9...N×RP 10 P-N3 N-N3 11 R×P is very much to White's advantage.

| 10 | B×B | N×B |
| 11 | B-N5 | Q-Q2?! |

After 11...P-KB3 12 Q-Q3 K-B2 13 P×P P×P White's advantage is somewhat less than in the game. But on 11...Q-B1 White can continue strongly with 12 N-K2 P-QB4 13 R-R3 N-N1! 14 N-N3 (also good is 14 P-QB4!) 14...N-Q2 15 N×P R-R2 when Black has insufficient counterplay for the pawn (Kostro-Sokolsky, Poland-Byelorussia match 1966).

12 Q-Q3

Also quite strong and even more effective is the immediate 12 N-K2 Q-B3 13 O-O N-N1 14 P-KB4 N-Q2 15 Q-Q3 N(Q2)-B1 16 P-B5, e.g. 16...P×P 17 R×P N-K3 18 QR-KB1 N×B 19 P×N O-O-O (or 19...O-O 20 N-N3 P-R5 21 N-R5 with a devastating attack) 20 R×P R(Q1)-N1 21 Q-B5ch K-N2 22 Q-Q7 and White won. Portisch-Ivkov, Zagreb 1965.

12	...	N-N1
13	N-K2	P-QB4

If 13...Q-B3 14 O-O Q-B5 15 Q×Q P×Q 16 P-B4 followed by P-B5 with a good game.

14	O-O	N-B3
15	N-N3	R-QB1

15...N(N3)-K2 followed by ...P-N3 would be a more passive approach to Black's problems.

16 P-KB4

16 P-R4 would transpose to the game Sakharov-Lein, USSR 1968, in which the advance of the QRP seemed to bear little relevance to the manner in which White won: 16...P×P 17 P×P N(N3)-K2 18 Q-Q1 N-B4 19 N×P! N(B3)×QP 20 B-B6! R-B5 21 P-QB3 N-B3 22 B×P N×B 23 N-B6ch winning.

The text is a direct attempt to take advantage of Black's K-side weaknesses.

16 ... N(B3)-K2

On 16...N(N3)-K2 I had originally intended 17 P-B5 P×BP 18 N×BP N×N 19 R×N P×P 20 P×P N×QP! 21 P-K6! e.g. 21...P×P? 22 R-K5 N-B3 23 Q-N6ch K-B1 24 R-KB1ch K-N1 25 R×KP; or 21...Q×P 22 R(B5)-B1, both of which are very good for White. But after 21...N×KP! 22 R×QP Q-B3 it is Black who stands better. So 16... N(N3)-K2 should be met by 17 B×N N×B and then 18 P-B5 P×P 19 N×BP N×N 20 R×N when Black's Q-side counterplay is too slow.

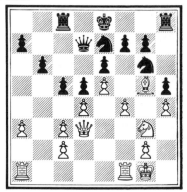

Similarly, 16...P×P 17 P×P N(N3)-K2 18 B×N Q×B 19 P-B5 is also good for White: 19...Q×KRP 20 P×P Q×Pch 21 Q×Q N×Q 22 P×Pch K-K2 23 QR-Q1 with much the better ending.

17	P-B5	N×BP
18	N×N	P×N
19	R×P	O-O

Saidy quipped that Petrosian would probably try to defend Black's position by 19...R-KN1 and then ...N-R1.

20	QR-KB1	P×P
21	P×P	R-B5

21...Q-R5 loses to 22 R×P! R×R 23 R×R K×R 24 Q-B5ch K-N1 25 Q×Rch K-R2 26 P-B3 followed by P-K6 and P-K7 etc.

22	P-B3	Q-B3
23	Q-B3	R×BP
24	Q×RP	R-KN6

Enticing the king to the KR2-QN8 diagonal so that after an eventual P-K6 Black may have a useful queen check (see, for example, the note to 27 R×P concerning the failure of 27 P×P).

If 24...R×P 25 Q-N4 and White wins because of the threat of 26 P-R5 N-R1 27 B-B6. 24...Q-B5 loses to 25 P-K6 Q×Pch 26 K-R1 P×P 27 R×Rch N×R 28 Q-B7ch K-R2 29 B-B6.

25	K-R2	R-Q6

26   R-B6!!

One point of this sacrifice is that if black declines it with (say) 26...Q-B2 White can win quickly by giving up his queen: 27 Q×N! P×Q 28 R×Rch K-R2 29 R-K8 and 30 R(B1)-B8 mating. Other queen moves fail either to the same idea or to 27 P-K6.

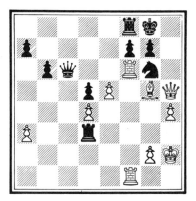

26	...	P×R
27	R×P	

Attempts to mate at KN7 permit Black to turn the tables: 27 B×P R×QP 28 Q-R6 Q×B! and 29...R×Pch, or 27 P×P Q-Q3ch 28 K-R1 R-B1 and now Q-R6 can be met by ...Q-B1.

27	...	Q-B7

My opponent, understandably, did not relish his position after 27...Q-B2 28 R×Nch (not 28 Q-N4? R×QP!) 28...P×R 29 Q×Pch Q-N2 30 Q×R, e.g. 30...Q-R2 31 Q-KN3 Q-N3 32 P-K6.

51

28	P-K6	Q-B2ch
29	K-R1	R×RP
30	P×Pch	R×P
31	Q×Nch	K-R1
32	B-B4	

Not 32 Q×R?? R-R8ch 33 R-B1 Q×Q.

32	...	Q-K2
33	B-K5	R-R8ch
34	K-R2	R-N2
35	R-B4	R-K8

If 35...Q×B 36 Q-R6ch and then I take the queen.

36	Q-R5ch	K-N1
37	B×R	Q×B

Played with only seconds to spare. But in any case Black cannot save his queen: 37...K×B 38 R-N4ch K-B3 39 R-N6ch K-B2 40 Q-R7ch K-K1 41 R-N8ch and 42 R-N7.

38	R-N4	**Resigns**

GAME 7

White: Honfi
Black: Farago

Hungarian Team Championship 1973

Notes by Csom

1	P-K4	P-K3

2	P-Q4	P-Q4
3	N-QB3	B-N5
4	P-K5	N-K2
5	N-KB3!?	

5	...	P-QB4
6	P×P	QN-B3
7	B-Q3	P-Q5

7...N-N3 is less happy after 8 B×N RP×B 9 B-K3 with a slight advantage to White.

8	P-QR3	B-R4
9	P-QN4	N×NP
10	P×N	B×P
11	O-O	

This is best: to complete his development as quickly as possible. It is weaker to play 11 B-QN5ch B-Q2! 12 Q×P B×Nch 13 Q×B(B3) B×B when Black has the better game.

11	...	B×N

52

If 11...P×N, 12 N-N5! is dangerous.

12 R-N1   P-KR3

This move is necessary to prevent N-N5.

13 N-Q2!?

A sharp and difficult struggle occurred in a correspondence game Zinser-Ackermann, 1964: 13 N-R4 Q-Q4 14 P-B4 B-Q2 15 P-B5 etc.

13 ...   B×N!

The knight cannot be allowed to reach Q6.

14 B×B   B-Q2?!

Farago would like to sacrifice his QNP in order to gain control of the diagonal QR1-KR8 as quickly as possible and then attack the pawns on K4 and QB4. Honfi, with the ensuing interesting, if somewhat over-bold conception, tries to win a different, more important pawn. In my opinion Black can equalize more quickly by means of 14...O-O 15 Q-N4 N-B4 16 Q-K4 B-Q2! 17 R×P (or 17 Q×NP) 17...Q-B1.

15 Q-N4   B-B3
16 R-N4!?

So he has his eye on the QP: of course 16 Q×NP loses to 16...R-KN1.

16	...	Q-Q4
17	R×QP	Q×KP
18	R-K1	Q×BP?

A sign of over-confidence. The only effective defence is 18...Q-B3 upon which White has two possible continuations:

a) 19 B-B3 O-O 20 R-QB4 Q-N4 21 Q-R3 N-N3 22 B×N P×B 23 Q×KPch K-R2 with equality;

b) 19 B-K3, which is not so good on account of 19...P-KR4 20 Q-R3 (if 20 Q-N3 then 20...P-R5 21 Q-N4 P-R6 22 P-N3 Q-B6) 20...P-KN4!?

We can safely write under the following diagram "White to move and win", for the following sacrifice tears Black's defences to shreds.

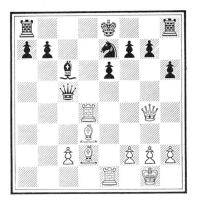

19 R×P!!   P×R

The sacrifice wins, whether accepted or not. 19...B-Q2 20 R×B! K×R 21 R-K5 dis ch P-B4 22 B×BPch wins the queen.

20 B-N6ch   K-B1

Or 20...N×B Q×Nch K-B1 22 B-N4 winning.

| 21 | R-KB4ch | Q-B4 |

Or 21...N-B4 22 B-N4.

22	B-N4!	K-N1
23	B×Q	P×B
24	Q-K2	N-N3
25	R×P	K-R2
26	R-B7	KR-K1
27	Q-Q1	K-N1
28	R-B7	N-B5
29	Q-N4	N-K3
30	B-B3!	Resigns

GAME 8

White: Ljubojevic
Black: Andersson

Amsterdam 1972

Notes by Balashov

1	P-K4	P-K3
2	P-Q4	P-Q4
3	N-QB3	B-N5
4	P-K5	P-QN3
5	Q-N4	B-B1
6	N-B3	Q-Q2
7	P-QR4	

| 7 | ... | B-R3 |
| 8 | N-QN5 | N-K2 |

Not 8...P-QB3? because of 9 N-Q6ch B×N 10 Q×NP.

9	Q-R5	N-N3
10	P-R4	P-QB3
11	N-B3	B×B
12	K×B	

It is clear that White has achieved nothing and stands worse.

12	...	P-QB4
13	P-R5	P×QP
14	N(KB3)×P	B-B4
15	N-N3	N-B3
16	P-B4	O-O
17	N×B	P×N
18	Q-Q1	P-B3

Black has succeeded in completing his development and proceeds to operate actively in the centre.

| 19 | P×P | |

19 ...   **N-Q5!?**

A very interesting continuation, which involves the sacrifice of a piece. Nevertheless, it would have been stronger to play the straightforward 19...R×P 20 N-K4 R-B2 21 N×P (21 N-N5 R-B4 gives White nothing) 21...Q-Q3 22 N-Q3 P-K4, with advantage to Black.

20	P-R5	N×KBP
21	P-KN3	

The knight at KB4 has nowhere to go, but Black has a menacing initiative in return for his piece.

21	...	R×P
22	P×N	P-K4
23	B-K3	QR-KB1

23...R-Q1 to defend the pawn at Q4 is also of interest, but the move played is more energetic.

24   R-KR2

A critical position, in which Andersson missed his chance of developing his attack.

24 ...   **K-R1?**

White would have repulsed the attack after 24...R×Pch 25 B×R R×Bch 26 K-N2 or 24...Q-KB2 25 K-N1 R×P 26 B×R Q×B 27 K-R1. The correct solution was 24...P-N4! After 25 P×P e.p. R×NP or 25 R-N2 Q-R6 26 Q-N4? Q×B 27 Q×Pch R-N3 Black keeps up a strong attack. It is a pity that Andersson failed to bring his conception to its logical conclusion.

25	K-N1	P×P
26	B×N	P×B
27	Q×P	Q-N5ch
28	R-N2	Q×P

If 28...Q-R6 then 29 P-KR6!

29	N×P	**Resigns**

GAME 9

White: Ciocaltea
Black: Hecht

Budapest 1973

1	P-K4	P-K3
2	P-Q4	P-Q4
3	N-QB3	B-N5
4	P-K5	P-QN3
5	P-QR3	B×Nch
6	P×B	Q-Q2

7	N-R3	B-R3
8	B×B	N×B
9	Q-N4	P-KB4
10	Q-R5ch	P-N3

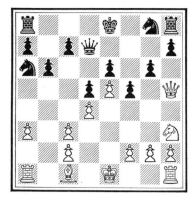

11	Q-K2	N-N1
12	P-QB4!?	

After 12 O-O N-QB3 13 P-QR4 N-R4 14 R-Q1 N-B5 15 R-Q3 P-KR3 16 N-B4 Q-B2 17 R-KR3 P-KN4 18 N-R5 O-O-O Black has good play. Bednarski-Andersson, Lund 1972.

12	...	N-QB3
13	P-QB3?	

White should play 13 B-N2 P×P 14 Q×P KN-K2 15 Q-Q3 R-Q1 16 R-Q1 P-QN4! with an unclear position.

13	...	KN-K2

Also good is 13...P×P 14 Q×P N-R4.

14	P×P	KN×P
15	B-N2	P-QN4!

A positional pawn sacrifice giving Black a clear superiority on the Q-side.

16	Q×P	

After 16 P-QR4 P-N5! 17 P-QB4 N-B6! 18 B×N P×B 19 P-Q5 P×P 20 P-K6 Q-Q3, Black has the advantage.

16	...	R-QN1
17	Q-K2	N-R4
18	P-QR4	

Better drawing chances are offered by 18 P-QB4 N×P 19 Q×N R×B 20 O-O Q-N4 with a slight plus to Black.

18	...	Q-B3
19	O-O	Q-B5!
20	Q×Q	

The exchange sacrifice also fails after 20 Q-Q2 N-N6 21 Q-R6 N×R 22 B×N Q-Q6! threatening ...R-N8.

20	...	N×Q
21	B-R3	K-Q2

An inexact move. It was important to complete the blockade by 21...P-QR4!

22	P-R5!	N×BP
23	B-B5	P-QR3
24	N-B4	R-N6

After 24...N-Q4 White obtains counterplay by 25 N×N P×N 26 P-K6ch.

25	P-R4	R-K1

25...KR-QN1 is better.

26	KR-B1	Drawn

GAME 10

White: Tringov
Black: Spiridonov

Varna 1973

1	P-K4	P-K3
2	P-Q4	P-Q4
3	N-QB3	B-N5
4	P-K5	Q-Q2
5	P-QR3	B×Nch
6	P×B	P-QN3
7	P-QR4	B-R3
8	B×B	N×B
9	Q-N4	P-KB4

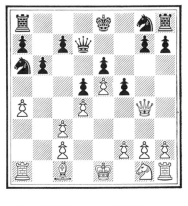

10	Q-R5ch	P-N3
11	Q-K2	N-N1
12	N-B3	N-QB3

13	P-B4	P×P
14	Q×P	P-KR3
15	B-N2	KN-K2
16	O-O	P-KN4
17	KR-Q1	P-N5

If 17...N-R4 18 Q-K2 Q-B3 19 N-Q2 O-O-O (not 19...Q×BP 20 B-R3 threatening both R-QB1 and Q-R5) 20 P-QB4 P-B5, and now in Tringov-Planinc, Athens 1971, 21 Q-Q3 would have given White the advantage.

18	N-Q2	R-Q1
19	Q-B1?	

This allows Black to take the initiative. Correct is 19 N-B1 O-O 20 Q-K2 (or 20 N-N3) with chances for both sides.

19	...	O-O
20	N-N3	N-N3
21	P-QB4	Q-B2
22	Q-K2	KR-K1
23	P-R5	K-R2
24	P-B3?	

This only helps Black.

24	...	R-KN1!
25	BP×P	N-B5
26	Q-B3	R×NP!
27	P-N3	

Acceptance of the sacrifice loses quickly after 27 Q×QN R×NPch 28 Q×R N×Q 29 K×N Q-R4! winning at least a piece.

57

27	...	Q-R4!
28	K-R1	

If 28 Q×QN QR-KN1! and there is no defence to the threat of 29...R×Pch.

28	...	QR-KN1!
29	P×P	

If 29 Q×QN R×P threatening 30...Q×Pch 31 K×R R-R6 mate. If 29 P×N R-N8ch! followed by mate in two.

29	...	RP×P
30	N-Q2	N-N5??

Endangering his well played attack. The correct move was 30...N-R4! 31 R×N (not 31 P×N N×P 32 N×N R-N8ch!) 31...P×R 32 P×N Q-R5! 33 R-KB1 R-N6! 34 Q-B2 Q-R6 35 N-B3 R-N7 36 Q-R4 R×Pch followed by mate.

31 B-B3??

Missing his one chance of saving the game by 31 P×N N-Q6 32 Q×N R-N7 33 N-B3 R(1)-N6 34 Q-B1 etc.

31	...	QN-Q6!
32	P-Q5	

If 32 P×N Black wins brilliantly by 32...R-N8ch!! 33 R×R Q×Qch 34 N×Q N-B7 mate.

32	...	R×P
33	Resigns	

GAME 11

White: Pachman
Black: Uhlmann

Dresden 1957

1	P-K4	P-K3
2	P-Q4	P-Q4
3	N-QB3	B-N5
4	P-K5	P-QB4
5	B-Q2	N-K2
6	P-QR3	

6	...	B×N
7	B×B	P-QN3

Or 7...QN-B3 8 N-B3 P×P 9 N×P (9 B×P equalizes) 9...N×P! 10 N×P B×N 11 B×N O-O 12 B-Q3 N-B3 13 B-N3 Q-B3! and Black has the initiative. Tringov-Uhlmann, Skopje Olympiad 1972.

8	P-QN4	Q-B2
9	N-B3	P×NP
10	B×P	B-R3
11	B-Q3	B×B

12	P×B	QN-B3
13	R-QB1	Q-Q2
14	B-Q6	O-O

More exact was 14...R-QB1 15 O-O N-B4 16 Q-R4 N×B 17 P×N O-O 18 R-B3 Q×P 19 KR-B1 N-K2 with the better ending. Not, however, 14... N-B4 15 O-O N×B 16 P×N with advantage to White.

15	Q-R4	KR-Q1!
16	K-K2	

Not 16 O-O N×KP winning a pawn.

16	...	QR-B1
17	P-N4	Q-N2
18	R-B3	P-QN4
19	Q-N3	N-R4!

The exchange of one pair of rooks helps Black to exploit his Q-side pawn majority.

20	Q-B2	R×R
21	Q×R	N(4)-B3
22	R-QN1	R-QB1
23	Q-N2	P-QR3
24	N-Q2	

24 P-QR4 offered better chances.

24	...	Q-N3!
25	B-B5	

25 N-N3 fails to 25...N-N3 followed by...Q-Q1-R5.

25	...	Q-Q1!

26	P-QR4	

The threat of ...N-N3 and ...Q-R5 forces White's hand.

26	...	P×P!
27	Q-N6	Q×Q
28	R×Q	P-QR4!
29	K-K3	P-R4!
30	R-N7	N-N3
31	P×P?	

31 B-Q6 offered better chances of counterplay, whereas now White's K-side is in ruins.

31	...	N-R5
32	K-B4	N-B4
33	N-B3	R-N1!
34	R-B7	

White dare not exchange rooks in view of his poor pawn position.

34	...	N-N5
35	R-R7	

Or 35 N-K1 P-R6 etc.

35	...	N(N5)×Pch
36	K-N5	R-N5!
37	K-N4?	N×BPch

Not, of course, 37...N×B 38 R-R8ch followed by mate in two.

38	K-B4	N-Q6ch
39	K-N4	N-B7ch
40	K-B4	N-K5!
41	P-R4	R-N8

Threatening 42...R-KB8

42	R-R8ch	K-R2
43	N-N5ch	N×N
44	P×N	R-KB8ch
45	K-N4	N-K6ch
46	K-N3	N-B5
47	R-KB8	R-B4
48	Resigns	

GAME 12

White: Jansa
Black: Korchnoy

Luhacovice 1969

1	P-K4	P-K3
2	P-Q4	P-Q4
3	N-QB3	B-N5
4	P-K5	P-QB4
5	Q-N4	N-K2
6	P-QR3?	

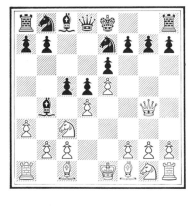

6	...	Q-R4!
7	P×B?!	

There is already no way of avoiding complications. If 7 B-Q2, P×P would be unpleasant.

7	...	Q×R
8	K-Q1	P×QP
9	N-N5	O-O

Eliminating all dangers.

10 N-KB3

The intended 10 N-B7 fails to 10...B-Q2 11 N×R N-R3 12 Q×QP N-B3 followed by 13...KN×NP. Or here 11 P-N5 Q-R4! 12 N×R B×P with a clear advantage to Black.

10	...	QN-B3
11	B-Q3	N-N3
12	R-K1	N×NP!
13	N-R3	

Trying in vain to trap Black's queen.

13	...	N×B
14	P×N	B-Q2
15	N×P	QR-B1
16	N(4)-B2	R×N!
17	K×R	R-B1ch
18	K-Q2	

A sad necessity. Having returned the exchange Black has kept the initiative and he still has an extra pawn.

18	...	P-N3
19	Q-N4	B-K1
20	N-B2	Q-R3

21 N-Q4   N-B5!

With the double threat on Q6 and
KN7. Black now wins a second pawn
and his material advantage is
decisive.

22	Q-R3	Q×Q
23	P×Q	N×NP
24	R-N1	N-B5
25	K-K3	N-N3
26	P-B4	B-Q2
27	B-N2	P-B3

Mobilizing his central pawn
majority.

28	P×P	P×P
29	P-KR4	

29 P-B5 P×P would give Black a
different passed pawn but the end
result would be the same.

29	...	K-B2
30	P-R5	N-K2
31	R-N2	P-K4
32	P×P	P×P
33	R-KB2ch	K-K1
34	N-B3	N-B4ch
35	K-Q2	P-K5!
36	P×P	P×P
37	R-K2	P-K6ch
38	K-K1	R-B5
39	N-K5	R-KR5
40	R-N2	R-R8ch
41	K-K2	B-N4ch
42	N-Q3	R-QN8!
43	Resigns	

GAME 13

White: Timman
Black: Hug

Nice Olympiad 1974

1	P-K4	P-K3
2	P-Q4	P-Q4
3	N-QB3	B-N5
4	P-K5	P-QB4
5	P-QR3	B-R4
6	P-QN4	P×QP
7	Q-N4	N-K2
8	N-N5	

This is a less often played continuation than the sharper 8 P×B
P×N which offers chances to both
sides.

8	...	B-B2
9	Q×NP	R-N1
10	Q×RP	QN-B3

This way Black will never get
White's KP, but after 10...P-R3 11
N×Bch Q×N 12 N-K2 B-Q2 13 B-N2

61

QN-B3 14 O-O-O O-O-O 15 N×P
N×N 16 B×N N-B4 17 Q-R3 N×B 18
R×N Q×KP 19 Q-K3! White would
still maintain the advantage.

11 P-KB4   P-R3

11...B-N1 12 N-KB3 P-R4 was
sharper and more consistent in connection with Black's 10th move (13
N-N5!? R×N 14 P×R B×P gives Black
counter-chances).

12	N×Bch	Q×N
13	Q-Q3	B-Q2
14	N-B3	N-B4

With the idea of playing
15...N(B3)-K2 and 16...B-N4.

15 P-N4!

An excellent idea, to capture the
initiative with this sacrifice of a
pawn.

15	...	N-K6

Or 15...R×P 16 B-R3 R-KN1 17
B×N with the advantage.

16	B×N	P×B
17	Q×KP	P-Q5
18	Q-Q2	

In the case of 18 N×P Black would
quickly bring his QB onto the long
diagonal and have very active
counterplay. Naturally White does
not wish such a reverse in his
superior position.

18	...	R×P
19	K-B2!	O-O-O
20	R-KN1	R×R
21	K×R	P-B3
22	P×P	R-B1

In case of 22...P-K4 23 P×P N×KP
24 Q-B4 R-N1ch 25 B-N2 B-B3 26 Q-
B5ch K-N1 27 Q×N R×Bch 28 K-B1!
B×N 29 Q×Qch K×Q 30 P-B7, White
wins easily.

23	R-K1	R×P
24	R-K4	R-N3ch
25	K-B2	Q-Q1
26	P-QR4	Q-N3!

This is the best chance now that
Black's knight is unstable.

27	P-N5	P×P
28	P×P	P-Q6ch
29	Q-K3	Q×P
30	B×P	Q-KR4
31	P-B5!	R-B3

Black's queen would be trapped
after 31...P×P 32 R-KR4, while
31...Q×BP 32 R-KB4 loses a whole
rook.

32	R-KR4	Q-K1
33	R-R4	K-B2?

Better was 33...K-N1, but after 34
N-K5 P×P 35 N×Nch R×N (a must
because of the threat 36 Q-B4ch) 36
R-Q4! Black would have little hope
of being able to survive the ending.

34	N-Q4	P×P

35	N-N5ch	**Resigns**

If 35...K-N1 36 R-R8ch!

GAME 14

White: Fischer
Black: Tal

Leipzig Olympiad 1960

Notes by Tal

1	P-K4	P-K3
2	P-Q4	P-Q4
3	N-QB3	B-N5
4	P-K5	P-QB4
5	P-QR3	B-R4
6	P-QN4	P×QP
7	Q-N4	N-K2
8	P×B	P×N
9	Q×NP	R-N1
10	Q×RP	QN-B3!
11	N-B3	Q-B2
12	B-QN5	B-Q2
13	O-O	

13	...	O-O-O

The most critical moment of the game. At this point I spent about 40 minutes assessing the position arising after 13...N×KP 14 N×N Q×N 15 B×Bch K×B 16 Q-Q3. At first sight it appears very attractive for Black. He has good chances both in the middlegame (in view of the open files on the K-side), and in the endgame, thanks to his far advanced pawn on B6. But at the board I somehow could not find a way to strengthen my position significantly, while at the same time the QN-file gives White considerable counterchances. For example: 16...QR-QB1 17 R-N1 K-B2 18 R-N5! K-N1 19 B-K3, and White has activated his forces. It is very difficult for Black to set his central pawn mass in motion, and therefore I rejected 13...N×KP, preferring the sharper move in the game.

14 B-N5

Now head-spinning complications arise, finally ending in perpetual check. White could also have continued 14 B×N, when I intended throwing caution to the winds: 14...B×B 15 Q×P P-Q5, with very sharp play.

[Editor's comment: In "My 60 Memorable Games" Fischer analyses this continuation out to a win: 16 Q×Pch B-Q2 17 Q×N R×Pch 18 K×R B-R6ch 19 K×B Q×Q 20 B-N5.]

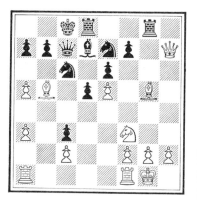

14 ...   **N×KP!**

Were it not for this move, Black's position would be unenviable. Now White has to switch to the calculation of intricate variations.

15 N×N!

Bad, of course, is 15 B×N N×Nch 16 K-R1 R-R1 with the threats of 17...R×Q and ...Q×KRP mate. In the case of 15 B×Bch Black has a choice between 15...K×B and 15...R×B 16 N×N Q×N 17 B×N R-R1 18 QR-K1 R×Q 19 R×Q R×B with the better chances in the ending. Now it is Black's move, and with it comes his turn to solve complicated problems.

15 ...   **B×B!**

The attempt to play in analogous fashion to a variation given previously, 15...Q×N, would lead after 16 B×N R-R1 (or 16...B×B 17

B×R R-R1 18 QR-K1 Q×R 19 R×Q R×Q 20 B-B6) 17 KR-K1! (not 17 QR-K1 Q-N1!) 17...Q×Rch 18 R×Q R×Q 19 B×R K×B 20 B×B K×B 21 R-K3 P-Q5 22 R-K4 to a certain advantage for White.

16 N×P   **B×R**

A curious variation could have resulted after 16...QR-B1 17 B-R6 B×R 18 B×R B×P 19 N-Q6ch! Q×N 20 B×N.

17 N×R   **R×B**
18 N×KP   **R×Pch**
19 K-R1!

White would lose after 19 K×B R×RP!

19 ...   **Q-K4**

When starting his combination with 14...N×KP, Black thought that, besides the move in the game which guarantees him a draw, he also could play the sharper 19...Q-QB5 20 Q×N R-N1, but on actually reaching this position he realized that after 21 N-B4! P-Q5 22 Q-K4! the stranded black bishop has no way of coming into play, whereas White can himself gradually build up a dangerous attack.

20 R×B   **Q×N**

Agreeing to the draw. Possible was 20...R-N3, but even then, by continuing 21 Q×N R×N 22 Q-B5ch K-

64

N1 23 P-R6!, White would be able to draw without difficulty.

21	K×R	Q-N5ch
22	Drawn	

GAME 15

White: Gligoric
Black: Pachman

Munich Olympiad 1958

1	P-K4	P-K3
2	P-Q4	P-Q4
3	N-QB3	B-N5
4	P-K5	P-QB4
5	P-QR3	B×Nch
6	P×B	N-K2
7	Q-N4	N-B4
8	B-Q3	P-KR4
9	Q-B4	Q-R5
10	N-K2	Q×Q
11	N×Q	N-K2
12	B-K2	

12	...	P-R5

If 12...P-KN3 then 13 P×P is

strong.

13   N-R5

Now 13 P×P would not be so clear after 13...QN-B3 14 N-Q3 P-Q5 with counterplay.

13	...	K-B1

In the game Gligoric-Foguelman, Belgrade 1962, play went 13...R-R2 14 B-KN5 P×P 15 P×P QN-B3 16 O-O-O N-N3 17 P-N4 B-Q2 18 P-KB4 P-R3 19 KR-B1 with the better game for White.

14	B-KN5	P×P?

14...QN-B3 is better.

15	P×P	P-QN3
16	P-N4	

Not 16 B×P N-B4 and 17...N×P.

16	...	P×Pe.p.
17	BP×P	B-R3
18	P-N4!	B×B
19	K×B	QN-B3
20	P-B3	R-B1
21	P-KR4	K-N1
22	KR-KB1!	N-N3
23	R-B3	R-B2
24	QR-KB1	

Black loses mainly because he cannot activate his badly placed KR.

24	...	R-R2
25	K-B2!	N-R4
26	K-N3	N-QB5

27	P-R4	N-B1
28	R(1)-B2	N-N3
29	N-B4	N×N
30	B×N	R-R1
31	B-B1	N-R4
32	B-Q2	N-B5
33	B-N5	N-R6
34	B-B1	

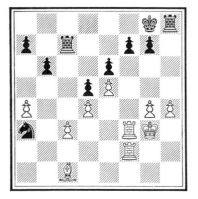

34 ...   N-N8?

A grave error; after 34...N-B5 White would have had to build up pressure by 35 P-KR5 followed by 36 R-KR2 and 37 P-N5.

35	B-N2	K-R2
36	R×P?	

It would be simpler to win the knight by 36 R-Q3 KR-QB1 37 R-QB2 followed by 38 R-B1.

36	...	KR-QB1
37	P-N5	N×P
38	B×N	R×R

Or 38...R×Bch 39 K-N4 R(1)-B2

40 K-R5 etc.

39	R×R	R×Bch
40	K-N4!	R-B5
41	K-R5	R×QP

Or 41...R×RP 42 R-K7.

42	R×RP	R-KB5
43	R-K7	P-Q5
44	P-N6ch!	

Not 44 R×KP? P-N3ch 45 R×P R×Pch drawing.

44	...	K-N1
45	R×KP	K-B1
46	K-N5	R-B6

If 46...R-K5 47 K-B5 R×RP 48 R×P wins.

47	R×P	**Resigns**

GAME 16

White: Unzicker
Black: Uhlmann

Varna Olympiad 1962

1	P-K4	P-K3
2	P-Q4	P-Q4
3	N-QB3	B-N5
4	P-K5	P-QB4
5	P-QR3	B×Nch
6	P×B	N-K2
7	Q-N4	Q-B2
8	B-Q3	P×P
9	N-K2	P×P
10	Q×NP	R-N1

11	Q×RP	QN-B3
12	B-KB4?!	B-Q2
13	O-O	O-O-O

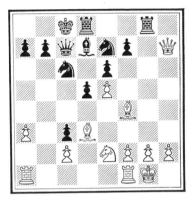

14	Q-R5	P-Q5
15	B-N3	B-K1!

A multi-purpose move, threatening ...P-B4 and guarding the KBP and QP.

16 Q-B3

The best defence is 16 B-K4.

16	...	N×P!
17	Q-KB6	B-B3!!
18	KR-K1	

18 B×N fails to 18...R×Pch and 19...R×BPch etc.

18	...	R×B

Forced, but very strong, as Black's well posted bishop ensures him the advantage.

19 N×R

The best reply, as 19 RP×R would rob White of his only trump-card, the passed KRP.

19	...	N×B
20	P×N	N-N3!
21	N-K2	

21...N-B5 must be prevented.

21	...	Q-Q2
22	P-KR4	P-K4
23	P-R5	Q-N5
24	N-N3	N-B5
25	P-R6	

White banks everything on this pawn. After 25 R×P N×QP 26 R-KN5 Q-K3! Black's passed pawns cannot be contained.

25	...	N×NP

Risky, when 25...Q-N3 26 Q×Q N×Q should give Black a won ending.

26	P-R7	Q-R6!
27	R×P??	

White should have played 27 Q-B5ch Q×Q 28 N×Q when 28...N×R produces an interesting situation in which White is allowed to queen his pawn. After 29 N-K7ch K-N1! 30 N-N8 N-B6ch 31 K-B1 P-K4!! (the point: White cannot play 32 P×P B-N4ch 33 K-N2 N-R5ch and 34...N-N3) 32 P-R8=Q P×P 33 Q-R7 P-Q7 34 N-B6 P-B7! 35 Q×QBP B-N4ch 36 K-

N2 N-K8ch, Black wins.

27	...	**N-K6**
28	**Resigns**	

GAME 17

White: Bronstein
Black: Uhlmann

Zagreb 1965

1	**P-K4**	**P-K3**
2	**P-Q4**	**P-Q4**
3	**N-QB3**	**B-N5**
4	**P-K5**	**P-QB4**
5	**P-QR3**	**B×Nch**
6	**P×B**	**N-K2**
7	**Q-N4**	**Q-B2**
8	**Q×NP**	**R-N1**
9	**Q×RP**	**P×P**
10	**K-Q1**	**N-Q2**

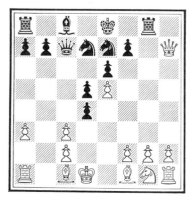

11 N-B3!

After 11 R-QN1 N-QB4 12 B-Q3 P×P 13 N-B3 B-Q2!? 14 B-KN5 B-B3

15 P-KR4? Black had the advantage in Yanofsky-Uhlmann. White should play 15 R-N4! with excellent prospects, but Black could earlier have played 13...N×Bch.

11	...	**N×P**
12	**B-KB4**	**Q×P**
13	**N×N**	**Q×Rch**
14	**B-B1**	**P-Q6?**

Better is 14...R-B1 15 B-N5ch N-B3 16 N×N B-Q2 with equality; or here 15 B-Q3 B-Q2 16 K-K2 N-B3 17 N×P! R×N 18 Q-N8ch R-B1 19 B-N6ch K-K2 20 Q-N7ch K-Q3 21 B-B4ch R×B 22 R×Q R-N5 23 Q-R6 N-K4 24 B-Q3 R×P with equal chances. But at the time this game was played, it was thought that 14...R-B1 15 B-Q3 was good for White (16...N-B3 had not yet been discovered) and Uhlmann's 14...P-Q6 was intended to improve on the older line. As the course of this game shows, the sharp attacking positions that arise from ...P-Q6 offer the better chances to White.

15	**Q×BPch**	**K-Q1**
16	**Q-B6**	**P×Pch**
17	**K-Q2**	**Q-Q5ch**
18	**B-Q3**	**K-K1**
19	**K-K2**	**B-Q2**
20	**B-K3**	**Q-N7**
21	**R-QB1**	**R-QB1**
22	**N×B!**	**P-Q5**

Now Bronstein could have gained the advantage with the problem move 23 N-N8!! or he could have tried 23

68

Q×KP P×B 24 N-B6ch K-B1 25 N-Q5! when Black's situation would have been much more difficult than in the game.

23	B-Q2	K×N
24	B-N4	KR-K1
25	B-N5ch	R-B3
26	K-Q2	N-Q4
27	Q-B7ch	R-K2
28	B(N4)×R	Q-B6ch
29	K-K2	P-Q6ch

This saves Black from losing the exchange. If 29...N×B, 30 B×Rch and 31 Q-R7 wins Black's most important passed pawn.

30	B×P	N×B
31	R×P	Q-K4ch
32	K-Q1	Q-R8ch
33	K-Q2	Q×P
34	R×R	P×R
35	B-B4	Q-N5ch
36	K-Q3	Q-N8ch
37	K-B3	Q-QB8ch
38	K-Q3	Q-QN8ch
39	Drawn	

White: Hansen
Black: Wirth

Correspondence Game 1973

1	P-K4	P-K3
2	P-Q4	P-Q4
3	N-QB3	B-N5
4	P-K5	N-K2
5	P-QR3	B×Nch
6	P×B	P-QB4
7	Q-N4	Q-B2
8	Q×NP	R-N1
9	Q×RP	P×P
10	K-Q1	QN-B3!
11	N-B3	P×P
12	N-N5	N×P
13	P-B4	R×N
14	P×R	N(K4)-N3
15	P-KR4!?	

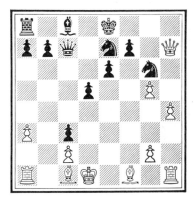

15 ...   Q-N6?

More solid was 15...P-K4 16 P-R5 N-B1 17 B-N5ch N-B3 18 Q-N7 B-N5ch 19 K-K1 O-O-O 20 B×N Q×B

21 P-R6 P-Q5 22 K-B2 (White lost after 22 Q×BP? in Presson-Hurt, Arkansas 1969) with unclear chances.

| 16 | P-R5 | N-B5 |

This was the point of Black's previous move.

| 17 | Q-R8ch | K-Q2 |
| 18 | B-N5ch | N-B3 |

The only move. 18...K-Q3 (not 18...K-B2 19 Q-K5ch!) 19 Q-Q8ch K-B4 20 Q×Nch K-Q5 (not 20...K×B 21 Q-N4ch winning the other black knight) 21 Q-N4ch K-K4 22 B×Nch Q×B 23 R-K1ch K-B4 24 R-KB1 is obviously bad.

| 19 | B(B1)×N | Q×B |
| 20 | Q×P | K-Q3 |

There is no time for 20...Q×P 21 P-R6!

21	P-R6	P-K4
22	Q-Q2	B-N5ch
23	K-B1	Q×Qch
24	K×Q	N-Q5
25	R-R4	B-B4
26	R-KB1	B-N3
27	R×N!	P×R
28	B-Q3	

With the exchange sacrifice White has rendered his opponent's central pawns worthless and his own K-side pawns very mighty.

| 28 | ... | K-K4 |

28...B×B 29 K×B is equally hopeless, or 28...B-R4 29 P-N4.

| 29 | B×B | P×B |
| 30 | R-B6 | **Resigns** |

If 30...R-KN1 31 R×P!

GAME 19

White: R. Byrne
Black: Uhlmann

Monte Carlo 1968

1	P-K4	P-K3
2	P-Q4	P-Q4
3	N-QB3	B-N5
4	P-K5	P-QB4
5	P-QR3	B×Nch
6	P×B	N-K2
7	Q-N4	Q-B2
8	Q×NP	R-N1
9	Q×RP	P×P
10	N-K2	QN-B3
11	P-KB4	B-Q2
12	P-R3	

12	...	P×P
13	P-N4	

This is the idea, countering the pressure down the KN-file, admittedly at the cost of some time.

13	...	0-0-0
14	Q-Q3	P-Q5
15	R-QN1	

Directed against ...Q-N3, but Black now produces the surprising sacrifice of a piece.

15	...	N×P!?

Based on the occupation of the long light squared diagonal and the exploitation of White's weak centre.

16	P×N	B-B3!
17	R-N1	N-N3!
18	B-B4	N×B
19	N×N	Q×Pch
20	N-K2	R-Q4!

The point of the sacrifice, threatening 21...B-N4 and thus giving White no time to consolidate.

21	B-N2	B-N4
22	Q-K4	P-Q6!

Thematic.

23	Q×Q	

After 23 R×B R×R 24 Q×Q R×Q 25 P×P comes 25...R-Q1 26 B-K4 P-B7! threatening both ...R×P and ...P-B4

with excellent play; or here 24 P×P Q-QB4 with unclear complications.

23	...	R×Q
24	R×B	

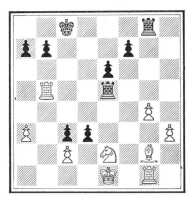

24	...	R×R?!

A great pity, as Black would have good winning chances with 24...R×Nch! 25 K-Q1 R-Q7ch 26 K-B1 R×BPch 27 K-N1 R-Q1! 28 B×Pch K-B2 29 B-K4 R-K7 etc; or here 25 K-B1 R×BP 26 B×Pch K-B2 27 B-K4 R-Q1!

25	N×P	P×P
26	K-Q2	R-N7
27	B-K4	P-B8=Qch
28	K×Q	R-N6
29	K-B2	R×RP
30	R-KB1	R-N2
31	R-B4	K-N1?

The simplest way to draw was 31...P-B4! 32 P×P R-QB2! 33 R-B3 P×P 34 B×BPch K-Q1 35 P-R4 R×Nch etc.

32	B-Q3	R-R8
33	P-R4	R-R8
34	P-N5	R-R7ch
35	K-N3	K-B2?

It was essential to play 35...P-R3 first, as Black is now lost.

36	N-N5ch	K-Q2
37	N×P	P-K4
38	R-QN4	P-N3
39	B-B5ch	K-B2
40	R-QB4ch	K-N2
41	N-N5	K-R3
42	N-Q6	P-N4
43	R-B6ch	K-R2
44	N×NPch	K-N2
45	R-B4	Resigns

GAME 20

White: Bogdanovic
Black: Uhlmann

Sarajevo 1963

1	P-K4	P-K3
2	P-Q4	P-Q4
3	N-QB3	B-N5
4	P-K5	P-QB4
5	P-QR3	B×Nch
6	P×B	N-K2
7	Q-N4	Q-B2
8	Q×NP	R-N1
9	Q×RP	P×P
10	N-K2	QN-B3
11	P-KB4	B-Q2
12	Q-Q3	P×P
13	Q×BP	N-B4
14	B-Q2	

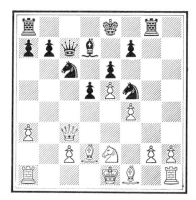

14	...	Q-N3!
15	P-QR4	

15 Q-QN3 is possible, when after 15...Q-B4 16 Q-QB3 Black must probably accept a repetition of moves. After 15 P-N3 R-QB1 16 Q-N3 N(B3)-Q5 Black has good play.

15	...	R-QB1
16	P-R5	Q-Q1
17	Q-Q3	P-R3!

In order to take the initiative on the Q-side with ...N-R2.

18	R-R3	N-R2
19	R-B3	B-N4
20	R×R	Q×R
21	Q-QB3	B-B5!
22	P-N3	N-N4
23	Q-N2	Q-B3

All Black's pieces have reached ideal posts, and 24 B-N2 now fails to 24...N-R5 25 R-N1 N×Bch 26 R×N P-Q5 when the black queen penetrates decisively into White's position.

24	R-N1	R-R1!
25	R-N2	

25 P-N4 loses to 25...N-R5 26 R-N3 P-Q5 27 K-B2 N-KB6! 28 R×N R×Pch 29 K-N3 B×N; or here 29 B-N2 R×Bch 30 K×R B×N 31 Q-N3 P-Q6, winning in both cases.

25	...	P-Q5
26	R-B2	Q-R8!

27 P-N4

There is no defence, as 27 Q-N4 fails to 27...B×N 28 R×B P-Q6! 29 P×P N(B4)-Q5 or 29 R-B2 N(B4)-Q5 30 Q-B5 N×Pch 31 K-Q1 R×P wins. If here 28 K×B Q-K5ch 29 K-Q1 N-K6ch 30 B×N N-B6ch wins, as

31 K-B1 loses to 31...N-R7ch.

27	...	R×P!

The culmination of Black's strategy. 27...N-K6 would have been a blunder in view of 28 N-N3! Q-N8 29 B×N P×B 30 R-N2 winning the queen.

28 P×N

After 28 R×R Q×R 29 P×N Q-R5ch 30 K-Q1 Q-B7! wins.

28	...	R×R
29	K×R	Q-R7ch
30	K-K1	

There is no defence, as Black wins after both 30 B-N2 B-Q4 or 30 K-B3 B-Q4ch 31 K-N4 P×Pch 32 K-N5 Q-R2! followed by ...Q-N3ch and ...Q-N5 mate.

30	...	Q-R5ch
31	K-Q1	Q-B7
32	B-K1	Q×KB
33	N-N3	Q-B6ch
34	K-B1	Q-K6ch
35	K-Q1	N-B6ch
36	B×N	P×B
37	Q-N6	Q-Q7 Mate

Chapter 2

The Nimzovich (Winawer) Variation
with 6...N-K2 7 P-QR4

White: Williams
Black: Keene

British Championship 1973

1	P-K4	P-K3
2	P-Q4	P-Q4
3	N-QB3	B-N5
4	P-K5	P-QB4
5	P-QR3	B×Nch
6	P×B	N-K2
7	P-QR4	

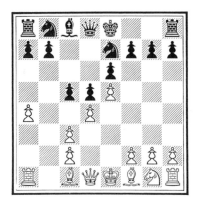

The quieter of the two plans at White's disposal. Instead of playing aggressively with his queen, White plans the more positional approach of holding fast in the centre and playing on Black's positional weaknesses and lack of mobility.

The direct point of the text move is two fold — it makes way for White's QB to occupy the QR3-KB8 diagonal and it prevents Black from blockading White's Q-side by the manoeuvre ...B-Q2 followed by ...B-R5 (see, for example, the continuation 7 N-B3 B-Q2 8 B-Q3?! B-R5 mentioned below). Also, Black sometimes carries out a similar manoeuvre with his queen (...Q-R4 followed by ...Q-R5). Since White's P-QR4 is virtually obligatory in the positional lines, he plays this move at once to retain as many options as possible for his minor pieces.

7 N-B3 B-Q2 8 P-QR4 transposes back to the text, but if White meets 7...B-Q2 with **8 B-Q3?!** he is soon in trouble after **8...B-R5!** which blockades the QRP and exerts permanent pressure on the backward QBP. e.g. 9 O-O Q-B2 10 R-K1 P-KR3 11 R-N1 N-Q2 12 P-B4 O-O 13 P×QP N×QP 14 B×P?! and Black managed to defend against the attack in Westerinen-Uhlmann, Halle 1963; or 9 R-QN1 Q-B2 10 O-O P-B5 11 B-K2 QN-B3 12 N-Q2 O-O-O with good play for Black. Kokkoris-Uhlmann, Varna Olympiad 1962.

After 7 N-B3 Black has four alternative possibilities to 7...B-Q2.

(a) 7...Q-R4 8 B-Q2 Probably the strongest reply, as unclear positions arise after 8 Q-Q2 P-QN3!? e.g. 9 P-B4 Q-R5! 10 P×QP KP×P 11 P-B4?! P×BP 12 P×P QN-B3 13 P×P O-O 14 B-K2 P×P 15 O-O B-B4 and Black stood better in Estrin-Khasin, Correspondence Game 1971. However, White could have tried 9 P×P P×P 10 P-B4! **8...Q-R5** After 8...P-B5 9 P-QR4 N-Q2 10 N-N5 P-KR3 11 N-R3 N-QN3 (11...N-KN3 12 B-R5 is unpleasant for Black) 12 N-B4 P-N3 13 P-R4 B-Q2 14 P-R5 P-N4 15 N-K2 O-O-O 16 P-N4 QR-N1 17 B-R3 N×P 18 P-B4 P×P 19 O-O White also has a good game. Bronstein-Saigin, Moscow 1945. In the game Ivkov-Broderman, Havana 1963, this blockading idea proved too great a loss of time: **9 P×P N-Q2 10 N-Q4 P-QR3 11 Q-N4 N-B4 12 Q-B4 P-KN4 13 Q×P N×N 14 P×N Q×QP 15 R-Q1 Q×KPch 16 Q×Q N×Q 17 B-B3 P-B3 18 P-B4 N-Q2 19 P-B5!** with the better ending.

(b) 7...Q-B2 8 P-QR4 If 8 B-Q3 P-QN3 9 P-QR4 B-R3 10 P-R5 (10 B-QN5ch B×B 11 P×B P-QR4 is also equal) 10...B×B 11 P×NP P×NP 12 R×R B-R3 13 R×B N×R 14 Q-Q3 N-QN1 with equal chances. Unzicker-Petrosian 1965; or 8 B-K2 B-Q2! 9 P-QR4! QN-B3 10 O-O P-B3 11 R-K1 (if 11 B-R3 P×KP 12 B×P P-K5 13 N-N5 P-KR3 14 N-R3 O-O; or 11 KP×P NP×P 12 P×P O-O-O with unclear positions in both cases) 11...P×KP 12 P×KP O-O 13 B-Q3 with equality.

After 8 P-QR4 we have transposed back to the main line.

(c) 7...P-QN3 8 B-QN5ch B-Q2 9 P-QR4 Q-B2 10 B-Q3 Again we have transposed to the main line.

(d) 7...QN-B3 8 P-QR4 After 8 B-Q3 Q-R4 9 O-O (9 B-Q2 P-B5 10 B-K2 Q-R5 is unclear; or Black can refrain from 10...Q-R5 and continue 10...B-Q2 11 O-O O-O-O 12 R-K1 P-B3 13 B-KB1 QR-N1 14 P-N3 P-B4 15 P-QR4 N-Q1 16 Q-B1 P-KR3 17 Q-R3 N(K2)-B3 18 KR-N1 P-KN4 with chances for both sides. Damjanovic-Gligoric, Porec 1974.) 9...P-B5! (not at once 9...Q×BP 10 B-Q2 Q-N7 11 R-N1 Q×RP 12 R-N3 Q-R7 13 Q-B1 P-B5 14 R-R3 winning the queen) 10 B-K2 Q×BP 11 B-Q2 Q-N7 12 R-N1 Q×RP 13 R-R1 White has only a draw. Better is 8 B-K2 Q-R4 9 O-O P-B5 10 B-Q2 Q-R5 (for 10...Q-Q2 see Szekely-Toth, Hungarian Correspondence Championship 1971/2. Illustrative game 21) 11 N-N5 B-Q2 with chances for both sides, or here 8...B-Q2 9 P-QR4 P-B3 10 KP×P P×BP 11 P×P Q-R4 12 Q-Q2 Q×P(B4) 13 B-R3 Q-R4 14 P-B4 and White stands better. **8...Q-B2** 8...Q-R4 transposes to the section on 7...QN-B3 in the notes to the main line. 8...B-Q2 transposes to Fischer-Larsen, 1st Match Game 1971 (illustrative game 22). **9 B-K2** If 9 Q-Q2 P-B3 10 KP×P P×BP 11 B-K2 P-B5 12 Q-R6 (if 12 O-O N-B4 13 P-N4 R-KN1! but Keres suggests 12 N-R4 with a slight plus for White) 12...N-N3 13 N-R4 R-KN1 14 B-R5 Q-N2 with equality. Smyslov-Bondarevsky, 1947; or 9 B-Q3 P×P 10 O-O (not 10 P×P N×QP 11 N×N Q-B6ch etc.) 10...P×P 11 R-K1 N-N3 12 B×N RP×B? (better is 12...BP×B 13 B-R3 N-K2 with an unclear position) 13 B-R3 N-K2 14 N-Q4 B-Q2 15 R-K3 and White has a strong attack. Vasyukov-Brenstadt, 1957. **9...B-Q2 10 O-O**

10...P-B3 If 10...P-KR3 11 B-R3 P-QN3 12 P×P P×P 13 B×P N×P 14 N×N Q×B 15 N×B K×N 16 B-N5ch K-B2 17 Q-R5 P-N3 18 Q-K5ch with good play for White. Smyslov-Botvinnik, USSR 1943; or 10...N-R4 11 R-K1 P×P (better

11...P-QN3) 12 P×P N-B5 13 B-Q3 P-KR3 14 N-Q2 with advantage to White. Fischer-Schweber, Buenos Aires 1970; or 10...P-B4 11 B-R3 P-QB5 12 N-R4 O-O 13 P-B4! with advantage to White. **11 KP×P P×BP 12 P-B4! O-O-O 13 B-R3 N-B4 14 B×P P×P 15 B×BP N(B3)×P 16 B×N Q×B 17 B×BP B-B3 18 N-K5! R×Q 19 N×Q R×R(B8)ch 20 K×R R-B1 21 B-K5 B-Q4 22 N-Q6ch** with the better ending for White. Gufeld-Bagirov, Leningrad 1960.

Let us now return the position after 7 P-QR4.

7   ...   Q-B2

7...QN-B3 8 N-B3 Q-B2 Transposes back to note (d) above, but instead of 8...Q-B2 Black can try **8...Q-R4** putting direct pressure on White's pawn at QB3 and threatening (though it is rarely good to execute the threat) to win White's QRP by ...B-Q2 followed eventually by moving away the QB3 knight. For 8...Q-R4 see Chapter 3.

8   N-B3

This position often arises from the alternative move order 6...Q-B2 7 N-B3 N-K2 8 P-QR4.

8   ...   P-QN3

The idea of this move is to exchange off Black's traditionally bad bishop by ...B-R3.

During the past few years this idea has become a popular way for Black to handle White's positional system, but the older **8...QN-B3** is also worthy of consideration.

77

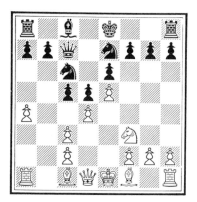

White now has several plausible continuations:

(1) **9 B-R3 P×P** Weaker is 9...P-QN3?! 10 B-Q3! P-KR3 11 O-O P-B5 12 B-K2 B-N2!? 13 R-K1 O-O-O 14 B-KB1 Q-Q2 15 P-N3 QR-K1 16 N-R4 with advantage to White because of his active K-side play. Mecking-Bronstein, Petropolis Interzonal 1973. **10 P×P Q-R4ch 11 Q-Q2 Q×Qch 12 K×Q N-B4 13 B-N2** with a slight endgame advantage to White.

(2) **9 Q-Q2** Transposes to note d, page 76 (subnote to White's 9th move).

(3) **9 B-K2** Transposes to the main part of note d, page 76.

(4) **9 B-Q3** Transposes to Fischer-Larsen, illustrative game 22.

9 B-QN5ch!

Virtually forcing Black to interpose with the bishop, and thereby preventing the exchanging manoeuvre ...B-R3.

The game Bertok-Geller, Zagreb 1955 continued 9 B-Q3 B-R3 10 O-O B×B 11 P×B N-Q2 12 B-R3 O-O with equal chances.

An alternative worth testing is 9 P-R5 B-R3 10 B×B N×B 11 O-O O-O (maybe better is 11...P-R3) 12 N-N5 with the initiative. But instead of 9...B-R3 Black may be able to capture the RP: 9...P×RP 10 B-Q3 B-R3 11 O-O B×B 12 Q×B N-Q2 13 B-R3 P-KR3 14 N-Q2 O-O 15 P-QB4 KR-K1 and Black might be able to hang on to the pawn. Scholl-Markland, Holland-England Match 1971.

9 ...   B-Q2

After 9...QN-B3 Black cannot exchange the light squared bishops by ...B-R3, while 9...KN-B3 10 O-O B-R3 11 N-N5 P-R3 12 N-R3 is good for White who will continue his attack with Q-N4 and N-B4-R5.

10   B-Q3

If 10 O-O B×B 11 P×B P-QR4 12 N-N5 (or 12 P×BP P×P 13 P-B4 P×P 14 Q-K2 N-Q2 with equality. Nezhmetdinov-Katalimov, USSR 1959) 12...P-R3 13 N-R3 N-Q2 14 N-B4 O-O 15 N-R5 K-R1 16 Q-N4 R-KN1 the position is approximately even. Ivkov-R. Byrne, Sousse Interzonal 1967.

10	**...**	**QN-B3**
11	**O-O**	**P-KR3**

Naturally 11...O-O?? would lose quickly to 12 B×Pch K×B 13 N-N5ch and the standard mating attack.

The alternative 11...P-B5 is examined in Fischer-Darga, Berlin 1960 (illustrative game 23), and Bannik-Tal, 25th USSR Championship 1958 (illustrative game 24).

The text is Krogius' move, first played against Gufeld in 1967. It prevents N-N5 and therefore prepares ...O-O.

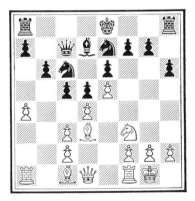

12   B-R3

12 R-K1 is more popular but not necessarily stronger. The move was used by Robert Byrne, Mecking and Karpov to good effect against Markland at

Hastings 1971/2. The British Master lost all three games (and another to Hartston who played 12 B-R3) and since then the British players have discovered new resources for Black. Let us look at some of these examples:

(1) **12...N-R4 13 Q-Q2** 13 B-R3 O-O transposes to Hartston-Portisch, Nice Olympiad 1974 (illustrative game 26) **13...R-QB1** Weaker is 13...O-O?! 14 Q-B4 P-B4?! 15 PxPe.p. QxQ 16 BxQ RxP 17 B-K5 R-B2 18 PxP PxP 19 B-B7! N(R4)-B3 20 P-B4! with a clear advantage for White. Mecking-Markland, Hastings 1971/2. **14 P-KR4** The immediate 14 Q-B4 is satisfactory for Black after 14...P-B4 15 PxPe.p. QxQ 16 BxQ PxBP; or 15 Q-N3 K-B2 followed by ...QR-KN1. Analysis by Karpov. **14...O-O** We are following Karpov-Markland, Hastings 1971/2 (illustrative game 25).

(2) **12...O-O** see Hartston-Portisch, Nice Olympiad 1974 (illustrative game 26).

12 ...   N-R4

The only reasonable way to deal with the problem of the attacked QBP.

13 N-Q2!

13 R-K1 O-O transposes to Hartston-Portisch.

13 ...   O-O

Not 13...BxP? 14 PxP, threatening 15 Q-N4.

14	PxP	PxP
15	N-N3	NxN

15...N(R4)-B3 16 BxP QxP 17 N-Q4! was successful for White in Hartston-Markland, Hastings 1971/2: 17...KR-Q1? (Better is Hartston's suggestion of 17...Q-B2 though after 18 P-KB4 Q-R4 19 B-R3 KR-Q1 20 R-B3 White has a firm grip on the position) 18 N-N5! B-K1 19 P-KB4 Q-B3 20 Q-K1 R-Q2 21 N-Q4! with a substantial advantage for White.

16 PxN   KR-B1

This move prepares for ...P-B5 but it has the disadvantage that it weakens Black's K-side. However, the suggested improvement 16...P-B3 17 PxP RxP seems to fail to Keene's strong innovation 18 P-QN4!, when Black has a bad game whether or not he exchanges pawns.

17	R-K1	N-N3
18	B-QB1!	

Intending 19 Q-K2.

18	...	N×P?!

This will create weaknesses along the K-file. Black is impatient and does not want to wait until White strengthens his position with 19 Q-K2. But 18...QR-N1 was playable, creating some pressure along th QN-file.

19	B-KB4	P-B3
20	R-K3!	B-K1
21	Q-K2	QR-N1
22	B-B2	P-B5

Short of action, Black weakens the dark squares in the centre even more, counting on the tactical break ...P-Q5.

23	P-QN4	R-Q1
24	R×N	P×R
25	B×KP	Q-Q2
26	B×R	R×B
27	Q-K5	R-Q1
28	Q-Q4	

Freeing the K5 square for the rook. 28 R-Q1 would regroup White's pieces less effectively, yet it was the more cautious choice.

28	...	Q-QB2?

Missing the only active chance: 28...P-K4 29 Q×KP P-Q5 30 P×P Q×QP 31 Q×Q R×Q because he was afraid of 32 R-Q1 when White has some winning chances in the end game (32...R×Rch 33 B×R B-N3 34 K-B1 P-B6 35 B-N3ch! and 36 K-K2).

29	R-K1	B-B2
30	P-R5!	R-K1
31	P-B4	

Black has a bad bishop, worthless blocked central pawns and he is doomed to passivity.

31	...	P-R3
32	R-K5	R-K2
33	K-B2	

White controls the whole board and he may activate his king as well.

33	...	Q-Q1
34	B-Q1	R-K1
35	P-N3	B-N3
36	B-N4	Q-B3
37	P-R4!	K-R2
38	P-R5	B-B2
39	K-N2	P-N3?

A mistake in a bad position on the eve of the time control.

40	R×QP	Q×Q
41	R×Q	P-K4
42	R-Q7	K-N1
43	P×NP	Resigns

White: Szekely
Black: Toth

Hungarian Correspondence
Championship 1971/2

Notes by Toth

1	P-K4	P-K3
2	P-Q4	P-Q4
3	N-QB3	B-N5
4	P-K5	N-K2
5	P-QR3	B×Nch
6	P×B	P-QB4
7	N-B3	QN-B3
8	B-K2	Q-R4
9	B-Q2	B-Q2
10	O-O	P-B5

11 N-N5!

The only possibility of weakening Black's K-side. That is why this is a typical move in this variation. In a game Bakulin-Khasin, USSR 1966, after 11...P-KR3 12 N-R3 N-N3 13 P-R4? O-O-O 14 Q-B1 P-B3 Black had the advantage on the K-side, but in the 3rd European Correspondence Championship Thiele improved on the variation: in a similar position against Cvachonceh he played 13 B-R5 (instead of 13 P-R4) and after 13...QN-K2 14 Q-N1 he had a good game. Under the influence of this game I decided to play the following paradoxical move.

11 ... P-B3!

"I am weakening the K-side so that my opponent does not weaken it"; this move is dynamic, attacking and tactically sound.

12	P×P	P×P
13	B-R5ch	N-N3
14	N-R3	O-O-O

With this move Black finishes his development. The open KN-file and a preponderance in the centre gives Black prospects of breaking through on K4. For this reason 12 P×P is questionable, but not a decisive mistake. The correct treatment of similar positions can be found, for example, in the strategic play of the first game of the Fischer-Larsen match (page 85), giving up the KP to open up the position.

15	Q-B3?	P-K4
16	KR-Q1	

If 16 Q×BP P×P 17 Q-B3 N(N3)-K4 18 Q-Q1 P×P 19 B-B4 P-Q5 and Black wins.

16	...	QR-B1
17	B-R6?	

An awkward place for the bishop. 17 K-R1 would have been better.

17	...	N-R5!
18	Q-K3	R(B1)-N1
19	K-R1	

This, though perhaps not the most attractive, gives the best hope of defence. If here 19 P-N4? either ...B×P or ...N-B4 wins a pawn. A grotesque picture: every square on the KR-file is occupied.

19	...	N×NP

This is not just a way of winning, but the beginning of a precisely calculated combination. See the note after move 27.

20	Q-B3	P-K5
21	Q×BP	B×N
22	R-KN1	Q-Q1!

If 22...Q×BP? 23 B-N7!

23	B-N7	Q×Q
24	B×Q	N-B5!
25	B×R	R×B
26	B-B7	N-K2
27	R-N7	P-KR4!

My previous move prevented the exchange of rooks — I need mine to create mating threats. My 27th move in retrospect looks a simple one, but I had to see it as early as the 17th move in the midst of hair-raising complications, and it was for this tactically quiet move that I rejected 19...P×P, which gains more material.

28	QR-KN1	B-N5
29	R-N3	N-K7
30	R(N7)×B	P×R

White's courageous resistance is hopeless now, because he cannot stop the black king's intrusion into the pawn phalanx.

31	B-K6ch	K-B2
32	R-K3	N-B5
33	B×NP	N(K2)-N3
34	P-B3	P×P
35	R×P	R-K1
36	R-N3	K-N3
37	B-B5	R-K8ch
38	R-N1	R×Rch
39	K×R	K-R4
40	K-B2	K-R5
41	B×N	N×B
42	K-N3	K×P
43	K-N4	K-N7
44	K-N5	N-R1
45	K-B6	P-R4
46	Resigns	

GAME 22

White: Fischer
Black: Larsen

1st Match Game 1971

Notes by Kholmov

1	P-K4	P-K3
2	P-Q4	P-Q4
3	N-QB3	B-N5
4	P-K5	N-K2
5	P-QR3	B×Nch
6	P×B	P-QB4
7	P-QR4	QN-B3
8	N-B3	B-Q2
9	B-Q3	Q-B2
10	O-O	P-B5
11	B-K2	P-B3
12	R-K1!	

Fischer develops his rook in preparation for an interesting pawn sacrifice.

12	...	N-N3

Black mistakenly thinks that this move forces White to take on B6. 12...O-O 13 B-R3 R-B2 14 P×P P×P was better, and if 15 N-R4 then 15...N-N3 16 B-R5 R-N2! with chances for both sides.
[After 12...O-O 13 B-R3 R-B2, White should continue 14 B-Q6 with similar play as in Bannik-Tal, illustrative game 24 — Gligoric.]

13	B-R3!	P×P?

A risky decision. Larsen is one of those players who happily accepts a challenge. The majority of Grandmasters would have castled long or as an extreme measure played 13...K-B2.

14	P×P	N(B3)×P
15	N×N	N×N

Against 15...Q×N there is the strong reply 16 B×P Q×BP 17 B×P O-O-O 18 R-K3, and as in the other case Black's king feels discomfort.

16	Q-Q4	N-N3

It is hard to find anything safer to recommend. 16...N-B3 fails to 17 B-R5ch! Nor is 16...O-O-O sufficient on account of 17 Q×RP N-B3 18 Q-R8ch Q-N1 19 Q×Qch K×Q 20 B-Q6ch K-R2 21 P-B4.

17	B-R5!

Fischer increases the pressure without wasting time capturing on N7.

17 ...   K-B2

If 17...O-O-O White does not win back the pawn (18 Q×RP P-N3 19 Q-R8ch Q-N1 20 Q×Qch K×Q 21 B-Q6ch K-N2 22 KR-N1 K-B3), but continues 18 P-R5!, after which Black's king has fallen out of the frying pan into the fire. On 18...K-N1 there would follow 19 B-B5 and the pawn cannot be defended. The same move is also unpleasant after 18...P-QR3. It is true that in this case Black could go into an opposite-coloured-bishop ending a pawn down: 19...P-K4! 20 Q×QP N-B5 21 Q×KP Q×Q 22 R×Q N×B 23 R×N. Possibily 17...O-O-O was the best chance for Black.

18   P-B4   KR-K1
19   P-B5   P×P
20   Q×QPch   K-B3

If 20...B-K3 then 21 R×B R×R 22 Q×KBPch R-B3 23 Q-Q5ch R-K3 24 R-KB1ch and White wins.

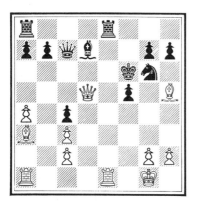

21   B-B3

It becomes clear that this is not the strongest continuation; both 21 B-Q6 and 21 P-N4! deserve consideration.

After 21 B-Q6, 21...Q-B3 fails to 22 Q-Q4ch K-B2 23 B-B3 Q-N3 24 B-Q5ch B-K3 25 B-B5 Q-Q1 (if 25...Q-R3 then 26 B×Bch R×B 27 Q-Q7ch) 26 R×B R×R 27 B×Rch K×B 28 R-K1ch K-B2 29 Q×BPch K-B3 30 Q-K6ch K-N4 31 B-K3ch P-B5 32 B×BPch! K×B 33 R-KB1ch K-N4 34 R-B5ch K-R3 35 Q-K3ch N-B5 36 Q×Nch P-KN4 37 R-B6ch K-N2 38 Q×Pch K-R1 39 Q-K5! etc.

Nor is it any use to play 23...Q-B1 (instead of 23...Q-N3) because of 24 B-Q5ch B-K3 25 R×B! R×R 26 R-K1 and Black's position is bad. 23...Q-R3 fails to 24 B-Q5ch B-K3 25 R×B R×R 26 B×Rch K×B 27 R-K1ch K-B2 28 Q-Q5ch K-B3 29 R-K6ch.

An attempt by the black king to slip off to R3 also leads to a fiasco: 22...K-N4 (instead of 22...K-B2) 23 B-B3 Q-N3 24 B-B5 Q-B2 25 P-R4ch K-R3 26 Q-Q2ch P-B5 27 B-Q6 Q-N3ch 28 K-R2 N×P 29 Q×Pch K-N3 (29...P-N4 30 Q-B6ch N-N3 31 K-N3!) 30 Q-N3ch K-B2 31 B-Q5ch B-K3 32 Q-B4ch etc.

The best move appears to be 21...Q-Q1 (instead of 21...Q-B3), but even then after 22 QR-N1 or 22 P-N4 Black still has the hardest part of the game ahead of him.

21 P-N4! is still more energetic for White. Then, in view of the threats of

22 R-KB1, 22 B-Q6 and 22 Q-Q4ch
K-B2 23 P×P B×P 24 R-KB1, it is
hard for Black to escape defeat. For
example, 21...Q-B3 22 Q-Q4ch K-
N4 (22...K-B2 23 P×P B×P 24 R-
KB1!) 23 P-R4ch! (23 B-B1ch? P-B5
24 B×Pch N×B 25 R-K5ch R×R 26
Q×Rch K-R3! 27 Q×Nch P-KN4
leads to very unclear play) 23...K×RP
24 B×N Q×B 25 B-K7ch R×B 26 R×R
and White wins. There is no
salvation in 24...P×B because of 25
B-K7ch P-KN4 26 P×Pch K-R4 27
Q×NP R-KN1 28 Q-R7ch K-N5 29
QR-Q1 R-R1 30 R-Q4ch K-B6 31
B×P!

21   ...   N-K4!

Larsen finds the best practical
chance! Other continuations were
weaker. For example, 21...B-K3 22
Q-Q4ch K-B2 23 QR-N1! (after 23
R×B? R×R 24 B-Q5 N-B5 25 R-K1
QR-Q1 Black has nothing to fear)
23...QR-Q1 24 Q×RP! B-B1 25 R×R
K×R 26 Q-B5! Q×Q 27 B×Q R-Q2 28
P-R5 and Black's position is difficult. If Black plays 23...KR-Q1
instead of 23...QR-Q1 then White
wins by 24 Q-K3 B-B1 25 R×P!
The attempt to simplify the
position would also be unsuccessful
after 21...R×Rch 22 R×R R-K1 23 Q-
Q4ch K-B2 24 R-N1! (after 24 R×R
K×R 25 Q×NP Q-N3ch! 26 K-B1 Q-
N8ch 27 K-B2 Q×Pch 28 B-K2 B-K3
29 Q×RP B-B2! the position is
extremely unclear) 24...P-N3 25 P-
R5, and it is very hard for Black to
meet the impending attack.

22   Q-Q4   K-N3
23   R×N   Q×R

Of course not 23...R×R because of
24 B-Q6!

24   Q×B   QR-Q1

Larsen put all his hopes in this
position, and indeed White's back
rank is so weak that Black's threats
look very strong.

25   Q×QNP

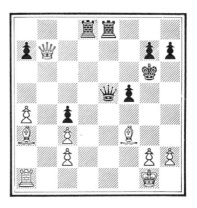

25   ...   Q-K6ch

Many commentators deprecated
this move believing that Larsen could
have achieved equality by playing
25...Q×BP. I. Zaitsev wrote in
"Shakhmatnaya Moskva" that after
26 Q-N1 R-K4! (a suggestion of
Murei) Black's counterplay is sufficient. In confirmation he adduced
the following variations: 27 B-N2 Q-
K6ch 28 K-R1 R-QN1 and 27 B-QN4
Q-Q5ch 28 K-R1 P-B6. The first of

these is unquestionable but the second raises some doubts. Black is threatening 29...R-QN1 and therefore 29 Q-N3 suggests itself in order to meet 29...R-QN1 with 30 B×P! However 29 Q-N3 is refuted decisively by 29...Q-Q8ch! with a win for Black! White must therefore play 29 B-R3 but then after 29...Q-Q7! Black's position is fine.

Alatortsev, however, in the weekly newspaper "64", disagreed with this assessment. He did not notice the move 26...R-K4! and gave 26...R-Q7 27 B-QN4 Q-K6ch 28 K-R1 R-B7 29 Q-Q1! etc. However, instead of 27...Q-K6ch, 27...Q-Q5ch 28 K-R1 R×BP! is not bad. It is true that in this case 29 B-B5! is unpleasant; but it is unclear which is the stronger, White's QRP or Black's QBP.

Black's twenty-eighth move ...R-B7 is also dubious; instead, the energetic continuation 28...P-B6 29 P-R3 Q-Q5 30 Q-N3 R-K6 gives Black the initiative.

In judging the move 26 Q-B6ch Zaitsev concludes that Black can draw with precise play. His analysis runs: 26 Q-B6ch K-N4 27 B-B1ch P-B5. (Here 27...K-R5 fails against 28 P-N3ch K-R6 29 B-KN2ch K-N5 30 P-R3ch K×NP 31 Q-B7ch [but not 31 R-R3 R-K8ch 32 B-B1 R×B (KB8)ch 33 K×R R-Q8ch 34 K-K2 R-K8 mate] 31...Q-K4 32 Q×Qch R×Q 33 B-N5! R-QB1 34 R-KB1 and there is no satisfactory defence against the threat of mate.) 28 P-R4ch K-B4! (if 28...K×P then 29 K-R2! Q×R 30 B×P and the threat of 31 P-N3 mate can-

not be countered) 29 P-N4ch! P×P e.p. 30 K-N2 Q-Q5! 31 K×P Q×R. Now the black queen has a check on KN8 as soon as White's bishop leaves the back rank; nor can White mate the enemy king without a quiet move. For example, 32 B-N4ch K-K4 33 Q-B5ch K-B3 34 Q-B2ch K-K4 35 Q-K1ch K-Q5 and White has nothing better than perpetual check.

| 26 | K-B1 | R-Q7 |

Larsen was counting on this tempting counter-attack, but bitter disillusionment awaits him.

27	Q-B6ch	R-K3
28	B-B5!	R-B7ch
29	K-N1	R×NPdbl ch
30	K×R	Q-Q7ch
31	K-R1	R×Q
32	B×R	Q×P(B6)
33	R-KN1ch	K-B3
34	B×P	

The passed QRP plays a decisive role in this ending. Black cannot hold it in the presence of the two strong bishops. A point of particular importance is the fact that they prevent the approach of the black king

| 34 | ... | P-B5 |

34...P-N4 is hardly any better, for then White can ensure the advance of his pawn by means of 35 B-N6 P-N5 36 P-R5 Q-N7 37 B-Q8ch K-N3 38 P-R6.

35	B-N6	Q×P
36	P-R5	Q-QN7
37	B-Q8ch	K-K3
38	P-R6	Q-R6
39	B-N7	Q-B4?

Black could have offered more stubborn resistance by playing 39...Q-N7! 40 R-K1ch K-Q3 41 B-N5, and White wins the KBP, deferring the advance of his own QRP. And if 39...P-QB6? White wins by 40 B-N6 P-B7 41 P-R7 P-B8=Q 42 R×Q! Q×Rch 43 B-N1.

| 40 | R-QN1 | P-QB6 |
| 41 | B-N6 | Resigns |

On 41...P-B7 there follows 42 R-K1ch.

GAME 23

White: Fischer
Black: Darga

USA — West Germany Match
Berlin 1960

1	P-K4	P-K3
2	P-Q4	P-Q4
3	N-QB3	B-N5
4	P-K5	P-QB4
5	P-QR3	B×Nch
6	P×B	N-K2
7	P-QR4	Q-B2
8	N-B3	P-QN3
9	B-QN5ch	B-Q2
10	B-Q3	QN-B3
11	O-O	P-B5
12	B-K2	

| 12 | ... | P-B3 |

The alternative is 12...P-B4 obtaining some space, avoiding problems along the K-file and hoping a little for a K-side pawn storm. But that move has the disadvantage that White's QB could be even safer and mightier on the QR3-KB8 diagonal in a blocked position.

12...O-O-O has also been tried, but after 13 N-N5 (less promising is 13 B-R3 N-B4 14 P-N4!? N-R3 15 B-Q6 Q-N2 [here it is an advantage for Black to have played ...P-QN3, which provides a bolthole for the queen, thus avoiding White's standard attack that results from B-Q6, ...Q-R4; KR-N1-N5] 16 N-R4 P-B3 and 17...N-B2) 13...QR-B1 14 B-N4 P-KR3 15 N-R3 P-B4 16 P×P e.p. R×P 17 P-B4 N-B4 18 N-B2 N-Q3!? 19 B-B3 P-KR4! 20 N-R3 (safer than 20 B×RP R(B3)-R3 21 B-N4 R×P! 22 N-R3?! R(R7)×N 23 P×R N-K5 with rather good compensation for the exchange. Moles-Henry, Ballyclare 1971) and White can keep the advantage.

13 B-R3!?

For 13 R-K1 see game 24. The move in the text is more aggressive, involving a pawn sacrifice. Fischer tried the same idea against Mednis in the 1962/3 US Championship with the slight but significant difference that Black's QNP was still on N2, and he came to the conclusion that it may well have been unsound.

13 ...   P×P

Mednis declined the pawn and castled, but after 14 R-K1! he had a cramped position (14...P×P is answered by 15 N×P! keeping the K-file open).

14 P×P

Black gains time and White has nothing after 14 N×P N×N 15 P×N Q×P 16 R-K1 Q×BP 17 B-R5ch P-N3 18 B-N4 (not 18 B×N K×B 19 Q×P? Q×QR!) 18...Q-B3.

14 ...   N×P

In case of 14...O-O 15 N-Q4! followed by P-B4, White would have sacrificed nothing and he would would have his KR even more favourably placed on KB1.

15 R-K1

The threat is 16 N×N Q×N 17 B-R5ch.

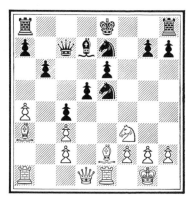

15 ...   N(K2)-B3

Better than 15...N(K4)-B3 (or 15...N(K4)-N3 16 P-R4! N-B3 17 N-N5 and Black's king has no good escape.) 16 N-N5! O-O (if 16...P-KR3 17 B-R5ch P-N3 18 N×P B×N 19 R×B P×B 20 Q×QP! R-Q1 21 Q×RPch K-Q2 22 QR-K1 regaining the piece) 17 B-KN4 Q-B5 (if 17...P-K4 18 B-K6ch K-R1 19 B×P!) 18 B×Pch! B×B 19 N×B Q×BPch 20 K-R1 R-B4 21 R-K2 Q-R5 22 N-Q4! R-R4 23 N-B3 Q-B3 24 Q-K1 R-K1 25 R-K6 Q-B2 26 Q-K2 R-R3 27 R-K3 followed by R-K1 and White is winning.

16 N×N   N×N
17 P-B4

Playable is 17 Q-Q4 (similar to Fischer-Larsen, illustrative game 22, where Black's QNP was on N2) 17...O-O-O (in the Fischer-Larsen game there occurred 17...N-N3 18 B-R5 K-B2 19 P-B4) 18 B-R5 N-N3 19 P-R5! P-N4 (or 19...Q-B5 20 B×N

QxQ 21 PxQ PxB 22 PxP PxP 23 B-K7 QR-K1 24 R-R7!) 20 P-N3 K-N2 21 P-R6ch K-R1 22 P-B4 with a bind on the dark squares. Pritchett-Markland, British Championship 1971.

17 ...   **N-B3**

Bad is 17...N-B2 18 B-R5 P-N3 19 P-B5! O-O-O 20 PxKP BxKP 21 RxB PxB 22 QxRP or 17...N-N3? 18 P-B5.

18   B-KN4

Better is the finesse 18 B-R5ch! P-N3 19 B-KN4 O-O-O 20 BxP BxB 21 RxB R-Q2 22 Q-B3 N-Q1 in order to be able to play 23 R-KB6! R-K1 24 R-Q1 etc.

18	...	O-O-O
19	BxP	BxB
20	RxB	R-Q2
21	P-B5	

Planning P-B6 and a grip on the KB-file. The game is even after 21 Q-B3 N-Q1 22 R-K5 Q-B3.

21 ...   **N-Q1!**

Driving his opponent's rook from its command outpost on the 6th rank.

22	R-K3	Q-B5!
23	R-B3	Q-K5
24	P-R5!	

Commencing operations against the king while Black's queen is temporarily cut off from the Q-side.

24 ...   **N-B3?**

Allowing the decisive opening of the QR-file. Correct was 24...P-QN4 with an even game.

25	PxP	PxP
26	Q-N1!	K-B2

Not 26...K-N2 27 B-B5 or 26...R-N2 27 P-B6 PxP 28 RxP P-Q5 29 Q-N5 etc.

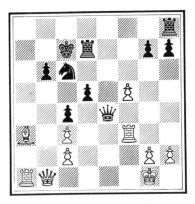

23   B-B1!   **Q-K8ch**

Black had no good defence against the threat 28 B-B4ch. If 27...N-K4, 28 B-B4 R-K1 29 Q-N5 wins

28	R-B1	QxP
29	B-B4ch	K-N2
30	Q-N5!	Resigns

GAME 24

White: Bannik
Black: Tal

25th USSR Championship, 1958

Notes by Bannik

1	P-K4	P-K3
2	P-Q4	P-Q4
3	N-QB3	B-N5
4	P-K5	P-QB4
5	P-QR3	B×Nch
6	P×B	N-K2
7	N-B3	Q-B2
8	P-QR4	P-QN3
9	B-QN5ch	B-Q2
10	B-Q3	QN-B3
11	O-O	P-B5

12	B-K2	P-B3
13	R-K1	O-O

Black has failed to annihilate the point K4, and so brings his king to safety in the hope of getting play on the open KB-file.

Botvinnik, the great expert on the French Defence, prefers castling long in this variation.

14	B-R3	R-B2
15	B-Q6	Q-Q1
16	B-B1	N-B4
17	B-R3	P×P
18	N×P	N×N
19	R×N	B×P
20	R×KP	Q-Q2
21	R-K5	B-B3

By exchanging the KP for the RP Tal thought that he would gain the advantage by means of ...N(KB4)-Q3-N4. However, he underestimated White's next move.

22 Q-R5!

Now 22...N-Q3 is followed by the unpleasant tactical blow 23 R×QP! and White wins material. For example, 23...B×R 24 Q×B R-Q1 25 Q×N Q×Q 26 B×Q R×B 27 B×P followed by 28 B×R.

White now has the open K-file, the square K5 and two active bishops. In addition Black has a lot of weaknesses. The QP is weak and the squares K3, K2 and K1 need to be defended. Tal correctly decides to exchange rooks, getting rid of the immediate threats. After that he can think about advancing his Q-side pawns.

22	...	P-KN3
23	Q-N5	Q-Q1
24	Q-N4	Q-Q2
25	P-KN3	

He has to prevent the threatened
...N(KB4)-Q3-N4. Now if 25...N-Q3
then White can play 26 Q×Q R×Q 27
B-R3 and if 27...R-Q1, 28 R-K6.

25	...	R-K1
26	QR-K1	R×R
27	R×R	N-Q3
28	Q-R4	N-B4

The knight cannot make the
bishop on R3 leave its guarding post.
On 28...N-N4 White can penetrate
decisively: 29 B-R3 Q-B2 30 R-K7
R×R 31 B×R and Black is defenceless
against the threat Q-B6 followed
shortly by mate.

29	Q-N5	N-N2
30	P-R4	

Black has defended the weak points
on the K-file, so White has to call up
the reserves.

30	...	R-B4
31	Q-K3	R×R
32	Q×R	P-KR4

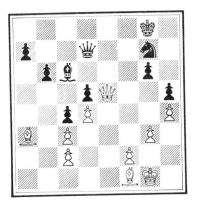

It is interesting that four of
White's pieces: a knight, both rooks
and the queen, have already been on
the key square — K5, and now it is
the turn of White's bishop to aim
there. With his last move Black
creates a refuge for his king and at
the same time prevents the further
advance of White's KRP.

33	Q-B6	Q-K3
34	Q-B8ch	K-R2
35	Q-QN8	Q-Q2
36	B-Q6	P-R4?

Black, in time trouble, has the un-
fortunate idea of advancing his Q-
side pawns. By playing 36...N-K1 37
B-K5 Q-QN2 38 Q-Q8 Q-Q2 39 Q-
N5 he could have ousted the queen
from the back rank and defended
himself.

37	B-K5	N-K1

This is forced. If the QRP is
advanced further then White
continues with a conclusive attack:
37...P-R5 38 Q-KB8 P-R6 39 B-R3
Q-N2 40 B-K6 with mate.

38	Q×P	P-R5
39	Q-B5	

39 B-R3 Q-QN2 40 Q-B5 P-R6 41
Q-KB8 N-N2 42 B-K6 would have
been more energetic, leading to un-
avoidable mate (42...P-N4 43 B-B7).

39	...	K-N1
40	B-R3	Q×B

| 41 | Q×B | K-B2 |
| 42 | Q-N7ch | |

This was the sealed move. White takes the QP and the BP after which he advances his own QP and QBP and so decides the game.

42	...	K-B1
43	Q×P	Q-B1
44	Q-N5	Q-R1
45	Q-B5ch	K-B2
46	Q×Pch	K-B1
47	P-Q5	P-R6
48	Q-B5ch	K-B2
49	P-QB4	P-R7
50	B-R1	Q-R3
51	Q-Q4	N-B3
52	P-Q6	Resigns

GAME 25

White: Karpov
Black: Markland

Hastings 1971/72

1	P-K4	P-K3
2	P-Q4	P-Q4
3	N-QB3	B-N5
4	P-K5	P-QB4
5	P-QR3	B×Nch
6	P×B	Q-B2
7	N-B3	N-K2
8	P-QR4	P-QN3
9	B-QN5ch	B-Q2
10	B-Q3	QN-B3
11	O-O	P-KR3
12	R-K1	N-R4
13	Q-Q2	R-QB1
14	P-R4	O-O

15	Q-B4	P-B4
16	P×P e.p.	R×P
17	Q×Q	R×Q
18	P×P!	

White gets rid of one weak pawn. After 18 N-K5 P×P! 19 P×P N(K2)-B3, Black would have the initiative thanks to his pressure along the QB-file. But now he cannot keep this pressure with 18...R×P? because of 19 B-R3.

18	...	P×P
19	N-K5	B-B1
20	P-QB4!?	

The alternative idea was 20 P-N3, planning B-KB4.

20	...	N(R4)-B3
21	B-N2	N-N5
22	P-QR5	R-B1
23	B-R3	P×P
24	N×P	R-B5
25	N-Q6!	

Not 25 P-N3? R×N 26 B×R N×P.

Also, 25 R-K4 N×B 26 P×N R×R 27 P×R N-B3 cannot be bad for Black.

25	...	N×B
26	P×N	R×RP
27	N-K4	

Weaker was 27 QR-B1 R-R5 28 B×P B-Q2!

27	...	R-R4
28	KR-QB1	B-N2
29	N×P	B-Q4
30	P-B3	R-B4
31	P-R6	

31 N-K4!? is less dangerous for Black.

31	...	R-B2
32	N-K4	N-B4

Threatening ...N-Q5.

33	B-B5	R-QB1
34	B-B2	R(B2)-B2
35	R×R	R×R
36	R-N1	N-K2
37	R-N8ch	K-R2
38	K-R2	N-N3

On 38...N-B1, 39 N-B5 and R-N7 would follow.

39 N-B5

Black has serious worries with his weak QR-pawn. The threat is R-N7.

39	...	R-B3

39...N-K4 40 R-N7 B×R 41 P×B N-Q2 (if 41...N-B3 42 B-N3) 42 P-Q4 puts up much less resistance.

40 R-Q8

Not now 40 R-N7? because of ...R×P!

40	...	R-B2
41	R-Q7	

Now Black's QRP will fall and the result of the ending is decided.

41	...	R×R
42	N×R	B-B3
43	N-N8	B-N4
44	B×P	N-K2
45	B-N6	

More precise than 45 B-B5? N-Q4 followed by ...N-B2.

45	...	N-B1
46	B-B5	K-N3?

White would have more technical problems after 46...B×QP 47 P-R7 N×P 48 B×N B-N4 49 P-B4.

47	P-R7	N×P
48	B×N	P-K4
49	P-Q4	P×P
50	B×P	K-B2
51	P-B4	P-N4
52	P×P	P×P
53	K-N3	K-N3
54	K-B3	K-B4
55	P-N3	

A grave mistake would be 55 P-N4ch?? K-N3 and White cannot win because his king is tied to the defence of the only remaining (weak) pawn on the light squares (the colour of Black's bishop).

| 55 | ... | **Resigns** |

GAME 26

White: Hartston
Black: Portisch

Nice Olympiad 1974

Notes by Krogius

1	P-K4	P-K3
2	N-QB3	P-Q4
3	P-Q4	B-N5
4	P-K5	P-QB4
5	P-QR3	B×Nch
6	P×B	N-K2
7	N-B3	B-Q2
8	P-QR4	QN-B3
9	B-K2	Q-B2
10	O-O	P-QN3
11	B-Q3	P-KR3
12	R-K1	O-O

This move is the hub of the chosen system. Black gets counterplay by means of ...P-KB3 or ...P-KB4. Unfortunately, in my game against Gufeld in the 1967 USSR Spartakiad, I feared a sacrifice on KR3 and played the weaker continuation 12...N-R4. After 13 N-Q2! O-O 14 Q-N4 P-B4 15 P×Pe.p. R×P 16 N-B3 QR-KB1 White could have gained

the advantage had he played 17 Q-N3.

However, as became clear later, the sacrifice on KR3 is not dangerous. The game Sutton—Moles, Skopje Olympiad 1972, went as follows: 13 B×P P×B 14 Q-Q2 (against 14 N-N5 Moles pointed out the following defence: 14...P×N 15 Q-N4 K-N2 [or 15...P-B4] 16 Q×NP ch N-N3 17 Q-B6ch K-N1 18 B×N Q-Q1! or 15 Q-R5 P-B4 16 P×P e.p. R×P 17 Q×Pch K-B2 18 Q-R5ch K-B1 19 Q-R8ch N-N1 20 B-R7 N-K2 21 R-K5 B-K1 22 R-N5 B-B2 23 B×N N×B 24 R×Nch B×R 25 Q×Rch Q-B2) 14...K-N2 15 Q-B4 N-KN1! (this is much stronger than 15...N-B4) 16 R-K3 QN-K2 17 N-R4 N-N3 18 R-N3 B-K1 19 R-K1 P-B5! 20 B×N P×B 21 Q-N4 N-K2 22 Q×KP Q-Q2 and Black soon won.

We should also note the game Williams—Moles (Oxford, 1971): 13 P-N4!? P-B5 14 B-B1 P-B3 15 P×P R×P 16 P-N5 P×P 17 B×NP QR-KB1! and Black got excellent play in return for the exchange.

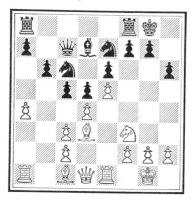

96

13 B-R3   N-R4

It is now clear why castling on the twelfth move was stronger: the placing of White's knight on Q2 (necessary in order for the queen to reach the K-side) forces the QB to take up a position on QR3, which is far from being an ideal place for it.

14 P×P   P×P
15 N-Q2   N-N3

Quite right. Black should not hurry with the advance ...P-B3. After 15...P-B3 16 P×P R×P 17 P-QB4 Black is in difficulties. It is not good to play 15...B×P because of 16 Q-N4 B-Q2 17 N-B3! (but not 17 P-QB4 P×P 18 N×P N×N 19 Q×N KR-QB1 with equal chances) and White has a strong attack because of the threat 18 B-QB1.

16 Q-R5   B-K1

This is the safest. After 16...N-KB5 17 Q-N4 N×B 18 P×N White unquestionably has the advantage because of his dangerous threats on the K-side. There are some quite interesting complications after 16...B×P 17 B×N P×B 18 Q×NP, when Black's position is very difficult to defend. For example: 18...B-Q2 19 N-B3 N-B5 20 B-B1 or 18...Q-B3 19 B-B1! (but not 19 N-B3 N-B5 20 B-B1 Q-K1 21 Q-N3 B×P 22 B×P Q-N3), or 18...QR-K1 19 B-B1 (in order to prevent the manoeuvre ...R(K1)-K2 and ...B-K1) 19...B-Q2 20 N-B3.

It seems that the only acceptable possibility is 18...Q-K2. And now if 19 N-B3, then 19...B-K1 20 Q-N3 N-B5 21 B-B1 K-R2 and Black is all right. But White could be more cunning and play 19 B-B1 and after 19...B-K1, 20 Q-N3 N-B3 21 N-N3 with the unpleasant threat of 22 B-R3. Still, 21...P-B5 22 B-R3 Q-N4 23 Q×Q P×Q 24 B×R P×N 25 B-R3 P×P 26 B-B1 P-N5 is possible, with sufficient compensation for the exchange. True, White can also play 17 Q-N4, but then 17...B-Q2 leads to the position which arose in the game a move later.

These numerous variations show that in the sharp position which arose in the game the outcome can depend on a single move. The first mistake can also prove to be the last!

17 Q-K2

If 17 N-B3 P-B4 18 P×P e.p. R×P, then White's queen is badly placed.

17 ...   B×P

A risky continuation, which demands very precise play on Black's part. 17...P-B4 18 P×P e.p. R×P was quite acceptable. After 19 N-B3 R-QB1 (19...N-KB5 is not so good because of 20 Q-K5) Black's position is quite good. For example: 20 P-N3 P-B5 21 B×N B×B 22 N-K5 B-K5 23 N-N4 R-B6 or 20 B-R6 R-N1 or 20 Q-K3 N-QB5.

18 Q-N4 B-Q2

18...N-QB5 is not satisfactory because of 19 N×N P×N 20 B×N, nor 18...Q-B3 19 N-B3 B-N4 because of 20 B×P! Q×B 21 R×N.

19 N-B3 N-QB5

Even this is playable. 19...N-B3 is not sufficient because of 20 B×N P×B 21 B×P R-B2 22 B-Q6 and 23 Q×NP, but 19...B-B1 gave good defensive chances. For example: 20 B-QB1 N-B3 21 Q-R5 P-B5 22 B×RP (22 B-B1 QN-K2) 22...BP×B 23 N-N5 N-B5 or 21 B×N P×B 22 Q×NP Q-B2 23 Q×Qch R×Q 24 B-K3 P-B5. It seems that in the last variation it is better to play 23 Q-N3 (instead of 23 Q×Q) in order to continue 24 B-K3 or B-R3. White's chances are somewhat better, but the struggle is still to come.

And in case of 20 P-R4 N-QB5 21 B-QB1 N(N3)×KP 22 N×N N×N 23 Q-N3 P-B3 24 B×P Q-B2 or 24 B-KB4 Q-B2 25 B×N P×B 26 R×KP P-QR4 Black has counter-chances.

20 B-QB1 B-B1?

A decisive mistake. He should have risked 20...N(N3)×P 21 N×N N×N 22 Q-N3 P-B3. After 23 B×P B-K1! (the only way—it iś essential to control the square KN3 and 23...N-B6ch is no good because of 24 Q×N P×B 25 Q-R5 Q-B5 26 R-K3) 24 B-KB4 P-B5! 25 B-KB1 P-R4 and the game is double-edged.

21 Q-R5 R-Q1

Alas! There is no satisfactory defence against the sacrifice on KR3.

22	B×P	P×B
23	Q×P	N-N7
24	N-N5	N×B
25	N-R7	**Resigns**

A fighting game, and an important one for the theory of the French Defence.

Chapter 3

The Nimzovich (Winawer) Variation

with 6...N-K2 and ...Q-R4

White: Smyslov
Black: Uhlmann

Mar del Plata 1966

1	P-K4	P-K3
2	P-Q4	P-Q4
3	N-QB3	B-N5
4	P-K5	P-QB4
5	P-QR3	B×Nch
6	P×B	N-K2
7	P-QR4	QN-B3

7...Q-R4 will transpose to the main line after 8 Q-Q2 QN-B3 or to the next note after 8 B-Q2 QN-B3.

8	N-B3	Q-R4

The main point of this idea is that if White defends his QB3 pawn with 9 B-Q2 he no longer has the possibility of deploying his bishop on its optimal diagonal (QR3-KB8). Nevertheless, it is not clear whether or not 9 B-Q2 is inferior to 9 Q-Q2.

9 Q-Q2

9 B-Q2 usually leads to a heavy positional struggle. **9...B-Q2 10 B-K2** In the game R.Byrne-Korchnoy, Nice Olympiad 1974, White tried the interesting move 10 B-QN5 and after 10...Q-B2 11 O-O O-O 12 R-K1 P-QN3 13 B-Q3 P-KR3 14 Q-B1 P-B5 15 B-K2 P-B3 16 B-B4 N-N3 17 B-N3 P×P 18 P×P N(N3)-K2 19 N-Q4 N×N 20 P×N N-B4 21 P-QB3 B-K1 22 B-N4 B-N3 23 Q-R3 Q-B2 24 P-B3 N×B 25 P×N P-KR4 26 B-R3 B-Q6, Black had slightly the better prospects. Black has nothing to fear either from 10 P-B4 Q-B2 11 P×QP KP×P 12 P×P O-O 13 B-K2 N×P! **10...P-B5 11 O-O** There is an interesting manoeuvre in 11 N-N5 P-KR3 12 N-R3 O-O-O 13 N-B4! (if 13 O-O P-B4 14 P-B4 K-N1, intending to win the RP by ...N-B1-N3. Stein-Uhlmann, Stockholm Interzonal 1962) 13...P-KN3 14 P-R4 QR-B1 15 P-N3 P-B3 with an unclear position. **11...P-B3 12 R-K1** For the alternative 12 P×P see Planinc-Hort, Wijk aan Zee 1973 (illustrative game 27).

In this position Black has to make the difficult decision about which side to castle. Both possibilities are playable and there is no need to castle at once:

(a) 12...0-0-0 13 B-KB1 P-B4 14 N-N5 QR-B1 15 P-B4 P-KR3 16 N-B3 R(B1)-N1 17 Q-B1 N-Q1 18 Q-R3 N(K2)-B3 19 KR-N1 Q-B2 20 R-R2 B-K1 with equal chances. Klovan-Vaganian, Sebastopol 1970.

(b) 12...0-0 13 B-KB1 QR-K1 14 P-N3 PxP 15 PxP?! Better chances are offered by 15 NxP NxN 16 RxN N-N3 17 R-K3 P-K4 18 PxP NxP 19 B-N2 B-N5 20 P-B3! with a slight advantage to White. **15...N-B1 16 B-N2** Better is 16 Q-K2 N-N3 17 KR-N1! with an unclear position. **16...N-N3 17 Q-N1 N-Q1 18 N-Q4 NxP 19 P-B4 K-R1 20 K-R1 P-QR3 21 Q-Q1 P-QN4 22 Q-R5 Q-B2 23 P-N4** After 23 B-QB1 NxP 24 B-QR3 Q-N3 25 BxR RxB Black's pawns should win for him. **23...B-B1 24 R-KB1** Black has the advantage after 24 R-K3 Q-B2 25 Q-R4 Q-K2. **24...N-B4 25 B-K3 N-K5 26 BxN PxB 27 Q-R4 N-B2** Threatening ...P-N4. **28 Q-N3 K-N1 29 P-R4 R-Q1 30 P-N5 R-Q4 31 P-R5?** White could obtain good play down the KN-file with 31 P-N6! e.g. 31...PxP 32 QxP Q-K2 33 R-B2 with a complex position. **31...N-Q1! 32 P-N6 P-R3 33 Q-R4 Q-Q2 34 N-K2 B-N2 35 K-N1 N-B3 36 N-N3 N-K2!** 37 Q-N4 N-B4 38 NxN PxN?! It was surely better to recapture with the rook. **39 Q-K2 R-Q1 40 K-B2 Q-K2 41 K-N3 Q-Q2 42 K-B2 K-B1 43 KR-QN1 K-K1 44 K-K1 Q-K2 45 Q-B2 R(Q1)-Q2 46 R-Q1 P-N5! 47 RxR RxR 48 PxP** Not 48 R-Q1 P-N6! **48...QxPch 49 K-B1 Q-N7 50 R-B1 P-B6** and Black should have won. Ciocaltea-Korchnoi, Hastings 1971/2.

(c) 12...P-B4 An interesting idea from the game Pritchett-Ivkov, Caorle 1972. **13 Q-B1 N-Q1 14 Q-R3 P-KR3 15 P-R4 P-KN3 16 KR-QN1 B-B3 17 Q-N4 Q-B2** 17...QxQ is rather drawish. **18 P-QR5 N-B2 19 B-QB1 R-KN1 20 B-R3 P-KN4** with good play for Black.

(d) 12...PxP 13 PxP 0-0 14 B-KB1 R-B4! 15 P-N3 QR-KB1 16 R-K3 16 B-N2 fails to 16...N-N3 **16...R(B4)-B2 17 B-N2 Q-B2 18 B-QB1 P-Q5!?** A subtle positional sacrifice of a pawn, allowing the black knight to reach the ideal square Q4. **19 PxP N-Q4 20 B-QR3!** White counters with a good move. Black would win after 20 R-K1 RxN 21 BxR N-B6 22 Q-Q2 RxB 23 K-N2 N-N5 24 KxR B-B3ch 25 K-N4 Q-B2 26 QxN Q-B4ch 27 K-R4 B-B6 etc. **20...N(B3)-K2** After 20...NxR 21 PxN followed by 22 N-N5 White is better. **21 B-Q6 Q-B1 22 R(K3)-R3 B-B3 23 Q-K2 P-B6! 24 R-KB1 N-KN3 25 BxR?** After this move Black's attack breaks through, whereas his sacrifice is insufficient after 25 N-K1 N(Q4)-B5 26 PxN NxBP 27 Q-K3! etc. **25...QxB 26 R(B1)-R1 N(Q4)-B5 27 PxN NxBP 28 Q-B4 NxB 29 N-N5** If 29 KxN RxN wins. **29...RxP! 30 R-KB1** If 30 QxKPch K-R1 31 P-Q5 N-K6! 32 PxB R-B8ch followed by mate. Or 30 NxKP

101

Q-B2 31 P-Q5 N-K6 with great advantage to Black. **30...R×Rch 31 Q×R Q×R 32 Q-B7ch K-R1 33 K-B2! N-B5!** The simplest way of reaching a won ending. **34 Q×N Q-K2 35 P-R5 P-KR3 36 N-K4 B×N 37 Q×B Q-N4 38 Q-Q3 Q-B5ch 39 K-K1 Q-R5ch 40 K-B1 Q-B5ch 41 K-K1 Q×RP** and Black won. Ciocaltea-Vaganian, Budapest 1973.

9 ...   **B-Q2**

It is wrong to release the tension immediately, as White has the better ending after 9...P×P 10 P×P Q×Qch 11 B×Q. In Smyslov-Letelier, Venice 1950, White gave an excellent demonstration of how this type of endgame should be handled. See illustrative game 28.

White also has the advantage after 9...O-O 10 B-R3 P-QN3 11 B-N5 B-R3 12 O-O P×P 13 Q-Q3.

The game Kuijpers-Korchnoy, Wijk aan Zee 1971 saw a third alternative: 9...P-B3! 10 B-R3 (more exact is 10 KP×P P×BP 11 P×P) 10...P×KP 11 P×KP Q×RP! 12 B-K2 P-QN3 13 P-B4 N-Q1! with an excellent game for Black.

Our main game (Smyslov-Uhlmann) reached this position by transposition.

10   B-K2

The alternative **10 B-Q3** is also very common:

(a) 10...P-B5 11 B-K2 P-B3 12 B-R3 Black has an excellent game after 12 KP×P P×BP 13 O-O N-B4 14 B-R3 O-O-O 15 KR-K1 P-R4 **12...N-N3** In the game

102

Stein-Vaganian, after 12...O-O-O 13 O-O P-R4 14 KR-K1 N-B4 15 B-KB1 P-R5 16 R-K2 QR-K1 17 Q-K1 N-Q1 18 P-N4! P×P e.p. 19 BP×P White had the edge. **13 O-O O-O-O 14 B-Q6** 14 KR-K1 P×P 15 P×P N(N3)×P 16 N×N N×N 17 Q-Q4 N-B3 18 Q×NP KR-N1 with an unclear position. **14...N(B3)-K2 15 N-R4 QR-K1** with equal chances. Fischer-Uhlmann, Buenos Aires 1960;

(b) 10...P-B3! **11 O-O** For 11 KP×P see Tringov-Vaganian, Vrnjacka Banja 1971 (illustrative game 29). **11...P×KP 12 N×P** Smyslov-Uhlmann, Havana 1964, went 12 P×KP O-O 13 R-K1 P-KR3 14 B-R3 B-K1 15 Q-K3 P-QN3 16 N-Q2 N-B4 17 Q-R3 Q×BP 18 B×N Q×N 19 QR-Q1 Q-B5 20 B×KPch B-B2 21 P-KB3 with an even game. **12...N×N 13 P×N O-O 14 P-QB4 Q×Q 15 B×Q B-B3** with equality. Fischer-Uhlmann, Stockholm Interzonal 1962.

Now, after 10 B-K2, White will be a tempo better off (than after 10 B-Q3) if Black intends the blockading ...P-B5 followed by castling Q-side. For this reason Black does better to put immediate pressure on White's central pawn structure.

10 ... R-QB1

A noteworthy alternative is 10...P-B3 11 KP×P (after 11 B-R3 P×QP 12 P×BP NP×P 13 N×P N×N 14 Q×N? [14 P×N is equal] 14...P-K4 15 Q-Q2 N-N3 16 B-QN4 Q-B2 17 Q×P N-B5 18 Q-B3 P-QR4, Black has the advantage) 11...P×BP 12 P×P O-O-O! 13 O-O P-K4 14 P-B4! P-Q5 15 Q-R6!? (Black stands very well after 15 Q×Q N×Q 16 N-Q2 P-B4, or here 16 B-Q2 N(R4)-B3 17 P-B3 B-N5 18 P-R3 B-R4 19 P-N4 P-Q6!) 15...N-N3 (or 15...P-K5!? 16 N-Q2 P-B4 17 N-N3 Q-B6 with an unclear position) 16 N-Q2! P-B4 17 N-N3 Q-B2 18 P-B4 N-N5 19 B-Q1 P-Q6 with complex play, as in Bogdanovic-Uhlmann, Sarajevo 1965.

11 P×P

Practically forced if White wishes to avoid a bad ending e.g. 11 B-R3 P×P 12 P×P Q×Qch 13 K×Q N-B4 14 P-B3 N-R4!; or 11 O-O P×P 12 P×P Q×Q 13 B×Q N-B4 and now the point of ...R-QB1 becomes clear, because 14 B-B3 fails to 14...N×KP, whereas 14 P-B3 N-R4 gives Black good play; or finally 11 B-Q3?! (losing a tempo) 11...P×P 12 P×P Q×Qch 13 B×Q P-QN3 14 R-R3 O-O 15 O-O R-B2 16 R-N1 P-KR3 17 K-B1 N-B4 18 B-B3 KR-B1 19 K-K2 P-B3?! (better is 19...N-R4) 20 P-N4?! (White has a slight advantage in the ending after 20 P×P P×P 21 B×N P×B 22 N-K1 N-R4 23 B×N P×B 24 K-Q2 R-B5 25 P-QB3 R×RP 26 R×R B×R 27 R-R1 B-N4 28 R×P P-R3 29 N-Q3 R-K1 30 N-B4) 20...N(B4)-K2 21 P×P P×P 22 P-R4 (better 22 K-Q2!) 22...B-K1 23 P-N5 B-R4 24 P×BP N-B4

25 B×N P×B 26 K-K3 K-B2 27 R-N5 R-Q2 28 P-R5 R-K1ch 29 N-K5ch N×N 30 P×N P-Q5ch and Black won. Timman-Korchnoy, Nice Olympiad 1974.

11	...	N-N3
12	O-O	

12	...	O-O

It seems more exact to play 12...N(B3)×P 13 N×N N×N 14 Q-K3 (after 14 Q-Q4 P-B3 15 B-R5ch P-KN3 16 P-KB4 N-B3 17 Q×BP R-B1 18 B×Pch P×B 19 Q×NPch K-Q1 the piece sacrifice looks unsound. However, 14 Q-N5 N-N3 15 P-QB4 is worth considering, when 15...P×P? loses to 16 P-B6!) 14...N-N3 15 B-R3 B-B3 16 P-KB4 O-O when White had great difficulty in finding play for his pawn. Hartston-Uhlmann, Hastings 1972/3.

13	Q-K3	Q-B2
14	N-Q4!	

An interesting manoeuvre aiming to place the knight on Q6. White's threat forces Black to exchange into an unfavourable ending.

14	...	Q×P

Again, the text is more or less forced. 14...N(N3)×P 15 N-N5 is unpleasant for Black and so is 14...N(B3)×P 15 N-N5 B×N 16 P×B as 16...Q×P fails against 17 Q×Q R×Q 18 B-R3 winning the exchange. Also, White was threatening to retain his pawn by 15 P-KB4.

15	N-N5	Q×Q
16	B×Q	

White has the better game owing to his two bishops with their wide range of activity and to his knight which will, from Q6, limit the movement of the black pieces.

16	...	P-QR3

Black has to weaken his Q-side to meet the threat of first 17 KR-N1, then 18 N-Q6. Now Black gets in ...R-B2 in time to defend his weak point, QN2, and his QN is freed from defending his QRP.

17	N-Q6	R-B2
18	P-R5	

White "fixes" Black's Q-side pawns which will be in constant danger in the later part of the endgame. He has also foreclosed at the proper moment on the possibility of ...N-QR4 by Black.

18	...	P-K4!

Black's main hope lies in his mobile pawn centre, and he uses his only counter-chance at the first opportunity.

19	KR-N1	N-Q1
20	R-Q1	B-B3
21	B-N4	

Using threats on different points, White gradually posts all his minor pieces aggressively.

21	...	N-K3

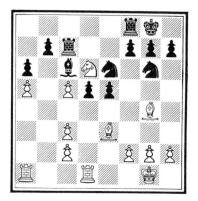

22 QR-N1

One of the rooks does belong on QN1, but it is preferable to get 22 P-N3 in first, allowing the king some luft.

22	...	N-K2
23	P-N3	P-B4
24	B-R3	P-KN3?

Black errs in feeling safe, and so he misses the opportunity of building counterplay by 24...P-KN4! (If White had played 22 P-N3 this chance wouldn't have come up.)

The next move makes Black realize how difficult is his position.

25 P-KB4!

Uhlmann sees the threat of having his pawn centre, upon the elasticity of which he so counts, blockaded.

25 ...   P-Q5

Black tries his last tactical possibility. He can expect nothing good of 25...P-K5 as White opens the position for his active pieces by 26 B-KB1 and 27 P-B4.

26	P×QP	N-Q4
27	B-B2	P×QP

On 27...N-B6 28 BP×P B-Q4 29 B-N2, Black wins the exchange and loses the game as he cannot stop the crowd of connected White pawns in the centre.

28	B×QP	N×B
29	R×N	R-K2
30	K-B2	

Not 30 B-N2 N-B6 winning the exchange.

30	...	N-B6
31	R-K1	R×R
32	K×R	N-K5
33	N×N	

More exact than 33 B-N2 N×BP 34 B×B P×B 35 R-B4 R-B3 with equality.

| 33 | ... | B×N |
| 34 | P-B3 | |

White is ahead by only a doubled pawn and still the ending is won for him. For Black's pawns are fixed on the colour of the white bishop and so his Q-side is desperately weak.

| 34 | ... | R-B3 |

Unfortunately 34...R-QB1 is out; it fails against 35 R×B.

| 35 | R-Q8ch | K-N2 |
| 36 | R-Q7ch | R-B2 |

36...K-N1 37 R-QB7 is not promising for Black, either.

| 37 | R×Rch | K×R |

White's good bishop and his advantage in space are enough to ensure the win.

38	K-Q2	K-K3
39	P-B4	

White must deny Q5 to Black.

39	...	K-Q2

Black is obliged to safeguard his Q-side and tries this attack on his opponent's pawns as his last chance.

If he leaves his king be and moves his bishop along the long diagonal, then White may exchange bishops via KB3. Or, if Black then leaves his bishop on QB3 and moves his king back and forth on K3 and KB3, White's bishop moves to Q5 at the proper moment taking one vital square from Black's king. And, with the bishops gone, the pawn ending is won. For, with kings on Q4 and QB3 for White and Black respectively, White can also gain a *zugzwang* position with appropriate K-side pawn moves: e.g. 1 P-KR3 P-KR3 2 P-N4 P×P 3 P×P P-R4 4 P-B5! P-R5 5 P×P P-R6 6 P-N7 P-R7 7 P-N8(Q) P-R8(Q) 8 Q-QB8 mate; or 1...P-KR4 2 P-KR4 K-B2 3 K-Q5 K-Q2 4 P-B6ch P×Pch 5 K-K5 K-K2 6 P-B5 etc.

40	K-K3	K-B3
41	K-Q4	K-Q2
42	K-K5	B-B6

The threat was 43 P-N4.

43	K-B6	K-B3
44	K-N7	K×P
45	K×P	B-R4
46	B-B1	K-N5
47	B-N2	K×RP

After 47...K×BP White wins by 48 B×P K-N4 49 P-R3 K×P 50 B-B8 followed by 51 P-N4.

48	B×P	K-N3

49	B-B8!	P-R4
50	B-Q7!	K-B4

Equally hopeless is 50...K-B2 51 B-N5 K-Q3 52 K-R6 and again the threat of K-N5 followed by P-R3 and P-N4 appears. Moreover, Black then has no time to play 52...K-K3 in view of 53 P-B5 K-B3 54 P-B6 etc.

51	P-R3	B-B6

Else 52 P-N4 traps the bishop.

52	K×P	B-B3
53	B×P	P-R5
54	B-N1	P-R6
55	P-B5	B-K5
56	B-R2	B-Q6
57	P-R4	K-Q5

On 57...B×QBP 58 B×B K×B 59 P-B6, the ensuing queen ending is also a loss for Black.

58	P-R5	K-K4
59	P-N4	K-B5
60	K-N7	Resigns

GAME 27

White: Planinc
Black: Hort

Wijk aan Zee 1973

1	P-K4	P-K3
2	P-Q4	P-Q4
3	N-QB3	B-N5
4	P-K5	P-QB4
5	P-QR3	B×Nch
6	P×B	N-K2
7	P-QR4	QN-B3
8	N-B3	Q-R4
9	B-Q2	B-Q2
10	B-K2	P-B5
11	O-O	P-B3

12	P×P	P×P
13	N-R4!?	

Weaker is 13 R-K1 O-O-O 14 B-KB1 N-B4 15 Q-B1 P-R4 16 Q-R3 QR-N1 17 QR-N1 N-Q1 18 R-N4 B-B3 with good play for Black. Suetin-Uhlmann, Berlin 1967.

13	...	N-N3!?

A risky idea, when 13...O-O-O 14 B-R5 P-K4 is possible.

14	B-R5	O-O-O

A pawn sacrifice for which there is theoretically insufficient compensation. After 14...R-KN1 then 15 Q-B3 is unpleasant, but 14...N-K2 is worth a try.

15	B×N	P×B
16	N×P	KR-N1?!

16...R-R2 seems better. In the game Klovan-Vaganian, USSR 1973, play went 17 Q-B3 R-B2 (worse is 17...N×P 18 Q×BP Q-B2 19 P-R3!) 18 B-B4 (there are unclear complications after 18 N-K5 N×N 19 P×N P-Q5!) 18...R-N1 19 N-R4 Q-Q1 20 Q-K2 (this move is necessary since both 20 B-N3 P-B4 and 20 Q-K3 P-K4 21 B-N3 P-B4 22 P×P P-B5 are obviously good for Black) 20...P-K4

21 B-N3 Q-K2 (the more obvious 21...P-B4 is no good because of 22 P×P P-B5 23 P-K6) 22 QR-K1 P-K5 and Black has an attack for the pawn.

17	N-B4	P-K4
18	N-K2	R-N5

Losing an important tempo, so 18...R-N2 was better.

19	P-B3!	R-N3
20	R-B2!	QR-N1
21	N-N3	K-N1?

Too slow; 21...Q-B2 offered better chances.

22	P×P	P×P
23	P-B4!	R-B3
24	Q-K2	P-K5

Or 24...B-N5 25 Q-K3! P-Q5 26 P×QP P×QP 27 Q×P with a great advantage.

25	P-B5!	K-R1
26	QR-KB1	N-K4
27	Q-K3!	R-B2

If 27...N-N5 28 Q-Q4.

28	R-B4	Q×RP
29	Q-Q4	R-K1
30	B-K3	Q-R4
31	R-Q1	B-R5

After 31...B-B3 32 R(4)-B1 White's attack down the QR-file is decisive.

32	Q×QP!	Q×Q
33	R×Q	B×P
34	P-B6	N-Q2
35	N-R5	B-Q6
36	P-N4!	R-K4?

This allows an immediate win but in any case there is no defence to the advance of the KNP.

37	R×N	R×R
38	P-B7	R×P
39	R×R	R-K1
40	N-B6	R-QB1 and
		Black
		resigned

GAME 28

White: Smyslov
Black: Letelier

Venice 1950

Notes by Kotov

1	P-K4	P-K3
2	P-Q4	P-Q4
3	N-QB3	B-N5
4	P-K5	P-QB4
5	P-QR3	B×Nch
6	P×B	N-K2
7	P-QR4!	Q-R4
8	Q-Q2!	QN-B3
9	N-B3	P×P

This continuation has been tried out in several games in the Soviet Union. Grandmaster Smyslov told me that at the dawn of his chess career he played a similar game with White against the Tbilisi Candidate

111

Master Shishov. The exchange of queens is to White's advantage because it reduces Black to waiting tactics: he can only hope to defend against his opponent's active bishops.

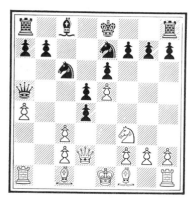

| 10 | P×P | Q×Qch |
| 11 | B×Q! | |

This reveals a deep understanding of the position. It is important for White not to allow the black knight to QB5 via R4. It gradually becomes clear that the advantage is on White's side: he has an important file on the Q-side and Black's pieces have no good squares for development.

| 11 | ... | N-B4 |

Smyslov considered this move wrong, since it merely forces White to carry out the plan of development he was intending anyway. He should have completed his development by simply playing 11...O-O, 12...B-Q2 and then doubling rooks on the QB-file.

12	B-B3	B-Q2
13	B-Q3	R-QB1
14	K-Q2	O-O
15	P-R5	R-B2
16	KR-K1	P-B3?

Black's position is cramped, but stable. By continuing 16...P-QR3, 17...KR-B1 and 18...N-R2 and then occupying QN4, Black would have kept a defensible position. Perhaps it was also worth moving the knight from B4 to K2.

The "active" move 16...P-B3 is a mistake because it creates in Black's position a significant weakness (Q4) which cannot easily be defended, especially since the open K-file and the important square K5 are at White's disposal.

| 17 | B×N! | |

A correct assessment of the position. White gives up the advantage of the two bishops, hoping to make use of the weak pawn on Q4.

17	...	P×B
18	P×P	R×P
19	QR-N1	P-KR3

He already has to prevent the threat 20 R-N5 B-K3 21 N-N5.

20	R-N5	B-K3
21	R(K1)-QN1	R(B3)-B2
22	N-K1	

The knight is marching to Q3 and from there it can go to B5 or K5, at the same time threatening to go to KB4, exchange the bishop and win the QP.

22	...	P-B5
23	P-B3	P-N4
24	N-Q3	K-R2

Here the king is placed too far from the "main theatre of military actions"; this allows Smyslov to carry out a decisive combination. 24...K-B1 would have been better.

| 25 | R-K1 | R-B3 |
| 26 | R-B5 | R-QB1 |

This makes it easier for White. It is difficult to defend against the threat of 27 N-N4, nevertheless Black should have given preference to 26...B-B2 27 N-K5 R-Q3 or 26...B-B2 27 B-N4 R-Q2.

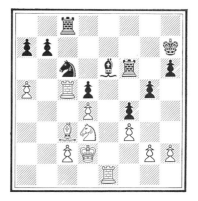

27 N-N4!

A smart combination which required deep and precise calculation. As a result of this move White gains a tremendous positional advantage with two connected passed pawns in the centre.

27 ...   N×N

After 27...N-K2 there comes a surprising attack: 28 N×P!! N×N (this seems to be the only possibility because if 28...B×N then 29 R×Nch and if 28...R×R? 29 N×Rch) 29 R×B! R(B1)×R 30 R×R N×R (if 30...R×B, then 31 R-Q6 N-B2 32 R-Q7ch! wins) 31 P×R N-Q2 32 K-Q3! N×Pch 33 K-B4 and White wins since the black king is too far away. This is why 24...K-R2 is a mistake.

28 R×B!   R×R(K3)

The only move, otherwise Black loses a piece.

29 R×R   N-B3

Of course not 29...N-R3 30 R-Q8, when the QP is indefensible.

30	P-R6!	P×P
31	R-B7ch	K-N3
32	R-Q7	N-K2
33	B-N4	N-B4

Black's last chance to attack White's K-side pawns. Otherwise after 33...K-B3 34 B×Nch R×B 35 R×QP White has an easy win.

34	R×QP	N-K6
35	R-Q8	N×NP
36	P-Q5	R-N3

37	B-B5	R-N2
38	R-QB8	N-R5
39	K-K2	N-B4
40	R-B6ch	K-R4

Black's fate is no better even after 40...K-B2 because of (for example) 41 K-Q3 and 42 K-K4.

41	P-Q6	R-Q2
42	R-B7	Resigns

After 42...R-Q1 43 P-Q7 he cannot defend against the threat of 44 R×P and 45 B-N6.

This fine positional game was conducted in masterly style by Smyslov. It is interesting that on the eve of the game Smyslov did not feel well, and he had to play the game with a high temperature because the tournament could not be prolonged by a single day.

GAME 29

White: Tringov
Black: Vaganian

Vrnjacka Banja 1971

1	P-K4	P-K3
2	P-Q4	P-Q4
3	N-QB3	B-N5
4	P-K5	P-QB4
5	P-QR3	B×Nch
6	P×B	N-K2
7	P-QR4	QN-B3
8	N-B3	Q-R4
9	Q-Q2	B-Q2
10	B-Q3	P-B3!

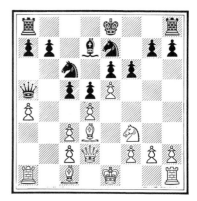

11	KP×P	NP×P
12	P×P	P-K4
13	B-K2?	

Play becomes very sharp after 13 P-B4! P×P! 14 B×BP O-O-O (better is 14...Q×BP) 15 O-O Q×BP 16 B-N3 B-N5 17 Q-R6 N-Q4 18 N-Q2 KR-N1 19 B-R3 Q-R4 20 N-K4 N-Q5 with a complex situation. Stein-Doroshkevitch, Riga 1970.

13	...	O-O-O
14	O-O	KR-N1
15	K-R1	N-N3!

Black's lead in development and strong pawn centre allow him to begin complications. Now 16 Q×P loses to 16...N-B5! 17 B×N B-R6!

16	P-B4	Q×Q
17	B×Q	P-K5!
18	N-N1	P-Q5
19	N-R3	B×N
20	P×B	P-B4

An imposing array of central pawns.

21	QR-Q1	N(N3)-K4
22	B-B4	P-Q6

Black's two knights and well placed rooks now continuously harass the two bishops.

23	P×P	P×P
24	B-R5	R-Q5!

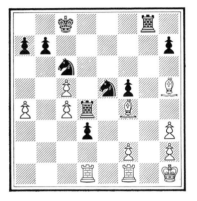

25 B-K3

It was relatively best to give up the

two bishops by 25 B×N N×B 26 KR-K1 N×P 27 B-B7 KR-Q1 28 B×N R×B, although White still has a bad ending.

25	...	R-R5
26	P-B4	N×P
27	B-B7	N×B
28	B×R	N-QN5

A useful gain of tempo.

29	KR-K1	N×R
30	R×N	R×BP
31	B×P	K-Q2
32	K-N2	K-K3!
33	K-N3	K-K4!
34	B-N8	R-K5
35	P-R5	R-K6ch
36	K-R4	P-B5
37	B-R7	K-Q5
38	K-N4	P-B6
39	K-N3	P-B7ch
40	K×P	R×P
41	B-B5	R×Pch
42	K-N3	R-R7
43	**Resigns**	

Chapter 4

The Nimzovich (Winawer) Variation with 6...Q-B2

White: Tal
Black: Botvinnik

1st Match Game 1960

1	P-K4	P-K3
2	P-Q4	P-Q4
3	N-QB3	B-N5
4	P-K5	P-QB4
5	P-QR3	B×Nch
6	P×B	Q-B2
7	Q-N4	

The most aggressive continuation. White can, of course, play quietly, along the lines of chapters 2 and 3. If he wishes to do so he must not play 7 P-QR4?? because of 7...P×P 8 P×P Q-B6ch 9 B-Q2 Q×QP, when White has nothing to show for the pawn. The positional way to meet 6...Q-B2 is **7 N-B3.** Now 7...N-K2 8 P-QR4 transposes to the main line of chapters 2 and 3. Alternatives to the transposition are:

(a) 7...N-Q2 Intending ...N-N3-R5, blockading White's QRP. **8 P-QR4! N-K2 9**

B-K2 P-B3 10 KP×P P×BP 11 P-B4! O-O 12 O-O P×BP 13 P×P! N×P 14 B×P R-Q1 15 Q-K2 with a clear advantage to White. Rakic-Lengyel, Belgrade-Budapest Match 1957.

(b) 7...QN-B3 Now White may play either 8 B-Q3, transposing into variations where Black does not have the exchanging resource ...P-QN3 and ...B-R3 at his disposal, or he can play 8 P-QR4, which will probably transpose to variations discussed in chapters 2 and 3 unless Black tries the double-edged 8...P×P 9 P×P N-N5!? 10 R-QN1!?

(c) 7...B-Q2 8 P-QR4 will also transpose to lines considered in chapters 2 and 3.

(d) 7...P-QN3 8 P-QR4 B-R3 This premature offer to exchange bishops is exposed in Epelman-Yurchenko, Quarterfinal USSR Championship 1973 (illustrative game 30).

7 ...   P-B4

7...N-K2 transposes to variations discussed in chapter 1, pages 30-37. 7...P-B3 is an idea worth noting. In the game Matulovic-R.Byrne, Sousse Interzonal 1967, play continued 8 N-B3 P-B5 (not 8...N-B3 9 Q-N3!) 9 B-K2 N-B3 10 O-O Q-B2 11 Q-R3 KN-K2 12 P-R4 B-Q2 13 B-R3 O-O-O 14 P-R5 P-R4 15 N-Q2 and now Black could have equalized with 15...N-B4.

8   Q-N3

Black has no worries after 8 Q-R5ch Q-B2 9 Q×Qch K×Q 10 N-B3 P×P 11 P×P N-K2 with equality; or 8 P×P e.p. N×P 9 Q-N3 Q×Q 10 RP×Q N-B3 11 N-K2 P-K4 with equality.

8   ...   N-K2

The sharpest move, which keeps Black's options on the Q-side and closes certain diagonals to White's QB.

If 8...P×P 9 P×P N-K2 10 B-Q2 O-O 11 B-Q3 P-QN3 12 N-K2 B-R3 (Diez del Corral-Petrosian, Palma 1969 went 12...R-B2 13 O-O B-R3 14 P-KR4 B×B 15 P×B QN-B3 with a good game for Black, but White can improve with Petrosian's suggestion 13 P-KR4!) 13 N-B4 Q-Q2 14 B×B (for 14 B-N4 see Hort-Petrosian, Kapfenberg 1970, illustrative game 31) 14...N×B 15 Q-Q3 N-N1 16 P-KR4 with a slight plus to White. Reshevsky-Botvinnik, World Championship Match Tournament 1948.

Another noteworthy alternative is 8...N-QB3 9 N-B3 P×P 10 P×P KN-K2 11 Q×P R-KN1 12 Q-R6 (if 12 Q×RP N×QP!) 12...B-Q2 13 Q-Q2 N-R4 14 P-N3 N-B5 and Black's positional advantage is well worth the pawn. Dely-Bondarevsky, Leningrad 1959.

9   Q×P

Consistent. Had Black played 8...P×P 9 P×P N-K2, this capture would not be possible because of (10 Q×P) R-N1 11 Q×P Q-B6ch winning. But now that Black has decided to maintain the tension surrounding the Q-side pawns, White is allowed to make this capture.

After 9 B-Q2 O-O 10 B-Q3 P-QN3 11 N-R3 B-R3 12 N-B4 Q-Q2 13 P-KR4 B×B 14 P×B QN-B3 15 B-K3 P×P 16 P×P QR-B1 Black has better counter-chances (Smyslov-Botvinnik, 14th Match Game 1957) because White does not have the possibility of activating his QB by B-N4 as in either the Reshevsky-Botvinnik game mentioned above or the Hort-Petrosian game (illustrative game 31).

	9	...	R-N1
	10	Q×P	P×P
	11	K-Q1	

This move offers the best prospects. After 11 N-K2 QN-B3 12 B-B4 B-Q2 ɩ3 R-Q1 P×P Black has the better game.

	11	...	B-Q2

Botvinnik's improvement, prepared for his first match with Tal. 11...
QN-B3 is weaker. See Gligoric-Petrosian, Belgrade 1959 (illustrative game 32).

12 Q-R5ch!

If 12 N-B3, then after 12...B-R5 13 B-Q3 Q×BP, his position immediately
becomes critical. On 12 N-K2, Black can likewise play 12...B-R5, with the
unpleasant threat of 13...P-Q6. It is easy to see how the move 11...B-Q2 kills
two birds with one stone: strategically it helps complete development and
prepare for castling long and tactically it readies the blow at (Black's) QB7. If
White does not want to come under strong attack, he must play extremely
actively. There is basis for this. With his move 7...P-KB4, Black got rid of his
pawn which was on KB2, for which the black king often has to play the
unpleasant role of "Guardian". But, on the other hand, the K1-KR4 diagonal
has been weakened, and this diagonal protects the black king when the KBP is
in its original square. Moreover, it has deprived Black's pieces of any future
"material" support in the diagonal. In spite of this, the white queen can now
return to "home shores" with a tempo. — Note by Tal.

12 ...   N-N3

12...K-Q1 has also been tried with the idea of avoiding the pin conceded by
...N-N3. White then has three possibilities:

(a) 13 B-KN5 In his notes to the main game Tal commented that this is how he
had intended to meet 12...K-Q1, "...going for the attack". Presumably
Botvinnik prepared an improvement after 13 B-KN5 because he tried 12...K-Q1
against Tal in the 12th game of their return match in 1961.

(b) 13 N-B3 This should be met by 13...B-R5! but Botvinnik played 13...Q×BP.
See illustrative game 33.

(c) 13 N-K2 P×P For 13...B-R5 see the brilliancy prize game Ivkov-Portisch,
Bled 1961 — illustrative game 34. 14 Q-B3 14 P-B4 seems suspect after 14...Q-
B4 15 Q-B3 P-Q5! 16 R-QN1 QN-B3 17 N-N3 N-R4 with an excellent game for
Black in Gipslis-Fuchs, Bad Liebenstein 1963. Or here 16 Q×NP QN-B3! 17
Q×Rch K-B2 18 Q×R N×Q 19 N-N3 Q-Q4 20 R-KN1 N-R4 with an attack.
14...QN-B3 15 Q×QBP According to Pachman White now has a slight plus, e.g.

15...N×P 16 Q×Qch K×Q 17 N-Q4 N-N5 18 K-K1 P-K4 19 P-KB3! N-KB3 20 N-N3 QR-QB1 21 B-N2, but the American Correspondence player F.K.Lobdell has found the improvement 19...P×N 20 P×N P×P when Black can probably hold the game. e.g. 21 B-KB4ch K-B3 22 R-QN1 P-R3 23 P-QR4 QR-K1 and now 24 K-Q2 N-B4 25 P-R5 B-B1 (not 25...N-K6?? 26 R-N6ch K-B4 27 B-Q6mate) 26 B-Q3 N-K6 27 R-N6ch K-Q2 28 R-K1 N-B5ch 29 B×N R×R 30 B×QP R(K8)-K1 with equality. Fawbush-Lobdell, 1971/2; or 24 K-Q1? N-B4 25 P-R5 N-K6ch 26 K-B1 N-B5 with a clear advantage to Black. Collins-Lobdell, 1971/2.

13   N-K2

White can repeat the position by 13 Q-R7 N-K2.

[From here on the notes are by Mikhail Tal.]

One must understand that such an agreement to a draw would be a considerable defeat. It would mean that I admitted that I was wallowing in a mire of confusion after the first innovation by my opponent.

White's 13th move attempts to take advantage of the pin. It threatens 14 N-B4 and on 14...K-B2, the quiet 15 B-Q3 could follow, or the sharper 15 P-N4. Now Black spent more than a half an hour deliberating over this position, from which it can be inferred that he had not covered all the subtleties of the variation in his home laboratory. The continuation 13...Q×KP 14 P×P or 13...P×P 14 N-B4 K-B2 15 B-Q3 (significantly stronger than 15 Q-R7ch, which was recommended by Vukovic) with a number of unpleasant threats (possible, for example, is the variation: 15...QN-B3 16 B×P P×B 17 P-K6ch B×P 18 Q-R7ch R-N2 19 Q×Rch!) is not at all satisfactory for Black. The straightforward 13...B-R5 runs up against the rejoinder: 14 N-B4 Q×BP 15 B-Q3 Q×R 16 N×N N-B3 17 N-B4ch! (stronger than the variation which I examined during the game, 17 N-K7ch K-Q2! 18 N×R R×N, with double-edged play). Likewise, the problem is not solved by 13...N-B3 14 P×P R-QB1 15 R-R2.

Botvinnik chooses the best continuation, which, at the cost of a pawn, further loosens White's king position. Now the game takes on a "gambit" character.

13 ...   P-Q6!

White's answer is forced.

14 P×P   B-R5ch

However strange it may seem, this natural move does not seem to be quite correct. Black takes advantage of the opportunity to break the pin on the K-side with a tempo, but in so doing, he drives the white king to K1, where it is considerably more secure.

White's problem would have been much more complicated after the simple 14...N-B3, followed by castling long. The white king, whose protection on the Q-side was quite unreliable, would have had to waste a tempo to get over to the other flank via K1. After 14...N-B3, I think that Black would have had some real compensation for his two sacrificed pawns.

15 K-K1   Q×KP

This is a fully understandable attempt by Black to regain some of his sacrificed material, but the text move loses a lot of time. 15...N-B3 might have been more in the spirit of Black's plan. Now, it is true, this move is not as strong, since White can continue 16 P-KB4 O-O-O 17 B-Q2, gradually freeing the pieces on his K-side. Sooner or later, Black will have to sacrifice a knight on K4. It is difficult to anticipate future events, but in any case, Black might have the initiative. It is tempting to look at the continuation used by the Czech Master Podgorny, 15...B-N4, but by continuing 16 B-N5! B×P 17 K-Q2, White seizes the initiative.

16   B-N5!

The basic problem which now confronts White is how to keep the black king in the centre. In this respect, the loss of White's KP has played into White's hands, since new threats can be created with the opening of the K-file. White's unusual plan is brought about by the "lateral" development of the rook.

16   ...   N-B3

The attempt to fight for the initiative via 16...P-B5 does not work in view of 17 P-Q4 Q-B4 18 N×P Q-B7 19 N-K2.

17   P-Q4   Q-B2

After 17...Q-K5 18 R-B1!, Black's queen finds that she does not have much room in the centre of the board. The transition to the endgame, 17...Q-R1 18 N-B4, likewise is not satisfactory for Black.

18   P-R4!

This was not played to begin the advance of the passed pawn (although it will play its role), but to bring White closer to his goal of getting the KR into the game and nearer the pressing developments in the centre. On more sluggish continuations, Black, by playing ...QN-K2 and preparing to castle long, obtains a dynamic position. Now there is no time for 18...QN-K2, inasmuch as White simply exchanges on K7 (19 B×N Q×B) and by continuing 20 Q-N5, carries the game into extremely prosaic channels. Therefore, Black is forced to meet him half-way, opening lines.

18   ...   P-K4
19   R-R3

Bringing up the reserves and incidentally countering the threat 19...P×P 20 P×P N×QP.

19 ...   Q-B2

Also possible here was 19...P-K5. In that case, Black's position would be rather solid, but he would be threatening absolutely nothing and White could go about realizing his extra pawn advantage without any hindrance. Bad would be 19...P-B5 20 Q-N4. All of Black's efforts are being directed to the driving back of the queen on KR5 with the rook on KR1, but he is never able to achieve this.

20   P×P   N(B3)×P

20... R-R1 is not possible in view of 21 P-K6 Q×P 22 R-K3 R×Q 23 R×Qch K-B2 24 R×N(N6)!

21   R-K3   K-Q2

Again, 21...R-R1 22 R×Nch K-Q2 23 R-K7ch Q×R 24 Q×N does not work.

22   R-N1

With this unusual manoeuvre, White brings his QR into the game; at the same time, Black's QNP is attacked.

22   ...   P-N3

It is difficult to imagine how, with the queen on KR5, the weakening of QR3 can play any role, but nevertheless, it does.

White's problem would have been complicated on 22...B-B3. I intended to sacrifice the exchange, transposing into a rather advantageous endgame with 23 N-Q4 P-B5 24 R×N! N×R 25 Q×Qch N×Q 26 B×P QR-K1ch 27 K-Q2, but this would have been the lesser of two evils for Black. The move 22...P-N3 has another disadvantage: White can take advantage of the position of the bishop on QR4, winning an important tempo for the development of the rook.

23   N-B4

White's pieces are poised like a latent mainspring. If Black now plays 23...R-

R1, then after 24 N×N N×N 25 Q-K2, the threat Q-R6 (see the preceding note) must be decisive.

23	...	QR-K1
24	R-N4!	

Preparing White's next move.

24	...	B-B3
25	Q-Q1!	

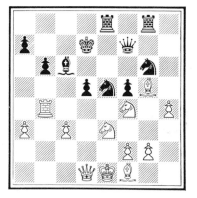

"The queen has done her job — she is now dismissed." Black never played ...R-KR1. A rather picturesque position has arisen: The white king and queen, after their long journeys, have returned to their original positions; the KB has not made one move at all, and nevertheless, Black has a very difficult position on his hands: White not only has a solid extra pawn, but he also has extraordinarily actively placed pieces — chiefly the rooks, which are effectively controlling the centre. The impressive mass of black pieces in this region is, in fact, harmless.

25	...	N×N

And after 25...N-N5 26 R-K2 or 26 R×R R×Rch 27 B-K2, Black is lost.

26	R(N4)×N	N-N3
27	R-Q4	R×Rch

On 27...P-B5, 28 Q-N4ch decides the issue.

28   P×R

There is no need to withdraw the bishop from its active position on KN5. The white KP can serve as a shield for the king if need be.
However, Black does not succeed in creating any threats whatsoever.

28	...	K-B2
29	P-B4	

This leads to a forced material advantage for White. On 29...N-K2, White continues 30 P×P B×P (or 30...N×P 31 B-QB4) 31 B×N Q×B 32 Q-B1ch, giving Black absolutely no chance.

29	...	P×P
30	B×P	Q-N2
31	B×R	

Not a bad course of events for the bishop, which had just made its first entrance into the game.

31	...	Q×B
32	P-R5	

Finally, the passed pawn has its say. **Black resigned.**

GAME 30

White: Epelman
Black: Yurchenko

Quarterfinal USSR Championship
1973

Notes by Epelman

1	P-Q4	P-K3
2	P-K4	P-Q4
3	N-QB3	B-N5
4	P-K5	P-QB4
5	P-QR3	B×Nch
6	P×B	Q-B2
7	N-B3	P-QN3
8	P-QR4	B-R3

9 B-QN5ch!?

White essays one of the sharpest variations. In his book "Spanisch bis Französisch" Keres gives the line 9 B×B N×B 10 Q-K2 N-N1 11 P-R5, with complex play. And the game Suetin-Donner, Havana 1968 continued 9 B×B N×B 10 Q-Q3 N-N1 11

O-O N-Q2?! 12 P-R5! with the better game for White.

9	...	B×B
10	P×B	P-QR4?!

It is naturally tempting to turn a backward pawn into an outside passed pawn, but the ending is still a long way off.

11	P-B4!	P×BP.
12	N-N5	P×P?

Black should definitely not just keep on taking everything — every tempo is precious for him now. For example, after 12...Q-N2 (hindering the moves Q-B3 and N-K4) 13 P-KB3 N-K2 14 N-K4 O-O 15 B-R3 N-Q2 16 N-Q6 Q-B2 17 N×QBP N-Q4 he could complete his development and put up a defence.

13	O-O	N-K2
14	Q-B3	N-Q4
15	B-R3!	

So White gets compensation for his two pawns in the shape of two diagonals, QR3-KB8 and KR1-QR8.

15	...	R-R2
16	B-Q6	Q-Q1
17	N-K4	P-B4

Or 17...R-Q2 18 B-R3 N-N5 19 N-Q6ch K-B1 20 P-B3 P×P 21 Q×QBP R×N 22 B×N P×B 23 Q×NP etc.

18	P×Pe.p.	P×P

19	KR-K1!	R-KB2
20	N-N5!	N-K2

The threat was Q×N.

21 B×N

Accuracy is needed to the very end. After 21 R×KP?! P×N 22 Q-Q5 P-R3! -23 QR-K1 KR-R2 Black can defend himself.

21	...	Q×B
22	N×KP!	Q-R2
23	Q-Q5	N-Q2
24	N×Pch	K-B1
25	Q-Q6ch	K-N2
26	N-B5ch	Resigns

GAME 31

White: Hort
Black: Petrosian

European Team Championship
Kapfenberg 1970

Notes by Nei

1	P-K4	P-K3
2	P-Q4	P-Q4
3	N-QB3	B-N5
4	P-K5	P-QB4
5	P-QR3	B×Nch
6	P×B	Q-B2
7	Q-N4	P-B4
8	Q-N3	P×P
9	P×P	N-K2
10	B-Q2	O-O
11	B-Q3	P-QN3
12	N-K2	B-R3
13	N-B4	Q-Q2

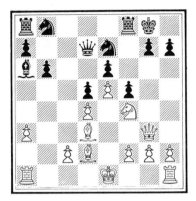

14 B-N4   R-B2!

The continuation in the game Spassky-Fuchs, Varna 1958, was weaker: 14...B×B? 15 N-R5 N-N3 16 B×R B-R3 17 B×P Q-N4 18 O-O-O N-B3 19 Q-R3 K-B2 20 P-N4! with advantage to White.

15 P-KR4

Black can defend against 15 N-R5 by 15...K-R1.

15	...	B×B
16	Q×B	QN-B3
17	R-R3	R-QB1!

Black's QR is bound for QB5.

18	R-N3	N-Q1
19	P-R5	R-B5
20	P-R6	N(K2)-B3
21	N-R5?	

According to Uhlmann, 21 P-QB3 is correct.

21 ...   P-N3!

The ex-World Champion has probably no equal in the playing of this type of position. He does not fear the loss of the exchange, for in the resulting position his cavalry will be poised for action. It should, incidentally, be observed that 21...R×QP? fails to 22 R×Pch R×R 23 N-B6ch.

22	N-B6ch	R×N
23	P×R	N-B2

The natural move 23...N×P was also strong.

24	Q-Q2

Against 24 P-QB3 Petrosian intended to play 24...P-K4 with more than enough compensation for the exchange.

24	...	R×QP
25	R-Q3	R-R5
26	R-R3	R-N5
27	K-B1	N-Q3
28	R-K1	K-B2
29	B-B3	N-K5
30	Q-Q3	N-B4
31	Q-Q1	R-QB5
32	B-N2	P-QN4
33	Q-K2	Q-Q3
34	K-N1	N-K5

White's scattered pieces are totally unable to co-operate, and Black unhurriedly strengthens his position.

35	R-Q3	Q-B4
36	R-QB1	P-K4
37	Q-K3	P-Q5
38	Q-K2	N×P(B3)

Black restores formal equality. White is helpless.

39	R(Q3)-Q1	N-Q4
40	Q-Q2	P-K5
41	Q-N5	N-B2
42	R-Q2	N-K3
43	Q-R4	P-R4

The sealed move. On resumption Black speedily realized his advantage.

44	R(B1)-Q1	R×P
45	R×R	Q×R
46	R-QB1	Q×B
47	R×N	P-Q6
48	R-R6	Q-Q5
49	Resigns	

GAME 32

White: Gligoric
Black: Petrosian

Belgrade 1959

1	P-K4	P-K3
2	P-Q4	P-Q4
3	N-QB3	B-N5
4	P-K5	P-QB4
5	P-QR3	B×Nch
6	P×B	Q-B2
7	Q-N4	P-B4
8	Q-N3	N-K2
9	Q×P	R-N1

10	Q×P	P×P
11	K-Q1	QN-B3

12 N-B3! N×P

White's next move is also strong against the alternatives 12...P×P and 12...B-Q2.

13 B-KN5 N(4)-N3

13...N-B2 fails to 14 B×N R-R1 15 Q-N7 Q×B 16 N-K5!

14 B×N

A strong alternative is 14 B-B6! R-B1 (if 14...B-Q2 15 N-R4!) 15 B-N7! followed by P-KR4-5.

14	...	N×B
15	P×P	B-Q2
16	B-Q3!	

Not 16 N-K5? Q-B6!

| 16 | ... | Q-Q3 |

Black has no time for 16...R×P 17 K-K2! and after 18 QR-KN1 White's pieces penetrate decisively on the K-side.

17	Q-R5ch	N-N3
18	N-K5	O-O-O
19	N×N	

19 N-B7 Q-B5 20 N×R Q×QP is unclear.

19	...	B-K1
20	Q-K2	

20 B×P P×B 21 Q×Pch B-Q2 would be a gross blunder.

20	...	B×N
21	P-N3	R-R1
22	K-Q2	R-R6
23	Q-K5	Q×Q
24	P×Q	QR-R1
25	K-K3	R×RP
26	R×R	R×R
27	P-KB3	

Better is 27 P-N4! P-B5ch 28 K×P B×B 29 K-N3! or here 27...P-Q5ch 28 K-B4! R×Pch 29 K-N5 B-R2 30 R-R1, or 27...R-R5 28 P-KB3 B-R2 29 K-B4 P×P 30 P×P B×B 31 P×B with a good rook ending for White.

27	...	B-K1
28	P-N4	

Better is 28 R-KN1!

28	...	P×P
29	P×P	K-Q1

30	R-QN1	P-N3
31	R-N4?!	R-R8!
32	R-KB4	R-K8ch
33	K-Q4	R-KN8
34	B-K2	K-K2
35	R-B6	R-QR8
36	R-B3	B-N3
37	R-B3	K-Q1
38	R-B6	B-B2
39	R-B3	B-N3
40	R-B6	B-B2
41	R-B3	Drawn

GAME 33

White: Tal
Black: Botvinnik

12th Match Game, 1961

Notes by Tal

1	P-K4	P-K3
2	P-Q4	P-Q4
3	N-QB3	B-N5
4	P-K5	P-QB4
5	P-QR3	B×Nch
6	P×B	Q-B2
7	Q-N4	P-B4
8	Q-N3	N-K2
9	Q×P	R-N1
10	Q×P	P×P
11	K-Q1	B-Q2
12	Q-R5ch	

12	...	K-Q1
13	N-B3	Q×BP
14	R-R2!	

This ugly move is practically forced. If 14 R-QN1 then 14...B-R5 threatens 15...P-Q6 and White would have to retreat his knight to K1. Even though Black would have had some difficulty in defending his pawns on K3 and N2 in this line, I was not thrilled by the prospect.

14	...	QN-B3

14...B-R5 would not have had the desired effect now because the square QB2 is defended and White could immediately chase the black queen away by 15 B-Q2.

15	R-N2	

Now that the threat of ...B-R5 has been dealt with the rook occupies the open QN-file.

15	...	K-B2

130

16 R-N5!

All of a sudden it becomes obvious that the black queen has nowhere to retreat and White is threatening to play 17 B-N2. Black has only two possibilities: the move played and 16...Q-R8. To the last move White would have replied 17 R-N2 and the black queen is under arrest. After 17...R-R1 18 Q-N5 R(QR1)-KN1 19 Q-Q2 the black queen has difficulty in gaining freedom, even though it is not directly threatened.

16	...	R-R1
17	Q×R	R×Q
18	B-N2	Q×Nch

After 18...P-R3 19 B×Q P×R 20 B×QP or 20 N×P Black would only have lost a pawn but his bad pawn formation together with the opposing passed pawn on the KR-file would have left him without much chance of defence. The exchange sacrifice was undoubtedly the best solution in the circumstances.

19 P×Q

An interesting position has arisen. White's pieces are not particularly well positioned, and moreover his pawn configuration is compromised. The KP is indefensible and if Black manages to win it fairly quickly and then advance his own KP then his pawn centre will become a serious force. White's hopes are mainly based on his passed pawn, which usually plays a major part in this variation.

19 ...   N-N3?

Black evidently under-estimated White's response. He should have stopped the advance of the White KRP by playing 19...R-R5, and if 20 B-B1, then 20...P-B5 after which it is hard for White to bring his bishops into play. After 20 P-KB4 R×BP 21 P-KR4 N×P 22 R-N3 Black would have had a hard struggle against White's passed pawn.

20 P-KR4!   N(N3)×KP

In the variation 20...R×P 21 R×R N×R 22 P-KB4 White would gradually have realized his material advantage.

21 P-R5   N-B2

Black did not have the courage to take the KBP. After 21...N×P 22 P-

R6 followed by R(N5)-QN3-KN3 he would have had to solve some very difficult problems.

22　P-KB4!

Now Black's central pawns are blocked and White brings his pieces into play.

| 22 | ... | N-Q3 |
| 23 | R-N3 | N-K5 |

Black cannot keep his knight on this excellent central square since White can chase it away by P-KB3 if necessary. First of all White gets rid of the pawn on Q4.

24	K-K1	R-R3
25	B-K2	B-K1
26	R-Q3	N-B3

The fate of White's KRP is sealed, but by sacrificing it White manages to get behind his opponent's front line.

27	B×P	N×B
28	R×N	B×P
29	R-Q3	R-R2

29...B×B 30 R×R B×R 31 P×B N-Q2 32 R×P N-B4 33 R-K3 would not have helped either.

30	R(Q3)-R3	B-N3
31	R×Rch	N×R
32	R-R6	N-B1

It becomes clear that Black is forced to lose the KP and any further resistance is useless.

33	R-R8	N-Q2
34	R-KN8	B-B2
35	R-N7	B-K1
36	R-K7	K-Q1
37	R×P	B-B2
38	R-KR6	K-K2
39	B-Q3	B-K3
40	R-R5	N-B3

In this position the game was adjourned and I sealed the move 41 R-N5. Convinced of the hopelessness of his position, **Botvinnik resigned** without resuming play.

GAME 34

White: Ivkov
Black: Portisch

Bled 1961

Notes by Keres

1	P-K4	P-K3
2	P-Q4	P-Q4
3	N-QB3	B-N5
4	P-K5	P-QB4
5	P-QR3	B×Nch
6	P×B	Q-B2
7	Q-N4	P-B4
8	Q-N3	N-K2
9	Q×P	R-N1
10	Q×P	P×P
11	K-Q1!	B-Q2
12	Q-R5ch	K-Q1
13	N-K2	

In the twelfth game of the Tal-Botvinnik duel in 1961, Tal continued with 13 N-B3, to which Black could have responded well with 13...B-R5! The move in this game is Ivkov's improvement. When necessary, the knight on K2 can take up the strong square KB4.

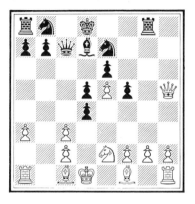

13 ... B-R5?

What would have been of good effect after 13 N-B3 is wrong here. Black should have discovered some other plan, perhaps 13...P×P or 13...P-Q6 14 P×P B-R5ch and 15...Q×KP.

14 N-B4!

After this move, the concept of Black's game can be said to have been smashed. Black has no real defence for the attacked pawn on K3 unless he opts for the time-wasting move 14...B-Q2.

14 ... Q×KP

After 14...Q×BP 15 R-R2 Black can not reply 15...Q-B3 because of 16 Q-B7 K-Q2 17 N-R5 etc., so he would be forced to play 15...B-Q2, which, after 16 B-Q3, would lead him into a dreadful situation. The move actually played is nothing more than an act of desperation. Clearly a catastrophe on K3 must soon come about.

15 Q-B7

More simply, 15 B-Q3 would be very strong.

| 15 | ... | B-Q2 |
| 16 | B-Q3 | Q-Q3 |

Black's position is utterly broken. White stands so well that with the simple 17 P×P he could be satisfied with one more pawn and a secure position. But quite justifiably he wants more than that and plays for the attack. Here or even on the following move Black could try ...QN-B3.

| 17 | R-K1 | P-K4 |
| 18 | P-QR4! | |

He threatens the fatal 18 B-R3.

| 18 | ... | B-K1 |
| 19 | Q-K6 | |

Correctly, White does not fight shy of exchanging queens. In so doing he destroys his opponent's pawn centre and with unimpaired strength involves the black king in the attack. The game is essentially already decided.

19	...	Q×Q
20	N×Qch	K-Q2
21	N-B5ch	K-B1
22	R×P	QN-B3
23	R-K2	R×P

Black could continue his resistance by 23...P×P, but after 24 B-KB4! he would certainly not escape defeat. However, the move actually made enables his opponent to execute a brilliant and conclusive attack, making this game rank as one of the finest at the Bled tournament.

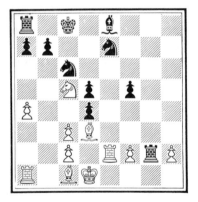

24 B×Pch!   K-Q1

The first fine mate variation appears after 24...K-B2 25 B-B4ch K-N3 26 R-N1ch K×N 27 R-N5ch K-B5 28 B-Q3ch K×P 29 B-Q2 mate. Black could extricate himself from a direct

mate only by 24...N×B 25 R×Bch N-Q1.

25   N×Pch   K-B2

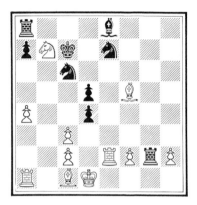

26   B-B4ch!   N-K4

After 26...K×N we have another mate variation: 27 R-N1ch K-R3 28 B-Q3ch K-R4 29 B-B7ch K×P 30 R-R1 mate.

27   R×N   N×B

In this way perhaps Black hopes to save his king, but something else materializes.

28	R-K7 dbl ch	K-B3
29	R-QB7ch	K-N3
30	R-N1ch	K-R3
31	R-B6ch!	

Yet another problem move, to vacate the square QB7 for the bishop. A third mate variation, 31...B×R 32 N-B5ch K-R4 33 B-B7 mate, forces **Black to resign.**

Part Two

Other Systems with 3 N-QB3

	1	P-K4	P-K3
	2	P-Q4	P-Q4
	3	N-QB3	

	3	...	N-KB3
	3	...	N-QB3
and	3	...	P×P

Chapter 5

√-7|6|76 -how to proceed in a R ending!

The Classical Variation

White: Shabanov
Black: Osnos

USSR 1961

1	P-K4	P-K3
2	P-Q4	P-Q4
3	N-QB3	N-KB3

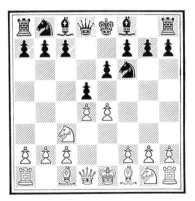

The oldest method of play in the French Defence has been somewhat neglected of late. Perhaps the reason for this is that Black cannot avoid concrete variations which tend to favour White, as practical results have shown. The move is less sharp than 3...B-N5 and therefore it offers less counterplay.

4   B-KN5

The most popular continuation and the logical way to increase the tension. Steinitz used to favour **4 P-K5** but after **4...KN-Q2** the fixed pawn centre gives Black sufficient counterplay by means of ...P-QB4 and ...P-KB3. e.g.:

(a) 5 QN-K2 P-QB4 6 P-QB3 N-QB3 7 P-KB4 P-B4 7...P-B3 is also perfectly playable. **8 N-B3 B-K2** and White cannot transpose to a favourable form of the Leningrad Variation (see later), as the knight on K2 is blocking the KB. The game Enevoldsen-Gilfer, Helsinki Olympiad 1952, continued: **9 N-N3 P×P 10 P×P O-O 11 B-K2 Q-N3 12 O-O P-KN4! 13 P×P N(B3)×KP** with an excellent game for Black.

(b) 5 P-B4 The most natural move which Steinitz himself preferred. **5...P-QB4 6 P×P** If White tries to defend his Q4 square, sharp variations arise e.g. 6 N-B3 N-QB3 7 B-K3 Q-N3 (there are wild complications after Korchnoy's suggested 7...P×P 8 KN×P Q-N3) 8 N-QR4 Q-R4ch 9 P-B3 P×P 10 P-QN4 N×NP 11 P×N B×Pch 12 B-Q2 B×Bch 13 N×B P-QN3! 14 R-QN1 B-R3 15 Q-N3 R-QB1 with chances to both sides. The game Bronstein-Portisch, Amsterdam 1964, continued 16 P-QR3 B×B 17 R×B R-B5 18 N-N2 R-B6 19 Q-N4 Q×P. **6...N-QB3 7 N-B3** Better than 7 P-QR3 B×P 8 Q-N4 O-O 9 N-B3 N-Q5 10 B-Q3 P-B4 11 Q-R3 P-QR3 12 B-Q2 P-QN4 13 O-O-O N×N 14 Q×N B-N2 15 N-K2 Q-B2 and Black had good play in Tarrasch-Marshall, 1905. **7...B×P 8 B-Q3 P-B3!** It is essential to attack the centre at once. **9 P×P N×P 10 Q-K2 O-O 11 B-Q2 N-Q5** Or 11...B-Q2 12 O-O-O K-R1 13 QR-K1 P-QN4, Tringov-Fuchs, Sofia 1958, leading to complex but rewarding (for Black) play. **12 N×N B×N** with even chances.

4   ...   B-K2

For 4...P×P see chapter 8 and for 4...B-N5 see chapter 7.

Now Black threatens 5...N×P and so White must solidify the centre.

5   P-K5

Anderssen's idea, **5 B×N B×B,** reduces Black's pressure on White's centre but only at the cost of conceding the two bishops. With careful defence Black can parry White's attack. e.g.:

(a) 6 N-B3 P-B4! Not 6...O-O?! 7 B-Q3 P-B4 8 P-K5 B-K2 9 P-KR4! P-B4 (not 9...P×P 10 B×Pch K×B 11 N-N5ch K-R3 12 Q-Q3 P-KN3 13 P-R5! B×N 14 P×Pch B-R5 15 Q-N3 P×P 16 R×Bch K-N2 17 R-N4 with a strong attack.) 10 P×P e.p. P×BP 11 N-KN5! with a good attack. **7 P×QP** Black has a comfortable game after 7 P-K5 B-K2 8 B-Q3 P×P 9 KN×P N-QB3. **7...KP×P 8 B-N5ch N-B3 9 Q-K2ch** Black has good play after both 9 O-O O-O 10 P×P Q-R4! 11 B-Q3 B-K3 and 9 P×P O-O! **9...B-K3 10 N×P** After 10 N-K5 O-O 11 B×N P×P Black has the advantage. **10...Q×N 11 P-B4 Q-Q1 12 P-Q5 Q-R4ch! 13 K-B1 O-O 14 P×B P×P 15 B×N P×B** with excellent chances for Black. Karaklaic-Gligoric, Yugoslavia 1949.

(b) 6 P-K5 B-K2 7 Q-N4 O-O 7...K-B1 8 B-Q3 is a little better for White. **8 B-Q3** White can also play 8 O-O-O which usually transposes. **8...P-QB4 9 P×P** Weaker is 9 Q-R3 P-KN3 10 P×P N-B3 11 P-B4 B×P 12 N-B3 P-B3 13 Q-R6 R-B2. Charousek-Maroczy, 1897. **9...N-B3 10 P-B4** Black has the advantage after 10 N-B3 P-B4 11 Q-R3 B×P 12 O-O B-Q2 13 P-KN4 N-N5 14 P-N5 P-Q5 15 N-K2 N×B 16 P×N P-B5. Richter-Stahlberg, Munich 1936. **10...P-B4 11 Q-R3 P-QN3** Or 11...Q-R4 12 O-O-O P-Q5 13 N-N1 N-N5! 14 B-B4 N×RPch (or 14...Q×BP) with a clear advantage to Black. **12 O-O-O P×P** and Black's strong centre guarantees him the better chances.

5   ...   KN-Q2

The natural retreat. Tartakower's move 5...N-K5 leaves Black with a weak pawn at K5 after B×B Q×B (even worse is 6...N×N 7 Q-N4 Q×B 8 Q×NP Q-N5 9 Q×Rch K-Q2 10 B-Q3 Q×NP 11 R-Q1 N×R 12 K×N Q×QP 13 Q×P, when

White has an important lead in development) 7 N×N P×N 8 Q-K2 P-QN3 (or 8...N-Q2 9 O-O-O P-KB4 10 P×P e.p. N×P 11 P-B3! P×P 12 N×P with pressure on Black's KP) 9 O-O-O B-N2 10 P-KN3 P-QB4 11 B-N2 N-B3 12 P×P Q-N4ch 13 K-N1 Q×KP 14 B×P Q×BP 15 N-B3 and White is somewhat better.

An even more peculiar idea is Nimzovich's 5...N-N1 which has been seen in some of Heidenfeld's games.

The most effective answer seems to be the retreat 6 B-K3, stressing the retarded development of Black's K-side by leaving Black's KN and KB on awkward squares. 6 B×B N×B is harmless, merely helping Black's KN to reach a good square (even 6...Q×B is playable, intending to develop the knight via KR3 to KB4 as in Marco-Albin, Carlsbad 1901). Also, the imitation of the Albin/Chatard/Alekhine Attack does not work well here: 6 P-KR4 B×B 7 P×B Q×P 8 N-R3 Q-K2 9 N-B4 (or 9 Q-N4 P-KB4, Dennehy-Heidenfeld, Dublin 1964; and Kraiko-Heidenfeld, Berne 1968) 9...P-KN3 and White has insufficient compensation for the pawn. Black's KN is better placed on KN1 than on Q2 because his Q-side pieces can be developed more quickly and his king will soon reach safety. Black's QN goes to KB1 via Q2 and after ...B-Q2 Black is ready to castle.

Let us now examine the possibilities after 6 B-K3: 6...P-QN3 7 P-KR4! The threat is 8 P-R5 and so Black must weaken his K-side in order to prevent this advance. But if White plays 7 Q-N4 P-KN3 and then 8 P-KR4, Black's reply 8...P-KR4 shows that White's queen is misplaced and it is easier for the second player to equalize. In the game Unzicker-Heidenfeld, Dublin 1967, White played 7 Q-N4 P-KN3 and then 8 N-B3. After 8...B-R3 9 O-O-O B×B 10 KR×B P-KR4 11 Q-N3 Q-Q2 12 B-N5 N-QB3 13 Q-B4 B×B 14 N×B N-Q1 15 P-KR3 P-QB3 16 P-KN4 Q-K2 17 Q-Q2 N-R3 18 R-R1 N-N2, Black castled Q-side and then equalized by attacking White's centre with ...P-KB3. Yet another possibility is the plan of simple development with 7 N-B3 B-R3 8 B×B N×B 9 Q-

K2 N-N1 10 O-O Q-Q2 as in Letelier-Heidenfeld, Havana Olympiad 1966, when White was unable to develop a significant initiative because of his obstructed QBP. **7...P-KR4 8 B-K2 P-N3** 8...B×P 9 P-KN3 B-K2 10 R×P R×R 11 B×R favours White. **9 N-B3 B-R3 10 Q-Q2 B×B 11 N×B** White has the advantage because he is ahead in development and ready for the thematic break P-QB4. The game Mikenas-Vistaneckis, Lithuania 1947, continued: 11...P-QB4? (Black should not open the position while he is behind in development) 12 P-B4! P×QP 13 N(B3)×P P×P 14 Q-B2 Q-Q4 15 N-B4! Q×KP? 16 O-O-O R-R3 17 N(B4)×KP! P×N 18 B×R N×B 19 Q×NPch N-B2 20 Q-N8ch B-B1 21 N×P! and White crashed through.

6   B×B

For 6 P-KR4 see the next chapter.

6   ...   Q×B

This is the standard position of the Classical Variation. White has a space advantage and he usually has the better bishop in an ending. Perhaps this is why Black's set-up has gone out of fashion.

7   P-B4!

Probably the strongest continuation, supporting the KP in preparation for meeting ...P-QB4 with P×P.

The principal alternative is **7 Q-Q2 O-O 8 P-B4** Even now this is the strongest move. **8...P-QB4 9 N-B3 N-QB3 10 P×P!** Black has good counterplay after 10 O-O-O P-B5! **10...N×BP** 10...P-B4 11 P×P e.p. Q×KBP 12 P-KN3 N×P 13 O-O-O transposes. **11 O-O-O** After 11 B-Q3 P-B3 12 P×P Q×P 13 P-KN3 N×Bch 14 Q×N (14 P×N P-K4!) 14...B-Q2 15 O-O QR-B1 16 QR-K1 B-K1 Black obtained equality in Bhend-Christoffel, Zurich 1961. **11...P-B3** After 11...P-QR3 12 B-Q3 P-QN4 13 N-K2 B-N2 14 N(B3)-Q4 N×N 15 N×N White had a positional advantage in Gligoric-Stahlberg, 7th Match Game 1949, in view of his beautifully centralized knight. **12 P×P Q×P 13 P-KN3 R-Q1 14 N-Q4 N-K5 15 Q-K3** and White's position is to be preferred.

Weaker possibilities for White are:

(a) 7 N-N5 N-N3 8 P-QB3 P-QR3 9 N-QR3 P-QB4 10 P-KB4 N-B3 11 N-B2 N-B5 12 R-N1 P-QN4 with equal chances. Lasker-Lilienthal, Moscow 1936;

(b) 7 B-Q3 O-O 8 QN-K2 P-QB4 9 P-QB3 P-B3 10 KP×P Q×P 11 N-B3 N-B3 12 O-O P-K4 with equality;

(c) 7 N-B3 O-O 8 B-Q3 P-QB4 9 P×P N-QB3 and White has insufficient control over his K5 square;

(d) 7 Q-N4 O-O 8 N-B3 P-QB4 9 B-Q3 (threatening 10 B×Pch K×B 11 N-KN5ch K-N1 12 Q-R5) 9...P-B4 10 P×P e.p. R×P 11 Q-R4 N-B1 12 P×P Q×P 13 O-O N-B3 14 QR-K1 B-Q2 with a good game for Black. Bernstein-Lasker, Zurich 1934.

7   ...   O-O

The exchange sacrifice 7...P-QB4 8 N-N5 O-O hardly seems good enough after 9 N-B7 P×P 10 N×R P-B3 11 N-B3 (or 11 N-B7 P×P 12 N-N5 P-QR3 13 N×P P×N 14 Q×P!) 11...P×P 12 P×P N-QB3 13 B-Q3 N(Q2)×P 14 O-O N-KN5 15 N-Q2! with advantage to White. Levenfish-Fahrni, Carlsbad 1911.

We must also mention 7...P-QR3 8 N-B3 P-QB4 9 P×P N-QB3 10 Q-Q2 Q×P 11 P-QR3 P-QN4 12 Q-B2 B-N2 13 Q×Q N×Q 14 O-O-O with a positional plus to White, as he can play B-Q3, KR-K1 and N-K2-Q4.

8   N-B3   P-QB4
9   P×P

Also possible is **9 B-Q3 P-B4** The threat was 10 B×Pch etc. **10 P×P e.p. R×P** After 10...Q×P White has chances with Bronstein's suggested 11 N-KN5, e.g. 11...Q×BP (if 11...P-KN3 12 Q-N4!) 12 B×Pch K-R1 13 Q-Q2 Q×QP (he should have tried 13...Q×Qch 14 K×Q R-B7ch) 14 Q×Q P×Q 15 N-N5 N-R3 16 N×QP N-B3 17 B-Q3 with the better ending for White. Ravinsky-Orlov, Moscow 1964.

11 Q-Q2 N-B3 12 P×P N×P 13 O-O N×B 14 P×N Q-KB2 No better is 14...B-Q2
15 QR-K1 Q-N5 16 P-KN3 B-K1 17 P-QR3 Q-N3ch 18 K-N2 with advantage to
White. Gligoric-Yanofsky, Dallas 1957. **15 N-K2 B-Q2 16 Q-K3 QR-KB1** (so
far as in Bronstein-Yanofsky, Saltsjobaden 1948) **17 Q×RP! P-QN3 18 Q-R3**
with advantage to White.

9	...	**P-B4**

9...P-B3 10 P×P is the same thing.

10	P×P e.p.	Q×KBP
11	P-KN3	N×P
12	B-Q3	N-B3
13	O-O	

It is worth delaying Q-Q2 in order to restrict Black's central activity.

13	...	B-Q2
14	Q-Q2	B-K1

The bad bishop tries to improve its position, but this involves a loss of time.

15	QR-K1	N×B
16	P×N	B-R4
17	N-K5!	

Once Black's knight is exchanged, White will have domination of the black
squares.

17	...	N×N
18	R×N	B-N5
19	Q-K3	Q-Q1
20	Q-Q4	Q-N3

The exchange of queens only helps White.

21	Q×Q	P×Q
22	P-QR3	QR-B1
23	N-N5	B-R6
24	R(B1)-K1	R-B7
25	R(K5)-K2	R×R
26	R×R	P-N4

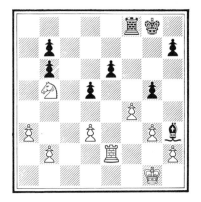

This tactic fails because of a counter-tactic.

27 K-B2!   B-N5

Not of course 27...P×P 28 P×P R×Pch? 29 K-N3 winning a piece.

28	R-K5	P-R3
29	K-K3	P×Pch
30	P×P	K-B2
31	N-Q4	R-KN1
32	P-B5!	B×P
33	N×B	P×N
34	R×BPch	K-K3

Black has managed to exchange minor pieces but the rook ending is lost.

35	R-R5	R-N3
36	K-Q4	R-N5ch
37	K-B3	R-N3
38	K-N4	K-Q3
39	K-N5	K-B2
40	P-N4!	

After 40 R×QP Black could play 40...R-N7.

40	...	R-Q3
41	R-B5	K-N1

Black is in zugzwang.

42	P-Q4!	K-R1
43	P-KR4!	K-N1
44	P-R5	K-R1
45	R-B8ch	K-R2
46	P-R4	

The zugzwang position is perfect, but this very fact allows a stalemate attempt.

46	...	R-Q1
47	R-B6	R-KB1
48	R×NP	R-B5
49	K-B5	Resigns

Chapter 6

The Albin/Chatard/Alekhine Attack

White: Gligoric
Black: Yanofsky

Saltsjobaden Interzonal 1948

	1	P-K4	P-K3
	2	P-Q4	P-Q4
	3	N-QB3	N-KB3
	4	B-KN5	B-K2
	5	P-K5	KN-Q2
	6	P-KR4!?	

This move leads to great complications about which no final judgement has yet been made. White offers a pawn for the sake of a lead in development and attacking chances on the K-side. In particular White hopes to take advantage of the half-open KR-file (if Black accepts the gambit) or just to obtain a space advantage on the K-side and to interfere with Black's normal development while at the same time maintaining the tension between the dark squared bishops.

6 ... P-QB4

The sharpest reply, allowing the wild complications arising from N-N5, but fighting for control of White's Q4 square.

Most of the alternative moves have disappeared from tournament play:

(a) 6...P-QR3 A move suggested by Maroczy, preparing ...P-QB4 without being worried by N-QN5. **7 Q-N4 P-KB4** Or here 7...K-B1 8 Q-B4 P-QB4 9 P×P N-QB3 10 N-B3 with the better game. **8 Q-R5ch P-N3 9 Q-R6 B×B 10 P×B K-B2 11 KN-K2 P-B4 12 N-B4 N-B1** Not 12...P×P 13 N×NP! etc. **13 P×P N-B3 14 P-KN4 N×P 15 B-K2 Q-B2 16 P×P N-B6ch 17 B×N Q×N 18 P-B6!** with a winning attack. Unzicker-Czerniak, Amsterdam Olympiad 1954.

(b) 6...P-KB3 7 Q-R5ch K-B1 White has the advantage after 7...P-N3 8 P×P N×P 9 Q-K2 P-B4 10 P×P N-B3 11 O-O-O O-O 12 N-R3. Sanguinetti-Benko, 1954. **8 P×P N×P 9 Q-B3 P-B4 10 P×P P-QN3** A pawn sacrifice recommended by Stahlberg. Acceptance gives Black good play. **11 P-R5! P-KR3** Black has no time for 11...P×P 12 P-R6 P-N3 13 O-O-O QN-Q2 (or 13...N-B3 14 N-K4 K-B2 15 N-R3 N-Q5 16 R×N P×R 17 B×N etc.) 14 R-K1 with a clear plus to White. Unzicker-Stahlberg, Stockholm 1960. **12 B×N B×B 13 N-R3!** and White is better.

(c) 6...P-KR3?! 7 B×B Q×B 8 P-B4 P-QR3 9 Q-N4 P-KB4 10 P×P e.p. N×P 11 Q-N6ch Q-B2 12 B-Q3 Q×Q 13 B×Qch K-K2 14 N-B3 R-Q1 15 O-O-O with a big advantage in the endgame. Velimirovic-Lontoc, Nice Olympiad 1974.

(d) It is not clear, however, that Black cannot afford to accept the gambit pawn: **6...B×B 7 P×B Q×P** This continuation has, perhaps wrongly, disappeared from tournament practice. **8 N-R3 Q-K2** After 8...Q-R3 9 N-QN5! N-R3 10 P-KB4 it is difficult for Black to find a good plan. **9 N-B4 P-QR3** After 9...N-B1 10 Q-N4 P-KB4 11 P×P e.p. P×P 12 O-O-O P-B3 13 R-K1 White had good play in Alekhine-Fahrni, Mannheim 1914. However, in the game Westman-Westerinen, Helsinki 1961, Black succeeded with 9...P-KN3! 10 Q-N4 N-QB3, followed by ...N-N3, ...B-Q2, ...O-O-O and a later Q-side attack. For a more detailed discussion of the possibilities for both sides see illustrative game 35. **10 Q-N4 P-KN3 11 O-O-O N-N3 12 B-Q3 N(N1)-Q2 13 R-R6 N-B1** and White's advantage is not easy to demonstrate.

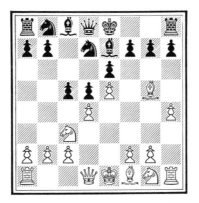

7 B×B!

The best way to retain some positional advantage. The alternatives are:

(a) 7 Q-N4 B×B After 7...N-QB3 8 B×B K×B 9 Q-N5ch K-B1 10 Q×Qch N×Q 11 P-B4 White has the better ending. White also has the advantage after 7...P-B4 8 Q-R5ch P-KN3 9 Q-R6 B-B1 10 B×Q B×Q 11 B-KN5. If 7...K-B1 8 N-B3 N-QB3 9 Q-B4 P×P 10 N-N5 P-QR3 11 N(N5)×P N-B4 with unclear play. **8 Q×B** If 8 P×B P×P! **8...Q×Q 9 P×Q N-QB3 10 P×P** After 10 N-N5 K-K2! is good for Black. **10...N(B3)×P 11 P-QN4 P-QR4 12 N-N5 K-K2 13 P-QB3 P-QN3** with good play for Black.

(b) 7 N-N5 P-B3! 8 **B-Q3** After 8 P×KBP N×P 9 B-KB4 O-O! 10 N-B7? N-K1! White is lost. **8...P-QR3 9 Q-R5ch K-B1 10 R-R3** White is committed to the attack. 10 N-KR3 fails to 10...P×QP 11 N-B4 N×P 12 N(N5)×P Q-N3 13 O-O-O Q×N 14 B-N5 Q×Rch 15 K×Q RP×B. Ragozin-Yanofsky, 1948. **10...P×N 11 B-R6!** Q-R4ch 12 B-Q2 Q-B2 13 R-N3 P×QP 14 N-B3 N×P There is no better defence to be found. **15 R×P! P-R3!** Not 15...N×Nch 16 K-Q1! or 15...K×R 16 B-R6ch winning. The text move sets a devilish trap, as now 16 B×RP loses to 16...R×B 17 Q×R B-N5ch and 18...Q×R. **16 B-R7! K×R 17 Q×Pch K-B2 18 Q-R5ch drawn** by perpetual check. Rossetto-Stahlberg, Vina del Mar 1947.

7 ...	K×B

According to the latest analysis, the sacrifice by **7...Q×B** is insufficient: **8 N-N5 O-O 9 N-B7 P×P 10 N×R P-B3** If 10...N-QB3 11 N-B3 P-B3 12 N×P P×P 13 N×P Q×N 14 N-B7 followed by 15 Q×P with advantage. Or 10...N×P 11 Q×P QN-B3 12 Q-Q2 P-QN3 13 B-K2 B-N2 14 N-B3 followed by 15 O-O-O as in Riumin-Lilienthal, Moscow 1935. Or finally 10...Q-N5ch 11 Q-Q2 Q×P 12 R-Q1 N-QB3 13 N-B3 N-B4 (13...N(Q2)×P 14 N×N N×N 15 Q×P!) 14 B-Q3 B-Q2 15 N-B7 R-B1 16 N(B7)×P P×N 17 O-O with good play for White. Christoffel-Guimard, Groningen 1946. **11 Q×P N-B3 12 Q-Q2 P×P 13 O-O-O N-B3 14 P-B3 Q-Q3 15 N-K2 B-Q2 16 N-B3 R×N 17 N-K4!** with some advantage to White. Bronstein-Stahlberg, 1950.

8 P-B4	Q-N3

Still the best move, as after 8...P×P 9 Q×P N-QB3 10 Q-Q2 Black has a permanent weakness on the dark squares.

9 N-B3	

Another good idea is 9 N-R4 Q-R4ch 10 P-B3 P×P 11 P-QN4, or here 9...Q-B3 10 N×P N×N 11 P×N Q×P 12 Q-Q2 with a positional plus.

9 ...	N-QB3

After this White obtains the better game, but 9...Q×NP seems dubious after 10 N-QN5 N-R3 11 P-QR3 threatening the powerful R-QN1 followed by Q-B1.

10 N-QR4!	Q-R4ch
11 P-B3	P×P

White has the advantage after 11...P-QN4 12 N×P N×N 13 P×N P-N5 14 N-Q4! etc.

12 P-QN4	Q-B2

After 12...N×NP 13 P×N Q×Pch 14 K-B2 P-QN4 15 B×P Q×B 16 N×P Q-R3 17 Q-N3 White has a strong attack for the pawn.

13	N×P	P-QR3
14	R-R3	N-N3
15	N-B5	B-Q2
16	P-R4	QR-QN1
17	P-QR5	N-B1
18	R-K3!	

Preventing Black's sole counterplay of ...P-B3.

18	...	N(B1)-R2
19	N-B3	P-KN3
20	Q-Q2	B-B1
21	Q-KB2	P-R4
22	Q-N3	K-K1
23	K-B2	N-K2
24	B-Q3	B-Q2
25	K-N1	

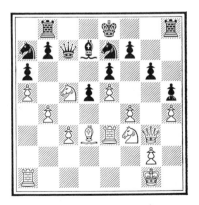

White can take time to prepare the final break-through as Black's weakness on the dark squares will sooner or later be fatal.

25	...	B-N4
26	B×B	N×B
27	R-Q3	N-R2
28	QR-Q1	N(R2)-B3
29	Q-B2	K-B1
30	N-N5	Q-B1
31	P-B4!	K-N2

White has a decisive attack after both 31...N×NP 32 R-QN3 and 31...P×P 32 R-Q7 etc.

32	P×P	N×QP
33	P-B5!	NP×P
34	R×N!	

An elegant final attack.

34	...	P×R
35	P-K6	P-B3

Or 35...P×P 36 N(B5)×KPch followed by 37 R×P winning.

36	N-B7	N-K2
37	Q-Q4	N-B3
38	Q×QP	R-Q1
39	N-Q7!	K-N3
40	R-KB1	N-K2
41	Q-Q4	Resigns

GAME 35

White: Westman
Black: Westerinen

Student Olympiad
Helsinki 1961

1	P-K4	P-K3
2	P-Q4	P-Q4
3	N-QB3	N-KB3
4	B-KN5	B-K2
5	P-K5	KN-Q2
6	P-KR4	B×B
7	P×B	Q×P
8	N-R3	Q-K2
9	N-B4	P-KN3!

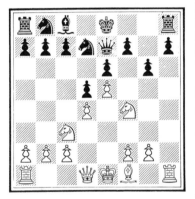

Depriving White of the use of his KR5 square.

10   Q-N4   N-QB3

By omitting ..P-QR3, Black has saved a tempo for the development of his Q-side. The disadvantage of this plan is that White is given the opportunity to play B-N5.

11   O-O-O   N-N3

Considerably less active is 11... N-B1 12 Q-N3 Q-N5 13 B-N5! with the possibility of a knight sacrifice on Q5. Balashov-Pismeni, Moscow Championship 1974.

12	R-R6	B-Q2
13	B-Q3?	

A serious strategic error. White's bishop plays no useful part in the attack on Black's K-side, whereas Black's B3 knight is useful and should be exchanged. After Keres' suggestion 13 B-N5, followed by B×N, White can build up on Black's KRP without worrying about a Q-side counterattack.

13	...	O-O-O
14	QR-R1	Q-N5!
15	N(B4)-K2	N×KP

Already White is lost.

16	Q-N3	N(K4)-B5
17	B×N	N×B
18	P-N3	Q-R6ch
19	K-Q1	N-Q3
20	R×PP	R×R
21	R×P	

Although White has regained one of the pawns, Black still has an easy win thanks to his strong Q-side attack.

21	...	P-QN4
22	N-B1	P-N5

23	N(B3)-K2	B-N4
24	Q-K5	Q-N7
25	N-B4	Q-B6
26	Q-K3	

The best chance. If Black exchanges queens White can manoeuvre a knight to K5 with good counterplay.

26	...	Q-N7
27	P-KB3	N-B4
28	Q-Q2	N×P
29	R×P	R-R1

30	N-R3	N-B4
31	Q×NP	N-K6ch
32	K-Q2	N-B5ch!
33	K-Q1	N-K6ch

Both players were short of time.

34	K-Q2	Q×BPch
35	K×N	Q×Nch
36	K-B2	Q-N7ch
37	K-N3	Q-K4ch
38	K-B2	B-K1

White lost on time.

Chapter 7

The MacCutcheon Variation

White: Uusi
Black: Chistiakov

Moscow 1956

1	P-K4	P-K3
2	P-Q4	P-Q4
3	N-QB3	N-KB3
4	B-KN5	B-N5

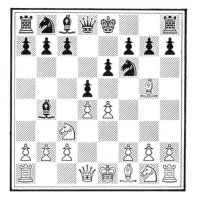

This is a more aggressive continuation than 4...B-K2 but one that allows White to make better use of his initiative. Although Black can soon get rid of the dangerous pin on his KN he does so only at the cost of conceding the bishop pair.

5 P-K5

The continuation 5 P×P Q×P 6 B×N P×B 7 N-K2!? was given a new lease of life in Vila-Mondragon, Siegen Olympiad 1970 (illustrative game 36), but Black can meet 5 P×P with 5...P×P, transposing to a satisfactory line of the Exchange Variation.

5	...	P-KR3
6	**B-Q2!**	

The move which introduces the richest variations and which has given White good play in practice. Black's only active reply is to keep his KN in the centre, but in order to do so he must first part with his KB which could have been useful in the defence of his K-side. Before we continue with the main line let us have a quick look at White's alternative sixth moves:

(a) 6 P×N P×B 7 P×P R-N1 8 P-KR4 P×P 9 Q-R5 Or 9 Q-N4 Q-B3 10 R×P Q×NP 11 Q×Q R×Q 12 R-R8ch B-B1 (12... K-Q2 is possible) 13 O-O-O P-QB3 and Black should equalize by ...N-Q2, ...P-N3, ...B-N2 and ...O-O-O **9...Q-B3 10 Q×RP Q×NP 11 N-B3 N-B3 12 Q-B4 B-Q3 13 Q-K3 N-K2** with equality.

(b) 6 B×N P×B 7 Q-N4 P×P 8 Q-N7 K-K2! 9 P×P Q-N1 with good play for Black.

(c) 6 B-K3 N-K5 7 Q-N4 Or 7 N-K2 P-QB4 8 P-QR3 B-R4 9 P-QN4 N×N 10 N×N P×NP 11 N-N5 with an attack for the pawn. Soller-Keres, 1934. **7...K-B1 8 P-QR3 B×Nch 9 P×B N×QBP 10 B-Q3** with some initiative for the pawn.

(d) 6 B-R4 P-KN4 7 B-N3 N-K5 8 N-K2 P-QB4 9 P-QR3 B×Nch 10 N×B Q-R4 11 Q-Q3 N-QB3 12 P×P B-Q2 13 O-O-O N×N 14 Q×N Q×Q 15 P×Q R-QB1 with an even game. Bernstein-Swiderski, Coburg 1904.

6	...	B×N
7	**P×B**	

If 7 B×B N-K5 8 B-N4 (or 8 B-R5?! O-O 9 B-Q3 N-QB3 10 B-B3 N×B 11 P×N P-B3 12 P-KB4 P×P 13 BP×P N-K2 14 N-B3 P-B4 15 O-O Q-R4 16 Q-K1 B-Q2 with a good game for Black. Fischer-Petrosian, Curaçao Candidates'

Tournament 1962) 8...P-QB4! 9 B×P (9 P×P? N×KBP!) 9...N×B 10 P×N N-Q2 11 Q-Q4 Q-B2 12 N-B3 N×BP with the better game for Black. Spielmann-Nimzovich, Göteborg 1920.

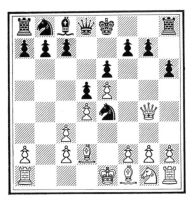

The disappearance of Black's minor pieces from the vicinity of his K-side makes things rather sensitive for him on that wing. The text move takes immediate advantage of Black's vulnerability and at the same time it helps White to complete his development.

8 ... P-KN3

8...K-B1 is also considered to be good for White: **9 P-KR4** An alternative is 9 B-B1 P-QB4 (9...N×QBP 10 B-Q3 P-QB4 transposes to the same position) 10 B-Q3 N×QBP 11 P×P Q-R4 12 B-Q2 Q-R5 13 P-KR3 N-K5 14 N-K2 N-QB3 15 B×N N×P 16 Q-R4 N-B3 17 N-B3 Q-B5 18 O-O-O P-B4 with unclear play. Vasyukov-Goldenov, Kiev 1964. **9...P-QB4** It is worth noting Dr. Euwe's recommendation 9...P-KB4 e.g. 10 P×P e.p. Q×P 11 N-B3 N-B3 12 Q-B4 (Possibly stronger is 12 P-R5 and if 12...P-K4 13 Q-R4 K-B2 [if Black exchanges queens White continues N-R4-N6] 14 B-QN5 P×P 15 P×P R-K1 16 N-K5ch K-N1 17 B-K3 N-N4 18 P-KB4 N-B2 as in Lilienthal-Sliwa, 1960, when 19 P-N4! gives White good attacking prospects.) 12...N×B 13 Q×N P-K4 when

White should continue 14 O-O-O P×P 15 P×P B-N5 16 N-K5! as in Tringov-Sliwa, Varna Olympiad 1962. **10 R-R3 Q-R4 11 B-Q3 N×B 12 R-N3! P-KN3 13 K×N P×P 14 Q×QP N-B3 15 Q-KB4 P-Q5 16 N-B3 Q×BPch 17 K-K2** and now if 17...Q×R White has a strong attack by 18 Q-B6 R-KN1 19 P-R5 etc.

9   B-Q3

The Duras move 9 B-B1 is also played here. After 9...P-QB4 10 B-Q3 N×QBP 11 P×P Q-R4 12 B-Q2 Q-R5 13 P-KR3 P-KR4! Black has at least equalized.

9	**...**	**N×B**
10	**K×N**	**P-QB4**
11	**Q-B4**	**N-B3**

Not 11...Q-N4 12 Q×Q P×Q 13 P-N4! and Black's KNP falls after 14 N-B3.

12	**N-B3**	**B-Q2**

Most other moves have led to no greater success for Black. e.g.:

(a) 12...Q-K2 13 P×P Q×P 14 N-Q4! P-R3 15 QR-QN1 N-Q1 16 P-KR4 with a clear advantage for White. Yudovich-Chistiakov, USSR Championship 1939.

(b) 12...P-B5 13 B-K2 Q-K2 14 Q-B6 Q×Q 15 P×Q N-N1 16 N-K5 with much the better endgame prospects. Panov-Zagoriansky, Moscow 1944.

(c) The manoeuvre **12...P×P 13 P×P B-Q2** also leaves White with an edge: **14 QR-QN1 N-R4 15 P-KR4 R-QB1 16 P-R5 P-KN4 17 Q-B6 Q×Q 18 P×Q.** This position was reached in the game Spassky-Panno, Amsterdam Candidates' Tournament 1956, and White was unable to realize his advantage: **18...P-N3 19 P-B3 N-B3 20 B-N5 N-N1 21 B-Q3** If White exchanges on Q7 his KB6 pawn will fall. **21...N-B3 22 B-R6?** This move shows that Spassky had not found a good plan. After 22 QR-K1! O-O or maybe 22...K-Q1!? 23 R-K3 R-K1 24 KR-K1, the manoeuvre N-R2-N4 would be a devastating positional threat. The move 24...P-N5 would no longer be satisfactory and Black has no good counterplay. **22...R-B2 23 KR-K1 P-N5 24 N-K5 N×N 25 R×N R-N1** and Black had little difficulty in holding the game.

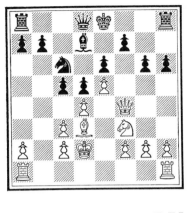

13	QR-QN1	P-B5
14	B-K2	P-N3
15	P-KR4	Q-K2
16	P-R5	P×P

Black admits to his positional defeat due to his dark squared weaknesses. After 16...P-KN4 17 Q-B6! Black would have a difficult endgame (compare Spassky-Panno above).

17	R×RP	O-O-O
18	QR-KR1	QR-N1
19	P-N3	Q-R6

A vain attempt at creating counterplay.

20   R×P

White is not tempted by 20 Q×BP R-B1 when Black has threats in connection with ...P-N4-N5 or ...R×N and ...N×QP.

20	...	R×R
21	R×R	N-Q1

Black is tied to the defence of his KBP and has no time for ...Q×RP.

22	N-N5	B-K1
23	B-R5	Q-K2

23...Q×RP 24 B×P R-B1 25 R-B6 is hopeless for Black.

24   N-R7

Black is a pawn down with a completely lost game. The rest is just desperate resistance.

24	...	B-R5
25	Q-B6	Q-R6

The only remaining chance.

26	B×P	Q×RP
27	B×Pch	N×B

Else, 28 B-B5 would follow.

28	Q×Nch	K-N2

Not 28...K-B2 29 Q-B7ch!

29	Q×QPch	K-R3
30	Q-K4	R-N5
31	Q-B5!	R×QPch

Nothing else is left to Black if he wants to get closer to his opponent's king — the only chance for an eventual perpetual check.

| 32 | P×R | Q-N7 |
| 33 | R-R1 | P-B6ch |

Or 33...Q×QPch 34 K-K2 P-B6 35 Q-Q3ch B-N4 36 R-R1ch wins.

34	K-K3	B×P
35	Q-QB8ch	K-R4
36	N-B6	B-N3
37	N-K4	B×N
38	K×B	Q-K7ch
39	K-Q5	Q-B6ch

White can afford that too.

40	K-Q6	Q×R
41	Q×Pch	K-N4
42	Q-N3ch	K-R3
43	P-K6	Q-KR1
44	Q-R4ch	K-N2
45	Q-B6ch	K-R3
46	P-Q5	Q-Q1ch
47	Q-Q7	Q-KB1ch
48	P-K7	Resigns

GAME 36

White: Vila
Black: Mondragon

Siegen Olympiad 1970

Notes by Levy

1	P-K4	P-K3
2	P-Q4	P-Q4
3	N-QB3	N-KB3
4	B-KN5	B-N5
5	P×P	Q×P
6	B×N	P×B
7	N-K2!?	

This idea turns out well, and indeed it is difficult to find a satisfactory reply. Usual is 7 Q-Q2 Q-QR4 8 KN-K2 N-Q2 9 P-QR3 N-N3 10 R-Q1 B-K2 which equalizes.

7	...	N-Q2

7...P-QB4? is bad: 8 P×P! Q×Qch (8...Q×BP 9 P-QR3!) 9 R×Q B×P 10 N-N5 N-R3 11 N(K2)-B3 and Black

is tied down. After 9 R×Q Black could improve with 9...N-Q2! but 10 P-QR3 B×BP 11 N-N5 O-O?! 12 N(K2)-B3 P-QR3 13 N-Q6 leaves White with the better ending because of his Q-side majority and better placed king.

If 7...N-B3 8 Q-Q2! B×N 9 N×B Q×QP 10 Q×Q N×Q 11 O-O-O P-QB4 12 N-K4! with an excellent game.

8	P-QR3	B×Nch
9	N×B	Q-QR4
10	Q-B3	P-B3

Before Black can develop his bishop he must contort himself to avoid leaving any pawns en prise. There is also the point that after 10...Q-N3 (say) 11 O-O-O, White would be threatening 12 P-Q5! P-K4 13 N-K4!

11	O-O-O	Q-KN4ch
12	K-N1	P-KB4
13	P-KR4	Q-N5

13...Q-B3 14 P-Q5! is no better.

14	Q-K3	P-N3
15	P-Q5	P-B5
16	Q-K1	B-N2
17	P×KP	P×P
18	P-B3	Q-N1
19	B-B4	O-O-O
20	B×P	Q-N2
21	Q-K4	P-B4
22	Q×BP	B-B3
23	R-Q6	K-N2
24	KR-Q1	KR-K1
25	R×B!	N-K4
26	R(B6)-Q6	Resigns

Chapter 8

The Rubinstein and Burn Variations

White: Gligoric
Black: Balashov

Skopje 1970

1	P-K4	P-K3
2	P-Q4	P-Q4
3	N-QB3	P×P

3...N-QB3 is rarely seen and with good reason. By blocking his QBP Black deprives himself of the traditional freeing move ...P-QB4 and he is normally saddled with a lifeless position. (The position after 3...N-QB3 can also arise via the move order 1 P-K4 N-QB3 2 P-Q4 P-Q4 3 N-QB3 P-K3.) For two examples of this move see Gligoric-Benko, Belgrade 1964, and Fischer-Petrosian, 3rd Match Game 1971 (illustrative games 37 and 38).

The text move relaxes the central tension too soon and gives White a good command of the centre. White has the better development, a pawn majority on the Q-side and he can frequently launch a strong attack on the K-side. Black's set-up is passive, his main problem being the development of his QB. It is not surprising, therefore, that 3...P×P is rarely seen in modern master chess.

A delayed form of this exchange is **3...N-KB3 4 B-KN5 P×P** which is known as the Burn Variation.

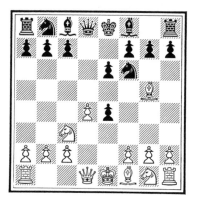

White still has a space advantage, but it is not easy to maintain this slight edge, and Black often succeeds in equalizing. **5 N×P** Better than 5 B×N P×B 6 N×P P-KB4 7 N-QB3 B-N2 8 N-B3 P-B4 9 B-N5ch (or 9 P×P Q-R4 10 Q-Q2 Q×BP 11 O-O-O N-B3) 9...B-Q2 and Black has an excellent game. **5...B-K2** Also possible is 5...QN-Q2 6 N-KB3 (for 6 N×Nch see Tal-Portisch, 4th Match Game 1965 — illustrative game 39.) 6...B-K2 7 N×Nch B×N 8 Q-Q2 (better seems 8 P-KR4 transposing to the Gligoric-Balashov game of the main line. White also stood better in Spassky-Porath, Lugano Olympiad 1968, after 8 B×B Q×B 9 B-B4 P-B4 10 Q-K2 O-O 11 O-O-O P-QR3 12 Q-K3 P×P? but Black could have equalized by 12...P-QN4) 8...B×B 9 N×B N-B3! 10 B-K2 (10 O-O-O seems to offer more prospects) 10...O-O 11 R-Q1 Q-Q3 12 O-O B-Q2 13 N-B3 KR-Q1 with equality (Fischer-Petrosian, Curacao Candidates' Tournament 1962). **6 B×N** Now, however, this exchange is the only way to give Black any problems. **6...B×B** Again 6...P×B comes into consideration. See Liberzon-Botvinnik, USSR Team Championship 1966 (illustrative game 40). **7 N-KB3 N-Q2** For 7...B-Q2 see Spassky-Petrosian 23rd Match Game 1966 (illustrative game 41). **8 Q-Q2** Also good is 8 B-B4 O-O 9 Q-K2! See Spassky-Czerniak, Goteborg 1971 (illustrative game 42). **8...P-QN3 9 B-N5 B-N2 10 N×Bch P×N 11 Q-B3 Q-K2 12 Q×P Q-N5ch 13 P-B3 Q×B 14 Q×B Q×P 15 O-O R-Q1 16 P-B4 Q-R6 17 KR-K1** with a slight plus to White. L. Steiner-Stahlberg, Stockholm 1948.

4   N×P   N-Q2

Other possibilities are:

(a) **4...N-KB3 5 N×Nch P×N** White is clearly better after 5...Q×N 6 N-B3. See for example, Gufeld-Alburt, USSR Team Championship 1974 — illustrative game 43. **6 N-B3 P-N3 7 B-KB4 B-QN2 8 P-B3 B-Q3 9 B-N3** and White has the more comfortable position.

(b) **4...B-Q2 5 N-KB3 B-B3 6 B-Q3 B×N 7 B×B P-QB3 8 O-O N-B3 9 B-Q3 QN-Q2 10 P-B4 B-Q3 11 P-QN3 O-O 12 B-N2** and White stands better, Spassky-O'Kelly, San Juan 1969.

(c) **4...B-K2 5 N-KB3 N-KB3 6 N×Nch** Perhaps even more accurate is 6 B-Q3 QN-Q2 7 Q-K2! when 7...N×N 8 B×N N-B3 fails to 9 B×NP B×B 10 Q-N5ch. **6...B×N 7 B-Q3 N-B3** For 7...N-Q2 see the main variation. **8 P-B3 P-K4 9 P×P N×P 10 N×N B×N 11 O-O B-B3** 11...O-O? 12 B×RPch! K×R 13 Q-R5ch wins. **12 Q-R4ch** with a lead in development.

5 N-KB3

Botvinnik's idea of 5 P-KN3 is worth noting. e.g. 5...KN-B3 6 N×Nch N×N 7 B-N2 P-B4 (if 7...P-K4 8 N-B3 P×P 9 N×P with the better development) 8 N-K2 Q-N3 9 O-O B-Q2 10 P-QB4 P×P 11 N×P R-Q1 12 B-K3 B-B4 13 P-QN4! Q×P 14 R-N1 Q-B6 15 R×P O-O 16 Q-K2! with advantage to White in Botvinnik-Guimard, 1946.

5	...	KN-B3
6	B-KN5	

After this developing move Black is unable to free his game straight away with 6...P-QB4?! because of 7 P×P! (compare variation 2 in the next note).

The alternative **6 N×Nch N×N** also keeps the initiative. **7 N-K5** Capablanca's idea. Alternatives are:

(1) 7 B-Q3 B-K2 (after 7...P-QN3 8 Q-K2 B-N2 9 B-KN5 B-K2 10 O-O O-O 11 QR-Q1 Black was very cramped in Tarrasch-Mieses, 1916. Or 7...P-B4 8 P×P B×P 9 B-KN5 B-K2 10 Q-K2 O-O 11 O-O-O with the better game for White in Spielmann-Petrov, Margate 1938) 8 Q-K2 O-O 9 O-O! (if 9 B-KN5 P-B4 10 P×P Q-R4ch 11 P-B3 Q×P (B4)) 9...P-QN3 10 P-B4 B-N2 11 R-Q1 and White stands better. Najdorf-Stahlberg, 1950.

(2) 7 B-KN5 P-B4 8 B-N5ch (sharp play arises after 8 B-QB4 which transposes to the Tal-Portisch game mentioned above — illustrative game 39) 8...B-Q2 9 B×Bch Q×B 10 B×N (10 Q-K2 is Simagin's suggestion) 10...P×B 11 P-B3 P×P 12 N×P B-B4 13 Q-B3 with a slight edge to White. Spassky-Petrosian, Moscow 1967.

7...Q-Q4 After 7...B-K2 8 B-Q3 O-O 9 O-O P-B4 10 B-K3 Q-B2 11 R-K1 P-QN3 12 Q-B3 B-N2 13 Q-R3 P×P 14 B×QP, White is better in view of the threat 15 N-N4. Or 7...B-Q3 8 Q-B3 P-B4 (if 8...P-B3 9 P-B3 O-O 10 B-KN5 B-K2 11 B-Q3 with advantage to White. Capablanca-Blanco, Havana 1913) 9 B-QN5ch K-B1 10 O-O P×P 11 B-KB4 B×N 12 B×B Q-Q4 13 Q×Q N×Q 14 KR-Q1 and White has the better endgame. Poulsen-Planas, Helsinki Olympiad 1952. **8 B-K2! P-B4** It is very risky to accept the pawn. After 8...Q×NP 9 B-B3 Q-R6 10 Q-Q3! the double threat of B-B6ch and Q-N5ch wins material for White. **9 B-K3 P×P 10 Q×P B-Q3 11 N-B4** and White's position is to be preferred.

6	...	B-K2
7	N×Nch	B×N

7...N×N 8 B-Q3 P-B4 9 O-O P×P 10 N×P, Portisch-Petrosian, 6th Match Game 1974; and 7...P×N 8 B-R4 P-QB4? 9 P-Q5! are both better for White.

8 P-KR4!

Gaining space on the K-side and allowing the KN to maintain control of the centre. After 8 Q-Q2 Petrosian has shown that 8...B×B 9 N×B N-B3! stresses the awkward position of White's KN which has gone astray from the centre, and therefore Black equalizes easily.

8	...	**P-B4**
9	**Q-Q2!**	

Developing and guarding against ...Q-R4ch. 9 P-Q5 is weaker.

9	**...**	**P-KR3**

The presence of White's QB is unpleasant and Black is committed to this weakening and the loss of a tempo. Another justification of White's 8th move!

10	**B×B**	**Q×B**

10...N×B costs Black his QBP.

11	**O-O-O**	**O-O**

White has a clearly better game, being ahead in development and having a Q-side pawn majority for the endgame.

12	**B-K2**

This gives away the best part of White's advantage. Stronger was 12 B-N5! forcing 12...P×P 13 Q×QP Q×Q 14 R×Q N-B3 15 N-K5, when White has the superior ending.

12	**...**	**P-K4!**
13	**P×KP**	

If 13 P-Q5 P-K5.

13	**...**	**N×P**
14	**N×N**	

In case of 14 Q-B3 N-N5 15 Q×P P-QN3 16 Q-Q4 Q×Q 17 R×Q N×P, Black has an even game.

14	...	Q×N
15	P-KB4	Q-K2

Now White has only a slight initiative.

16	B-B3	B-B4?

Better was 16...B-K3.

17	QR-K1!	Q-B3
18	R-K5	

White's pressure has increased and there are multiple threats to Black's Q-side pawns.

18	...	KR-K1

Black tries to defend actively, since a pawn is lost in any case.

19	P-KN4!	B-R2
20	B×P	QR-Q1
21	R×Rch	

Capturing the pawn with gain of tempo.

21	...	R×R
22	P-N5	Q-K3
23	B-Q5	Q-N5
24	B-B4	

Now Black is tied to the defence of his first rank and there is no threat of ...R-K7 any more. In addition, White is threatening 25 P-R5 and 26 P-N6.

24	...	**P-KR4**
25	**P-N3**	**B-B4**
26	**K-N2**	**B-K3**
27	**R-K1**	**R-KB1**

Not 27...Q×RP? 28 P-B5 B-Q2 29 Q×B!

28	**B×B**	**P×B**
29	**Q-Q6**	**Q×RP**

Or 29...Q×BP 30 Q×KPch K-R1 31 R-K4.

30	**Q×KPch**	**K-R1**
31	**R-K4!**	

Black is lost now. He cannot play 31...R×P because of 32 P-N6!

31	...	**Q-N5**
32	**Q-KN6!**	**P-R5**
33	**R-K7**	**R-KN1**
34	**Q-B7!**	**Q-Q8**

There is no time for 34...P-R6 because of 35 P-N6 threatening 36 Q×R!

35   R-Q7

Preventing 35...Q-Q5ch.

35 ...	**Resigns**

GAME 37

White: Gligoric
Black: Benko

Belgrade 1964

1	P-K4	P-K3
2	P-Q4	P-Q4
3	N-QB3	N-QB3
4	N-B3	N-B3
5	P-K5	

For 5 P×P see Fischer-Petrosian, game 38.

5	...	N-K5
6	B-Q3	N×N

A possible alternative is 6...B-N5 7 B-Q2 N×B 8 Q×N P-B3 with unclear play. The pawn sacrifice 7 O-O N×N 8 P×N B×P 9 R-N1 P-KR3 (9...B-N5!?) 10 B-R3 P-KN4 11 B-N5 B-Q2 12 P-R3 P-QR4 13 Q-Q3 B-N5 led to unclear complications in Nezhmetdinov-Lein, USSR 1967.

7	P×N	B-K2
8	P-KR4!	P-KR3
9	N-R2	P-QN3

After the risky 9...B×P 10 Q-N4 K-B1 11 N-B1! B-K2 12 R-R3 White has a strong attack.

10	Q-N4	B-B1
11	N-B1	P-KR4
12	Q-N3	N-K2
13	B-KN5!	Q-Q2
14	N-K3	B-N2
15	Q-B3!	

Black's weak KBP and the dominating position of the bishop on KN5 promise White a lasting initiative.

15	...	N-B3
16	R-R3	B-K2
17	R-N3	P-N3
18	B-B6	R-KN1
19	K-B1	O-O-O
20	K-N1	N-R4
21	Q-B4	B×B
22	Q×B	R-R1

Passive defence only helps White. 22...P-B4 was required.

23	R-Q1	QR-B1
24	P-QB4	

Opening up the centre at the right moment.

| 24 | ... | P×P |
| 25 | N×P | N-B3 |

After 25...Q×P 26 N×N P×N 27 B-K2 followed by 28 B-B3 White's heavy pieces can launch a winning attack on the Q-side.

26	P-QB3	Q-Q1
27	Q-B4	N-K2
28	N-K3	N-B4
29	B×N	NP×B
30	P-Q5!	Q-K2
31	P-B4	QR-N1
32	P-Q6	P×P
33	P×P	Q-Q2
34	P-B5	

The opening of the QB-file settles matters.

34	...	P×P
35	R-QB1	R×R
36	R×Pch	K-N1
37	Q×R	R-QB1
38	R×Rch	B×R
39	N-B4	B-R3
40	N-R5	P-B3

There is no defence

41	Q-N3ch	K-B1
42	Q-B2ch	K-N1
43	Q-Q1	B-N4
44	N-N3	Q-B3
45	Q×P	

The simplest way to win.

45	...	Q×QP
46	Q-R8ch	K-B2
47	Q×P	Q-Q8ch
48	K-R2	Q-Q3ch
49	K-R3	B-Q2
50	Q-B3ch	K-Q1
51	N-B5	B-B1
52	N-Q3	P-B5
53	Q-KB6ch	K-B2
54	N-K5!	Q-Q5
55	P-B3	P-R4
56	P-R5	Resigns

GAME 38

White: Fischer
Black: Petrosian

9th Match Game 1971

Notes by Shamkovich

1	P-K4	P-K3
2	P-Q4	P-Q4
3	N-QB3	N-QB3?!

Played after three minutes thought, so clearly decided upon in advance. This extravagant move of Nimzovich's is hard to find in the openings books and is supposed to be bad, since it blocks the QBP. However, I'm not so certain that it is bad. In any event there are a number of French systems in which one defers advancing the QBP e.g. Olafsson-Petrosian, Bled 1961, which went 3 N-QB3 B-N5 4 P-K5 Q-Q2 5 Q-N4 P-KB4 6 Q-N3 P-QN3 7 P-KR4 B-N2 8 B-Q3 N-QB3 9 N-K2 O-O-O. Nimzovich played the moves in the sequence 1 P-K4 N-QB3 2 P-Q4 P-Q4 3 N-QB3 P-K3 and after 4 P-K5 KN-K2! 5 N-B3 P-QN3 6 N-K2? B-R3 7 P-B3 Q-Q2 8 N-N3 B×B 9 N×B P-KR4 10 B-N5 N-R4 had good play on the white squares. Brinckmann-Nimzovich, Kecskemet 1927.

| 4 | N-B3 | N-B3 |
| 5 | P×P! | |

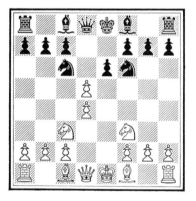

Fischer finds the weak link in the chain. The books give 5 P-K5 N-K5 6 B-Q3 B-N5 7 B-Q2 N×B or 5 B-KN5 B-K2 6 P-K5 N-K5 7 B×B Q×B 8 B-Q3 Q-N5!? 9 B×N P×B 10 P-QR3!

Q×NP 11 N×P with advantage to White as in Keres-Lein, Baku 1961. However, 8...N×N 9 P×N O-O 10 O-O N-R4 would give Black a decent game.

| 5 | ... | P×P |

Against Antoshin I once had this position and replied 5...KN×P without getting complete equality. Petrosian prefers symmetry which, at first sight, looks to ensure early equality.

6 B-QN5

Showing that the position is not all that simple. Thus, maintaining symmetry by 6...B-QN5 is met by 7 O-O not 7 N-K5 O-O! 8 N×N Q-K1ch, or 8 B×N P×B 9 N×QBP Q-K1ch 10 N-K5 B-R3! with active play. 7...O-O 8 B-N5 B-N5? 9 B(KN5)×N and 8...B-K3 9 N-K5 both favour White.

Black should probably play 6...B-K2 7 N-K5 B-Q2 while after 7 O-O O-O 8 N-K5 N-N1! he would be well on the way to equalizing.

| 6 | ... | B-KN5 |
| 7 | P-KR3 | |

Forcing an exchange that gives White the two bishops and the better development.

| 7 | ... | B×N |

It is clearly not nice to allow 7...B-R4 8 P-KN4 B-N3 9 N-K5.

| 8 | Q×B | B-K2 |
| 9 | B-N5 | P-QR3 |

Now the QP is in danger, and it is not easy to guard it without compromising the position. Yet after 9...O-O 10 O-O-O Black had two ways to try and keep it level, one quiet, one very sharp.

The first is 10...N-Q2 11 B×B (If 11 B-K3 N-N3! 12 B×N P×B with counterplay by ...N-B5) 11...N×B 12 QR-K1 N-KB3 13 P-KN4 P-B3 14 B-Q3 Q-Q3 but after 15 P-N5 N-Q2 16 P-KR4 and White has a dangerous initiative.

Better chances for Black are to be found in the second alternative 10...N-K5!? 11 B×B Q×B 12 N×P Q-N4ch 13 N-B4 (or 13 N-K3 N×BP! 14 B×N N×R) 13...Q×B! (Now 13...N×BP fails to 14 B×N N×R 15 B-R4 winning material) 14 Q×N N-N5 15 K-N1 Q-R5 16 P-QR3 KR-K1 winning the pawn back with a fine game.

10	B×Nch	P×B
11	O-O	O-O
12	KR-K1!	

The start of awkward pressure on the K-file.

12	...	P-KR3
13	B-R4	Q-Q2
14	R-K2	P-QR4
15	QR-K1	B-Q1
16	P-QN3	R-QN1
17	N-R4	

The main drawback to Black's position is the weak, split nature of his Q-side pawns. Having taken control of the K-file, Fischer now starts to attack these pawns, though Black's next move does yield some counterplay.

17	...	N-K5
18	B×B	QR×B!
19	Q-B4	

Why not the more natural 19 Q-Q3.? Possibly Fischer didn't want to allow the slightest counter-chance and feared 19...KR-K1 20 P-KB3 N-N6 when Black gets counter-chances after the exchange of both rooks, but 21 R-K5! would keep the advantage e.g. 21...P-B3 22 N-B5 Q-B2 23 R-K6! R×R 24 R×R R-K1 25 Q-K3 R×R 26 Q×R Q×Q 27 N×Q with a won ending.

The text does give Black a chance, namely 19...P-N4, and if 20 Q-N4 Q-Q3 cramping the queen. After six minutes thought Petrosian offers the exchange of queens, and thus goes into a poor ending which Fischer, as usual, plays confidently and well.

| 19 | ... | Q-Q3? |
| 20 | Q×Q | P×Q? |

The natural way to recapture, keeping out the knight from QB4. But 20...N×Q was a more stubborn defence with the idea 21 R-K7 KR-K1 22 K-B1 (22 R×Rch N×R) 22...R×R 23 R×R N-N4 24 P-QB3 K-B1 etc. However, after 21 K-B1!

Black is still in trouble.

21	P-QB4!	N-B3
22	R-QB1	

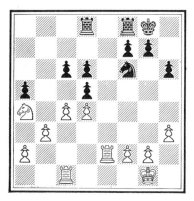

22	...	R-N1
23	P×P	P×P
24	P-B3	N-R4

Holmov feels that Black has better chances by 24...KR-B1, activating the other rook. Then if 25 R(2)-QB2 R×R 26 R×R R-N5 27 R-B8ch K-R2 28 R-QR8 R×QP 29 R×P R-Q7 and why is Black any the worse off? Possibly White must try 27 R-Q2 followed by playing his king to K3, but this is not clear. Now, however, White's rook is very active.

25	R-B6	N-B5
26	R-Q2	KR-K1
27	R×P	R-K8ch
28	K-B2	R-KR8
29	K-N3	N-R4ch
30	K-R4	P-N3
31	R×QP	R-K1
32	R×P	

One can say in all confidence that Petrosian has never before sacrificed such a lot of pawns.

32	...	R(1)-K8
33	N-B3	N-B5
34	K-N4	N-K3
35	R-K5	P-B4ch
36	K-N3	P-B5ch
37	K-R4	K-R2
38	N-K4	P-N4ch
39	K-N4	N-N2
40	N×Pch!	

Finally dispelling Black's illusions. The piece sacrifice decides at once.

40	...	P×N
41	R×R	R×R
42	K×P	N-K3ch
43	K-B5	R-K7
44	R×R	N×Pch
45	K-K5	N×R
46	P-QR4	Resigns

GAME 39

White: Tal
Black: Portisch

4th Match Game 1965

Notes by Tal

1	P-K4	P-K3
2	P-Q4	P-Q4
3	N-QB3	N-KB3
4	B-KN5	P×P
5	N×P	QN-Q2

172

Up till 1962 this variation was not especially popular, and was adopted only rarely — in those cases when Black very much wanted a draw. In the Candidates' Tournament at Curacao, Petrosian played this variation against me in round eight, as did Benko two rounds later. In the game with Petrosian I played 6 N×Nch N×N 7 N-B3 P-B4, and after an hour's thought chose the absolutely unique plan of 8 Q-Q3 B-K2 9 B×N B×B 10 Q-N5ch. White naturally lost very quickly. The game with Benko developed more normally, but during the game with Portisch I could not recall the exact order of moves (up till now I have fairly successfully endeavoured to forget all the games which I played at Curacao).

6   N×Nch

Probably the most accurate. After 6 N-KB3 B-K2 Black succeeds in simplifying the position, since on 7 N×Nch, 7...B×N is possible.

6	...	N×N
7	N-B3	P-B4
8	B-QB4	

I think that it is in this way, without trying to refute Black's opening, that White reaches the most promising position. Attempts to force matters by 8 N-K5 or 8 B-N5ch do not achieve anything against accurate defence.

8	...	P×P
9	0-0	B-K2
10	Q-K2	P-KR3

Black's desire to rid himself of the bishop on N5 is understandable. But in the future the pawn on KR3 will draw the attention of the white pieces directed against Black's K-side. KR6 is a very convenient square on which to sacrifice. 10...0-0 11 QR-Q1 N-Q4 12 B×B N×B was more in the spirit of the variation, when Black's knight can follow his white opponent. Against N-K5 there can follow ...N-N3, while with the white knight on Q4 Black can play ...N-B3. In positions of this type the exchange of knights is to the advantage of the defending side.

11	B-B4	0-0
12	QR-Q1	B-Q2
13	R×P	

White thought for about half an hour over this move. It was difficult to decide which was stronger — the openly aggressive move in the game, or the more reserved 13 N×P, after which White could play his rook along the third rank without loss of time. In nearly all variations White's attack would develop absolutely unhindered. But what didn't much appeal to me was the fact that Black could reply 13...N-Q4 14 B-K5 B-KB3 15 B×N P×B 16 B×B Q×B, and although White has an undisputed positional advantage, it may prove insufficient to win. White can easily obtain three quarters of a point, but after a defeat one wants more.

| 13 | ... | Q-N3 |
| 14 | Q-Q2! | |

It was with this continuation in mind that White decided on his previous move to capture the pawn with his rook. I did not consider any other moves. Therefore I was most astonished when after the game Portisch told me that only here had we diverged from the path of the Tal — Benko game, where White had chosen the ridiculous, in my (present) opinion, continuation 14 R-Q3. It is not surprising that here, having come up against an innovation, Portisch thought for about forty minutes.

| 14 | ... | B-B3 |

Black could also defend his bishop, and meet the coming bishop sacrifice, by 14...KR-B1. Against this I was intending to check once again the sharp variation 15 B×RP

P×B 16 Q×P Q×R! 17 N×Q R×B 18 R-Q1 with dangerous threats, and if this proved insufficient I had in reserve the unpretentious retreat 15 B-QN3, keeping an attractive position. Now White's reply is practically forced, otherwise the move 14 Q-Q2 is simply a waste of time.

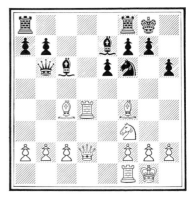

| 15 | B×RP | N-K5 |

The only move. In the case of 15...P×B White continues his attack by 16 Q×P, and now on 16...B×N decisive is 17 Q-N5ch K-R1 18 R-R4ch N-R2 (or 18...B-R4 19 B-Q3 with the irresistible threat of 20 R×Bch) 19 Q×B, when 19...R-KN1 fails to 20 Q-B6ch. 16...N-K5 is answered very strongly by 17 B-Q3. If Black changes the move order by playing 15...B×N, then White can, if he wishes, transpose into the variation already considered by 16 B×NP. Besides this, the simple 16 P×B P×B 17 K-R1 is also not bad.

| 16 | Q-B4 | P×B |

174

17 R×N

This gives the game rather a different direction. In return for the sacrificed exchange White counts on keeping a persistent-initiative. The attempt to force matters by 17 Q×RP achieves its goal after 17...B-B4 18 N-N5!, or 17...KR-Q1 18 B×P!, or 17...Q-B4 18 B-Q3, but after the only move 17...QR-Q1!, keeping the KB2 square defended, White has nothing better than to force a draw by perpetual check: 18 B×P R×R 19 B-B5 N-B3.

17 ...   B×R
18 Q×B

Here Portisch once again thought for a considerable time. He has on his side a minimal advantage in material — the exchange for a pawn. But the exposed position of his king and (once again) the presence of opposite-coloured bishops calls on him to be extra-careful. Thus 18...Q×NP loses almost immediately to 19 N-K5!, when it is impossible to defend against the various sacrifices on K6 and KB7 (19...B-B3 20 B-Q3). I thought that the best defensive resource was 18...B-B3 19 B-Q3 KR-Q1 20 Q-R7ch K-B1 21 Q×RPch K-K2 (weaker is 21...B-N2 22 Q-B4 or Q-R5) 22 P-QN3, but here White has already two pawns for the exchange, while his initiative shows no signs of diminishing. Portisch attempts to include his rook in the defence.

18 ...   QR-Q1!
19 P-QN3

The prospect of re-establishing material equality by 19 B-Q3 R×B and 20...Q×NP did not appear good enough.

19 ...   B-B4

Now the idea behind Black's defence is revealed. First of all, he for the moment restricts White's rook by attacking the point KB7. He plans for the black bishop to take part in the defence via the square Q5. The following manoeuvre by White is aimed at further weakening Black's K-side. It involves the calculation of a long variation, a calculation which, unfortunately, is inaccurate. Meanwhile, by continuing simply P-B3, White could have maintained all the advantages of his position, and the defence would have involved great difficulties. White's oversight is, however, rather amusing.

20 Q-B4   K-N2
21 Q-K5ch

This forces the advance of the pawn, since it is hopeless to allow the queen in on B6.

21 ...   P-B3
22 Q-N3ch

White naturally did not even consider capturing on K6.

22	...	K-R2
23	R-K1	R-KN1

23...R-Q3 would lose to 24 N-R4 R-KN1 25 B-Q3ch P-B4 26 B×Pch! This was White's idea — to "free" the square K7. But here Black had at his disposal a very interesting defensive possibility — 23...B-N5. I had taken this into account, and had prepared a winning variation, or so I thought: 24 B×P B×R 25 B-B5ch K-R1 26 Q-N6 B×Pch (if 26...Q×BPch, then 27 K-R1 Q-B8ch 28 N-N1) 27 K-B1 R-Q8ch 28 K-K2 Q-K6ch 29 K×R. But while Portisch was thinking over his move, White, to his horror, ascertained that by playing 28...R-K8ch, Black would be the first to mate. White would probably have had to move his rook, or else force a draw by 24 P-B3 B×P 25 N-R4 B×R 26 Q-N6ch. After the mistake committed by Black, White's attack gains in strength with every move.

24	Q-R4	R-Q3
25	K-B1	

I do not want to attach an exclamation mark to this move. It appears completely logical. White frees his queen from the defence of his KBP, since nothing is gained by capturing it without check. But here he had at his disposal a fine opportunity to gain a decisive advantage, by playing 25 P-B3 P-QR4 26 P-QR3!! (Koblentz pointed out this possibility straight away after the game). Now, in view of the threat of 27 P-QN4,

Black is forced to move either his queen or his rook. But then White captures one of the pawns — on K6 or KB6 — with decisive effect. For example: 26...R-B3 27 Q×BP B×BPch 28 K-B1 R×B 29 R×P, or 26...P-B4 27 P-QN4 P×P 28 RP×P R-N5 29 Q-K7ch R-N2 30 P×B Q×P 31 Q-B8! R-N1 32 Q-B7ch R-N2 33 N-N5ch! P×N 34 Q-R5ch K-N1 35 R×P. Fortunately, White's omission does not alter the overall assessment of the position. It is extremely difficult for Black to defend against the numerous threats, especially when in severe time trouble.

25	...	P-B4
26	P-KR3	

Preparing for the KNP to come into play in the role of a "battering-ram".

26	...	R-N3

Perhaps 26...Q-B3, which prevents White's next move, would have held out longer. Even then, by continuing 27 Q-B6, White would keep all the advantages of his position.

27 P-KN4!

This destroys, once and for all, the black king's shelter. Black gains nothing by 27...P×P 28 P×P Q-B3 because of the simple 29 N-K5, when he does not have a single check. Here the best defence was perhaps the immediate 27...Q-B3 28 P×P Q×N 29

P×Rch K×P, but White is now material up with an active position. The move made by Portisch loses immediately.

27	...	R-Q2
28	R×P!	

It was still possible to fall into a trap: 28 B×P? B×P!, and Black succeeds in simplifying the position. Now it is all over.

28	...	R-Q8ch
29	K-N2	R×R
30	B×R	P×P
31	Q×NP	R-Q1
32	N-K5	Resigns

GAME 40

White: Liberzon
Black: Botvinnik

USSR Team Championship 1966

Notes by Baranov and Moiseyev

1	P-K4	P-K3
2	P-Q4	P-Q4
3	N-QB3	N-KB3
4	B-KN5	P×P
5	N×P	B-K2
6	B×N	P×B

The usual move is 6...B×B. The move played leads to great complications.

7	N-KB3	P-KB4
8	N-B3	B-B3

In his book "The French Defence" Keres considers 8...P-QB3 9 Q-Q2 N-Q2 10 O-O-O R-N1 11 P-KN3 P-N3 12 B-N2 B-N2 with somewhat better play for White. Belavenets-Kasparyan, Moscow 1937. 8...B-B3 is considered to give White the advantage after 9 Q-Q2 N-B3 10 B-N5 B-Q2 11 O-O-O.

9	Q-Q2	P-B4!

This is a much more active move than 9...N-B3. Now 10 P-Q5 can be met by 10...P-K4, whereas after 10 P×P N-Q2 11 B-N5 O-O Black's position is quite promising (12 P-B6 P×P 13 B×P R-N1 with a strong attack).

10	O-O-O	P×P
11	N×P	N-B3

Or 11...B×N 12 Q×B Q×Q 13 R×Q B-Q2 and White has only a minimal

177

advantage.

12 B-N5   B-Q2

Play suddenly becomes sharp. The
quiet continuation 12…B×N 13 Q×B
Q×Q 14 R×Q B-Q2 gives White a
minimal advantage.

13 N×BP   P×N
14 Q-Q6!

14 KR-K1ch B-K3 is not
dangerous for Black. After the text
move 14…B-K3 is bad on account of
15 B×Nch P×B 16 Q×Pch B-Q2 17
R×B etc. and 14…B-K2 is no good
because of 15 KR-K1 with the threat
of 16 N-Q5.

14 …   B-K4!
15 KR-K1   Q-N4ch
16 K-N1

16 R-Q2 would also be met by
16…O-O-O, which leads to an advantage for Black after 17 R×B B-
K3.

16 …   O-O-O
17 R×B   B-K3!

Of course, 17…N×R is impossible
because of 18 N-Q5!!

18 Q-B5

The only move. White is obliged to
pin the knight on B6 which is attacking his rook on K5.

18 …   R×Rch

19 N×R   R-Q1
20 N-B3

He cannot play 20 R-K1 because of
20…Q-Q7 nor 20 N-K3 because of
20…Q×N 21 Q×Q R-Q8ch 22 Q-B1
R×Qch 23 K×R N×R.

20 …   Q×P
21 R-K1   K-N1
22 B×N   Q×B
23 Q-K5ch

23 Q×Q P×Q 24 N-K2, to weaken
Black's pawns, is slightly better for
White.

23 …   Q-B2
24 Q×Qch   K×Q
25 N-K2   R-KN1
26 R-N1   R-N5
27 P-KB3   R×Rch
28 N×R   K-Q3
29 P-N3   K-K4
30 K-B1   B-Q4
31 K-Q2   P-N4
32 P-QR3   P-B5
33 K-Q3   Drawn

GAME 41

White: Spassky
Black: Petrosian

23rd Match Game 1966

Notes by Tal

1 P-K4   P-K3
2 P-Q4   P-Q4

3	N-QB3	N-KB3
4	B-KN5	P×P
5	N×P	B-K2
6	B×N	B×B
7	N-KB3	B-Q2

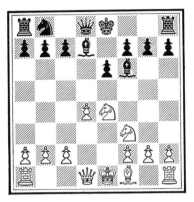

It would be interesting to know what Spassky would have played if Petrosian had repeated the plan he used in the 21st game — 7...N-Q2 with a subsequent ...P-K4.

The German master Teschner often plays the variation in which the QB is developed via Q2 to QB3. In Soviet competitions it was once used by Keres against Polugayevsky. It happened in the last round of the 29th Soviet Championship, when Polugayevsky had to win to catch up with the leader (who happened to be Spassky). After 8 B-Q3 B-B3 9 P-B3 N-Q2 10 Q-K2 B-K2 11 O-O (the energetic move 11 P-KR4 deserved consideration) 11...O-O 12 QR-Q1 N-B3, Keres obtained a thoroughly satisfactory position.

8	Q-Q2	B-B3
9	N×Bch	Q×N

It was worth thinking about 9...P×N, though it seems to me that White's position is slightly preferable after 10 Q-B4.

10	N-K5	O-O
11	O-O-O	N-Q2

Petrosian allows his pawns to be weakened in the interests of completing his development. It is interesting that after this Black slips almost automatically into a lost position. The crucial point is that the counterplay down the open QN-file, on which Petrosian was counting, turns out to be too slow.

Many commentaries on this game recommend, in place of the text move, 11...R-Q1, to be followed by ...B-K1 and then either ...N-B3 or ...P-QB4 according to circumstances. I believe that against this continuation White could have preserved all the advantages of his position (including the possibility of an attack on the king) by playing 12 B-Q3 or, as in the game, 12 P-KR4.

Another possibility after 11...R-Q1 is 12 Q-K3 B-K1 13 P-KN3 N-Q2 14 B-N2 P-B3 15 P-KB4 Q-K2 16 P-KR4 with the better game for White. Spassky-Donner, Leiden 1970.

12	N×B	P×N
13	P-KR4!	

This aggressive-looking move is far from being the beginning of a pawn-storm. Spassky will oppose the attack down the QN-file by the manoeuvre R-R3-QN3. It turns out that this manoeuvre serves not only to defend, but also to attack Black's weakened Q-side. At the same time White creates the positional threat of playing Q-N5 and exchanging into a favourable ending.

13	...	QR-N1
14	R-R3	P-B4

Played from a natural desire to get rid of the doubled pawns and somehow liven up play on the Q-side. White's task would have been somewhat harder after 14...R-N3 15 Q-N5 KR-N1. Still, even then, after 16 B-B4 (or the preliminary 16 Q×Q, followed by B-B4) White would retain a clear advantage. (White's QNP cannot be taken because of 17 B-N3).

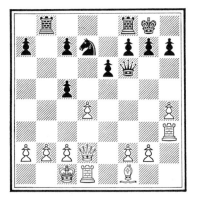

15 Q-N5!

A tactical resource (15...Q×BP is impossible because of 16 R-KB3 Q-N8 17 B-N5) serving purely positional ends. After the exchange of queens Black's Q-side weaknesses will tell.

15	...	P×P
16	Q×Q	N×Q
17	R×P	

Now we can take stock. Black's QRP and QBP are weak and White's bishop is significantly stronger than his opponent's knight. The only black piece showing any signs of activity — the rook at QN1 — will disappear from the board after White's R-QN3, and after that Black's position will be not only difficult, but even hopeless.

17	...	R-N2
18	R-QN3	R×R
19	RP×R	R-R1
20	R-QB4!	

There are many alluring continuations for White — 20 P-N3, 20 B-K2 or 20 R-QN4, but Spassky's choice is the simplest and most precise.

20 ... N-K1

After 20...N-Q4, 21 R-B5 is unpleasant for Black.

21	R-R4	N-Q3
22	P-N3	

The outcome of the game is now plainly visible to the naked eye. 22...P-QR4 loses a pawn to 23 P-QN4.

22	...	K-B1
23	B-N2	R-B1
24	R×P	K-K2
25	K-Q2	P-R3
26	P-QB4	P-N4
27	P×P	P×P
28	K-B3	K-Q2
29	P-QN4	R-KR1
30	P-N5	R-R7
31	B-B6ch	K-Q1

Here **Petrosian resigned** without waiting for his opponent's move. I should point out that the winning move is not the obvious 32 P-N6, which only complicates White's task after 32...P×P 33 R-Q7ch K-B1 34 R×N K-B2, but 32 P-B5!

GAME 42

White: Spassky
Black: Czerniak

Goteborg 1971

1	P-K4	P-K3
2	P-Q4	P-Q4
3	N-QB3	N-KB3
4	B-KN5	P×P
5	N×P	B-K2
6	B×N	B×B
7	N-KB3	N-Q2

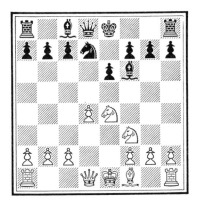

8	B-B4	O-O
9	Q-K2!	N-N3
10	B-N3	B-Q2
11	O-O	B-B3
12	N×Bch	P×N

Perhaps over-optimistic; he should play 12...Q×N 13 N-K5 B-K1.

13	QR-Q1	K-R1
14	P-B4!	Q-K1
15	KR-K1	R-KN1
16	P-Q5!	B-Q2

It was surely better to simplify by 16...P×P.

| 17 | Q-K4! | Q-KB1 |

Now there is no time for 17...P×P in view of 18 Q-B4.

18	Q-R4	R-N3
19	B-B2	R-R3
20	Q-K4	P-K4
21	N-Q2	N-B1
22	Q-K3	N-Q3
23	P-B5	N-B4

24	B×N	B×B
25	N-B1	R-R5
26	N-N3	B-Q2
27	P-Q6	P-B3
28	Q-N3	R-N1
29	R-K4	R×R
30	N×R	Q-R3?

30...Q-N2 was essential.

31	Q×BP	B-N5
32	P-B3	R-KB1

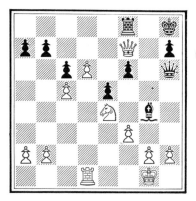

33   Q×Rch

This pretty queen sacrifice forces a rapid win.

33	...	Q×Q
34	P×B	Q-Q1
35	P-Q7	K-N1

If 35...K-N2 36 N-Q6!

36	N×Pch	K-B2
37	N-K4	K-K2
38	N-Q6	Resigns

GAME 43

White: Gufeld
Black: Alburt

USSR Team Championship 1974

Notes by Alburt

⑴	P-K4	P-K3
2	P-Q4	P-Q4
3	N-Q2	P×P
4	N×P	N-KB3
5	N×Nch	Q×N
6	N-B3	

This position is rightly considered to be to White's advantage. The threat of 7 B-KN5 is distinctly unpleasant; for example 6...B-Q2 7 B-KN5 Q-N3 8 B-Q3 P-KB4 9 P-KR4! N-B3 10 Q-K2 P-KR3 11 B-KB4 is good for White (Tarrasch-Lasker, match 1908).

6	...	P-KR3
7	B-Q3	N-B3

Or 7...B-Q3 8 O-O O-O 9 Q-K2 with advantage to White.

8	O-O	B-Q3
9	P-B3	O-O
10	N-Q2!	

While I was preparing for the match the Odessa master Lerner showed me the variation 10 Q-K2 P-K4! 11 Q-K4 P-KN3 12 B×P B-KB4 13 Q-K3 P×P 14 P×P KR-K1 15 Q-Q2 N×P 16 N×N B×B 17 Q×B Q-R5 and Black regains the pawn advantageously. The move played is undoubtedly stronger.

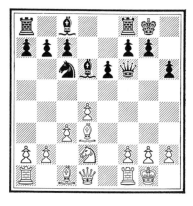

10 ...   P-K4?!

Here and on the next move the transfer of the queen to R5 deserved consideration. Black underestimates the force of 12 Q-R5.

11 N-K4   Q-Q1
12 Q-R5!

White's energetic opening play has given him a great advantage. The threat of 13 B×P cannot be parried.

12 ...   P×P
13 B×P   P×B?!

After thinking for half an hour I succumbed to the temptation to try the fortunes of three pieces against queen and pawn. An objectively stronger continuation was 13...P-KN3 14 Q-B3 (14 Q-KN5 Q×Q 15 N×Q̄ also gives White the better end-

ing), and now Black has two continuations, neither of which suffices for equality.
1) 14...Q-R5 15 N×B Q×B 16 N×B, and after either 16...QR×N 17 P×P Q-N2 18 B-R6 P×B 19 Q×N Q×P or 16...P×P 17 P×P QR×N 18 B-K4 White has an extra pawn;
2) 14...B×Pch 15 K-R1 Q-R5 16 B-KN5 Q-R1 17 N-B6ch K-N2 18 N-R5ch! Q×N 19 B-B6ch K-N1 20 Q×Q P×Q 21 K×B. Black stands worse, despite his extra pawn, because of the exposed position of his king. Of course, these two variations do not exhaust the possibilities of the position.

14 Q×RP   B-KB4
15 P-KB4

After 15 N-B6ch Q×N 16 Q×Q B×B 17 KR-K1! (17 Q-N5ch is also good) Black hardly has time to take on B3, so White will have queen and two pawns against three minor pieces. In view of the precarious position of Black's king this should be enough to win.

15 ...   R-K1

The idea is to defend against the threatened R-B3-N3 by means of ...R-K3-N3. After 16 N-B6ch Q×N 17 Q×Q B×B 18 R-B3 there could follow 18...R-K6.

16 N×B?!

An interesting conception, but one

based on an oversight in a main variation.

[White could have won by playing 16 R-B3 R-K3 17 R-N3ch R-N3 18 B-B4 B×N (or 18...R×R 19 N-B6ch Q×N 20 Q×Q) 19 R×Rch B×R 20 Q×Bch K-R1 21 Q-R5ch K-N2 22 Q×Pch K-R1 23 Q-R5ch K-N2 24 R-K1 P×P 25 Q-B7ch K-R1 26 R-K3. — Averbakh]

16	...	R-K3!
17	Q-R5	

Here White might have contemplated a queen sacrifice by 17 N×BP.

17	...	B-N3
18	N×BP	B×Q

After 18...B×N White has two pawns and an attack for the piece.

19	N×Q	N×N
20	B-B4	

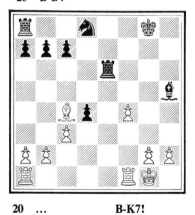

| 20 | ... | B-K7! |

Gufeld did not see this move when he played 16 N×B. Material will be equal (two minor pieces for a rook and two pawns) but Black gains a strong passed pawn on Q6.

21	B×Rch	N×B
22	P-B5	

White shouldn't have been in such a hurry to sacrifice the exchange.

22	...	B×R
23	R×B	

Possible is 23 K×B!?

| 23 | ... | N-Q1! |

This second retreat of the knight to Q1 is the way to win. White offered a draw at this point, but in view of his material advantage Black played on in the hope of more.

24	P×P	N-B3
25	P-KN4!	

White's passed pawns are decidedly dangerous. Black resolved to polish off White's Q-side and try to reach a won rook ending after giving up his knight on the K-side.

25	...	R-Q1
26	K-N2	R×P
27	K-N3	R-Q7
28	P-N5	R×NP
29	P-KR4	R×P
30	R-QN1	

Ingenious, but insufficient to save the game.

30	...	N-Q5
31	R×P	N×Pch
32	K-N4	N-K6ch

Possible was 32...N-N2!?

33 K-B3

Better was 33 K-B4 to be followed by 34 K-K5.

33	...	N-Q4
34	K-K4	R-R4
35	P-R5	K-B2
36	K-Q4	

36 K-K5 deserved consideration.

36	...	P-R3
37	K-K4	K-K3
38	P-R6	R-R5ch
39	K-B3	K-B4
40	R-N8	R-R6ch
41	K-B2	R-R6
42	R-N8	N-B5
43	R-N7	N-K3
44	K-N2	R-R4

Black can also win by means of 44...N×R 45 P×N R-R4.

45	R-N8	R×NPch
46	K-R1	R×R
47	P-R7	R-KR1
48	**Resigns**	

185

Part Three

The Tarrasch Variation

1	P-K4	P-K3
2	P-Q4	P-Q4
3	N-Q2	

Chapter 9

/11/9/83 ✓

The Tarrasch Variation
with 3...N-KB3

White: Geller
Black: Uhlmann

Skopje 1968

1	P-K4	P-K3
2	P-Q4	P-Q4
3	N-Q2	

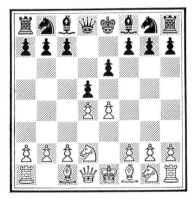

Here we have one of the main modern lines of the French Defence. Its advantage lies in the prevention of the pin ...B-N5 and the possibility of supporting the centre by P-QB3. In comparison with the Advance Variation, 3 P-K5, the text move develops a piece and supports the KP. Its disadvantage is that it blocks the QB. All in all the Tarrasch is a less aggressive continuation that is more likely to appeal to positional players.

Black has three methods of defence:

3...N-KB3, 3...P-QB4 and 3...N-QB3.

The first of these is the most complex. For years it was considered adequate, but the latest results favour White.

3	...	N-KB3
4	P-K5	KN-Q2
5	B-Q3	

This was the most popular move for many years, but more recently **5 P-KB4** has come into vogue. White opts for a fixed centre with an advantage in space. Black must play energetically if he is to obtain counterplay against this set-up. **5...P-QB4** 5...P-QN3 is too slow e.g. 6 QN-B3 B-R3 7 N-K2 N-QB3 8 P-KN4! Q-K2 9 P-B3 O-O-O 10 P-KR4 P-KR4 11 P×P K-N2 12 N-N3 B×B 13 K×B P-B3 14 Q-K2 Q-B2 15 B-Q2 and White managed to press home his advantage, as Black had no counterplay. Gipslis-Taimanov, Leningrad 1972. **6 P-B3 N-QB3 7 QN-B3!** Black has a comfortable game after the inexact 7 KN-B3 P×P 8 P×P Q-N3 9 N-N3 P-QR4 10 R-QN1 P-R5 11 N-R1 B-N5ch 12 K-B2 P-B3, Nahlik-Berthold.

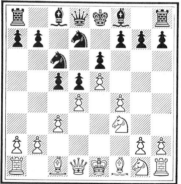

This is the basic position of the modern system.

7...P×P Transposing into the Leningrad System. This is the most popular move at this point but Black has tried a plethora of alternatives:

(a) 7...P-B4 8 B-Q3 Q-R4 (or 8...B-K2 9 N-K2 O-O 10 P-KR3 P-B5 11 B-B2 P-QN4 12 N-N5 N-N3 13 P-KN4 and White's attacking chances on the K-side were the more dangerous. Korchnoy-Larsen, Belgrade 1964.) 9 K-B2 B-K2 10 N-K2 P-QN4 11 B-Q2 Q-N3 12 P-KR3 P-N5 13 P-N4 P-N3 14 B-K3 B-R3 15 R-KN1 with some space advantage. Penrose-Uhlmann, Hastings 1966/67.

(b) 7...P-B5 (an idea that has received the support of Botvinnik) 8 P-KN4 (if 8 P-QN3 P-QN4) 8...P-KR4 (or 8...P-QN4 9 N-K2 N-N3 [possibly better is 9...P-KR4] 10 B-R3? [10 N-N3! is clearly better for White] 10...P-KR4 with an even game. Ostojic-Botvinnik, Wijk aan Zee 1969) 9 P×P N-N3 10 N-K2 R×P 11 N-N3 R-R1 12 B-N2 B-K2 13 O-O K-Q2 (or 13...P-N3 14 N-N5 with a clear advantage) 14 N-N5 Q-N1 15 P-B5 with a strong K-side attack. Parma-Pietzsch, Havana 1965.

(c) 7...Q-N3 8 P-KN3! (the most accurate treatment. For 8 N-K2 see Hamann-Uhlmann, Halle 1963 — illustrative game 44). 8...P×P. We have transposed to page 190, note to Black's 8th move.

(d) 7...B-K2 8 B-Q3 Q-R4 9 K-B1 (Keres recommends 9 B-Q2 Q-N3 10 N-K2 offering a promising pawn sacrifice. If 9 K-B2 then 9...Q-N3 is an awkward move to meet. See Kostro-Uhlmann, Poland-East Germany Match 1974 — illustrative game 45.) 9...P×P (better is 9...P-QN4 10 P×P P-N5 with even prospects.) 10 P×P P-QN3 11 B-Q2 B-N5 12 B-K3 B-R3 13 N-K2 B-K2 14 P-QR3 B×B 15 Q×B P-QN4 16 K-B2 P-B4 17 P-R3 P-N3 18 P-KN4 with the better game for White. Botvinnik-Uhlmann, Varna Olympiad 1962.

(e) 7...Q-R4!? (a move which conjures up great complications) 8 K-B2 (interesting is 8 B-K3 P×P 9 N×P N×N 10 B×N N-N1 11 N-B3 B-Q2 12 B-Q3 B-N4. Saharov-Doroshkevich, USSR 1973. 8 N-K2 is not so good e.g. 8...P-QN4! 9 B-Q2 P-N5 10 P-N4 P×BP 11 NP×P N-N3! 12 B-R3 N-N5 13 O-O P-R4! 14 B-B1! P×NP 15 B×P P-N3 16 N-N5 N-K2 with advantage to Black. S. Garcia-Korchnoy, Skopje Olympiad 1972. Perhaps White's best chance on the Q-side, after 7...Q-R4, is 8 P×P Q×P(B4) [otherwise P-QN4 can be played] 9 B-Q3 B-K2 10 N-K2 Q-N3 11 N(K2)-Q4! N×N 12 N×N B-B4 13 B-B2 N-N1! 14 N-N3 B-K2 15 Q-K2 B-Q2 16 B-K3 Q-B2 17 O-O with some advantage to White. Minic-Udovcic, Zagreb 1970.) 8...P-QN4 9 B-Q3 P-N5 10 N-K2 N-N3! (White has the better game after 10...B-R3 11 P-B5! see Lutikov-Kapengut, USSR Cup 1970 — illustrative game 46; or 10...P-N3 11 P-N4 P-R4 12 P-KR3 B-QR3 [weaker is 12...P×BP 13 NP×BP P×QP 14 P×QP N-N5 15 B-N1 P×P 16 P×P R×R 17 Q×R] 13 R-KN1 B×B 14 Q×B P×NP 15 RP×P P×BP 16 NP×P P×P 17 P×P N-N5 18 Q-Q1 Q-R3 19 N-K1 R-R7ch 20 R-N2 R×Rch 21 K×R with unclear play.) 11 B-Q2?! (a sharper line is 11 P-N4 P-N3 [Portisch recommends 11...P×BP 12 NP×P N-R5] 12 P-KR4 P×BP 13 NP×P P×P 14 P×P N-N5 15 B-N1 Q-R5 16 Q×Q N×Q

189

17 P-R3 N-B3 18 P-R5! with advantage. Portisch-Hug, Skopje Olympiad 1972. For 11 K-N3 see Savon-Portisch, Petropolis 1973 — illustrative game 47.) 11...B-R3 12 P×NP P×NP 13 Q-QN1 N-B5 14 B-B1 B-K2 15 P-QN3 N-R6 16 B×N P×B 17 R-QB1 N-N5 18 N-K1 K-Q2! and Black had a minimal advantage. Matulovic-Korchnoy, Ohrid 1972.

Now let us examine the position after **7...P×P.**

8 P×P P-KR4 More exact than 8...N-N3 9 P-KN4! P-KR4 10 P×P R×P 11 N-K2 P-N3 12 N-N3 R-R1 13 P-KR4! B-K2 14 P-R5 P×P 15 N×P with the better prospects for White.

Black can also try 8...Q-N3 9 P-KN3! B-N5ch (it is not advisable to play the immediate 9...P-B3 e.g. 10 B-R3! P×P 11 BP×P B-N5ch 12 K-B1! [preventing ...N×KP] 12...N-B1 13 N-K2 N-N3 14 K-N2 O-O 15 B-N4 B-Q2 16 P-KR4 with advantage to White. Portisch-Tal, Oberhausen 1961) 10 K-B2! P-B4 (once again, after 10...P-B3 11 K-N2 P×P, the opening of lines only favours White.) 11 K-N2 (or 11 N-K2 Q-B2 12 P-KR3 N-N3 13 P-N4 P-N3 14 R-KN1 B-Q2 15 P×P NP×P 16 P-R3 B-K2 17 N-B3 P-QR3 18 B-K3 O-O-O with equal chances. Haag-Uhlmann, Zinnowitz 1965.) 11...Q-Q1 (also possible is 11...N(Q2)-N1 12 N-R3 B-Q2 13 N-B2 P-QR4 and Black has good play, but not the weaker 13...N-R3 14 R-QN1 N-B2 15 N-Q3 with advantage to White. Suetin-Uhlmann, Sarajevo 1965 — illustrative game 48.) 12 B-Q3 N-N3 13 N-K2 B-Q2 14 P-KR3 B-K2 15 P-KN4 P-N3 16 N-B3 and White has the initiative. Liberzon-Uhlmann, Leipzig 1965.

9 B-Q3 N-N3 10 N-R3! The best move, threatening in many variations to go to KN5 with possible sacrifices on KB7 or K6. 10 N-K2 B-Q2 has also been tried, and now:

(1) 11 P-QR3 P-R4 12 O-O P-QR5 13 Q-K1 N-R4? (Black should try 13...P-N3 with unclear play) 14 P-B5! P×P 15 P-K6!! P×P 16 Q-N3 K-B2 17 N-B4 with a winning attack. Wade-Uhlmann, Skopje 1968.

(2) 11 O-O B-K2 (or 11...P-R4 12 N-B3 P-N3 13 P-QR4 N-N5 14 B-K2 B-K2 15 B-K3 R-QB1 16 P-KN3 K-B1 with equality. Matanovic-Pietzsch, Moscow 1963.) 12 P-QR3 P-R4 (too slow is 12...P-R3 13 B-Q2 P-N3 14 Q-N1! K-B1 15 N-N5! Q-K1 16 R-B3! K-N2 17 R-N3 R-KR3 18 N-KB3 R-KR2 19 P-B5 with a clear advantage to White. Estrin-Pietzsch, 1969) 13 B-Q2 P-QR5 14 R-B1 P-N3 15 Q-K1 K-B1 16 R-QB2 N-R2! 17 B-N4 B-QN4 with equality. Matanovic-Uhlmann, Skopje 1968.

10...B-Q2 11 O-O P-N3 12 P-R3 Weaker is 12 B-Q2 N-B5! 13 B×N P×B 14 N(R3)-N5 N-K2! 15 Q-K2 Q-N3! 16 P-QR4 R-B1 17 KR-B1 N-Q4 with the better game for Black. Matulovic-Uhlmann, Skopje 1968. But a plausible alternative to the text is the immediate 12 N(R3)-N5. **12...P-R4 13 Q-K2 B-K2 14 N(R3)-N5 P-QR5 15 Q-KB2 N-R4 16 B-Q2 N-N6 17 QR-Q1 N-B5 18 B-B3 R-QB1 19 Q-N3 R-KN1 20 Q-K1** and after successfully blockading the Q-side, White obtained the initiative with P-KR3 and P-KN4. Maric-Uhlmann, Skopje 1968.

Now let us return to the main line continuation 5 B-Q3.

Now that the white KB has been developed, the KN is free to go to its most natural square K2 while the QN aims at KB3. All White's minor pieces are thus directed towards the K-side where Black has a disadvantage in space. On the other hand, this development of White's KB does not contribute to the protection of his exposed pawn chain on Q4 and K5 and therefore the move 5 B-Q3 does less to give White a lasting advantage in space than the alternative 5 P-KB4.

5 ... P-QB4

So far 5...P-QN3 has been little tested. Both 6 P-KB4 and 6 N-K2 are good continuations for White.

6 P-QB3

The pawn sacrifice 6 KN-B3 P×P! is insufficient after 7 O-O N-QB3 8 R-K1 B-N5! 9 R-K2 Q-B2 10 Q-K1 Q-N1, threatening ...B-R4-B2.

6 ... N-QB3

The normal move, putting pressure on the QP. Here are some examples of the alternative **6...P-QN3:**

(1) 7 P-KB4 N-QB3 8 QN-B3 P-N3 9 N-K2 B-QN2 10 O-O Q-B2 11 B-Q2 B-N2 12 P-QN3 O-O-O with an unclear position. Fridstein-Goldberg, USSR 1949.

(2) 7 Q-K2 P×P 8 P×P N-QB3 9 QN-B3 N-N5! 10 B-KN5 B-K2 11 B×B N×Bch 12 Q×N Q×B with good play for Black as he can take control of his QR3-KB8 diagonal. Maric-Ugrinovic, Belgrade 1959.

(3) 7 N-R3 B-R3 8 B×B N×B 9 O-O B-K2 (better is 9...N-B2 10 Q-N4 P-B5!) 10 Q-N4! P-N3 11 N-B3 P-R3 12 N-B4 N-N1 13 P-QN3 with advantage to White.

(4) 7 Q-N4 B-R3 8 B×B N×B 9 N-K2 N-B2 10 O-O P-B5 11 P-QN3 P-QN4 12 P×P NP×P 13 P-QR4 P-N3 14 N-B3 P-KR4 15 Q-N3 N-N1 16 B-N5 with the better game for White. Ravinsky-Golovko, Moscow 1959.

(5) 7 KN-B3 B-R3 8 B×B N×B 9 Q-K2 N-B2 10 O-O B-K2 11 R-K1 P-KR3 12 N-B1 Q-B1 13 N-N3 Q-R3 14 Q-K3 P-N3 15 P-N3 P-B5 16 P×P P×P 17 P-QR4 N-Q4 18 Q-Q2 P-QN4 with unclear play. Browne-Petrosian, Zagreb 1970.

(6) 7 N-K2 B-R3 8 B×B N×B 9 O-O N-B2 10 N-KB4 and White has the initiative. See Keres-Dvoretsky, Triangular Team Tournament, Moscow 1973 — illustrative game 49.

Now back to the main line.

7 N-K2

White can try a promising pawn sacrifice by 7 KN-B3 Q-N3 8 O-O P×P 9 P×P N×QP 10 N×N Q×N 11 N-B3 Q-N3 12 Q-R4! The idea is to switch White's queen to the K-side and to hinder the development of Black's pieces. After 12...Q-N5! (it is risky to play 12...B-K2 13 Q-KN4 P-N3 14 B-KR6 when White has the initiative) 13 Q-B2 Q-B4 (Black achieves equality by returning the pawn. If instead 13...P-KR3 14 B-Q2 Q-N3 15 QR-B1 B-K2 16 Q-R4, White has the advantage. Korchnoy-Udovcic, Leningrad 1967) 14 B×P P-QN3 15 B-B4 (or 15 Q-N1 B-R3 16 B-K3 Q-N5! with good play) 15...B-R3 16 KR-B1 Q×Q 17 B×Q N-B4 18 N-Q4 B-K2 with equality. Furman-Uhlmann, Polanica Zdroj 1967.

After 7 KN-B3, if Black tries to attack both the head and tail of White's pawn chain, he has severe problems along the K1-KR4 diagonal. An amusing exhibition game of Tal's (Latvia 1970) went: 7...P×P 8 P×P P-B3? 9 N-N5!! P×N 10 Q-R5ch P-N3 11 B×Pch P×B 12 Q×P(N6)ch K-K2 13 N-B4! B-R3 14 B×Pch B×B 15 Q-N7ch K-K1 16 N-Q6mate.

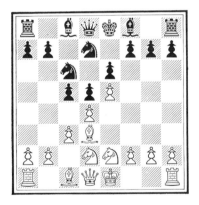

7 ...   Q-N3

The logical continuation, putting pressure on the QP which forces N-B3, thus preventing P-KB4 strengthening White's centre. Instead Black has two other moves that are worthy of serious consideration:

(a) 7...P-B3 8 N-KB4 White finds it hard to castle after 8 P-KB4 P×QP 9 P×QP P×P 10 QP×P (10 BP×P? N×QP 11 N×N Q-R5ch) 10...B-B4. However, 8 KP×P is a solid continuation ensuring White a small positional plus after 8...Q×P 9 N-B3 P×P 10 P×P B-N5ch 11 B-Q2! (not 11 K-B1 O-O 12 N-B4 B-Q3 13 N-R5 Q-B2 14 N-N3 P-K4 with good play for Black) 11...B×Bch 12 Q×B O-O (or 12...P-K4 13 P×P N(Q2)×P 14 N×N Q×N 15 O-O O-O 16 QR-K1 Q-B3 17 B-B2 B-K3 18 N-B3 QR-Q1 19 B-N3 N-Q5? 20 R×B! N×R 21 N×P Q-Q5 22 Q-K2 N-B4 23 N-B6 dbl ch K-R1 24 N×P! with a clear advantage. Gorjanov-Ovetchkin) 13 O-O. Now, after ...P-K4, we have variations similar to those in the above note. Perhaps Black's best after 8 KP×P is 8...N×BP 9 N-B3 B-Q3 transposing into the main line. **8...Q-K2 9 KP×P** Again the best chance. After 9 Q-R5ch Q-B2 10 B-N6? P×B 11 Q×R P×QP 12 P×QP N×QP 13 O-O N×P Black has a mighty centre. Nor does 9 N-B3 seem satisfactory, e.g. 9...P×QP (not 9...P×KP 10 N-N6 P×N 11 B×Pch K-Q1 12 B-N5 N-B3 13 P×KP with a strong central attack) 10 P×QP P×P 11 N-N6 P×N 12 B×Pch K-Q1 13 B-N5 N-B3 14 P×P Q-N5ch 15 K-B1 B-K2 16 P×N P×P 17 B-K3 and Black has an excellent game. Euwe-Kramer, 1940. **9...Q×P** If 9...N×BP 10 N-B3 P-K4 11 P×KP N×P 12 O-O N×Nch 13 Q×N B-N5 14 B-N5ch B-Q2 15 B×Bch Q×B 16 R-Q1 O-O-O 17 N×P! N×N 18 P-B4 winning a pawn, or here 15 N×P N×N 16 Q×N B×B 17 B-N5! B-B3 18 Q-B5 B-K5 19 Q-B4 Q-K3 20 KR-K1 winning. **10 N-B3 P×P** White stands better after 10...B-Q3 11 N-R5 Q-K2 12 Q-B2! (or 12 O-O P-KN3 13 P×P B×BP 14 N-B4 and the K-file spells trouble for Black) 12...P-KN3 13 P×P B×BP 14 B-KN5 Q-B2 15 N-B4 N(Q2)-K4 16 N×N N×N 17 O-O-O. Stoljar-Shagalovich, USSR 1955. **11 O-O!** Not 11 P×P B-N5ch 12 K-B1 (12 B-Q2?? Q×N) 12...B-Q3 13 N-R5 Q-K2 with good play down the KB-file. **11...N(Q2)-K4** Black has no time for 11...B-Q3 because of 12 N×KP. 11...P×P also fails to 12 N×KP P×P 13 B×NP Q×B 14 R-K1. Finally 11...N-B4 12 R-K1 is better for White. **12 N×N N×N 13 B-N5ch N-B3** If 13...B-Q2 14 B×Bch K×B (14...N×B 15 R-K1!) 15 R-K1 R-K1 (not 15...P×P 16 N×QP P×N 17 Q×Pch B-Q3 18 Q×Pch K-K3 19 P-B4! with great advantage) 16 P-B4!! B-N5 17 R×N! Q×R (or 17...B-Q3 18 Q-R4ch K-B1 19 R-K1 B×N 20 B×B Q×B 21 P×P wins) 18 N-Q3! winning the bishop. **14 R-K1 B-K2 15 P×P O-O 16 B-K3** and Black's backward KP gives White a positional plus.

(b) 7...P×P 8 P×P N-N3 A system worked out by masters from Leningrad. Black intends to counter White's K-side action by ...P-KN3 and possibly ...P-KR4, and build up Q-side play on his QN5 and QB5 squares. It is clearly a positional set-up in which Black dare not make the slightest mistake. Instead of 8...N-N3 he could of course still play 8...P-B3 or 8...Q-N3, transposing to (a) above or to the main line, respectively. **9 O-O B-Q2**

10 P-B4 The most aggressive continuation, intending an eventual P-B5. In addition to the text White has two other natural developing moves:

(1) 10 P-QR3 P-QR4! 11 P-QN3 P-R5 12 P-QN4 R-B1?! (better is 12...B-K2 13 B-N2 P-B4! with equal chances but White can also improve with 13 P-B4 P-B4 14 P×P e.p. B×BP 15 N-KB3 O-O 16 Q-B2 P-KN3 17 B×P! P×B 18 Q×Pch B-N2 19 N-N5 R-B3 20 Q-R7ch K-B1 21 P-B5! threatening N-B4. Ivkovic-Hecht, Vrsac 1973) 13 B-N2 B-K2 14 N-KN3 P-N3 15 R-B1 and White has more space. Or here 10...R-B1 11 P-QN4 P-QR3 12 N-QN3 N-B5 13 N-B4 P-QN3 14 Q-N4 N-K2 15 N-KR5 B-R5 16 N-Q2 N-N3 17 N-B3 Q-Q2 18 B-N5 Q-B3 19 KR-B1 and White stands better. Neikirch-Fuchs, East Germany 1957.

(2) 10 N-KB3 B-K2 11 N-B4 (other attempts are: 11 B-Q2 N-N5 12 B×N [better is 12 B-N1] 12...B×B 13 P-QR3 B-K2 14 R-B1 O-O 15 Q-B2 P-N3 16 Q-Q2 K-N2 with equality. Or 11 P-QN3 P-QR4 12 P-QR4 N-N5 13 N-B3 N-B1 14 B-K2 N-R2 and Black controls the Q-side, with the break ...P-QN4 in the air) 11...P-QR4 (more exact is 11...P-N3; or first 11...R-QB1 12 P-KR3 N-N5 [12...P-N3 also equalizes] 13 B-N1 Q-B2 14 N-R5 P-N3 15 N-B6ch B×N 16 P×B B-N4 17 R-K1 N-B7 with equality) 12 N-R5! P-N3 (not 12...O-O 13 Q-Q2! threatening N×P followed by Q-KR6) 13 N-B6ch B×N 14 P×B Q×P 15 B-KN5 Q-N2 16 Q-N3 (or 16 Q-Q2 with good chances) 16...N-N5 17 B-N1 P-R3 18 B-B4 B-R5 19 Q-K3 N-B5 20 Q-B3. with advantage to White.

10...P-KN3 If 10...N-N5 11 B-N1 P-QR4 12 P-QR3 N-B3 13 P-B5 P×P 14 B×P B×B 15 R×B P-N3 16 R-B1 B-N2 17 N-KB3 O-O 18 B-N5 P-B3 19 P×P B×P 20 B×B Q×B 21 N-B3 P-R5 22 Q-Q3 with a minimal advantage to White. **11 N-KB3** Weaker alternatives are:

(1) 11 R-B3 P-KR4! 12 P-QR3 R-B1 13 P-QN4 N-K2 and Black can post his minor pieces on the light squares.

(2) 11 P-QR3 P-QR4 12 P-QN3 (or 12 N-KB3 P-R4 13 N-B3 P-QR5 14 Q-B2 R-KN1 15 Q-B2 N-R4 16 Q-N3 N(R4)-B5? [better 16...R-B1] 17 P-B5! with advantage to White. Szabo-Troianescu, 1950) 12...P-R4 13 N-KB3 (better 13 B-N2) 13...P-QR5! 14 P×P (if 14 P-QN4 N-R2) 14...N×RP 15 R-N1 N-R4 16 N-N5 N-N3 17 N-QB3 R-B1 18 Q-B2 R-KN1 with an unclear position.

11...P-KR4

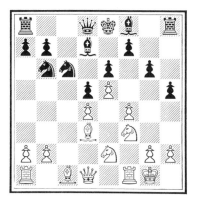

This position has been reached several times in master games. Although no definite assessment can yet be given we should state that the practical results tend to favour White. Here are some examples:

(1) 12 B-Q2 N-N5 13 B-N1 N-B5?! (better is 13...P-R4 14 P-QR3 N-B3 15 P-QR4 N-N5 with equal chances) 14 B-B1 P-R4 15 P-QN3 N-N3 16 P-QR3 N-B3 17 P-QR4 with a positional plus.

(2) 12 N-B3 P-R4 13 P-QR4 N-N5 14 B-K2 B-K2 15 B-K3 R-QB1 16 P-KN3 K-B1 17 P-R3 K-N2 18 K-N2 N-B5 19 B-B1 Q-B2 20 N-K1 P-B4! 21 P×P e.p.ch B×P 22 N-B3 Q-N3 23 N-K5 B-K1 24 P-N4 N-Q3 with complications and chances for both sides. Matanovic-Pietzsch, 1963.

(3) 12 P-QR3 P-QR4 13 Q-K1 (in the game Hennings-Rittner, Black clearly stood better after 13 Q-B2 R-KN1 14 B-K3 P-QR5 15 N-B3 N-R4 16 B-B2 B-K2

17 N-KN5 R-QB1 18 P-R4 N-N6 19 QR-Q1 N-B5) 13...N-K2? (the correct move is first 13...P-QR5 14 Q-N3 and then 14...N-K2 and 15...N-B4) 14 P-R3! P-QR5 15 N-N5 N-B5 16 P-KN4 P×P 17 P×P P-N4 18 K-N2 Q-R4 19 Q-Q1 B-N2 20 R-R1! with a positional advantage. Udovcic-Ivkov, Yugoslavia 1952.

(4) 12 K-R1 N-N5 13 B-N1 B-N4 14 R-N1 B×N 15 Q×B Q-B2 16 P-QR3 N-B3 17 B-Q3 N-B1 18 B-K3 N(B1)-K2 19 N-R4 N-B4 20 N×N NP×N 21 P-QN4! with a space advantage on the Q-side. Matanovic-Wade, Stockholm Interzonal 1952.

8   N-B3   P×P —✓

Making White's QP susceptible to a direct attack and obtaining the square QN5 for the use of Black's pieces.

9   P×P   P-B3! —✓

This immediate attack on the centre has proved to be best. 9...Q-N5ch 10 B-Q2 Q×NP is dubious after 11 R-QN1 Q-R6 12 R-N3 Q-K2 13 O-O Q-Q1 14 N-B4 B-K2 15 N-R5 O-O 16 Q-K2 with advantage to White. Zhuravlev-Prutovich; Or 9...B-N5ch 10 B-Q2 B×Bch 11 Q×B Q-N5 12 R-QB1 Q×Qch 13 K×Q! N-N3 14 P-QN3! K-K2 15 P-KR4 B-Q2 16 R-R3 with the better ending. Keres-Flores, Buenos Aires 1939. In reply to 9...B-N5ch White can also play 10 K-B1 with complications which favour him after 10...P-B3 (10...O-O? 11 B×Pch!) 11 N-B4! P×P 12 N(B4)×KP N-B3 (if 12...P-K5 13 B-KB4! P×N 14 B-B7 N-B3 15 B×Q [not 15 N×Pch K-B2 16 B×Q B-N5! 17 P-KN3 B-KR6ch 18 K-N1 K×N 19 B-B7 KR-K1 with an excellent game for Black. Spielmann-Stoltz, 1930] 15...B×N 16 B-QB5 B-N5 17 Q-R4 P×Pch 18 K×P with a clear advantage to White. Berner-

Wiese, 1954) 13 N×NPch K-B1 (13...K-B2 14 N-R5! N×N 15 N-N5ch and 16 Q×N) 14 B-KR6 K-N1 (there is no defence; if 14...N-N5 15 Q-B1! and if 14...P-K5 15 N-R5ch K-K2 16 N×N K×N 17 Q-B1! P×B 18 Q-N5ch K-K3 19 Q-N4ch!) 15 Q-B1! P-K5 (15...N-N5 16 N-B5) 16 Q-N5 K-B2 17 N-R5 N×N 18 Q×Nch K-K2 19 B-KN5ch K-B1 20 N-K5! N×N 21 B-KR6ch K-K2 22 Q×Nch winning. Rotaru-Diaconescu, Romania 1961.

10 P×P

In this poisition 10 N-B4 is not so effective. e.g. 10...P×P 11 P×P (not 11 N(B4)×KP P-K5 12 B-KB4 N(Q2)-K4!! 13 P×N B×N 14 N-N5 B-KB4 15 B-K2 B-QN5ch 16 K-B1 Q-Q1 with advantage to Black. Barden-Wade, England 1959) 11...B-N5ch 12 K-B1 N(Q2)×P 13 N×N N×N 14 Q-R5ch N-B2 15 B×P. Black now has two good possibilities. Either 15...B-Q2! 16 N-N6 B-N4ch 17 K-N1 B-B4 with excellent attacking chances for the exchange. Or 15...Q-Q5!? 16 B-K3 Q×P 17 R-B1 Q-K4 18 Q-Q1 R×B 19 Q-R4ch B-Q2 20 Q×B(N4) R-B1 21 R×Rch B×R 22 N-N6 Q-B3 with advantage to Black. Menke-Wilde, 1957.

| 10 | ... | N×BP |
| 11 | O-O | B-Q3 |

Black has no time for 11...B-Q2 12 R-K1 B-Q3 13 B-KB4 B×B 14 N×B when Black's weak KP is exposed.

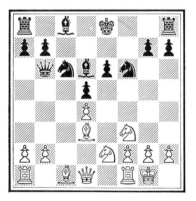

White now has a wealth of moves at his disposal and it is difficult to say which is the best.

12 N-B3

Perhaps the most positionally consistent continuation. Before we examine this move in detail we must first consider eight(!) alternative tries:

(a) 12 N-N3 Or 12 R-K1 O-O 13 N-N3 12...O-O 13 R-K1 K-R1! and White's QP is just as weak as Black's KP.

(b) 12 P-QR3 O-O 13 P-QN4? P-K4! **14 P×P N×KP 15 N(B3)-Q4** Or 15 N×N B×N 16 B-K3 Q-B2 with advantage to Black. Stoltz-Schmid, Helsinki Olympiad 1952. **15...N(B3)-N5! 16 P-B4?** If 16 P-R3 N×B! **16...N×B 17 Q×N B-KB4** with advantage. Kolarov-Pietzsch, 1965.

(c) 12 P-QN3 O-O 12...P-K4 is shown to be premature after 13 P×P N×P 14 N(K2)-Q4 O-O 15 B-K3 with a positional plus. **13 B-N2** Not 13 B-KB4 N×P! 14 N(B3)×N P-K4 with a good game. **13...B-Q2 14 N-N3 K-R1 15 B-N1 P-QR4 16 P-QR3 QR-B1 17 R-K1 N-K2 18 N-K5 B-K1 19 R-K3 B×N!** 20 P×B N-Q2 21 B-Q4 Q-Q1 22 B-Q3 B-N3 with equality. Florian-Uhlmann, Balatonfured 1959.

(d) 12 R-N1. For a long time this move was held to be an improvement on White's play until Uhlmann came up with a satisfactory answer: **12...O-O 13 B-KB4 N×P!** This is Uhlmann's idea. Not 13...B×B 14 N×B Q-B2 15 P-KN3 P-K4 16 P×P N×P 17 N×N Q×N 18 Q-N3 with the better game. **14 N(B3)×N P-K4** Also possible is 14...B×B 15 N×B P-K4 16 N×QP Q×N with equality. **15 B-K3 P×N 16 B×QP** If 16 N×QP? B×Pch! **16...Q-B2 17 P-KR3 B-Q2** with even chances.

(e) 12 B-Q2 O-O Not 12...Q×NP 13 R-N1 Q-R6 14 R-N3 Q-R5 15 B-QN5 Q×RP 16 N-B1 winning. If 12...P-K4 13 P×P N×P 14 N×N B×N 15 B-B3 and White has a lead in development. **13 B-B3 B-Q2.** The chances are about even. See Zinn-Uhlmann, East Germany 1964 (illustrative game 50), and Weinitschke-Trescher, East German Correspondence game 1970-74 (illustrative game 51).

(f) 12 Q-Q2?! O-O 13 Q-N5 B-Q2 14 Q-R4 N-QN5 15 B-N1 B-N4 16 R-K1 N-Q6 with advantage to Black. Milic-Udovcic, Yugoslavia 1957.

(g) 12 B-KB4 B×B 13 N×B Q×NP! The only move to equalize e.g. 13...O-O 14 R-N1! Q-B2 15 P-KN3 P-K4 16 P×P N×P 17 N×N Q×N 18 R-K1 and Black's isolated QP is a permanent weakness. Aronin-Kotkov, USSR 1960. If here 14...K-R1 White can immediately plunge into favourable tactics by 15 N-N5 N×P 16 N×RP! N×N 17 N-N6ch K-N1 18 N-K7ch K-B2 (or 18...K-R1? 19 B×N

winning) 19 N×B QR×N **20** Q-R5ch with advantage. **14 R-K1** White can force a draw immediately by 14 R-N1 Q×RP (not 14...Q-R6 15 N-N5 Q-Q3? **16 N(B4)×KP!** B×N 17 N×B Q×N 18 R-K1 N-K5 19 B×N P×B 20 P-Q5 Q-K4 21 P×N P×P 22 Q-N3! Q-Q4 23 Q-N4 with a clear advantage to White. Minev-Uhlmann, Berlin 1962. 15...O-O is better.) **15** N-N5 O-O **16** R-R1 Q-N7 **17** R-N1 with a draw by repetition. **14...O-O 15** N×KP The zwischenzug 15 R-K2 has no importance after 15...Q-R6 16 N×KP B×N 17 R×B QR-K1 18 R×R R×R 19 B-N5 with equality. Estrin-Filzer, 1957. **15...B×N 16** R×B QR-K1 **17** R×R R×R **18 Q-QB1!** 18 R-N1 Q×RP 19 R×P N-K5! is unclear. **18...Q×Qch** Or 18...Q-N3 19 R-N1 Q-R4 20 P-KR3 P-QR3 21 R×P N×P 22 Q-N5 N×Nch 23 P×N Q-K8ch 24 K-N2 R-K2 25 R-N8ch R-K1 Drawn. Fuchs-Uhlmann. **19** R×Q R-QB1 with equal chances. Platz-Uhlmann, East Germany 1962.

(h) 12 N-B4 O-O 13 R-K1 B-Q2! This pawn sacrifice guarantees Black adequate resources. If instead 13...B×N 14 B×B Q×NP? 15 B-Q6 R-K1 16 B-K5 Q-R6 17 B×N P×B 18 N-R4! R-K2 19 R-K3 then White has a winning attack. Ciric-Smederevac, Yugoslavia 1957. White also has the advantage after 13...N-K5 14 P-KN3 B×N 15 B×B Q×NP 16 R-K2. **14 N×KP KR-K1** The chances are even. See Georgadze-Doroshkevich, Tbilisi 1971 (illustrative game 52).

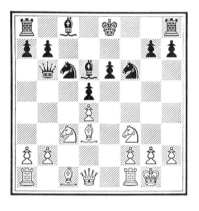

12	...		O-O
13	**B-K3**		

This prevents the freeing move ...P-K4 and White prepares to build up calmly} ?
on the Q-side.

because of discovered attack on Black Q

13	...		B-Q2

200

14 P-QR3!

14 N-K5 is proved to be premature after 14...B×N 15 P×B Q×P 16 P×N Q×N 17 P×P Q×P with an extra pawn for Black. However, a good alternative is 14 R-B1 QR-B1 15 N-K5 B-K1 16 Q-Q2 N-K2 17 P-B3 Q-Q1 18 B-KB2 P-QR3 19 N-K2 R×R 20 R×R Q-N1 21 R-K1 N-B3 22 P-B4 N-K2 23 N-B3 Drawn. Trifunovic-Uhlmann, Halle 1963. Another possibility occurred in Barden-Uhlmann, Hastings 1958/9, which went 14 R-K1 K-R1 15 P-KR3 P-QR3 16 R-QB1 N-K2 17 N-QR4?! B×N 18 Q×B N-B4 19 B-KN5 (19 N-K5 was essential) 19...B-N5! 20 Q-N3 N-Q2 21 R-K2 N×P 22 N×N Q×N 23 B-K3 Q-R5 24 R-B7 (if 24 P-N3 Q×RP 25 Q×B N-K4 wins; Or 24 P-R3 B-Q3 25 Q×NP N-K4 with advantage) 24...N-K4 25 R×QNP P-QR4 26 P-R3 P-Q5! with a clear advantage for Black.

14 ... Q-Q1!

Having done her duty on the Q-side the queen now heads for the other wing, at the same time preventing the possibility of N-K5. Other moves which have been played are:

(a) 14...QR-K1 15 P-QN4 P-QR3 16 R-B1 Stronger is 16 N-K5! 16...K-R1 17 B-N1 R-K2 18 B-N5 B-K1 19 P-R3 B-N1 20 N-K2 P-QR4 21 P×P Q×RP 22 Q-N3 B-Q3 23 R-B3 R(K2)-KB2 24 B-R4 Q-R3 with equal chances. Palmasson-Uhlmann, Prague/Marianske Lazne 1954.

(b) 14...P-QR3 15 P-QN4 Q-Q1! 16 R-K1 Q-K1 17 P-R3 R-B1 18 R-QB1 K-R1 19 B-N1 Q-R4 with equality. Dr. Szily-Uhlmann, 1959.

15	P-R3	R-B1
16	R-K1	K-R1
17	R-QB1	Q-K1

White has the better game after 17...P-K4 18 P×P N×P 19 N×N B×N 20 B×QRP B×N 21 R×B R×R 22 P×R Q-R4 23 B-Q4 Q×RP 24 Q-N1.

| 18 | R-B2 | P-QR3 |
| 19 | R(B2)-K2 | R-QB2 − ? |

This move can be criticized. 19...Q-R4 would give equal chances.

201

20	B-B1	P-QN4
21	B-N1	N-Q1
22	Q-Q3	Q-B2
23	N-K5	Q-N1
24	B-B4	

The space advantage and Black's weak KP give White the better position.

24	...	B-K1
25	Q-Q2	N-N2
26	N-Q3	B-N3
27	R×P	B×B
28	N×B	B×B
29	R×B	N-KR4?!
30	N(B4)×QP!	

The most clear-cut solution.

30	...	R×N
31	R-K5!	R(B6)-B1
32	R×N	Q-B2
33	R-K5	N-Q3
34	N-K3!	Q-N3
35	R-KB1	P-R3
36	P-Q5	N-B5
37	N×N	R×N
38	R-K2	R-Q1
39	R-Q1	R-Q3
40	Q-K1!	R-B4
41	R-K5	K-R2 and Black Resigned

GAME 44

White: Hamann
Black: Uhlmann

Halle 1963

1	P-K4	P-K3
2	P-Q4	P-Q4
3	N-Q2	N-KB3
4	P-K5	KN-Q2
5	P-KB4	P-QB4
6	P-B3	N-QB3
7	QN-B3	Q-N3
8	N-K2	

8	...	P-B3!
9	P-KN3	P×QP
10	P×QP	

In the game Barczay-Farago, White played 10 N(2)×P N×N? 11 P×N P×P (or 11...B-N5ch 12 B-Q2 O-O 13 B×B Q×Bch 14 Q-Q2 with the better ending for White) 12 BP×P B-N5ch 13 K-B2 O-O 14 K-N2! with advantage. However, Black could play instead 10...P×P and if 11

N×P(6)? P-K5! 12 N×B P×N, or here 12 N(3)-Q4 N-B3 with the better game for Black. So White must play 11 P×P B-B4! 12 B-Q3! (if 12 N×P N(2)×N 13 N×Pch K-B1 with unclear play) 12...P-N3! 13 N×P B-B7ch with complications.

10	...	B-N5ch
11	B-Q2?	

Correct is 11 N-B3 O-O 12 P×P (not 12 B-R3 P×P 13 B×Pch K-R1, nor 12 B-N2 P×P 13 BP×P R×N! 14 B×R N×QP with advantage to Black) 12...N×BP with equal chances.

11	...	P×P!
12	BP×P	O-O
13	B-N2	N(2)×P!!

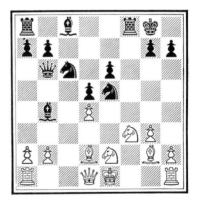

A fine piece sacrifice giving Black a decisive advantage.

14	P×N	N×P
15	N(2)-Q4	

If 15 N-B4 Q-K6ch 16 K-B1 B×B

17 N×N (17 N×B P-KN4!)
17...Q×N(K4) 18 Q×B P-KN4 19 R-K1 Q-Q3 and Black wins.

15	...	N-Q6ch
16	K-K2	N×P
17	Q-N3	Q-R3ch!
18	K-B2	B×B
19	Q×N	Q-Q6!
20	QR-Q1	Q-K6ch
21	K-B1	P-QN3

The entry of Black's QB into the game forces the win.

22	Q×B	B-R3ch
23	N-K2	R×Nch
24	B×R	Q×Bch
25	K-N1	B×N
26	R-K1	B-Q6!
27	Resigns	

GAME 45

White: Kostro
Black: Uhlmann

Poland-East Germany Match 1974

1	P-K4	P-K3
2	P-Q4	P-Q4
3	N-Q2	N-KB3
4	P-K5	KN-Q2
5	P-KB4	P-QB4
6	P-B3	N-QB3
7	QN-B3	B-K2
8	B-Q3	Q-R4!?
9	K-B2?!	

In my (Uhlmann) game against Botvinnik at the Varna Olympiad 1962, White played 9 K-B1 and after 9...P×P 10 P×P P-QN4 gained the advantage. However, the correct play for Black is 9...P-QN4 10 P×P P-N5 with equal chances. The pawn sacrifice 9 B-Q2 Q-N3 10 N-K2 Q×P is unclear.

9	...	Q-N3!
10	N-K2	P-B3

We now see the difference between this line and the main variation in which White has usually played P-KN3 giving his king a safe square on KN2. Black now threatens to win a pawn by 11...P×QP 12 P×QP P×P 13 P×P N(2)×P.

11 Q-N3

White clearly did not relish this move but there seems to be nothing better. Adorjan tried 11 K-N3 in his game with Vaganian at Teesside 1974, but after 11...P-N4 White was in trouble: 12 R-K1 P×QP 13 N(K2)×P (If 13 P×QP P×BPch 14 N×P P×P 15 P×P N-B4, Black has a good game.) 13...P×BPch 14 B×P P×P 15 N×P(K5) N(Q2)×N 16 R×N (If 16 B×N, then 16...N×B 17 R×N B-Q2 [17...B-Q3 is bad because of 18 Q-R5ch K-Q1 19 Q-N5ch] followed by castling. By sacrificing the exchange White gets a strong position, the only disadvantage of which is his unsettled king.) 16...N×R 17 B×N R-KN1ch 18 K-R3 R-N4 19 B-N5ch! (Adorjan plays with imagination. 19 N-B3 loses because of 19...Q-K6 and 19 Q-K2 B-Q2 20 N-B3 R-R4ch 21 K-N4 O-O-O 22 K×R R-N1 is also insufficient.) 19...K-Q1 (If 19...B-Q2, then 20 B×Bch K×B 21 Q-R4ch K-Q1 22 R-K1 with a strong attack.) 20 Q-K2 B-Q2 (Now this move is possible because the queen cannot check from R4.) 21 B-Q3 K-B1! (This prepares 22...B-Q3 and at the same time threatens 22...R×B 23 Q×R B-KB3! 24 Q×B P-K4ch, winning the queen.) 22 N-B3 R-KN1 23 P-B4! K-Q1! (23...B-Q3 24 R-KB1 B×B 25 N×B P-Q5 26 P-B5 gives White a dangerous initiative.) 24 B×P R-KB1 25 Q-Q2 R-QB1 26 P-QN3 R-QB4! (The rook comes into play with great effect. 27...P×P is threatened.) 27 R-Q1 K-B1! (Vaganian manoeuvres skilfully in the face of strong enemy pressure.) 28 B-Q3 P×P 29 B×P Q-B3 30 B-K2 (White defends against the threat of 30...R×N, but instead succumbs to a different blow.) 30...R×B! 31 N×R R-R1ch 32 K-N3 B-R5ch 33 K-B4 R-

B1ch 34 Resigns (After 34 K-N4 Q×Pch 35 K×B Q-B7ch, mate is inevitable.)

11	...	Q×Q
12	P×Q	P×QP
13	P×QP	O-O
14	B-Q2	P-KN4!

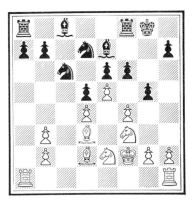

This move smashes White's imposing pawn centre and activates Black's pieces. An alternative idea is a piece sacrifice by 14...P×P 15 BP×P N(Q2)×P!? 16 P×N N×P with active play.

15 P×BP

15 P-N3 loses a pawn after 15...P-N5 16 P×P B×P.

| 15 | ... | B×P |
| 16 | P×P | B-N2! |

The point. Not 16...B×QPch 17 N×B N×N 18 B-N4! R-B2 19 P-N6 P×P 20 B×P R-B3 21 B-B3 with some advantage to White.

205

17	B-B3	P-K4!
18	P×P	N(Q2)×P
19	KR-Q1	B-N5
20	N-N1?	

Better is 20 B×N N×B 21 N-N1 when Black has only a slight edge.

20	...	P-Q5!
21	B-K1	N×Bch
22	R×N	N-K4
23	R-Q2	R-B4

Now Black regains his pawn with the better game.

24	P-R3	B×N
25	N×B	P-QR3!

A neat zwischenzug.

26	K-K2	

Or 26 K-N3 N×N 27 P×N R×NPch with advantage to Black.

26	...	N×N
27	P×N	R-K1ch
28	K-Q1	

If 28 K-B2 R-K6 and the pawn harvest is gathered in.

28	...	R×BP
29	P-R4	P-Q6!
30	R-KR2	

Or 30 R-KB2 R×R 31 B×R R-K7 winning both Q-side pawns.

30	...	R-B8
31	K-Q2	B×P

32	R-R2	

Or 32 R-N1 B-R6! followed by 33...R×B 34 R×R B-N5ch.

32	...	B-K4
33	R-KB2	B-B5ch
34	Resigns	

GAME 46

White: Lutikov
Black: Kapengut

USSR Cup 1970

Notes by Chaplinsky

1	P-K4	P-K3
2	P-Q4	P-Q4
3	N-Q2	N-KB3
4	P-K5	KN-Q2
5	P-KB4	P-QB4
6	P-B3	N-QB3
7	QN-B3	Q-R4
8	K-B2	P-QN4
9	B-Q3	P-N5
10	N-K2	B-R3?
11	P-B5!	

206

11	...	NP×P
12	BP×P	P×KP
13	NP×P	P×P
14	P×P	N-N5

It would have been better to exchange bishops. After 14...B×B 15 Q×B B-K2 16 N-B4 (16 B-N5 O-O) 16...N-Q1 followed by castling, Black can defend himself. Now, though, White has a clear advantage.

15	B-N1	B×N
16	Q×B	B-K2
17	P-KR4	Q-R3
18	Q-Q1	R-QB1
19	B-N5?	Q-B5?

After 19...Q-R6! 20 B×B K×B Black's chances are no worse because of the threat of ...Q-N7ch or ...Q-B6. Instead of 19 B-N5 White should have played 19 P-R3!, keeping a positional advantage.

20	B×B	K×B
21	P-R3	Q-B6

If 21...N-QB3, then 22 Q-Q2 with strong threats.

22	B×P	Q-N7ch
23	K-N3	R×B
24	P×N	R-B7
25	Q-KB1	R-R3
26	P-R5	P-N3
27	R×P	R-K7

Black's position is indefensible: for example, 27...R×RP 28 R×P P×R 29 Q-N5! R×Pch 30 K-R3 or 27...Q×NP

28 Q-Q3 Q-N7 29 R-KN1 P×P 30 Q-R6. In both cases White must win.

28	R-KR4	R×RP
29	R×R	P×R
30	N-Q2!	

The more obvious 30 N-N5 R×NPch! 31 Q×R Q×QP gives Black chances of salvation.

30	...	R×KP
31	P×R	Q×KPch
32	Q-KB4	P-R5ch
33	K-N4	Resigns

GAME 47

White: Savon
Black: Portisch

Petropolis Interzonal 1973

Notes by Bihovsky

1	P-K4	P-K3
2	P-Q4	P-Q4
3	N-Q2	N-KB3
4	P-K5	KN-Q2
5	P-KB4	P-QB4
6	P-B3	N-QB3
7	QN-B3	Q-R4
8	K-B2	P-QN4
9	B-Q3	P-N5
10	N-K2	N-N3
11	K-N3	

11	...	P×BP
12	NP×P	B-R3

12...N-R5 was worth considering.

13 P-KR4

An interesting idea; he intends to advance the KRP further. Black should prevent this by playing 13...P-R4, which would oblige White to play 14 P-B5 (since otherwise 14...P-N3 blocks the position), and after 14...P×BP 15 B×P B×N 16 Q×B Q×BP the complications favour Black, since both 17 B-N2 and 17 P-K6 can be met by 17...N×QP.

13	...	B-K2
14	P-R5	B×B
15	Q×B	Q-R5
16	P-B5	Q-B5
17	Q×Q	N×Q

Although the exchange of queens shows up a number of weaknesses in White's position he still has the better chances, thanks chiefly to the "wedge" on R6.

18	P-R6	P-N3
19	P×KP	P×KP
20	R-QN1	O-O
21	N-B4	N-Q1

Black must separate his rooks, since 21...K-B2 is met by the unpleasant reply 22 R-N7, threatening N-N5ch.

22 N-R3

Aiming to conquer the important point KN5.

22	...	R-B1
23	R-K1	

If 23 B-N5 B×B 24 N(R3)×B N-K6, Black manages to get his knight to KB4.

23	...	P×P
24	P×P	N-R6
25	R-N3	N-B7
26	R-Q1	

This concludes preparations for B-N5.

26	...	R-QB5
27	B-N5	N-B3
28	R-N7	R-B2
29	R(Q1)-QN1!	R-N5

It becomes clear that the pawn on Q4 is immune: 29...N(B7)×P? 30 N×N N×N 31 B×B N-B4ch 32 K-R2 N×B 33 R×N R×R 34 R-N8ch K-B2

208

35 N-N5 mate. The stubbornest defence was 29...B-B1. After the exchange of bishops Black's position is difficult.

| 30 | B×B | R×R(N2) |
| 31 | R×R | N×B |

32 R-N8ch

A regrettable oversight in time-trouble. He could have won by 32 R-N2! N-B4ch (or 32...N-K6 33 N(R3)-N5) 33 K-R2 N(B7)×P 34 N×N N×N 35 N-N5 R-B4 36 R-N8ch R-B1 37 R-N7. Black should therefore have played 31...R×B (instead of 31...N×B), though even then his position is difficult after 32 R-N2 N-K6 33 N(R3)-N5.

32	...	R-B1
33	R×Rch	K×R
34	N(R3)-N5	N-B4ch
35	K-B4	K-K2
36	N×RP	N×RP
37	P-N4	N-B2
38	N(R7)-N5	N-Q1

39	N-R4	N×P
40	N×NPch	K-K1
41	**Drawn**	

GAME 48

White: Suetin
Black: Uhlmann

Sarajevo 1965

Notes by Suetin

1	P-K4	P-K3
2	P-Q4	P-Q4
3	N-Q2	N-KB3
4	P-K5	KN-Q2
5	P-KB4	P-QB4
6	P-B3	N-QB3
7	QN-B3	Q-N3
8	P-KN3	P×P
9	P×P	B-N5ch
10	K-B2	P-B4
11	K-N2	N(Q2)-N1
12	N-R3!	

12 N-K2 is the usual move here, striving for active play on the K-side: P-KR3, P-KN4, N-KN3 and so on. In this game White choses a different plan: he plays N-KR3-KB2-Q3, aiming at the important squares on the Q-side, where the main strategic battle takes place.

12	...	B-Q2
13	N-B2	N-R3
14	R-QN1	

In line with his plan White prepares P-QN4.

14	...	N-B2
15	N-Q3	

15	...	B-K2

This natural move is an almost imperceptible, but nevertheless serious, mistake. Black should not have been afraid of exchanging his bishop on N5 and should have played 15...P-QR4! in order to frustrate White's intention — a Q-side attack. If 16 N×B P×N!, then Black has active counterplay on the R-file and he exerts pressure on Q5 and QB5.

16	B-K3	N-R4
17	B-B2	B-QN4
18	P-QN4	

Black obviously underestimated this long-prepared move. Now he is in very serious difficulties, for if 18...N-B5 19 P-QR4! B-Q2 20 N-B5 then the threat of 21 B×N P×B 22 N×B K×N 23 P-Q5! immediately decides the game. So the following exchange is really forced.

18	...	B×N
19	B×B	N-B3
20	P-N5!	

Continuing with a determined attack. 20...N-R4 21 Q-R4 O-O 22 B-K1 N-B5 23 B×N P×B 24 B-R5 leads to the loss of Black's queen. The following moves are forced for Black.

20	...	N-N1
21	Q-R4!	

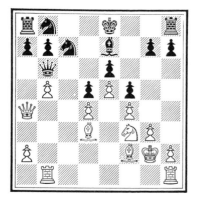

This queen thrust, which threatens the manoeuvre B-K1-R5, places Black in a critical position.

21	...	O-O
22	KR-QB1	

Not immediately 22 B-K1 P-QR4! 23 P×Pe.p. Q-R2 because Black's defence is then quite stable.

22	...	N-K1
23	R-B8	

The only way! Now the threat of B-

K1 is strong again. 23 B-K1 immediately is refuted by 23...Q-Q1.

23	...	N-B2
24	R×Rch	

It is true that the tempting 24 B-K1 R×R 25 B-R5 N-Q2 26 B×Q P×B gives White a queen for a rook and a minor piece, but Black can then build up a firm stronghold.

24	...	K×R
25	B-K1	

At last the leitmotif sounds!

25	...	P-QR4
26	P×Pe.p.	Q-R2

If 26...R×P, 27 Q-B2! Q-B3 28 Q×Q R×Q 29 R×P and White has an easily won ending.

27	Q-N3	

This is the simplest winning line.

27	...	P×P
28	Q-N7!	N-Q2
29	B-R5	N-N4

In order to sharpen up the game a little.

30	Q-B6	K-B2
31	B×P!	

The decisive tactical blow. After 31...P×B 32 P-K6ch K-B1 33 P×N Black is completely destroyed.

31	...	N-B1
32	B-QN6	Q-N1
33	B-Q3	Q-B1
34	R-QB1	Q×Q
35	R×Q	N-R6
36	R-B7	K-K1
37	R×Bch!	

One more blow, and this time, the last one.

37	...	K×R
38	B-QB5ch	Resigns

GAME 49

White: Keres
Black: Dvoretsky

USSR Team Tournament
Moscow 1973

Notes by Dvoretsky and Rosenberg

1	P-K4	P-K3
2	P-Q4	P-Q4
3	N-Q2	N-KB3
4	B-Q3	P-B4
5	P-K5	KN-Q2
6	P-QB3	P-QN3
7	N-K2	B-R3
8	B×B	N×B
9	O-O	N-B2
10	N-KB4!	

Against 10 P-KB4 Black gets a good game by playing 10...P-KB4! Now, though, 10...P-KB4? is bad because of 11 Q-R5ch.

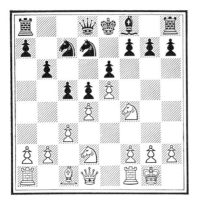

| 10 | ... | B-K2 |
| 11 | R-K1 | |

The line recomended in "64" is not dangerous for Black: after 11 P-B4 P×QP 12 P×P N×KP 13 R-K1 Black has the simple move 13...N-N3. The piece sacrifice 14 P×P N×N 15 P×Pch K-B1 is of dubious value.

11 ...   O-O

In Keres's book on the French Defence which was published in East Germany, this position is assessed as favourable for White.

12 N-B1

This move is given in the book, but 12 Q-N4 and 12 N-B3 deserve attention. These moves make it harder for Black to advance the KBP to B4.

12 ...   Q-B1

The immediate 12...P-B3 is weaker because of 13 KP×P R×P 14

Q-N4.

13 N-N3

Against 13 Q-N4 Black was intending to play 13...P-B4 14 P×Pe.p. N×P 15 Q-R3 B-Q3!, when White achieves nothing by 16 P×P P×P 17 N×KP because of 17...R-K1 18 N×N (18 B-B4? R×N!) 18...R×R 19 N×R Q×N with sufficient compensation for the pawn. 13 Q-B3! is quite interesting (instead of 13 Q-N4) and if 13...P-B4, then 14 P-B4! (less clear is 14 N×KP N×N 15 Q×QP K-B2).

| 13 | ... | P-B4 |
| 14 | P-B4! | |

The same could have followed after 13...P-B3. A continuation leading to roughly level play (after 13...P-B3) is 14 KP×P N×P 15 N-Q3 (15 Q-K2 B-Q3! 16 N×KP R-K1) 15...B-Q3 16 B-B4 B×B 17 N×B Q-Q2 18 N-Q3 Q-Q3.

14 ...   P-KN4

Perhaps the only continuation, as otherwise Black has to give up the square Q4. For example, 14...P×BP? 15 P-Q5 P×P 16 N×QP N×N 17 Q×Nch K-R1 18 P-K6 with a clear advantage. Or 14...P×QP? 15 P×P P×P 16 Q×P B-B4 17 Q-Q3 winning a pawn.

15 N×KP!

Neither 15 N(B4)-R5 P×QP nor 15

N-R3 Q-Q1 16 Q-R5 P-B5 are dangerous for Black, whereas the piece sacrifice sets him a difficult task.

15	...	N×N
16	P×QP	N×QP
17	P-Q6	B-Q1
18	P-K6	B-B3

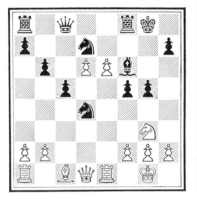

19 N-R5

White has two methods of continuing the attack besides this move:

a) 19 P-K7 R-B2 (if 19...R-K1 then 20 N×P N×N 21 Q-Q5ch K-N2 22 Q×N and Black's pieces are bottled up) 20 P-K8=Qch Q×Q 21 R×Qch R×R. In our opinion Black can hold this position.

b) 19 N×P N×N 20 Q-Q5 K-R1 21 Q×N B-Q5 22 P×N Q-B3! and Black can even win!

19 ... Q-B3!

The alternatives 19...P-N5 20 B-R6, 19...P-KR3 20 P-KR4 and

19...P-KB5 20 Q-N4 are bad, allowing White to strengthen his attack decisively.

At this point the Grandmasters in the press-room thought that Black's position was about to collapse. In particular, 20 P-KR4 was suggested. If then 20...Q×QP 21 P×N Q×P then 22 B×P! B×B 23 P×B and White wins. Keres, however, rejected 20 P-KR4, correctly considering that Black would get dangerous counterplay by means of 20...P×P!, and if 21 B-R6, then 21...P-R6! 22 P-B3 N-K4.

| 20 | P×N | Q×P(Q3) |
| 21 | N×Bch | |

Here, however, 21 P-KR4 deserves careful study. After 21...P-KR3 22 P×P P×P 23 N×Bch Q×N 24 Q-R5 P-KB5 25 R-K8 R-Q1 26 B-Q2 R×P 27 QR-K1 White retains the initiative.

21	...	Q×N
22	B-K3	QR-Q1
23	Q-R4!	Q-Q3
24	B×P	R×P

The position has simplified. Black has returned the extra pawn and warded off the immediate threats. Nevertheless, White could still have tried for an advantage by means of 25 B-B4! Q-QB3 26 Q-B4ch Q-Q4 27 Q×Qch R×Q 28 R-K3. With the next move Keres accepts a transition into an equal four-rook ending.

| 25 | B-K3 | P-KB5 |
| 26 | B×N | Q×B |

27	Q×Q	R×Q
28	R-K2	P-B6
29	P×P	R×P
30	QR-K1	K-N2
31	Drawn	

GAME 50

White: Zinn
Black: Uhlmann

East Germany 1964

1	P-K4	P-K3
2	P-Q4	P-Q4
3	N-Q2	N-KB3
4	P-K5	KN-Q2
5	B-Q3	P-QB4
6	P-QB3	N-QB3
7	N-K2	P×P
8	P×P	Q-N3
9	N-KB3	P-B3
10	P×P	N×BP
11	O-O	B-Q3
12	B-Q2	O-O
13	B-B3	B-Q2

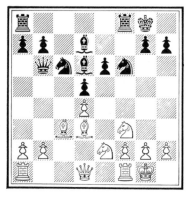

14   Q-Q2?!

Better is 14 N-N3 QR-K1 15 N-K5 R-K2 16 K-R1! B-K1 17 P-B4 K-R1 with roughly equal chances.

| 14 | ... | QR-K1! |
| 15 | QR-K1 | R-K2 |

For 15...N-KN5 see Weinitschke-Trescher, game 51.

| 16 | N-N3 | N-KN5! |
| 17 | P-KR3 | |

After 17 Q-N5 N-R3 18 R-K2 R×N!? 19 P×R N×P 20 B×N Q×B 21 R-Q1 Q-N3 22 Q-K3 B-B4 Black had an excellent game in Westerinen-Uhlmann, Halle 1964.

| 17 | ... | N-R3 |
| 18 | B-N1 | B-B5! |

In the game Hennings-Uhlmann, East Germany 1963, White had a clear advantage after 18...B×N 19 P×B P-K4 20 Q-N5 N-B2? (better 20...P×P) 21 Q-R5 P-K5 22 Q×QP.

19	Q-B2	P-N3
20	N-K2	B-N1!
21	Q-Q2	N-B4
22	N-B1	N-Q3
23	N-R4?	N-B5!
24	Q-R6??	

The quickest way to lose, but even after 24 Q-B2 Black wins by 24...R-B5 25 N-B3 R×N! 26 P×R Q-B2 27 P-B4 Q×P 28 P-B3 N-K6 etc.

| 24 | ... | B-B5 |
| 25 | Resigns | |

GAME 51

White: Weinitschke
Black: Trescher

East German Correspondence
Tournament 1970/74

Notes by Weinitschke

1	P-K4	P-K3
2	P-Q4	P-Q4
3	N-Q2	N-KB3
4	P-K5	KN-Q2
5	B-Q3	P-QB4
6	P-QB3	N-QB3
7	N-K2	Q-N3
8	N-B3	P×P
9	P×P	P-B3
10	P×P	N×BP
11	O-O	B-Q3
12	B-Q2	O-O
13	B-B3	B-Q2
14	Q-Q2	QR-K1
15	QR-K1	N-KN5
16	Q-N5	

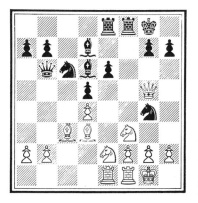

I saw this move for the first time in the game Essegern-Kahn, 1968, with both QR's still on QR1.

16	...	P-K4
17	P×P	R×N!?

This double-edged exchange sacrifice is based upon the exposed position of White's queen. It would of course be safer to capture the KP, but then Black would have an isolated QP, as so often happens in this variation. In the post mortem analysis Black suggested that he should have sacrificed on the previous move, a possibility which is worth a try e.g. 16...R×N 17 P×R N×RP 18 Q-R5 P-N3 19 B×P P×B 20 Q×NPch K-B1 21 K-N2 or White can take a draw by perpetual check.

18 P-K6!

Doubtless the strongest move, threatening mate as well as to win back the piece.

18	...	N(N5)-K4
19	P×B	R(K1)-KB1
20	B×Pch	K×B
21	Q-R5ch	K-N1
22	P×R	

The game now seems over, as White is the exchange and two pawns up and 22...N×BPch 23 K-R1 N×R fails to 24 Q×Pch K-R1(?) 25 Q×B R×P? 26 Q-R6ch!; or here 24...K-R2 25 Q×B R×P 26 R-N1 wins. However, Black finds a resource.

22	...	P-Q5!
23	P-B4	P×B
24	P×N	N×P
25	N×P	N-B6ch
26	Q×N!	

This leads to an ending with an extra pawn, whereas 26 K-R1 is unclear and risky.

26	...	R×Q
27	R-K8ch	R-B1
28	P-Q8=Q	Q×Q
29	R×Q	R×R
30	R-Q1	B-B2
31	R×Rch	B×R
32	K-N2	P-KN4?

This rash pawn move makes White's task easier. Black should centralize his king.

33	K-B3	K-N2
34	K-N4	K-N3
35	N-K4	P-N3
36	P-KR3	B-K2

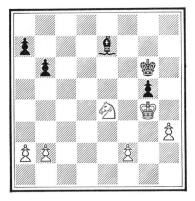

White now has a simple winning

plan. He creates a passed pawn on the K-side then switches his king to the Q-side to attack the QRP and QNP.

37	P-B4	P×P
38	K×P	P-N4
39	K-K5	P-R4
40	K-Q5	P-R5
41	N-B3	B-B3
42	N-Q1	P-N5
43	K-B4	B-K2
44	K-N5	P-R6
45	P-N3	K-B4

White simply threatens to mop up the blockaded pawns, so Black's last chance is to march his king to QN8.

46	N-B2	K-B5
47	N-Q3ch	K-K6
48	N×P	K-Q7
49	N-Q5	B-Q3
50	N-N6	K-B7
51	N-B4	B-K2
52	K-R4	K-N8
53	N×Pch	K×P
54	N-B4	K-N8

There are some endings in which the bishop can draw against knight and two pawns, but this is impossible here, as the pawns are too far apart.

55	N-K3	K-B8
56	P-N4	K-Q7
57	N-N2!	Resigns

If the black king attacks the knight, White can allow it to be captured, as the bishop cannot stop both the pawns.

GAME 52

White: Georgadze
Black: Doroshkevich

Georgia-RSFSR Match, Tbilisi 1971

1	P-K4	P-K3
2	P-Q4	P-Q4
3	N-Q2	N-KB3
4	P-K5	KN-Q2
5	B-Q3	P-QB4
6	P-QB3	N-QB3
7	N-K2	P×P
8	P×P	Q-N3
9	N-KB3	P-B3
10	P×P	N×BP
11	O-O	B-Q3
12	N-B4	O-O
13	R-K1	B-Q2!
14	N×KP	KR-K1

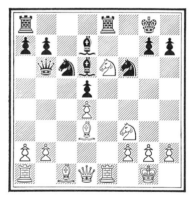

15   B-B5

Not 15 N-B5 N×P 16 N×B N(Q5)×Nch 17 P×N N×N 18 B-B5 N-B3 19 B-N5 B×Pch 20 K-N2 B-K4 and Black stands better.

15 ...   B-N5!

Probably the best reply, though 15...N-QR4 also seems playable. 16 B-N5 B×N 17 B×Bch (or 17 R×B B×Pch 18 N×B R×R 19 B×Rch Q×B 20 B×N Q×B Drawn. Gligoric-Schmid, Dublin 1957) 17...R×B 18 R×R P×Pch 19 K×B Q×R 20 B×N Q×B 21 Q-K2 N-B3 22 R-K1 R-KB1 with equal chances.

If Black plays less actively, however, he runs into trouble, e.g.:
1) 15...N-K2!? 16 B-R3 N-N3 17 N(K6)-N5 N-N5 18 B-K3!? Q×NP 19 Q-Q3 Q-R6! 20 Q-N1 Q-N5 21 N-K5 Q×Q 22 QR×Q N(N3)×N 23 P×N B×P with even chances. White can, however, play better with 18 B×N B×B 19 R×Rch R×R 20 P-KR3! B-KB4 21 N-K5! with some advantage.

2) 15...R-K2? 16 B-N5! QR-K1 17 N×P! K×N (if 17...R×Rch 18 N×R K×N 19 B×Nch K×B 20 B×B; or 17...R×N 18 B×B R×Rch 19 Q×R N×B 20 Q-K6ch K-R1 21 B-R6! [not 21 Q×B N×P] 21...R-N3 22 Q×N R×B 23 R-K1 N-K2 [23...R-B3 24 R-K8ch B-B1 25 N-N5 wins] 24 R×N B×R 25 Q-K8ch K-N2 26 Q×Bch with a clear plus to White. Karker-Jarkovsky, 1956) 18 B×Nch K×B 19 B×B R×Rch 20 N×R winning.

16   R-K2

It is not clear which move is best in this position. If 16 R-K3 N-QR4 17 P-QR3 B-KB1 18 B-Q2 (in the game Ciric-Jovcic, Black had a won game

217

after 18 Q-K1 N-N6 19 R-N1 QR-B1 20 N(B3)-N5 R×B 21 R×R N×R 22 Q×N P-KR3 23 B-N6 P×N 24 B×R B×N) 18...N-B5 19 R-N3 Q-B3? 20 N-K5! N×N 21 P×N and White is better. Thurner-Vosta, 1966. But Black could equalize with 19...B-R5 20 R×Q B×Q 21 R×B P×R 22 N-B7 N×P. Another improvement is possibly 16 R-K3 N-Q1.

Probably stronger than the text, however, is 16 B-Q2! B×B 17 Q×B N-K2! (a move first played by Heemsoth. The obvious 17...N-K5 fails to the pretty combination 18 B×N P×B 19 N(K6)-N5!! P×N 20 Q-Q3! P-N3 21 Q-B4ch K-N2 22 Q-B7ch K-R3 23 P-KR4 winning) 18 N×P! (the best chance, as 18 B-R3 fails to 18...N-K5, and Black has the advantage after 18 P-KN4 N×B 19 P×N N-K5 20 Q-K3 B×N 21 P×B R×P. Riedmuller-Heemsoth, Correspondence game 1957) 18...K×N 19 Q-N5ch N-N3 20 B×B (not 20 B×N?! P×B 21 N-K5 B-B4 22 P-KN4 B-K5 23 QR-Q1 N-R2 with advantage to Black) 20...N×B 21 P-KR4! P-KR3 22 Q×QP N-B3 (or 22...Q-QB3) 23 Q-KB5 and White is no worse in view of his three pawns for the piece and Black's weakened K-side.

| 16 | ... | N-Q1! |
| 17 | P-QR3 | B-Q3?! |

Black could obtain the advantage

with 17...B×N!? 18 B×Bch N×B 19 P×B Q×NP, or he can play for equality with 17...B-B1 18 N×B B×B 19 R×R N×R 20 N-R4 Q-KB3 21 Q-R5 P-KN3 22 Q×RPch K×N 23 B-R6ch N-N2 24 P-KN4 B-K5 25 P-N5 Q×QP 26 N×Pch B×N 27 Q×B.

| 18 | N(B3)-N5 | P-KR3 |
| 19 | N×N | R×R |

Not 19...B×B? 20 R×Rch N×R 21 Q-B3 winning.

20	B×B	R-K2
21	B-K6ch	K-B1
22	B-R3!	

Not 22 N(Q8)-B7 P×N 23 N×P B-B2!

22	...	R×N
23	N-K6ch	R×N
24	B×R	B×KRPch
25	K×B	Q×B
26	B-B4	Q-B4
27	Q-B3	K-B2

Weaker is 27...N-K5 28 B×P!

28	R-QB1	R-QB1
29	R×R	Q×R
30	B-K5	Q-N5
31	Q-QN3	Q-Q2
32	Q-KB3	Q-N5
33	Q-QN3	Q-Q2
34	Q-KB3	**Drawn**

Chapter 10

The Tarrasch Variation
with 3...N-QB3

White: Estevez
Black: Hubner

Leningrad Interzonal 1973

1	P-K4	P-K3
2	P-Q4	P-Q4
3	N-Q2	N-QB3

A move which at first sight seems anti-positional, as the knight blocks the QBP which constitutes Black's main offensive weapon in the French. The idea of the text-move is to attack the centre by a later ...P-KB3, then aim for ...P-K4, but as White can neutralize this manoeuvre, this method of defence has lost its popularity.

4 KN-B3   N-B3

Black deliberately provokes White's advance, hoping that White's KP has insufficient pawn support. Black plans to free his game by undermining White's centre, but the idea takes time and Black must also sacrifice some space so the plan can never be quite successful.

5 P-K5   N-Q2

Not 5...N-K5 when White has a good game after both 6 B-Q3 and 6 P-B3. See Vaganian-Murei, Moscow 1972/3 (illustrative game 53).

6 N-N3!

The best method of refuting Black's set-up.

Black's main difficulties lie in the cramped nature of his position and in his passive QB. White's natural text-move will help to complete his development and strengthens his control over certain central squares. Other attempts are:

(a) **6 P-KN3 B-K2 7 B-R3** Possible is 7 P-KR4!? **7...P-KR4 8 B-N2** If 8 O-O?! P-KN4! **8...P-R5 9 O-O** with equal chances.

(b) **6 P-QN3 P-B3 7 B-N2 B-K2 8 P-QR3 O-O 9 B-N5 P-QR3 10 B×N P×B 11 P×P B×BP 12 O-O P-B4 13 R-K1 Q-K2** with an even game. Mednis-R. Byrne USA 1964.

(c) **6 P-B4 P×P 7 N×P N-N3 8 N×N RP×N 9 B-Q3 N-N5 10 B-K4 B-Q2 11 B×NP R×P** with equality.

(d) **6 B-N5 P-QR4** Or 6...P-QR3 7 B×N P×B 8 N-N3 P-QB4 9 B-N5 B-K2 10 N-R5 N-N1 11 B×B Q×B 12 P-B3 O-O 13 O-O B-Q2 14 Q-Q2 and White stands a little better. Kuprejanov-Marovic, Belgrade 1964. **7 O-O N-R2 8 B-Q3 P-QB4 9 P-B3 P-B5 10 B-B2 P-QN4** with unclear play.

(e) **6 B-K2 P-B3 7 P×P Q×P** Or 7...N×BP 8 O-O B-Q3 9 P-B4 O-O 10 R-K1 B-Q2 11 P-B5 B-B5 12 N-B1 N-K5 13 B-N5 P-K4 with unclear complications. Liberzon-Gusev, 1957. **8 N-B1 B-Q3** For 8...P-K4 see Makarichev-Vaganian, Tbilisi 1973 — illustrative game 54. **9 N-K3 O-O 10 O-O Q-N3 11 P-B4 N-B3 12 P-KN3** with a slight plus for White.

(f) **6 P-B3 P-B3!** The key move in all lines. If White now tries for tactical complications they only favour Black: e.g. 7 N-R4 Q-K2 8 B-Q3 P×P 9 Q-R5ch Q-B2 10 B-N6 P×B 11 Q×R P-K5 12 N-N3 N-B3 13 P-B3 B-Q2; or 7 B-Q3 P×P 8

220

N×P N(Q2)×N 9 P×N N×P 10 Q-R5ch N-B2 11 B×P, with the better chances for Black in both cases. **7 B-N5 P×P** 7...P-QR3! **8 P×P P-QR3 9 B×N P×B 10 0-0 P-B4** and Black stands well.

6	**...**	**B-K2**

It seems that the only way to justify 3...N-QB3 is to attack the centre at once with **6...P-B3 7 B-QN5 B-K2** Not 7...P×P 8 P×P N-B4 9 N-N5 B-Q2? 10 B×N P×B 11 Q-R5ch P-N3 12 Q-B3 Resigns. Tal-Vaganian, Dubna 1973. **8 B-KB4** Best seems 8 P×P B×P 9 0-0 0-0 10 R-K1 with lasting pressure on the weak KP. **8...0-0 9 P×P P×P 10 0-0 N-N3** 10...P-QR3 is an improvement, but White stands better after 11 B×N P×B 12 R-K1 N-N3 13 N-R5. **11 R-K1 B-Q3 12 B-N3 P-QR3 13 B-Q3 N-R5 14 R-N1** with positional pressure. Botvinnik-Boleslavsky, USSR 1944.

7 B-QN5

Or 7 P-B3 0-0 8 B-Q3 P-B3 9 Q-K2 Q-K1 10 0-0 P×P 11 P×P Q-R4 12 R-K1 N-B4 13 N×N B×N, and now both 14 B-K3 and 14 P-QN4 give White some positional advantage.

7	**...**	**P-QR3**

The two other possibilities are 7...0-0 8 0-0 N-N3 9 R-K1 B-Q2 10 B-Q3 N-N5 11 B-B1 N-R5 12 P-B3 N-R3 13 N-R5! with advantage to White; and 7...N(B3)-N1 8 0-0 0-0 9 B-KB4 P-QN3 10 R-B1 B-R3 11 B×B N×B 12 Q-K2 N(R3)-N1 13 P-B4 when White is better developed and has a space advantage.

8	B×N	P×B
9	N-R5	N-N1

Better is 9...B-N5ch 10 B-Q2 B×N 11 B×B P-QB4.

10	O-O	P-QB4
11	P-B4!	

This opening up of the centre is the correct way to exploit White's lead in development.

11	...	O-O

After 11...P×BP 12 B-K3 P×P 13 N×QP Black stands badly.

12	P×BP

White also has some advantage after 12 B-K3 P×QP 13 N×P B-Q2 14 P-B5! Minic-Espig, Berlin 1968.

12	...	B×P
13	B-N5!	Q-Q2

If 13...B-K2 14 B×B Q×B 15 P×P R-Q1 16 R-B1 R×P 17 Q-K1, or the dubious 13...P-KB3 14 P×BP NP×P 15 B-R6 R-B2 16 P×P when Black's pawn position is ruined.

14	N-N3	B-R2
15	R-B1!	B-N2?

After this move the loss is inevitable. It was essential to play 15...P×P although White still stands better.

16	P-B5!	P-KB3
17	B-B4!	N-B3
18	R-K1	QR-K1
19	N(N3)-Q4	N-Q1
20	P-QN4	P-B3
21	P-QR4	B-N1
22	B-N3	P-R3
23	P-R4!	

Preventing any expansion by ...P-B4 and ...P-N4.

23	...	Q-KB2
24	Q-Q2	Q-R4
25	P-N5!	

Increasing his advantage.

25	...	R-B2
26	R-N1	B-B2
27	Q-Q3	RP×P
28	P×NP	P×NP
29	Q×P	R(K1)-B1
30	P-B6	B-B1
31	R-R1!	P×P
32	B×P	B×B
33	R×B	Q-N3
34	R-R8	R-B2
35	Q-N6	Q-B2
36	R-K2!	

There is now no defence to 37 N-K5 etc.

36	...	Q-B5
37	P-N3!	R×P

White wins a piece after 37...Q-B8ch 38 R-K1 R×P 39 R×Q.

38	Q×R	Q×N(B6)
39	Q×B	Q-Q6
40	Q-B5	Resigns

GAME 53

White: Vaganian
Black: Murei

Training tournament, Moscow
1972/73

Notes by Murei

1	P-Q4	P-K3
2	P-K4	P-Q4
3	N-Q2	N-QB3
4	KN-B3	N-B3
5	P-K5	N-K5!?

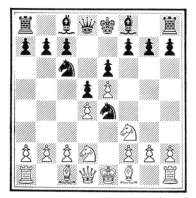

5...N-Q2 is the usual move. The point of Black's move is to exchange off his knight, and thereby reduce the conglomeration of pieces which can be so unpleasant for Black in view of his opponent's advantage in space.

6 B-Q3

6 P-B3 is more effective. It would have constrained the black knight on B3, which stands in the way of the QBP. Shamkovich-Lein, USSR 1965, went as follows: 6...N×N 7 B×N P-B3 8 B-QN5 B-Q2 9 Q-K2 Q-K2 10 P×P P×P 11 B-KB4 O-O-O 12 O-O R-K1 13 P-B4 with advantage to White. In return for the weakness of K4 and of his pawn on K3 Black has quite good play for his pieces.

6	...	N×N
7	B×N	N-N5!

Now White has either to allow the exchange of one of his bishops or waste time in retreating the bishop on Q3, and consequently allow ...P-QB4.

8	B×N	B×Bch
9	P-B3	B-K2
10	P-KR4!	

White keeps an advantage in space and also brings his rook into play to attack on the K-side. 10 P-QN4 P-QB3 11 P-QR4 P-QR4 12 Q-N3 P×P 13 P×P Q-N3 14 R-QN1 Q-R2 is weaker.

10	...	B-Q2
11	R-R3	P-QB4
12	P×P	

A debatable solution. White did not want to allow the Q-side to be closed by ...P-B5. It is also possible that he was not satisfied with his prospects after ...P×P.

12	...	Q-B2

Black is preparing to castle Q-side. 12...B×QBP is dangerous, because of 13 N-N5.

13 Q-K2

Now 13 N-N5 is not possible because of 13...B×N 14 P×B Q×KPch and 15...Q×NP. 13 P-QN4 P-QN3 14 P×P Q×BPch 15 K-B1 P×P is to Black's advantage.

13	...	B×BP
14	R-N3	

14 N-N5 P-KR3 15 N×BP K×N 16 Q-R5ch K-K2 17 R-B3 QR-KB1 gives White nothing.

14	...	P-KN3
15	P-R5	O-O-O
16	O-O-O	

After 16 N-N5 I was going to play 16...B-K1 threatening to counter-attack by means of 17...P-KR3 and ...P-KN4

16 ... QR-B1

After the game Vaganian said that he expected 16...P-Q5 and that he was going to play 17 P×QP B×Pch 18 K-N1. I rejected 16...P-Q5 because of 17 P-B4!

17 K-N1

Essential prophylaxis. Furthermore White intends to make use of the QB-file.

17 ... P-B3

It is essential to hurry because 18 N-Q4 and then P-KB4 is threatened. 18 N-Q4 would come even after 17...Q-N3. For example, 18...B×N 19 P×B Q×Q^p 20 B×P.

18 P×NP P×NP

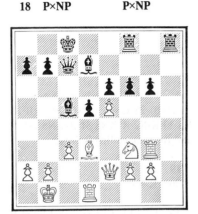

19 R×P?

This gives up the advantage. White achieves little by 19 P×P R×P 20 R×P R×R 21 B×R because of 21...R-N1 22 N-K5 B-Q3 23 N×B R×B 24 Q-R5 R×P 25 N-B6 Q-K2 26 Q-R8ch Q-Q1 27 Q×Qch K×Q 28 R-K1 K-K2 29 N×Pch K-B2 and then 30...R×P.

But White had a stronger continuation in 19 R-KB1! I was going to answer this move by 19...P×P 20 N×P R×P 21 R×R B×R 22 R×P (22 R-B3 R-R8ch 23 K-B2 B-B4 24 R-B7 B-R5ch 25 P-QN3 Q-R4! or 25 K-Q2 Q-N3) 22...B-QR5. However, when we looked at this variation after the

game Vaganian showed me the move
23 K-R1!, after which the difference
in material and the unsafe position of
the black king make themselves felt.
For example, 23...B-Q5 24 N-B3 (24
P×B Q-B8ch 25 B-N1 Q×Bch 26 K×Q
R-R8ch) 24...B×P 25 Q×Pch B-Q2
(or 25...Q-Q2) 26 R-N8ch, and
White wins. While writing this com-
mentary I found the intermediate
move 22...B-K1. Now 23 R×P is met
by 23...R-R8ch 24 K-B2 B-QR5ch 25
P-QN3 B-Q5 26 B-B4! (26 P-B4 Q-
R4 27 Q-Q2 B×Pch!) 26...B×N 27
P×B Q×B (27...P×B 28 R-K8ch K-Q2
29 R×B) 28 Q×Qch P×Q 29 R×B R-
R8 30 K-N2 R-KN8 31 R-KN5 P-R4!
and the rook ending is drawn.

| 19 | ... | P×P |
| 20 | R-N7 | |

He should have reconciled himself
to a draw: 20 Q×P Q×Q 21 N×Q R×P
22 N×B K×N 23 B-N5ch K-K2 24 R-
K1 R-B3 25 R-N7ch R-B2.

20	...	P-K5!
21	B×P	R(R1)-N1
22	R×R	R×R
23	B-Q3	R×P
24	R-R1	Q-B5
25	R-R8ch	K-B2
26	R-R7	

If 26 Q-K5ch then 26...B-Q3! re-
taining an advantage.

| 26 | ... | K-Q3 |

Here White could achieve the

draw: 27 Q-K5ch Q×Q 28 N×Q B-K1
29 N-B7ch. However, I was already
short of time, and Vaganian decided
to take advantage of the fact.

| 27 | P-N4 | B-N3 |
| 28 | P-B4 | P×P |

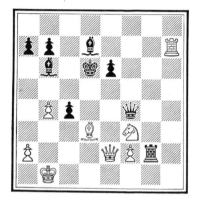

| 29 | B-K4 | |

White overlooks an effective reply.
Against 29 B×P, 29...Q-B4ch 30 B-
Q3 B-N4! wins. After the game I
could not decide whether the dia-
grammed position was won for
Black. Analysis showed, however,
that White could draw by playing 29
Q-Q1! Here are the key variations:

a) 29...P×B 30 Q×Pch B-Q5 31
N×B R-N8ch 32 K-N2 Q-B8ch 33 K-
N3 Q-Q8(N8)ch 34 Q×Q R×Q 35 K-
B3;

b) 29...B-B3 30 B-B5ch! B-Q4 31
R-Q7ch! K×R 32 Q×Bch K-B2 33
Q×KP B×P 34 Q-K7ch K-N3 35 Q-
B6ch K-B2 (35...K-N4 36 B-Q7ch);

c) 29...K-B2 30 R×Bch K×R 31
B-B1ch;

226

d) 29...B-B3 30 B-B1ch B-Q4 31 B×R Q-B4ch 32 Q-B2 B-K5 33 R-Q7ch! K×R 34 N-K5ch Q×N 35 Q×B. Or 32...Q×Qch 33 K×Q B-K5ch 34 K-B3 B×R 35 N-Q4 K-K4 36 N-B3ch K-B5 37 N-Q4 P-K4 38 N-K2ch. Nor does 35...B×Nch 36 K×B P-N4 37 P-B4 change matters.

| 29 | ... | B-Q5! |

A tactical device based on decoy and double protection. White was counting on 29...P-K4 30 R×Bch K×R 31 N×Pch Q×N 32 B-B6ch K-Q3 33 Q×Qch K×Q 34 B×R with a draw.

30	R-R4	Q×R!
31	N×Q	R-N8ch
32	K-B2	B-R5ch
33	K-Q2	P-B6ch
34	K-Q3	B-N4ch
35	K×B	B×Q
36	K×P	R-N5
37	B-B3	R×N
38	B×B	R-R7
39	B-Q1	R×P

Here the curtain can be drawn: **White resigned** a few moves later.

GAME 54

White: Makarichev
Black: Vaganian

41st USSR Championship
(First league)
Tbilisi 1973

1	P-K4	P-K3
2	P-Q4	P-Q4
3	N-Q2	N-QB3
4	KN-B3	N-B3
5	P-K5	N-Q2
6	B-K2	P-B3
7	P×P	Q×P
8	N-B1	P-K4!

Courageous and well timed. After 8...B-Q3 9 N-K3 O-O 10 O-O Black would have to put up with the sad fact of a backward pawn on K3 (...P-K4 becomes impossible because of the weakness of Q4).

9 P×P

An important moment. The logical 9 N-K3 is considered to be stronger. In that case 9...P×P 10 N×P(Q5) Q-Q3 11 B-QB4 N(Q2)-K4 (or 11...N-N3 12 Q-K2ch and 13 B-B4) 12 N×N Q×N(K4)ch 13 K-B1! leads to White's advantage. Korchmar-Khudoshin, Saratov, 1948.

Or 9...P-K5 10 N×P Q-Q3 (if 10...B-N5ch 11 P-B3! Q-Q3 12 N×B P×N 13 B×P N×N 14 P×N and Black loses a pawn) 11 P-B4. With this move White supports the centralized knight, intending after 11...P×N 12 B-B4 to make his opponent pay heavily for the piece. In the well-known twenty-five-year-old game Korchmar-Aratovsky, Saratov, 1948, 12...P×B (the combination 12...P×P 13 R-KN1 Q×B is refuted by the intermediate move 14 B-R5ch) 13 Q×Pch N(Q2)-K4 14 P×N Q-Q1 15 O-O-O gave White a decisive attack.

This variation is not entirely clear, however; instead of 14...Q-Q1 one might try, for example, 14...Q-N3 15 O-O-O N-N5! 16 N×Pch K-B2 with abundant complications.

| 9 | ... | N(Q2)×P |
| 10 | Q×P? | |

A risky business. Correct is 10 N-K3 N×Nch 11 B×N P-Q5 12 N-Q5.

10	...	B-K3
11	Q-N5	P-QR3
12	Q-R4	

Not 12 Q×NP because of 12...R-R2.

| 12 | ... | O-O-O |
| 13 | N×N | |

After 13 N-K3 there follows 13...B-QN5ch 14 P-B3 B×BPch 15 P×B N×Nch. It becomes apparent that White has been too ambitious in taking the central pawn. He has difficulties with his development and Black's attacking prospects are starting to be felt.

13	...	Q×N
14	P-QB3	B-QN5!
15	P×B	B-B5

Is this effective? It is, but "Man has already trodden here". In the game A. Petrosian-Panchenko, Odessa, 1973, White tried to save himself by 16 N-N3 but lost after 16...B-N4! 17 Q-R3 R-Q6 18 B-B4 Q-K3 19 P-N3 R×N 20 O-O R×KNPch! 21 K×R B×B. The present attempt is not succesful either.

16	N-K3	B×B
17	K×B	N-Q5ch
18	K-K1	

After 18 K-B1 KR-B1 there is no satisfactory way of defending KB2.

| 18 | ... | KR-K1 |

Now 19...Q-K5 is threatened with a two-fold attack on KN7 and QB7.

19	B-Q2	Q-K5
20	K-Q1	Q-Q6
21	R-K1	N-N6
22	R-K2	N×R
23	K-K1	R×N
24	P×R	N-B7ch
25	K-Q1	N×KPch
26	K-K1	Q-N8ch
27	K-B2	N-N5ch
28	Resigns	

Chapter 11

/- 9/4/81

The Tarrasch Variation
with 3...P-QB4

White: Karpov
Black: Korchnoy

8th Match Game 1974

1	P-K4	P-K3
2	P-Q4	P-Q4
3	N-Q2	P-QB4

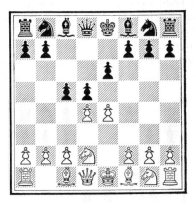

An immediate attempt to release the tension in the centre. In practice this line is the most popular, allowing Black free play for his pieces. The main disadvantage lies in the isolated QP which often becomes a fixed weakness.

4   P×QP

The most popular continuation by far, leading quickly to positions in which Black's QP is isolated. Black has no difficulties after 4 P×BP B×P 5 N-N3 (Or 5 B-Q3 N-KB3 6 P-K5 KN-Q2 7 KN-B3 N-QB3 8 Q-K2 Q-B2 9 N-N3 B-N3 10 B-KB4 P-B3 with advantage) 5...B-N3 6 P×P P×P 7 N-B3 N-QB3 8 B-QN5 N-K2 9 O-O O-O 10 KN-Q4 P-QR3 11 B-K2 N-K4 with an even game. Haag-Korchnoy, Gyula 1965. The main alternative is **4 KN-B3** which aims at preserving the central tension for as long as possible. **4...N-QB3** Also played is 4...N-KB3 when 5 P×QP gives White some positional advantage (but not necessarily 5 P-K5 KN-Q2 6 P-B4 [after 6 P-B3 N-QB3 7 B-Q3 Q-N3 White can try the promising pawn sacrifice we mention on page 193] 6...P×BP [6...N-QB3 seems more accurate] 7 N×P P×P 8 Q×P with some space advantage for White) e.g. 5...N×P 6 N-N3 P×P 7 QN×P B-K2 8 B-Q3 (also strong is 8 P-KN3 O-O 9 B-N2 B-B3 [or 9...B-Q2 10 O-O N-QB3 11 N×N B×N 12 N-K5 Q-B2 13 N×B Q×N 14 Q-K2 P-QN4 15 B-K3 B-B3 16 QR-Q1 with a small plus to White. Jansa-Korchnoy, Nice Olympiad 1974] 10 O-O N-B3 11 P-B3 Q-N3 12 N-N3 with the better game for White. Keres-Stahlberg, Budapest 1952) 8...B-B3 9 O-O O-O 10 P-B4 N-N5 11 B-K4 Q-K2 12 Q-K2 N(N1)-B3 13 B-K3 B-Q2 14 KR-Q1 N×N 15 Drawn. Torre-Korchnoy, Nice Olympiad 1974.

There is another possibility in 4...P-QR3, preventing a later B-QN5, but the loss of time has its dangers: e.g. 5 P×BP! (5 P×QP is also possible, but not 5 B-Q3 P-B5) 5...B×P 6 B-Q3 N-QB3 7 O-O (or 7 P-QR3 KN-K2 [not 7...N-B3 8 O-O Q-B2 9 P-QN4 B-K2 10 Q-K2 O-O 11 P-B4 with advantage to White. Ciric-Marovic, Yugoslavia 1969] 8 O-O O-O 9 P-QN4 B-R2 10 B-N2 N-N3 11 N-N3 with a positional plus for White. Matanovic-Kupper, Opatija 1953) 7...KN-K2 8 N-N3 B-Q3 9 Q-K2 Q-B2 10 B-KN5! P×P 11 B×KP P-B3 12 B-K3 P-K4 13 QR-Q1 B-KB4 14 N-B5 B×N 15 B(K3)×B B×B 16 Q×B O-O 17 B-Q6 Q-B1 18 N-Q2 with advantage to White. Parma-Uhlmann, Sarajevo 1968. **5 B-N5** This move leads to sharp positions. (Instead White can reach the main line with 5 P×QP.)

In this position Black must decide how he intends to deal with the tension in the centre.

5...P×KP This is just one way to solve the problem — destroy White's pawn centre. Five other moves deserve consideration:

(1) 5...B-Q3 6 P-K5 B-N1 7 P×P N-K2 8 O-O O-O 9 R-K1 N-N3 10 B×N P×B 11 P-QN4 (it seems safer to play 11 P-QN3 Q-R4 12 B-N2 Q×BP 13 P-B4 P-B3 14 R-QB1 Q-K2 15 P×BP NP×P 16 N-B1 N-B5 with an unclear position. Gufeld-F. Portisch, Tbilisi 1971. 11 N-N3 seems risky, as Black obtains a mobile pawn centre after 11...P-B3) 11...P-B3 (or 11...P-QR4 12 P×P R×P and Black has good play for the pawn in view of White's weak Q-side pawns and the possibility of the break ...P-B3) 12 B-N2 P×P 13 N×P N×N 14 B×N B×B 15 R×B Q-R5 16 P-QB3 with a possible plus to White (Westerinen-F. Portisch, Vilnus 1969) although Black should hold the balance by 16...Q×BPch 17 K-R1 P-QR4! 18 P-QR3 P×P 19 BP×P Q-Q5 20 Q-K1 Q-N7 21 R-K3 P-K4!

(2) 5...P-QR3 6 P×QP (in Suetin-Petrosian, Moscow 1967, Black equalized after 6 B×Nch P×B 7 O-O P×QP 8 N×P P-QB4 9 N-B6 Q-B2 10 P×P P×P 11 R-K1ch B-K3 12 N-K5 B-Q3 13 N(Q2)-B3 N-K2 14 P-B4 O-O 15 P×P N×P) 6...P×B 7 P×N P×BP 8 P×P B×P 9 O-O N-B3 10 N-N3 (after 10 Q-K2 B-K2 11 R-Q1 Q-N3 12 P-B4 O-O Black had no difficulties in Radulov-R. Byrne, Leningrad Interzonal 1973) 10...Q×Q 11 R×Q B-K2 (or 11...B-N3 12 B-K3!) 12 N-K5 B-N2 13 B-K3 N-Q4 14 B-B5 with a positional advantage to White. Tseitlin-Steinberg, USSR 1971.

(3) 5...N-B3 6 P×QP Q×P (6...KP×P is not to be recommended e.g. 7 O-O B-K2 [not 7...P-B5 8 P-QN3 P×P 9 N-K5 with advantage; nor 7...B-K3 8 R-K1 B-Q3 9 P×P B×BP 10 N-N3 and White is better. Euwe-Broadbent, London 1948] 8 P×P O-O [if 8...B×P 9 R-K1ch B-K2 10 Q-K2 with advantage] 9 N-N3 N-K5 10 B-K3 B-N5 11 B×N P×B 12 P-B3 R-K1 13 Q-Q4 and White retains his extra pawn. Pachman-Opocensky, Brno 1944) 7 P-B4 Q-Q1 8 O-O P×P 9 N-N3 and White has more space. If instead of 9 N-N3 White plays 9 N-K5 B-Q2 10 N×B Q×N 11 N-B3, Black equalizes by 11...R-Q1 12 N-K5 Q-B2 13 B-KB4 B-Q3 14 Q×P O-O. Westerinen-Andersson, Berlin 1971.

(4) 5...Q-N3 (a move without much practical testing) 6 Q-K2 P×KP 7 N×P P×P 8 O-O B-Q2 9 B-KB4 P-QR3 10 B-R4 N-B3!? with chances for both sides.

(5) 5...P×QP 6 N×P B-Q2 7 N×N P×N (after 7...B×N 8 B×Bch P×B 9 P-QB4! P-Q5 10 O-O P-QB4 11 P-B4 White has the better prospects) 8 B-Q3 Q-B2 9 Q-K2 N-K2 10 N-B3 N-N3 11 P-K5 R-QN1 12 O-O B-K2 13 R-K1 P-QB4 14 P-B4

O-O with equal chances. Tal-Korchnoy, Moscow 1971.

6 N×P B-Q2 7 B-N5! "First and foremost development. The open nature of the position makes every tempo prescious." — Tal. The text was played by Tal against Uhlmann in a sensational game at Moscow 1971. A few rounds later Stein played 7 B-K3 against Uhlmann but was unable to achieve anything in the opening (see illustrative game 55). **7...Q-R4ch** On 7...Q-N3 Tal was planning 8 Q-K2 P×P 9 O-O-O. **8 N-B3 P×P** In view of the threat of P-Q5, Tal thought this exchange to be practically forced. **9 N×P B-N5?** Correct is 9...B-K2 10 Q-Q2 (or 10 B-K3 Q-B2 with equality) 10...N-B3 (not, of course, 10...B×B 11 Q×B N×N 12 B×Bch) 11 O-O-O with chances for both sides in the lively struggle ahead. **10 O-O B×N 11 P×B Q×BP?** Better is 11...P-QR3 though after 12 B×B B×B 13 N×B Q×B 14 Q-Q6 N-K2 15 KR-Q1! N×N 16 Q-Q7ch K-B1 17 Q×NP White still has the advantage. **12 N-B5! P×N 13 R-K1ch B-K3 14 Q-Q6** Now White threatens to transfer his bishop to the QR3-KB8 diagonal. There is also the possibility of 15 QR-Q1. **14...P-QR3 15 B-Q2 Q×P 16 B-N4 P×B 17 Q-B8ch K-Q2 18 KR-Q1ch K-B2 19 Q×R Resigns** Since 19...N-B3 20 Q×R N-K5 is met by 21 B-K1. Tal-Uhlmann, Moscow 1971.

Let us now return to the main line, **4 P×QP**

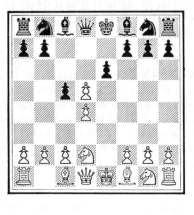

| **4** | **...** | **KP×P** |

Black can avoid the problems of the isolated QP with **4...Q×P,** but that move gives White an important tempo and it still leaves Black's QB as a problem child: **5 KN-B3** More exact than 5 P×P B×P 6 KN-B3 N-KB3 7 B-B4 Q-Q1 8 O-O O-O 9 Q-K2 N-B3 10 P-B3 Q-B2 11 N-K4 B-K2 12 B-KN5 N-Q4 with equality. Pirc-Eliskases, Noordwijk 1938, although White could have tried 10 N-N3 and 11 B-KB4. **5...P×P** If 5...N-KB3 6 B-B4 e.g.6...Q-B3 7 P-QR4 Q-B2 8 O-O P×P 9 N×P B-Q2 10 Q-K2 N-B3 11 N(Q2)-B3 P-QR3 12 P-R3 N×N 13 N×N B-K2 14 P-QN3 with some positional advantage. Andersson-Petrosian, Wijk aan Zee 1971; or 6...Q-Q3 7 O-O N-B3 8 N-N3 P×P 9 N(N3)×P P-QR3 10 N×N Q×N 11 N-K5 Q-B4 (if 11...Q-B2 12 B-B4 B-Q3 13 Q-K2 followed by 14 QR-Q1) 12 Q-K2 B-K2 13 P-QR4! O-O 14 R-R3 with advantage to White. Jansa-Augustin, Czechoslovakia 1974. **6 B-B4**

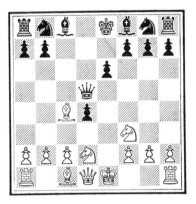

6...Q-Q1 The alternative is 6...Q-Q3 7 O-O N-KB3 (after 7...N-QB3 8 N-K4 Q-Q1 9 B-B4 N-B3 10 Q-K2 B-K2 11 QR-Q1 the position is unclear; or 8 R-K1 P-QR3? [8...N-B3] 9 P-QR4 Q-B2 10 N-K4 B-Q2 11 N×P B-K2 12 N-KB5! with a clear advantage to White. Ofstad-Uhlmann, Halle 1963. Again the most solid continuation is 8 N-N3 N-B3 transposing to the main line, since 8...P-K4 9 N-N5 N-R3 10 P-B4! gives White a strong attack) 8 N-N3 N-B3 and:

(1) 9 R-K1 P-QR3 (if 9...B-Q2 10 N(N3)×P P-QR3 11 B-KN5 Q-B4 12 B-N3 O-O-O 13 P-B3 with advantage to White. Liebert-Uhlmann, East Germany 1963) 10 P-QR4 B-K2 11 N(B3)×P N×N 12 Q×N B-Q2 13 B-B4 Q×Q 14 N×Q R-QB1 15 B-QN3 and White has the better ending. Averbach-Stahlberg, Zürich 1953.

(2) 9 N(N3)×P The simplest way of obtaining a slight positional plus. 9...N×N 10 N×N (even the ending after 10 Q×N Q×Q 11 N×Q is not easy for Black e.g. 11...P-QR3 12 B-B4 B-K2 [12...B-B4 13 N-N3 B-K2 14 B-K2! and Black has difficulties on the Q-side] 13 KR-K1 with pressure) 10...P-QR3 (or 10...B-K2 11 P-QN3 O-O 12 B-N2 P-K4 13 N-N5 Q×Q 14 KR×Q B-KB4 15 QR-B1 with an endgame advantage for White. Tal-Uhlmann, Moscow 1967) 11 B-N3 (other

good moves are P-QN3, P-QR4, P-QB3, R-K1 and B-K3) 11...Q-B2 12 Q-B3 B-Q3 13 P-KR3 O-O 14 B-N5 with the more comfortable game.

7 O-O N-QB3 8 N-N3 B-K2 If 8...N-B3 9 Q-K2 B-K2 (or 9...P-QR3 10 R-Q1 P-QN4 11 N(N3)×P N×N 12 R×N Q-N3 13 B-Q3 B-N2 [if 13...B-B4 14 R-KR4 B-N2 15 P-QN4 with good chances] 14 P-QR4! B-B4 15 R-KR4 P-N5 16 P-R5! and White stands well. Andersson-Sax, Hilversum 1973) 10 R-Q1 O-O 11 N(N3)×P Q-B2 12 N×N P×N 13 B-KN5 B-N2 14 Q-K5 Q×Q 15 N×Q KR-Q1 16 N-Q7 P-B4 17 N×Nch B×N 18 B×B with the better endgame for White. Keres-Eliskases, Noordwijk 1938. **9 Q-K2** or 9 N(N3)×P N×N 10 N×N P-QR3 11 B-K3 B-B3 12 P-QB3 N-K2 13 Q-R5 O-O 14 QR-Q1 with the better game for White. Smyslov-Stahlberg, Helsinki Olympiad 1952. **9...B-B3 10 R-Q1 P-QR3** Or 10...KN-K2 11 N(B3)×P B×N 12 B-K3 N-B4 13 N×B N(B3)×N 14 B×N N×B 15 Q-K3 with a lead in development. **11 N(N3)×P B×N 12 B-K3 KN-K2 13 B×B N×B 14 R×N Q-B2 15 QR-Q1 O-O 16 Q-K5** with advantage. Averbach-Stahlberg, Stockholm Interzonal 1952.

5 KN-B3

This has recently become the most popular move thanks largely to the games of World Champion Karpov. Instead, White may play more actively with **5 B-N5ch** in an attempt to provoke complications, and now:

(a) 5...B-Q2 6 Q-K2ch White achieves very little with 6 B×Bch N×B 7 N-K2 (if 7 KN-B3 Q-K2ch) 7...B-Q3 8 O-O KN-B3 (more exact than 8...N-K2 9 N-KB3 P-B5 10 B-B4 Q-B2 11 Q-Q2 O-O 12 KR-K1 KR-K1 13 B×B Q×B 14 N-N3 with some initiative. Larsen-Uhlmann, 3rd match game 1971) 9 N-KB3 O-O 10

P×P N×P 11 B-K3 R-K1 with equality. Larsen-Uhlmann, 5th match game 1971.
6...B-K2! White has an endgame advantage after 6...Q-K2 7 B×Bch N×B 8 P×P
N×P 9 N-N3 (or 9 QN-B3 Q×Qch 10 N×Q N-B3 11 B-K3 N(B4)-K5 12 O-O-O B-
B4 13 B×B N×B 14 N-B4 with the better ending. Averbach-Szabo, Sczawno
Zdroj 1950) 9...Q×Qch (or 9...N-R5 10 N-Q4 P-QR3 11 B-K3 N×P 12 N-B5 Q-
N5ch 13 B-Q2 Q-K5 14 R-N1 N-B5 15 B-B3 threatening R×P and N×P) 10 N×Q
N-R5 (if 10...N×N 11 RP×N B-B4 12 N-B3 N-B3 13 N-R4! followed by B-K3
with the better position. Even worse here is 12...O-O-O 13 R-R5! Ivkov-Hort,
Wijk aan Zee 1970) 11 N(N3)-Q4 and the isolated QP puts Black at a dis-
advantage. Parma-Vaganian, Yugoslavia-USSR match 1971. **7 P×P N-KB3 8 N-
N3!** The natural move, making it difficult for Black to achieve full equality.
Weaker is 8 KN-B3 O-O 9 O-O B×P 10 N-N3 R-K1 11 Q-Q3 B-N3 (or 11...P-
QR3 12 B×B QN×B 13 B-N5 B-R2 with equality. Botvinnik-Bronstein, 3rd
match game 1951) 12 B-N5 (or 12 B×B QN×B 13 B-Q2 N-B1 14 B-B3 N-K3 15
B-K5 N-K5 16 QR-Q1 N(K3)-N4 with equality. Beni-Korchnoy, Luhacovice
1969) 12...B×B (or 12...N-B3 13 P-B3 N-K4 14 N×N R×N 15 B×B R×B 16 B-R3
Q-Q3 with equality. Padevsky-Antoshin, Zagreb, 1965) 13 Q×B QN-Q2 14 P-
QR4 P-QR3 15 Q-Q3 R-K5 with an even game. Fuderer-Petrosian, Göteborg
Interzonal 1955. Or here 14 N(N3)-Q4 Q-B2 15 P-B3 P-QR3 16 Q-Q3 N-K5 with
equality. Polugayevsky-Kholmov, USSR 1956. **8...O-O 9 B-K3 R-K1 10 N-B3!**
Play is unclear after 10 O-O-O P-QR4 11 P-QR4 N-R3 12 B×B Q×B 13 Q-N5
Q×Q 14 P×Q N-B2 15 P-B6 P×P 16 P×P P-R5 17 N-Q4 P-R6! 18 P×P N-K5!
Böhnisch-Fuchs, East Germany 1966. Or 10 O-O-O P-QR3 11 B×B (11 B-Q3 P-
QR4!) 11...QN×B 12 N-R3 N×P 13 B×N B×B 14 Q-B3 B-R2 15 N-B4 with
equality. Kuzmin-Korchnoy, USSR 1973. **10...P-QR3** Well worthy of
consideration is 10...B×P 11 B(N5)×B QN×B 12 N×B N×N 13 Q-N5! (after 13 O-
O N-N5 Black equalizes, but 13...P-Q5 is risky in view of 14 KR-Q1 Q-N3 15
N×P Q×P 16 N-N5 Q-K4 17 Q-B4 with advantage) 13...R-QB1 (weaker is
13...N(B4)-K5 14 O-O Q-B2 15 P-B3 with a positional plus. Castaldi-Porath,
Hilversum 1947. White also stands better after 13...N-K3 14 O-O Q-B2 15 P-B3
P-QR3 16 Q-N6. Keres-Bondarevsky, USSR 1948) 14 O-O P-QR3 (White has
the better ending after 14...Q-Q2 15 Q×Q N(B4)×Q 16 P-B3) 15 Q-N4 R-K5 16
Q-Q2 P-R3 17 QR-Q1 R-K1 18 P-B3 N(B4)-K5 19 Q-Q3 Q-B2 with a minimal
advantage to White. Browne-Uhlmann, Hastings 1972/3. **11 B×B** Not 11 B-Q3
B-R5! **11...QN×B 12 O-O N×P 13 N(B3)-Q4** with a slight positional plus to
White. For 13 KR-K1?! see Parma-Korchnoy, Moscow 1971 (illustrative game
56).

(b) 5...N-B3

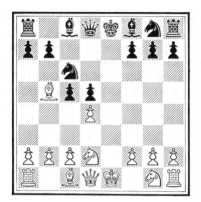

This move avoids the complications of 5...B-Q2. **6 Q-K2ch B-K2** Once again 6...Q-K2 is better for White after 7 P×P Q×Qch 8 N×Q B×P 9 N-QN3 B-N3 10 P-QR4 N-K2 11 P-R5 B-B2 12 B-KB4! Szabo-Barcza, Stockholm Interzonal 1952; or here 10 B-Q2 B-Q2 (10...N-K2 11 B-N4! Euwe-Botvinnik, World Championship Match Tournament 1948) 11 B-B3 P-B3 12 O-O KN-K2 13 B-Q4 with a positional advantage. **7 P×P N-B3 8 N-N3 O-O 9 B-K3** After 9 N-B3 Black can also equalize with accurate play: 9...N-K5 10 B-K3 R-K1 11 O-O-O (or 11 O-O N×QBP 12 Q-Q1 N-K5 13 N(B3)-Q4 Q-B2 with equal chances. Gerstenfeld-Boleslavsky, USSR 1940) 11...N×QBP 12 B-QB4 N×Nch 13 B×N B-K3 with equal chances. Florian-Katetov, Prague 1943. Weaker, however, is (9 N-B3) R-K1 10 B-K3 (10 O-O B×P 11 Q-Q3 B-N3 12 B-N5 also offers White a slight advantage according to Keres) 10...P-QR3 11 B-Q3 (11 B×N P×B 12 O-O P-QR4 13 R-K1 Q-B2 is unclear. Poljak-Khasin, USSR 1949) 11...B-N5 12 O-O-O with advantage to White. Smyslov-Uhlmann, Cienfuegos 1973 (illustrative game 57). **9...R-K1** Here or the next move the complications arising after ...P-QR3 have not yet been exhausted e.g. 9...P-QR3 (White has the advantage after both 9...B-N5 10 P-KB3 B-Q2 11 O-O-O P-QR3 12 B-R4. Ribli-Enklaar, Wijk aan Zee 1972; and 9...N-KN5 10 O-O-O N×B 11 Q×N R-K1 12 N-B3 B-B3 13 Q-Q2. Poljak-Sokolsky, USSR 1951) 10 B-R4! (if 10 B-Q3 P-Q5 11 B-KN5 P-QR4 12 P-QR4 B-K3 13 N-B3 B×N 14 P×B B×P with good play for Black. Hübner-Uhlmann, Palma Interzonal 1970) 10...R-K1 11 O-O-O N-KN5 (if 11...N-K5 12 Q-B1 B-B4 13 N-K2 R-QB1 14 P-QR3 with the advantage. Ribli-Farago, Hungarian Championship 1971) 12 N-B3 (If instead 12 Q-B3 N×B 13 P×N B-N4 Black has a strong attack for the pawn.) This is the critical position which needs further examination. One example is 12...B-B3 13 KR-K1 (after 13 P-B4 the play becomes wildly complicated. Black can play 13...B-K3 or the sharp 13...P-Q5) 13...N×B 14 P×N R-K5! with the better game for Black. Kupreichik-Gulko,

USSR 1973. **10 O-O-O P-QR4 11 P-QR4 B-Q2 12 N-B3 N-R2 13 N(B3)-Q2 N-K5!** with chances for both sides, but not 13...N-N5 14 K-N1 N×B 15 P×N B-N4 16 Q-B3! with a clear advantage for White. Parma-Vaganian, Yugoslavia-USSR Match 1972.

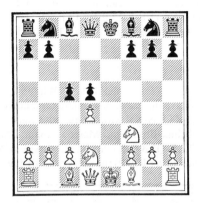

5   ...   **N-QB3**

(a) 5...N-KB3 The disadvantage of this move is that in many variations the knight is needed on K2 e.g.: **6 B-N5ch B-Q2** Not 6...N-B3 which transposes to note (3) on page 231). **7 B×Bch QN×B 8 O-O B-K2 9 P×P N×P 10 N-Q4** Also good for White is 10 N-N3 N(B4)-K5 11 N(B3)-Q4 Q-Q2 12 Q-B3 O-O 13 N-KB5 KR-K1 14 N×Bch R×N 15 B-K3. Keres-Ivkov, Bamberg 1968. **10...O-O** If 10...Q-Q2 11 N(Q2)-B3 O-O 12 N-K5 Q-B1 13 B-N5 R-K1 14 N-Q3 with some positional advantage. Botvinnik-Bronstein, 15th match game 1951. **11 N-B5 R-K1 12 N-QN3 N-K3** After 12...R-QB1 13 B-K3 B-B1 14 B-Q4 N-K3 15 P-QB3 N×B 16 Q×N, as in Khasin-Sokolsky, USSR 1957; or 12...N(B4)-K5 13 N×Bch Q×N 14 B-K3 Q-B2 15 B-Q4 N-Q2 16 Q-Q3 as in Parma-Donner, Busum 1968, White has some advantage in the ending. **13 B-K3 Q-B2 14 P-QB3 QR-Q1 15 Q-B3** with strong pressure. Geller-Stahlberg, Zürich Candidates' Tournament 1953.

(b) 5...P-QR3 Now that White has exchanged pawns this move seems playable, since 6 P-B4 N-KB3 7 B-K2 N-B3 8 P×QP KN×P 9 O-O P×P 10 N-N3 B-K2 11 N(B3)×P O-O 12 B-B3 B-B3 13 N-B2 N(Q4)-K2 gives White nothing.

Szily-Botvinnik, Budapest 1952. **6 P×P** After 6 B-K2 P-B5 7 O-O B-Q3 8 R-K1 N-K2 9 N-B1 QN-B3 10 B-N5 O-O 11 P-B3 P-B3 12 B-Q2 P-QN4 the position is unclear. Gipslis-Korchnoy, Tallinn 1967. **6...B×P 7 N-N3 B-R2 8 B-Q3** If 8 B-KN5 N-KB3 9 N(B3)-Q4 O-O 10 B-K2 Q-Q3 11 O-O N-K5 12 B-K3 with equality. Keres-Botvinnik, World Championship Match Tournament 1948; or 8 B-K2 N-KB3 9 O-O N-B3 10 B-KN5 O-O 11 P-B3 R-K1 12 N(N3)-Q4 Q-Q3 with equality. Estevez-Korchnoy, Leningrad Interzonal 1973. **8...Q-K2ch 9 B-K2** If 9 Q-K2 N-QB3 10 O-O B-N5 11 P-KR3 B-R4 12 B-KB4 Q×Q with equal chances. **9...N-KB3 10 O-O O-O 11 N(B3)-Q4** Better is 11 B-KN5! **11...N-B3 12 R-K1 N-K5 13 B-K3 N-K4 14 N-Q2 P-B4.** Ciric-Korchnoy, Yugoslavia-USSR match 1967.

(c) **5...P-B5** Bronstein's move, designed to leave White's Q4 occupied by the QP so that White will not have the use of this square for a knight. **6 P-QN3 P×P** Not 6...P-QN4 7 P-QR4 Q-R4 8 N-K5! with a clear advantage for White. **7 B-N5ch** For 7 RP×P see Bebchuk-Bronstein, Moscow Team Championship 1974—illustrative game 58. **7...B-Q2 8 Q-K2ch** with advantage to White because of his lead in development and (after RP×P) the half-open QR-file.

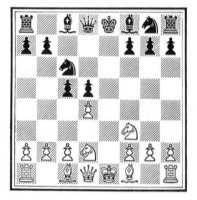

6   B-N5

There is nothing in 6 P×P B×P 7 N-N3 (not the blunder 7 B-N5?? B×Pch 8 K×B Q-N3ch winning a pawn) 7...B-N3 8 B-Q3 N-B3 9 O-O O-O 10 B-KN5 Q-Q3 with equal chances.

6   ...   B-Q3

6...P-B5 is not to be recommended. White has both 7 Q-K2ch Q-K2 8 P-QN3 with the better ending (compare note (c) on 5...P-B5 above) and 7 O-O B-Q3 8 P-QN3 PxP 9 P-B4 N-K2 10 PxQP NxP 11 QxP O-O 12 N-K4 N-R4 13 Q-N2 B-K2 14 B-Q2 with advantage. Keres-Stahlberg, Marianske Lazne 1965.

Equally dubious is the attempt to solve Black's problems by 6...P-QR3, see Gligoric-Stahlberg, 3rd match game 1949 (illustrative game 59).

One final alternative to the main line is 6...Q-K2ch 7 B-K2 PxP 8 O-O Q-Q1 (or 8...Q-B2 9 N-N3 N-B3 10 N(N3)xP B-K2 11 P-B3 when White has the edge.) 9 N-N3 B-Q3 10 N(N3)xP KN-K2 11 P-QN3 O-O 12 B-N2 N-N3 13 P-B4 N(B3)-K2 14 R-B1 N-B5 15 P-B5 B-N1 16 R-K1 NxBch 17 QxN with the better game for White. Tal-Holm, Kapfenberg 1970.

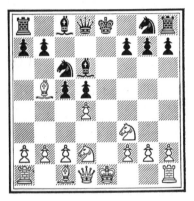

7 PxP

At the present time this sequence of moves is the most common. After **7 O-O PxP 8 N-N3** Not 8 NxP at once because of 8...BxPch 9 KxB Q-R5ch 10 K-N1 QxN equalizing immediately. Geller-Ivkov, USSR-Yugoslavia match 1969. **8...N-K2 9 N(N3)xP O-O,** we reach a position identical to that after move 10 in the main line (in the main line White has used an extra tempo on 7 PxP whereas Black has used two extra tempi with his bishop [7...BxBP and 8...B-Q3] but saved one by omitting 7...PxP). The difference in move order is significant inasmuch as in the main line White has the option, at move 10, of playing something other than 10 N(N3)-Q4. We should point out that in the main line Black has the option, at move 9, of retreating his bishop to QN3 rather than Q3, but this should not be considered a disadvantage for White since 9...B-N3 is inferior.

7 ...   BxBP

Here too Black gains nothing by 7...Q-K2ch 8 Q-K2 B×BP 9 N-K5 (for 9 N-N3 see Balashov-Vaganian, USSR Championship 1973 — illustrative game 60.) 9...B-Q2 10 N×B K×N 11 N-N3 Q×Qch 12 K×Q R-K1ch 13 K-B3 B-Q3 14 B-K3 P-QR3 15 B×Nch P×B 16 P-B4 with an attack down the centre.

8 O-O   N-K2
9 N-N3

The interesting attempt to set up a blockading position with 9 P-B4 proved dubious in the game Mestel-Uhlmann, Hastings 1973, when Black obtained a strong attack on the K-side after 9...O-O 10 N-N3 B-Q3 11 B×N P×B 12 P-B5 B-N1! 13 B-N5 Q-B2! 14 N(N3)-Q4 N-N3 15 Q-R4 B-Q2 16 Q-R6 P-B3 17 B-Q2 N-K4! 18 P-KN3 B-B1 19 Q-R4 Q-Q2 with the better chances.

9 ...   B-Q3!

The retreat **9...B-N3** has the disadvantage that White wins a tempo after R-K1 and B-K3, as the black bishop can be exchanged at an appropriate moment, giving White the better ending. e.g.: **10 R-K1** More exact than the immediate 10 B-K3 B×B 11 P×B (or 11 B×Nch P×B 12 P×B B-N5! first played in Matanovic-Gligoric, Sousse Interzonal 1967, 13 Q-Q4 B×N! 14 R×B O-O 15 QR-KB1 N-N3 16 N-B5 Q-K2 17 P-QR4 QR-K1 18 P-QN3 N-K4 with equality. Geller-Ivkov, Sousse Interzonal 1967) 11...O-O 12 Q-Q2 Q-N3 13 P-QR4 B-B4 14 N(B3)-Q4 N×N 15 P×N Q-N3 with equality. Or 10 B-N5 O-O 11 R-K1 Q-Q3 12 Q-Q2 B-N5 13 B×N(B6) N×B 14 B-B4 Q-Q2 15 N-K5 N×N 16 B×N QR-K1 17 B-Q4 B×B 18 N×B P-QR3 with only a slight edge for White. Radulov-Schmid, Nice Olympiad 1974. **10...O-O** White had the advantage after 10...B-N5 11 B-N5 P-B3 12 B-K3 B×B 13 R×B in Geller-Matulovic, Skopje 1968. **11 B-K3** In the game Karpov-Vaganian, USSR 1973, after 11 B-N5 P-KR3 12 B-KR4 P-N4?! 13 B-N3 N-B4 14 Q-Q2 White had the better game, but Black should play 12...P-B3 13 B-N3 N-B4 with an unclear position according to Karpov. **11...B-KB4** White stands better after 11...B-N5 12 B×B Q×B 13 B×N. Karpov-Krogius, USSR 1970. **12 P-B3 B-K5 13 N(N3)-Q4 Q-Q3 14 B-KB1 Q-B3 15 Q-R4 P-KR3 16 QR-Q1** with a more comfortable game for White. Ghizdavu-Botez, Romania 1972.

With 9...B-Q3! we reach a position that must be considered critical for the Tarrasch Variation, and hence for the theory of the French Defence in general. Whether or not White can take advantage of his opponent's isolated QP will determine the assessment of the whole variation. Karpov reached this position no less than seven times during his Candidates' Match with Korchnoy at the end of 1974, and it is therefore with particular pleasure that R.H.M. welcomes the following contribution by World Champion Karpov. Karpov's analysis of this critical variation extends to the end of the main game, and his contribution was written specially for this volume.

The most popular position in the Tarrasch Variation. Its most important features are the presence of the isolated pawn and the fact that each side controls different squares in the centre. The open king file is also important. What general considerations do modern players have in mind when dealing with this position?

Nimzovich stressed that the important point in such positions is not so much the isolated pawn itself (the weakness of which is more often than not illusory) as the blockading square in front of it. For this reason White attempts to get an unshakeable grip on his Q4 square, while Black disposes his forces in such a way as to try and challenge this grip. In short, White strives to make Q4 a base for his pieces and Black hopes to expel them from that square.

At the start of this battle White adopts a firm stance whereas Black has a more mobile set-up. The extent of the zones of activity of each side is normally clearly marked out. White solidifies his position in the centre and eyes the weaknesses that arise on the Q-side. His ideal is to win the QP. Black counters in the centre and tries to create threats on the K-side. His ideal is to achieve the advance ...P-Q5. We therefore have a case of statics versus dynamics!

Let us now consider concrete lines which give rich food for thought.

10   N(N3)-Q4

The classical line which has held the stage for many years. The same position can be reached but in one move less by adopting the move order **1 P-K4 P-K3 2 P-Q4 P-Q4 3 N-Q2 P-QB4 4 KP×P KP×P 5 KN-B3 N-QB3 6 B-N5 B-Q3 7 O-O P×P 8 N-N3 N-K2 9 N(N3)×P.** For simplicity of exposition and to avoid any confusion over move order we are going to assume that the position has been reached by the more normal move order, i.e. in ten moves. Generally speaking the move 7...P×P has independent significance only in cases of definite deviations from recognised theory, e.g. 8 R-K1ch N-K2 9 N×P O-O 10 N-B1, but there are no known examples of this continuation; or 8 N×P which is mentioned on page 239.

The text is by far from being the only move played at this juncture. Six other moves also come into serious consideration:

(a) 10 B-N5 Until recently this was the most common line. One of the ways of playing against the isolated QP is to carry out appropriate minor piece exchanges so as to gain various positional advantages. This tendency is most clearly seen after the text move. **10...O-O**

Originally the various plans here were considered to be of equal strength:

(a1) 11 R-K1 Black equalised easily in Pogats-Portisch, Hungary 1958, which went 11 Q-Q2 Q-B2 12 P-KR3 P-KR3 13 B-K3 B-KB4. **11...Q-B2** This is more elastic than 11...B-KN5 12 P-KR3 (not so convincing is 12 B-K2 Q-B2 13 P-KR3 B-K3 14 N(N3)-Q4 which led to near equality in Kan-Khasin, Moscow 1949) 12...B-R4, since in this case Black has to reckon with the possibility of 13 B×QN P×B 14 N(N3)-Q4 R-B1 (14...Q-Q2 is bad because of 15 B×N B×B 16 N-K5, while 14...Q-B2 15 B×N B×B 16 N×P Q×N 17 R×B Q-B3 18 R-N7 QR-N1 19 R-N3 R×R 20 RP×R B×N 21 Q×B Q×NP 22 R×P Q×BP 23 R-Q7 leaves Black a pawn down in the ending) 15 P-B4 P-KR3 (15...P×P? 16 N-B5) 16 B×N B×B 17 Q-R4 and White has the initiative. The direct attempt to get rid of the pin by 11...P-KR3 favours White since, as we shall see, it helps his subsequent manoeuvre B-KR4-KN3. Admittedly, in Larsen-Andersson, Siegen Olympiad 1970, White even got a slight advantage after 12 B-K3 B-KN5 13 P-KR3 B-R4 14 B-K2 R-K1 15 N(N3)-Q4 P-R3 16 Q-Q2 B-N3 17 QR-Q1 Q-B2 18 B-Q3 N-K4 19 N×N B×N 20 B×B N×B 21 P-QB3, but the main reason for this was Black's play which can be strengthened by 15...Q-Q2, 16...Q-B2 and 18...QR-Q1.

The idea 10 B-N5 O-O 11 R-K1 Q-B2 was treated in a fresh manner in the 18th game of my match with Korchnoy: **12 P-B3!** 12 P-KR3 wastes time: 12...P-KR3 13 B-Q2 B-KB4 14 N(N3)-Q4 B-K5 15 B-B3 QR-Q1 16 B-Q3 with complicated play and approximate equality, e.g. 16...Q-N3 (16...B-QB4 is not so good — 17 B×B P×B 18 R×P N-B4 19 N×N(B5)! with an attack) 17 B×B P×B 18 R×P and now not 18...B-B4 19 Q-K1! N×N 20 N×N B×N 21 R×N (Toran-Kramer, Beverwijk 1957), but simply 18...N-Q4. **12...B-KN5 13 P-KR3 B-R4**

14 B-K2! P-KR3 15 B×N! N×B 16 N(B3)-Q4! B×B 16...B-N3 makes no difference because of 17 B-Q3 and now Black also has to reckon with N-N5 **17 Q×B P-
R3 18 Q-B3 QR-Q1 19 QR-Q1 R-Q2 20 N-KB5 N×N 21 Q×N KR-Q1 22 R-K3**
and White has a slight but definite advantage. However, in the sequel Korchnoy
managed to save the half point by inventive play.

(a2)   11 B-KR4

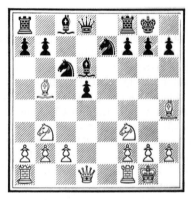

This move was first tried some years ago and it gave the line 10 B-N5 a new
impetus. It was played in Bronstein-Furman, 14th USSR Championship 1946,
but this game was then completely forgotten, and only twenty-five years later
was it resurrected. **11...Q-N3** The most modern approach, but 11...Q-B2 and
11...B-KN5 have also been played:

**(1)   11...Q-B2 12 B-N3 B×B 13 RP×B B-N5 14 R-K1 QR-Q1 15 P-B3 Q-N3 16
B-Q3** Threatening 17 B×Pch and 18 N-N5ch. **16...N-N3 17 Q-B2 B×N 18 P×B R-
Q3** Probably he should prefer 18...P-Q5 although even then, after 19 P-KB4
P×P 20 P×P, Black's knight cannot get into play and White has a definite advan-
tage. **19 P-KB4 KR-Q1 20 P-R3!** White has a definite advantage, and what is
probably more important a clear plan of action. Karpov-Kuzmin, Leningrad
Interzonal 1973 (illustrative game 61).

(2)   A step forward for Black was made in a few games where he tried **11...B-
KN5,** starting an immediate fight for the central squares. **12 B-K2** Other moves
are:

(i)   12 R-K1 R-B1 (or 12...R-K1 13 B-N3 B×B 14 RP×B Q-N3 15 B-Q3 with the
better game for White. Balashov-Uhlmann, Moscow 1971) 13 P-B3 N-K4?! 14

243

B-K2 N-B5? 15 N(B3)-Q4, and in view of the fact that the pawn cannot be taken (15...N×P? 16 Q-B2 B×B 17 Q×B) Black has to retreat by 15...B-Q2 when his difficulties are just as great after 16 B×N P×B 17 N-Q2 R-K1 18 N-K4 B-N1 19 Q-B3. Browne-S. Garcia, Madrid 1973.

(ii) 12 B-N3 (this is rather premature) 12... B×B 13 RP×B Q-N3 14 B-Q3 (with the threat of 15 B×Pch) 14...N-B4 (if 14...N-K4 15 R-K1 N(2)-B3 16 B-K2 B×N, and now, by 17 P×B, White could keep the initiative, Ivanovic-Farago, Prstina 1973) 15 B×N B×B, although here too White still has slightly the better of it after 16 P-B3.

12...B-R4 The point of this retreat is to meet 13 N(B3)-Q4 by 13...B-N3 avoiding the exchange of bishops. In addition to this far from stereotyped plan there is also 12...Q-N3 13 B×N! N×B (the pawn sacrifice 13...B×B 14 Q×P QR-Q1 15 Q-B4 is inadequate) 14 Q-Q4! Q×Q 15 N(B3)×Q B-Q2 (15...B×B 16 N×B QR-B1 seems more stubborn) 16 QR-Q1 KR-Q1 17 KR-K1 K-B1 18 P-QB3, when the endgame favours White. Kuzmin-Uhlmann, Leningrad Interzonal 1973 (illustrative game 63). Uhlmann improved the defence against R Byrne in their game from the same event by 12...R-K1! 13 R-K1 when a draw was agreed! This improvement was more clearly shown in Vogt-Uhlmann, Potsdam 1974: 12...R-K1 13 R-K1 Q-N3 14 N(B3)-Q4 (or 14 B×N R×B! 15 Q×P QR-Q1 with active piece play for the pawn) 14...N-N3! (after 14...B×B 15 R×B B-K4! White missed the following tactical turn in Schmid-Portisch, Nice Olympiad 1974: 16 N-B3 B×P 17 R-N1 B-B6 18 R-K3 with chances for both sides) 15 N×N (not 15 B×B R×Rch 16 Q×R N×N winning) 15...R×B! 16 R×R (if 16 N(B6)-Q4 R-K5 17 P-KB3 B×BP! with a clear advantage) 16...P×N 17 B-N3 and Black has no problems. This Vogt-Uhlmann encounter is given in full as illustrative game 64. **13 R-K1 Q-N3 14 N(B3)-Q4 B-N3 15 P-QB3** Gaining a slight but persistent advantage by his strangehold on Q4. **15...KR-K1 16 B-B1 B-K5 17 B-N3 B×B 18 RP×B P-QR4** Wrongly weakening his QN4 square. 18...QR-Q1 was called for: **19 P-QR4 N×N 20 N×N** An unpleasant surprise for Black. 20 P×N B-N3 is level, whereas now if 20...Q×P, 21 N-N5 wins material. **20...N-B3 21 B-N5! KR-Q1 22 P-KN4!** Preparing for the ending by cutting off the bishop from the useful KB4-QB1 diagonal. **22...N×N 23 Q×N Q×Q 24 P×Q QR-B1 25 P-B3 B-N3 26 R-K7 P-N3 27 QR-K1** and Black had a very difficult position. Karpov-Uhlmann, Madrid 1973 (illustrative game 62).

Let us now return to the position after **11...Q-N3.**

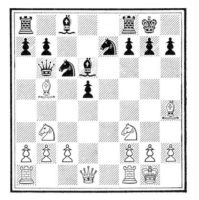

The year 1974 was crucial for this variation. In a number of games the Moscow Champion Boris Gulko succeeded in showing that after **12 B-Q3 P-QR4!** Black has full equality, e.g.

(1)   13 P-R4 N-B4 14 B×N B×B 15 B-N3 (15 Q×P B×BP 16 Q×B B×N is equal) 15...B×B 16 P×B B-K5 with advantage to Black. Balashov-Gulko, Moscow Championship 1974.
(2)   13 P-R4 N-B4 14 B-N3? B×B 15 P×B N×P 16 R-K1 N-R4 17 Q-Q2 B-N5 with a sound extra pawn. Belyavsky-Gulko, Daugavpils 1974.
(3)   13 P-B3 P-R5 14 N(N3)-Q4 N-N3 15 N-QN5 B-B5 16 B-N3 B×B 17 P×B B-N5 18 R-N1 N-K4 with excellent play. Zhidkov-Gulko, Daugavpils 1974.

The line has also worked out well in a number of other games. Thus Wittman-Vaganian, Teesside 1974 went 13 P-B4 P-R5 14 P×P N-N5 15 N(N3)-Q4 N×B 16 Q×N R-R4! 17 N-KN5 (if 17 B×N B×B 18 N-B5 B-B3 with a clear advantage to Black) 17...N-N3 18 N-B5 B×N 19 Q×B Q-Q1 and the threats of ...R×P and ...P-R3 make White's position unpleasant.

Nor could White hope for much from Timoschenko-Farago, Rimavska Subota 1974, which went 13 P-R4 N-B4 14 B-QN5 N×B 15 N×N B-K4 16 P-B3, and now, by means of 16...R-Q1 17 N-B3 B-N5, Black could have equalized quickly. He actually got the worse of it after 16...P-Q5 17 N-B3 B-KN5 18 B×N! P×B 19 N(N3)×QP Q×P 20 Q-Q3!

In answer to 11...Q-N3 one can mention 12 P-QR4 and 12 B-K2, but neither is dangerous for Black. In Janosevic-Raicevic Black soon got the better game after 12 P-QR4 B-KN5 13 B×N(B6) P×B 14 P-R5 Q-B2 15 B-N3 P-QB4 16 R-K1 QR-N1. In Pinter-Farago, Hungary 1974, Black gradualy got the upper hand after 12 B-K2 N-B4! 13 Q×P (13 P-B3 is sounder) 13...N-N5 14 Q-Q2 N×B 15 N×N R-Q1 16 B-Q3 (16 Q-N5!?) 16...B-K4 17 QR-Q1 B-N5 18 R-N1 N×B 19 P×N Q-Q3 20 Q-N5 B-K7 21 KR-K1 B×Pch.

(b) Now the move **10 N(B3)-Q4** is worth mentioning. By playing in this way White avoids the pinning of this knight, a pin that often causes him a lot of trouble. However, the move conflicts somewhat with the other positional considerations which we mentioned earlier. In particular, White's K-side could well become a firing range for the enemy pieces. Nevertheless, the variation is not without bite. **10...O-O 11 B-N5** Or 11 Q-R5 N-K4 12 P-KR3 P-QR3 13 B-Q3 N×B 14 P×N P-R4 with equality. Aronin-Portisch, 1959. **11...N-K4 12 R-K1 P-B3?! 13 B-KR4 N(2)-N3 14 B-N3 P-B4 15 N-K2.** White stands better but this is a consequence of 12...P-B3. 12...Q-B2 would seem to leave the position level.

(c) **10 B×Nch** is once again gaining in popularity. Now 10...N×B 11 R-K1ch B-K2 12 N(B3)-Q4 O-O 13 N×N P×N 14 B-K3 allows White to start playing on the enemy's weak dark squares. The main line is **10...P×B 11 Q-Q4** Black has no difficulties after 11 B-K3 O-O 12 B-B5 B-N5 13 Q-Q3 P-QR4 14 P-QR4 B×B 15 N×B Q-Q3. Ingerslev-Bronstein, Moscow 1956. **11...O-O 12 B-B4 N-B4** 12...P-QR4 is weaker: 13 B×B Q×B 14 KR-K1 N-N3 15 P-QR4 R-N1 16 Q-B3 R-N5 17 N×P P-QB4 18 N-N3 R-B5 19 Q-Q2 and White has every justification for hoping to realize his extra pawn. Adorjan-Maric, Novi Sad 1973. In this line it is also quite possible for White to consider the natural-looking move 15 N-K5. **13 Q-Q2 Q-N3** Black failed to equalize after 13...R-N1 14 KR-K1 R-N5 15 B×B Q×B 16 P-B3 R-N5 18 QR-Q1. Hulak-Raicevic, Yugoslavia 1974. **14 B×B** Not 14 N-R4? B-QN5 15 P-B3 B×P 16 Q×B N×N, while after 14 N(B3)-Q4 B×B 15 Q×B N×N 16 N×N P-QB4 or 16 Q×N Q×Q 17 N×Q P-QB4 White cannot hope to get any advantage. Still it may be better to play 14 KR-K1 hoping to get the better development. **14...N×B 15 P-QR4 N-K5 16 Q-Q4 B-K3! 17 P-R5 Q-N4 18 Q-Q3 Q-N5** when Black (unlike his opponent) has nothing to grumble about. Velimirovic-Vaganian, Kragujevac 1974.

(d) **10 B-K3** is nowadays played very rarely. Then comes **10...O-O 11 Q-Q2** White gets nowhere from 11 B-B5 B×B 12 N×B Q-N3 13 B×N Q×N 14 B-R4 B-N5. **11...B-KN5 12 B-K2 B×N 13 B×B N-K4** and Black gets full equality from

246

his threat to exchange one of the enemy bishops. Gligoric-Petrosian, Stockholm Interzonal 1952.

(e) **10 B-Q2 O-O 11 B-B3** should be met by **11...Q-B2 12 R-K1 B-KB4 13 QN-Q2 B-N3,** but not 13...B-K5 14 B-Q3!

(f) **10 P-B3 O-O 11 N(N3)-Q4** transposes to the text, and that, in fact, was the order of moves adopted in the main game.

Now let us return to the main line, after **10 N(N3)-Q4.**

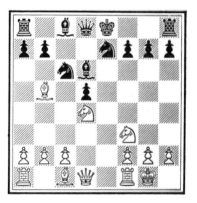

10	...		O-O
11	P-B3		

Once again White has a wide choice of alternatives:

(a) **11 B-K3 B-KN5** The straightforward 11...N×N 12 N×N N-B4 13 N×N B×N 14 P-QB3! P-QR3 15 B-R4 Q-B2 16 P-KN3 B-K3 17 R-K1 QR-Q1 18 Q-B3 left Black with an unpromising position in Matulovic-Maric, Yugoslavia 1974. **12 Q-Q2** The problem of the pin on the knight has been resolved in a number of ways. Janosevic-Bronstein, Sarajevo 1971 went 12 P-KR3 B-R4 13 B-Q3? N×N! 14 B×N N-B3 15 P-B3 (15 B-B3 P-Q5 16 B-Q2 B-B2 is good for Black who has the simple plan of playing for mate). 15...N×B 16 P×N Q-B3 17 P-KN4 B-N3 18 R-K1 Q-B5! 19 B×B BP×B 20 R-K3 P-KR4! with a decisive attack. Another game went 12 B-K2 R-K1 13 Q-Q2 Q-Q2 14 KR-K1 (14 N-QN5 is better) 14...QR-Q1 15 QR-Q1 B-N1 16 B-KB4 B×B 17 Q×B N-N3 18 Q-Q2 R-K5! 19 N×N P×N and again Black had the initiative. Theory recommends the move order 12 P-KR3 B-R4 13 Q-Q2, which normally is a harmless transposition. There is the difference, however, that Black can then play 13...R-B1 hoping for 14 B-K2 B-N1 15 P-B3 Q-B2 16 P-KN3 Q-Q2 when he stands no worse. Hence the reason for the text whereby White refrains from weakening pawn moves for the time being. **12...Q-B2 13 P-KR3 B-R4** Exchanging bishop for knight leaves White with the preferable position: 13...B×N 14 N×B QR-Q1 15 Ṗ-B3 N-K4 16 N×N B×N 17 KR-K1. Larsen-Matulovic, Belgrade 1964. **14 N-R4** Until quite recently the impression created by the game Matanovic-Jansa, Tel-Aviv 1964, was that Black should not allow this move: 14...N×N 15 B×N B-B5 16 B-K3 B×B with the better game for White. But Black can improve with **14...B-N3! 15 N×B RP×N 16 B×N P×B 17 P-QB4 Q-Q2!** Not 17...P×P 18 QR-B1 QR-Q1 19 R×P P-QB4 20 N-N5 B-R7ch 21 K-R1 R×Q 22 N×Q B×N 23 B×R with a technically won game. **18 N-N3?! P×P 19 N-B5 Q-B2 20 QR-B1** and the game soon ended in a draw. Matulovic-Suetin, Belgrade 1974.

(b) A special position is occupied by the hybrid line **11 B-N5** Due to the efforts of Grandmaster Uhlmann the following continuation has become well known: **11...P-B3** An alternative is 11...Q-B2 12 P-KR3 (or 12 R-K1 N×N 13 Q×N B-K3 14 B-Q3 with the better game for White. Sigurjonsson-Uhlmann, Raach 1969) 12...P-B3 (12...B-Q2 13 B-Q3 P-QR3 14 P-B3 KR-K1 is also possible. Krogius-Uusi, USSR 1959) 13 B-K3 N-K4 14 P-QN3 (or 14 R-K1 P-QR3 15 B-KB1 with play for both sides) 14...P-QR3 15 B-K2 B-Q2 16 Q-Q2 P-QN4 17 QR-Q1 K-R1 18 N-K1 N(4)-N3 19 N-Q3 P-B4 20 B-N5 P-B5 and Black gradually outplayed his opponent by exploiting the attack on the K-side. Neikirch-Uhlmann, Potsdam 1974 (illustrative game 65). **12 B-K3!** After 12 B×N NP×B 13 N×P B×Pch 14 N×B N×N White has lost all of his opening initiative. Or 12 B-KR4 B-KN5 13 Q-Q2 Q-N3 14 B×N P×B 15 B-N3 P-QB4 and White has come to a strategical dead end. **12...N-K4! 13 R-K1 P-QR3 14 B-KB1 K-R1 15 P-KR3 B-Q2 16 P-B3 R-B1 17 P-QR4 R-K1 18 N×N P×N 19 N-B3 P-R3.** This position occurred in the game Geller-Uhlmann, Amsterdam 1970. The position is sharp and complicated as can be seen from the variation 20 Q-Q2 B-KB4 21 B×KRP!? P-K5! 22 N-Q4 P×B 23 Q×Pch K-N1 24 P-QB4! (But not 24 P-KN4 Q-N3, nor 24 Q-N5ch B-N3 25 N-K6 Q-Q2 26 Q-B6 B-K4!) 24...Q-N3 25 N×B N×N 26 Q-N5ch! N-N2 27 Q×Pch.

(c) On the basis of existing games in the line **11 P-KR3** the plan introduced by this precautionary move has little force. E.g. 11...N×N 12 Q×N B-KB4 13 P-B3 B-K5 14 N-N5 N-B4 15 Q-Q1 Q-B3 16 R-K1 B-B4! 17 Ṅ×B P×N 18 R×P B×Pch

248

and Black had the initiative in Tukmakov-Uhlmann, Hastings 1972/73; or 11...Q-B2 12 B-R4 N×N (after 12...P-QR3 White hardly has anything) 13 N×N N-B4? 14 N×N B×N 15 Q×P with an extra pawn and the better position for White. Tukmakov-Petkevich, USSR 1972.

(d) After **11 B-Q3 N-N3 12 B-KN5 B-K2 13 B×B Q×B 14 R-K1 Q-B3** the position is level. Jansa-Matanovic, Varna Olympiad 1962.

(e) After **11 P-QN3 B-KN5** we get tenser positions. Note that 11...N×N 12 N×N B-K4 or 12 Q×N N-B3 is simpler. One can also recommend 11...P-QR3 12 N×N P×N 13 B-Q3 N-N3 14 B×N RP×B 15 B-N2 P-QB4 16 Q-Q2 B-N2 17 B-K5 P-Q5 18 Q-B4 B×B 19 N×B as in Shamkovich-Smederevac, Polanica Zdroj 1970. Another logical line is 11...Q-R4 12 B-N2 B-QR6 13 B×B Q×QB 14 R-K1 B-N5 15 B×N N×B 16 Q-Q2 with equality. Karaklajic-Petrosian, Belgrade 1956. After **12 B-N2 Q-N3** a game Bondarevsky-Alatortsev, Kiev 1940, went **13 N×N** Nor does Black have problems after 13 B-K2 QR-Q1 14 P-KR3 B-R4 15 Q-Q2 KR-K1. Gipslis-Korchnoi, 38th USSR Championship 1970. The lines 13 P-QR4 QR-Q1 14 Q-Q2, Krnic-Lekovic, Yugoslavia 1963, and 13 P-QR4 B-K4 14 N×N N×N 15 B×B N×B 16 B-K2 N×Nch, Krnic-Uhlmann, Vrsac 1973, also tend to lead to equality. **13...P×N 14 B-Q3.** White has a sound position while Black has active pieces. The chances are equal.

Now let us return to the 8th game of the Karpov-Korchnoy match, 1974.

The plan behind 11 P-B3 was developed to a considerable degree during my match with Korchnoy. The idea had already occurred in Matanovic-Portisch, Yugoslavia-Hungary Match 1959. Black did not defend very accurately in that game and after 11...B-KN5 12 Q-R4 N×N? 13 N×N N-N3 14 P-KB4 P-QR3 15 B-Q3 he stood worse. At the time it was suggested that Black could keep things level by 12...Q-Q2.

11   ...   B-KN5

Korchnoy played **11...Q-Q2,** the move recommended by theory, only in the 16th game, and after **12 B-K3 P-QR3 13 B-K2 N×N 14 Q×N N-B3 15 Q-Q2 KR-K1 16 QR-Q1 QR-Q1 17 B-N6 B-B2 18 B×B Q×B 19 KR-K1 P-R3 20 P-KR3** White had only a minute advantage.

12   Q-R4

This position has certain special features. In principle Black has two fine bishops which harrass White, and the exchange of either pair of bishops gives White's pieces the chance to find new and firmer footholds. On the other hand Black's knights are more static, being restricted to certain squares. The course of the match did not resolve the problem of the isolated pawn which stands in the midst of all these developing events. Is it a strength or a weakness?

The side with the isolated pawn always has the problem of where to put his queen. It can hardly stay in the centre since there are no handy squares there in view of the play on the open files. Hence it has to be put somewhere further afield, but on the best possible square. White's QR4 is a reasonable citadel for the most powerful piece.

I preferred the modest **12 B-K2** only in the 4th game of my match with Korchnoy. There followed **12...R-K1 13 R-K1 P-QR3 14 B-KN5 P-KR3 15 B-R4 Q-N3 16 Q-N3 B-QB4 17 Q×Q B×Q 18 B-Q3 K-B1** when the ending is still somewhat in White's favour.

12   ...   B-R4
13   R-K1

Naturally not 13 B×N P×B 14 N×P N×N 15 Q×N B×N which can hardly appeal to White.

Two other moves were tried during the Karpov-Korchnoy match:

(a) **13 B-K3,** as in the 12th game, finally produced a draw after a hard fight: **13...Q-B2 14 P-KR3 N-R4! 15 B-Q3** Or 15 QR-Q1 P-QR3 16 B-Q3 N-B5 17 B-B1; or 15...N-B5 16 B×N Q×B 17 Q×Q P×Q 18 N-QN5 B×N 19 P×B B-N1 20 R-Q7 when Black probably stands no worse. **15...N-B5 16 N-N5 Q-Q2! 17 B×N P×B 18 KR-Q1 N-B4!** 18...P-QR3 is weaker: 19 R×B Q×N 20 Q×Q P×Q 21 N-Q4. **19 Q×BP B×N 20 P×B N×B 21 P×N Q×P** etc.

(b) **13 B-Q3 P-KR3** Naturally not 13...B-N3 14 B×B RP×B 15 N-KN5 when the threatened Q-R4 will give White a powerful attack. However, 13...B-B4!? as in the 14th match game is quite feasible: 14 R-K1 P-KR3 15 B-K3 B-QN3 16 P-KR3 Q-Q3 17 B-K2 KR-K1 18 QR-Q1 Q-B3 and Black has solved his opening problems satisfactorily. **14 B-K3 P-QR3 15 KR-K1** There is also the interesting 15 QR-K1 R-K1 (more accurate than 15...Q-B2 16 P-KR3 N-R4 17 Q-B2 N-B5 18 B-QB1 when White has some advantage). 16 P-KR3 R-B1 17 Q-B2 B-N1! and Black has achieved full equality, Matulovic-Vaganian, Kragujevac 1974. **15...Q-B2 16 P-KR3 N-R4!** a frequently seen move by means of which Black tries to drive the enemy pieces from their strong posts. **17 N-R4** Black also gets full equality after 17 QR-Q1 N-B5 18 B-QB1 P-QN4 19 Q-B2 B-B4. **17...N-B5 18 Q-B2** After 18 N(Q4)-B5 N×P 19 Q-Q4 N×N 20 N×N B-K4 Black retains the extra pawn. **18...N×B** and Black has an easy game as in the 10th game of the match.

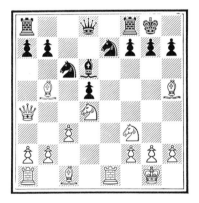

13	...	Q-B2
14	P-KR3	B-N3

15 B-N5   P-QR3

Deciding to force some clarification of the position. Black has to keep nagging at the enemy bishops, since otherwise he cannot develop his major pieces. Moreover, White must always keep an eye on exchanges which might prove unfavourable to him.

16	B-KB1	P-R3
17	B×N	N×B
18	QR-Q1	

By keeping a firm blockade on Q4 White maintains the better position.

18	...	N-B3
19	B-Q3	B-R4!

The straightforward 19...N×N 20 Q×N B-QB4 21 Q-KN4 (not 21 Q×QP? QR-Q1 winning); or 20 N×N B×B 21 R×B Q-B5 22 Q-B2, would leave White with the advantage, whereas now Black stands no worse.

20	P-KN4	B-N3
21	Q-B2!	

Naturally 21 B×B P×B 22 N-K6 Q-B2 23 N×R Q×N(B6) was considered by both players and assessed as being in Black's favour in view of the threats of ...R×N and ...Q×RP. On the other hand the advance 21 N-B5 would be met by 21...B×N 22 B×B QR-Q1 or 22...B-B4 when the bishop at KB5 may well prove to have no great role to play.

21	...	B×B
22	Q×B	QR-Q1
23	R-K2	KR-K1

Black cannot abandon the K-file, e.g. 23...B-B4 24 QR-K1 R-Q3 25 R-K8 and Black's defence is difficult.

24 N-B5

After 24 R×Rch R×R 25 N×N P×N 26 Q×RP P-KB4, or 26...B-B4 27 N-Q4 (27

K-N2 P-B4) 27...R-K3 Black might well seize the initiative on the K-side.

24	...	R×R
25	Q×R	B-B5
26	R-K1	P-KN3

26...K-B1 also looks satisfactory, avoiding simplification.

27	N-K7ch	N×N
28	Q×N	Q-N3
29	K-N2	K-N2
30	R-Q1	B-Q3

Not 30...R-Q3 31 R-Q4 when 32 R-QN4 will win a pawn.

31	Q-K2	B-B2
32	R-Q3	Q-K3
33	Q-Q1	B-N3
34	R-Q2	Q-K5
35	P-N3	

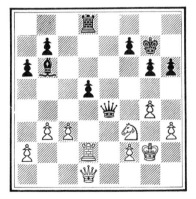

This threatens P-B4 and invites Black to play 35...R-QB1? 36 R-K2 Q-KB5 37 Q×P R×P 38 Q×NP, while 35...B-R4 36 R-Q4 Q-K2 37 P-N4 is equally bad for Black.

After 35...P-KN4 36 R-K2 (36 P-B4 is risky because of 36...P-KR4! when both 37 P×P P-N5 38 P×P Q×Pch and 37 R×P P×P 38 R×Pch K-B3 are catastrophic for White) 36...Q-KB5 37 R-K5 P-Q5 38 Q-Q3, the weakness of Black's KB4 shows up.

36   P-B4   **P-KR4**

36...P-Q5 is dangerous because of 37 P-N4. Now, however, after 37 P-N5 P-Q5 38 P-N4 B-Q1, Black is all right.

37	R×P	R×R
38	Q×R	Q×Q
39	P×Q	P×P
40	P×P	K-B3
41	K-B1	

The endgame is drawish. There followed

41	...	K-K2
42	N-Q2	B-B2
43	N-K4	P-B4
44	P×P	P×P
45	N-B5	K-Q3
46	N×Pch	K×P
47	P-N4	K-B5
48	N-B5	B-N3
49	N×P	K-N4
50	N-B5	K×P
51	N-N3	K-R6
52	Drawn	

Summing up: The moves 10 B-N5, 10 N(N3)-Q4, 10 B×N and in particular 10 P-B3, lead, in modern practice, to a complicated manoeuvring game with a lot of pieces on the board. Hundreds of games have been played with these moves and the majority of them have revolved around one and the same subject — The fate of the isolated QP.

GAME 55

White: Stein
Black: Uhlmann

Moscow 1971

1	P-K4	P-K3
2	P-Q4	P-Q4
3	N-Q2	P-QB4
4	KN-B3	N-QB3
5	B-N5	P×KP
6	N×P	B-Q2
7	B-K3	

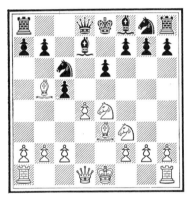

7	...	Q-R4ch
8	N-B3	P×P
9	N×P	B-N5
10	O-O	B×N
11	P×B	KN-K2
12	R-QN1	O-O
13	B-Q3	N×N

A good alternative is 13...P-K4 14 N-N5 B-K3 15 N-Q6 P-QN3 with complications.

14	P×N	B-B3

15	P-QB4	QR-Q1
16	Q-N4	

Provoking Black's next move, but 16 Q-K2 was safer, with equal chances.

16	...	P-B4!
17	Q-K2	P-B5!

A far-sighted pawn sacrifice.

18	B-Q2	Q-KN4
19	Q×Pch	K-R1
20	Q-R3!	

The best defence. Not 20 P-Q5 N×P 21 P×N R×P! with deadly threats.

20	...	P-KR3

Not 20...N-N3 21 B×N Q×B 22 P-Q5 B-Q2 23 Q-R4 and White is clearly better.

21	B-B3	

Again 21 P-Q5 fails to 21...N×P 22 P×N R×P 23 R-N3 KR-Q1, winning back the piece with advantage.

21	...	B-Q2!
22	Q-B3	B-N5!
23	Q-K4	

Not 23 Q×NP N-Q4!! 24 P×N B-B6 25 P-N3 P×P 26 BP×P Q-K6ch 27 R-B2 B×P 28 Q-N2 Q×B followed by placing the queen on the long, light-squared diagonal.

23	...	**B-B4**	
24	**Q-K2**	**QR-K1!?**	

More accurate is 24...B×B 25 Q×B
P-B6 26 P-N3 N-N3! 27 K-R1 Q-N5
28 KR-K1 N-B5! when White can
choose between 29 Q-K4 Q-R6 30
Q×BP N-Q4!! winning, or 29 Q-B1
N-K7 30 B-R1 Q-B1! winning back
the pawn with the better game. If
White defends by 28 R-KN1 then
28...R-B4! 29 R×P R-KR4 30 Q-B1
(if 30 R-N5 N-K4! 31 Q-B1 R×RPch!
32 K×R Q-R4ch 33 Q-R3 N-N5ch
followed by mate) 30...R-R6 31 R-N5
R-K1 and White is completely tied
up, since both P-B5 and P-Q5 fail to
...Q-R4, while if 32 Q-N1 N-B5 33
P×N R×Pch 34 K×R Q-R5 mate, or
32 Q-B1 R-K7 33 B-K1 Q×QP with a
great advantage for Black.

25   Q-Q2?!

White chooses not to play 25 B×B
N×B 26 Q-B3 N-R5 27 Q-R3 P-B6 28
P-N3 N-N7 with unclear complica-
tions.

25	...	**N-N3**
26	**R-N5**	**N-R5**
27	**P-B3**	**P-R3**
28	**R-Q5**	**R-K6**
29	**B×B**	**R(B1)×B**
30	**R×R**	**Q×R**
31	**P-Q5?**	

31 B-R1 was essential.

31	...	**Q-N3!**
32	**P-Q6**	

There is no defence to the double
threat of ...R×B and ...N×BPch.

32	...	**R-Q6**

Even simpler is 32...N×BPch 33
R×N R×R 34 P-Q7 Q-N8ch 35 Q-K1
Q×Qch 36 B×Q R-Q6 winning.

33   Q-K2

33 Q-QB2 is the best chance.

33	...	**R×B**
34	**P-Q7**	**Q-N3ch??**

A gross time-trouble blunder
which loses a well-played game.
34...R-Q6 35 Q-K8ch K-R2 36 P-N4
P×Pe.p. 37 P-KR3 P-N7 would have
won easily.

35	**P-B5!!**	**Resigns**

The QP cannot be stopped.

GAME 56

White: Parma
Black: Korchnoy

Moscow 1971

1	**P-K4**	**P-K3**
2	**P-Q4**	**P-Q4**
3	**N-Q2**	**P-QB4**
4	**P×QP**	**KP×QP**
5	**B-N5ch**	**B-Q2**
6	**Q-K2ch**	**B-K2**
7	**P×P**	**N-KB3**

8	N-N3!	O-O
9	B-K3	R-K1
10	N-B3!	P-QR3
11	B×B	QN×B
12	O-O	N×P
13	KR-K1?!	

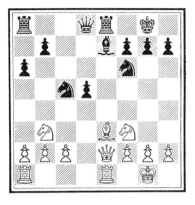

13	...	Q-B2
14	KN-Q4	N-R5
15	N-KB5!	B-B1!

15...N×P? fails to 16 N×P K×N 17 B-Q4 N-B5 18 Q-N4ch followed by 19 Q-N5 with great advantage.

16	Q-B3	Q×BP
17	B-Q4	R×Rch
18	R×R	R-K1

A fine defensive move giving White no time for N-R6ch.

19	R-KB1	R-K3
20	N-K3	Q-K5
21	Q×Q	

This offers the best drawing chances in view of the QB-file and well

posted bishop on Q4.

21	...	P×Q
22	R-B1	N-K1
23	R-B4!	

Again the best move, as 23...P-QN4 would be dubious because of 24 R-B8 N-Q3 25 R-R8 with a strong attack.

23	...	N-N3!
24	B×N	R×B
25	R×P	

White's active defence has allowed him to win back his pawn, but no more.

25	...	N-Q3
26	R-Q4	P-N3
27	K-B1	R-B3
28	R-Q2	P-B4
29	N-Q4	R-B8ch
30	R-Q1	R×Rch
31	N×R	B-N2
32	N-B2	

32 N-K6 is better.

32	...	K-B2
33	K-K2	K-K3
34	P-B4	N-K5
35	N(B2)-K3	P-KR4
36	P-KN3	B-B3
37	K-Q3	P-QN4
38	P-QN4	P-R5
39	P-N4!	B-K2
40	P×Pch	P×P
41	N-QB2	B-Q3
42	N-Q4ch	K-B3

| 43 | N-K3 | B×BP |
| 44 | N(K3)×P | **Drawn** |

GAME 57

White: Smyslov
Black: Uhlmann

Cienfuegos 1973

1	P-K4	P-K3
2	P-Q4	P-Q4
3	N-Q2	P-QB4
4	P×QP	KP×QP
5	B-N5ch	N-B3
6	Q-K2ch	B-K2
7	KN-B3	N-B3
8	P×P	O-O
9	N-N3	R-K1
10	B-K3	P-QR3
11	B-Q3	B-N5
12	O-O-O	

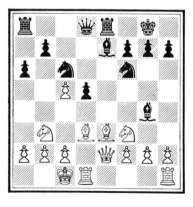

12	...	N-K4
13	P-KR3	B×N
14	P×B	Q-B2
15	K-N1	N(K4)-Q2

As expected, Black will win back the pawn, but Smyslov has a subtle plan in mind.

16 P-QB4!   P×P

Parrying the threat of 17 P×P N×QP 18 B×KRPch. Black might have tried 16...N×P 17 P×P (not 17 N×N B×N 18 P×P B×B 19 P×B Q-K4 20 P-K4 N×QP) 17...N×N in the hope of exploiting the various pawn weaknesses, but the white position contains dynamic possibilities.

17 B×BP   N×P

Uhlmann had been aiming for this position but failed to notice the following "petite combinaison".

18 B×BPch

Strangely enough, this is the third time that Smyslov has surprised Uhlmann with a sacrifice on the KB2 square (Moscow 1956 and Moscow 1971 were the two previous occasions).

| 18 | ... | K×B |
| 19 | B×N | P-QN4 |

Not 19...B×B 20 Q-B4ch K-B1 21 N×B and Black is in great trouble.

20	B×B	R×B
21	Q-Q3	R-Q2
22	Q-B5	QR-Q1

Black need not avoid simplification, in view of White's doubled pawns, so it was better to play at once 22...R×Rch 23 R×R R-K1 with good defensive chances.

| 23 | R-QB1! | Q-N3 |
| 24 | KR-K1 | R-Q4 |

After 24...Q×P White has 25 Q-K6ch and 26 Q×RP.

| 25 | Q-B2 | Q-Q3 |
| 26 | N-B5 | R-K1 |

The threat of 27 N-N7 could not be prevented by 26...R-QB1 or 26...R-Q7.

27	R×R	K×R
28	N-K4	Q-Q2
29	Q-N3	P-QR4

If 29...Q-B4 Smyslov gives 30 K-R1 N×N 31 R-K1 K-B1 32 P×N Q×BP 33 Q-N4ch Q-B4 34 R-KB1ch followed by 35 Q-N3 with a decisive attack.

| 30 | Q-K3 | K-B2 |
| 31 | P-R3 | R-Q6? |

Of course 31...R-Q8?? fails to 32 Q-N3ch but 31...P-R5! would still give Black a chance to set up a stiff resistance.

32	N×N	P×N
33	Q-R6	Q-B4
34	K-R1	R-Q2
35	R-KN1	P-R5
36	Q-N7ch	K-K3
37	Q-N8ch	K-Q3
38	R-Q1ch	K-B2
39	R-QB1ch	K-N2

Or 39...K-Q3 40 Q-KB8ch K-K4 41 Q-B5ch R-Q4 42 R-K1ch K-B5 43 Q-K3 mate. Or 39...K-N3 40 Q-N8ch R-N2 41 Q-Q6ch K-R2 42 R-B6 etc.

| 40 | Q-QB8ch | K-R2 |
| 41 | R-B7ch | Resigns |

GAME 58

White: Bebchuk
Black: Bronstein

Moscow Team Championship 1974

Notes by Bronstein

1	P-K4	P-K3
2	P-Q4	P-Q4
3	N-Q2	P-QB4
4	P×QP	KP×P
5	KN-B3	P-B5

259

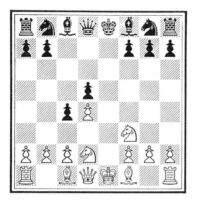

So far Black has a perfectly normal position but who knows what striking plan they'll dream up next? By playing 5...P-B5 Black deprives White's knight of the square Q4 and sets his opponent some unusual problems.

| 6 | P-QN3 | P×P |
| 7 | RP×P | B-QN5 |

The move 7...B-QN5 had not been played before. Why did I play this way? I had in mind my game against Lebedev from the Moscow Championship 1953. In that game I played 7...B-Q3, but in view of the threat of P-QB4 and then P-QN4-QN5 I had to waste a tempo by playing B-QN5.

Here is the game: 8 B-Q3 N-K2 9 O-O O-O 10 R-K1 QN-B3 11 P-B4 B-QN5 12 Q-B2 N-N3 13 B-N2 B-K3 14 QR-Q1 Q-B3 15 R-K3 B-Q3 16 Q-B3 N-B5 17 N-K5 B-KB4 18 P-N3 B×N 19 P×B Q-R3 20 B×B P-Q5 21 Q-B2 P×R 22 P×N P×N 23 Q-K4 QR-Q1 24 B-B3 Q-R4 25 P-B3 N-K2 26 B-KN4 Q-R5 27 Q×NP N-N3 28 Q-K4

P-KR4 29 P-B5 P×B 30 P×N Q-N4 31 P-B4 Q×NP 32 Q×Q P×Q 33 R×P R×R 34 B×R R-Q1 35 B-R5 R-Q6 36 P-N4 R-Q5 37 P-QB5 R×BP 38 P-N5 R-K5 39 P-B6 K-B2 40 B-B7 R-QB5 41 P-N6 P×P 42 B×P R×P 43 B-B2 K-K3 44 Resigns.

The reader may well ask whether it was really necessary to play ...B-QN5 since the bishop had to retreat to Q3 anyway. What can I say? White changed his plan and Black had to change as well. Such is chess. The person whose mind is more flexible wins.

8 B-N5ch

The natural 8 B-Q3 is simpler and better.

| 8 | ... | B-Q2 |
| 9 | Q-K2ch | |

This is altogether useless. Now Black not only finishes his development successfully but also he is able to harass the white queen with his rook from K1.

| 9 | ... | N-K2 |
| 10 | O-O | |

In all probability my opponent wanted to play 10 B×Bch Q×B 11 N-K5 but then realized that after 11... Q-K3 12 Q-N5ch QN-B3 13 Q×NP O-O Black has too dangerous an attack for his pawn.

| 10 | ... | O-O |
| 11 | B-R3 | |

No variations can prove the claim that it would have been better to exchange white-squared bishops, but intuition and experience show that this is so. My opponent did not expect the bishop on Q2 to refuse exchange, since according to the usual reckoning that bishop is bad whereas the bishop on QN5 is good. However, the excellent working diagonal QB1-KR6 and the half open character of the whole position justifies the exceptional assertion that the bishop on Q2 is good while that on QN5 is bad. These are just minor details which do not usually influence the outcome of the game.

11	...	B(N5)×B
12	R×B	QN-B3
13	P-B4	

This is a committal move. If White wanted to play for a draw he could have played 13 P-B3 and prevented the intrusion of the knight on KB5 by P-KN3; if Black's bishop had turned up on KR6 then he needn't have been ashamed of exchanging it by playing B-B1. An early draw would have been the most likely result.

| 13 | ... | R-K1 |
| 14 | Q-Q3 | N-N3 |

All of a sudden White is faced with certain difficulties. It is a pity to take the knight on QB6 with the bishop: he may have to play P-KN3 and then the absence of a white-squared bishop could be costly. He should

have taken the risk and played 15 P-N3 immediately. Black could have played 15...P-QR3 16 B-R4 Q-K2 17 KR-R1 QR-B1, keeping the tension up but without any clear breakthrough to the king.

After a long pause White came to a different decision: to relieve the pawn tension in the centre. The drawback of this plan is in his spoiled pawn formation.

| 15 | P×P | N-N5 |

After 15...N-B5 16 P×N N×Q 17 P×B R-K2 Black is left with no minor pieces.

| 16 | Q-B4 | |

| 16 | ... | P-QR4 |

It is hard to believe that this simple pawn move at the very least assures Black's strategic victory and may even win the game altogether. It threatens to trap the queen, nor does there seem to be an adequate defence against the intrusion of the black knight on N3, which is preparing to fork the queen and the rook from QB6. (17 R-Q1 N-B5 18 Q-KB1 B×B 19 Q×B N-K7ch 20 K-R1 N-B6). At this critical moment, instead of defending passively (17 B×B Q×B 18 R-Q1 N-B5 19 Q-KB1 P-QN4), White allows a smart finish.

17	R-Q1	N-B5
18	B×B	Q×B
19	N-K5	R×N!
20	P×R	Q-N5
21	Q-KB1	N-R6ch
22	K-R1	Q×R
23	Q×Q	N×BPch
24	K-N1	N×Q

White made another move, 26 P-Q6, out of sheer inertia, but then **resigned.**

GAME 59

White: Gligoric
Black: Stahlberg

3rd Match Game 1949

1	P-K4	P-K3
2	P-Q4	P-Q4
3	N-Q2	P-QB4
4	P×QP	KP×P
5	KN-B3	N-QB3
6	B-N5	P-QR3?!

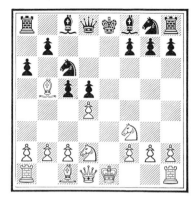

7	B×Nch	P×B
8	O-O	B-Q3

White has the advantage also after both 8...B-K3 9 R-K1 N-B3 10 N-N5 P×P 11 QN-B3! Lilienthal-Trupan, USSR 1949; and 8...P×P 9 R-K1ch B-K2 10 N-N3 K-B1 11 Q×P B-Q2 12 B-Q2 R-N1 13 B-R5 Q-B1 14 B-N6. Keres-Koberl, Sczawno Zdroj 1950.

9	P×P	B×BP
10	N-N3	B-Q3

After 10...B-N3 11 B-K3 B×B 12 R-K1 N-K2 13 R×B White stood better in Boleslavsky-Rossetto, Helsinki Olympiad 1952.

11	Q-Q4!	P-B3

If 11...N-B3 both 12 B-N5 and 12 R-K1ch are good for White.

12	B-B4	N-K2
13	KR-K1	O-O
14	B×B	Q×B
15	Q-B5!	Q×Q

262

16	N×Q	R-R2
17	P-QN4	

17 N-Q4 N-B4 would only ease Black's defence.

17	...	N-B4
18	N-N3	R-QB2
19	P-B3	K-B2
20	N(B3)-Q4	N-Q3

Now the exchange of knights brings Black no relief: after 20...N×N 21 N×N P-QB4 22 N-N3, Black's QP is weak.

21	N-QB5	R-K1
22	R×R	K×R
23	P-B3!	

After the immediate 23 P-QR4 Black can sacrifice a pawn by 23...N-K5 24 R-K1 K-B2 25 N×N P×N 26 R×P P-QB4 with counterplay.

23	...	K-B2
24	K-B2	P-N4
25	P-QR4	P-KR4
26	P-R5	

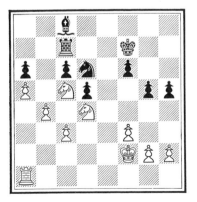

Fixing the QRP and the QB!

26	...	N-B5
27	R-K1	N-K4
28	P-N3	R-K2
29	R-K2	R-B2
30	P-KB4	P×P
31	P×P	N-N3
32	K-N3	N-K2
33	R-K1	R-R2
34	K-B2	

If 34 K-R4 N-N3ch.

34	...	R-R1?

He should play 34...K-N3.

35	N-R4	B-R6
36	R-K3	B-Q2
37	N-N6	R-R2
38	R-K1	

Not 38 R×Nch K×R 39 N-B8ch B×N 40 N×Pch K-Q3 41 N×R B-Q2 trapping the knight.

38	...	N-B4
39	N×N	

Black would have active play after 39 N×B N×N 40 N-N8 N-B4 41 N×BP R-B2.

39	...	B×N
40	N-R4	B-Q6
41	N-B5	B-N4

After 41...B-B4 42 P-R4 the white king would later go to Q4 winning.

42	P-B5	R-R1

If 42...R-B2 43 N-K6 and 44 R-KN1.

43	N-N7!	K-N2
44	R-KN1ch	K-B2
45	R-K1	K-N2
46	N-Q6	P-R5
47	K-B3	R-Q1
48	R-K7ch	K-N1
49	R-K6	K-N2
50	K-K3	

The safest method, as Black has swindling chances after 50 N-K8ch K-B2 51 N×P P-Q5, and 50 K-N4? P-Q5! 51 P×P B-B5! is good for Black.

50	...	B-R5
51	K-Q4	R-KN1
52	K-B5	K-R2
53	N-K8!	R-N7
54	N×Pch	K-N2
55	N-Q7!	R-KB7
56	P-B6ch	K-N3
57	N-K5ch	K-R4

On 57...K-B4, 58 K-Q6 wins.

| 58 | P-B7 | P-Q5 |
| 59 | R-K8 | **Resigns** |

GAME 60

White: Balashov
Black: Vaganian

39th USSR Championship
Leningrad 1971

Notes by Razuvayev

1	P-K4	P-K3
2	P-Q4	P-Q4
3	N-Q2	P-QB4
4	KN-B3	N-QB3
5	P×QP	KP×P
6	B-N5	B-Q3
7	P×P	Q-K2ch

8	Q-K2	B×BP
9	N-N3	Q×Qch
10	K×Q!	B-N3
11	B-K3	N-B3?!

A risky move. Black avoids weakening QB4 at the cost of doubled pawns.

12	B×B	P×B
13	N(B3)-Q4	B-Q2
14	KR-K1	O-O-O
15	P-KB3	N-K1

An interesting manoeuvre. The knight is transferred to Q3, where it can control the important squares QB5 and KB4.

Balashov plays to exchange his active knight on Q4 for the knight on

264

Q3; simplification favours White because of the weaknesses in Black's pawn formation.

16	B-Q3	N-Q3
17	K-Q2	KR-K1

17...N-B5ch is of course bad, because of 18 K-B3 and Black is forced to retreat.

18	N-N5	N×N
19	B×N	K-B2
20	B-Q3	K-Q3
21	R×R	R×R
22	P-B3	

An interesting moment. After the move played Vaganian manages to exchange his knight for the bishop and at the same time to get rid of his weak pawn on Q4. 22 P-KB4 would have been better. Here are some continuations: 22...P-Q5 23 P-B5 (preventing the bishop's transfer to Q4) 23...K-Q4 24 R-KB1 P-B3 25 R-B4 R-K4 26 P-QR3! and Black is hard put to defend against the threat of 27 N×P N×N 28 P-B4ch K-B4 29 P-QN4ch and so on. Or 24...N-K4 25 R-B4 N×B 26 R×Pch K-B3 27 R×N! and 27...B×P is not possible because of 28 N-Q4ch. And if 23...K-K4 24 P-QR3 K-B3, then 25 R-KB1 R-K4 26 R-B4 and Black is in difficulties. For example, 26...K-N4 27 P-N3 B×P 28 P-KR4ch K-N3 29 R×B R×R 30 P-N4 and White wins.

22	...	N-K4
23	N-Q4	N-B5ch

24	B×N	P×B
25	P-KR4	R-K4?

The beginning of all his troubles. The rook advances to the fourth and Black tries, quite unnecessarily, to keep it there for the rest of the game. Vaganian probably over-estimated his position. He should have stood firm since White could not create any real threats.

26	R-K1	R-QR4
27	P-R3	R-KR4
28	P-KN3	P-R3
29	R-K2	R-QB4

29...P-KN4 is bad because of 30 R-R2 P×P 31 P-KN4. On the next move this advance would have been bad because of 31 BP×P, after which White has an advanced passed pawn on the KR-file.

30	P-B4	R-QR4
31	K-K3	P-R4
32	R-Q2	K-K2

33 N-B2!

A strong move which sets Black a lot of problems. The knight is going to K3, where it will be very active. 33...R-QN4 would have been best now: for example, 34 N-N4 B-K3 35 K-Q4 P-B3 and Black can hold the position. 33 K-K4 B-B3ch 34 N×Bch P×N 35 R-Q4 P-KB4ch 36 K-K3 P-QN4 would not have gained anything: the game is level.

33	...	B-K3
34	K-K4!	B-B4ch
35	K-Q4	B×N

Vaganian puts his hope in a rook ending, but in vain. However, it's now hard to find a good recommendation. For example: 35...B-K3 36 N-K3 R-R1 37 K-K4 and Black has difficulty in defending against P-B5. Or 36...R-QB4 37 P-B5 B×P 38 N×P R-B3 39 N-K3 B-K3 (even worse is 39...R-Q3ch 40 N-Q5ch K-Q2 41 K-B4 and White wins) 40 P-B4 with advantage to White.

36	R×B	R-QB4
37	R-K2ch	K-B3
38	R-K8	

But not 38 R-K5? R×R 39 P×Rch K-B4 40 K×P K-N5 41 K-N5 K×P 42 K×P K×P 43 K×P K-N6 44 P-B4 P-R5 45 P-B5 P-R6 46 P-B6 P-R7 47 P-B7 P-R8=Qch.

38	...	R-QN4
39	R-K2	R-QB4

40	P-R4	P-N3
41	R-K8	R-B2

This was the sealed move. Balashov played the endgame so accurately that it could serve as an instructional text. The transfer of the rook to QN5 is specially noteworthy.

42	R-K5	R-B3
43	R-QN5!	K-K3
44	K-K4	K-B3
45	P-B5	P-N4
46	R-Q5	P×P
47	P×P	K-K2
48	K-K5!	

An excellent move. The white king is working very hard in this game. Black is obliged to weaken his second rank.

48	...	P-B3ch
49	K-Q4	R-B1
50	R-N5	R-B3
51	P-R5!	P×P
52	R×NPch	K-B1
53	K-Q5!	R-B1
54	R-N5	R-K1
55	K×P	R-K5ch
56	K-Q5	R×P
57	R×P	K-N2
58	P-N4	R-R8
59	P-N5	P-R5
60	P-B4	P-R6
61	R-R2	P-R7
62	K-B5	K-B2
63	R-K2	K-B1
64	P-N6	K-N2
65	R-QN2	**Resigns**

GAME 61

White: Karpov
Black: Kuzmin

Leningrad Interzonal 1973

Notes by Karpov

1	P-K4	P-K3
2	P-Q4	P-Q4
3	N-Q2	P-QB4
4	P×QP	KP×P
5	KN-B3	N-QB3
6	B-N5	B-Q3
7	P×P	B×BP
8	O-O	KN-K2
9	N-N3	B-Q3 .
10	B-N5	O-O
11	B-KR4	Q-B2

A wasted tempo. He should have started the battle for the central squares by playing 11...B-KN5. I was going to play 12 B-N3 B×B 13 RP×B Q-N3 14 B-Q3, threatening 15 B×RPch K×B 16 N-N5ch, and after 14...N-B4 15 B×N B×B 16 P-QB3 White has a slight advantage.

12	B-N3	B×B

It was still better to play 12...B-KN5.

13	RP×B	B-N5
14	R-K1	QR-Q1
15	P-B3	Q-N3
16	B-Q3	

The player who has the isolated pawn aims either to gain the initiative on the K-side or to advance the isolated pawn.

Since Black has no attack here he has only one plan: to advance the QP. If he does not achieve this White will have a clear advantage.

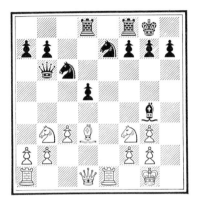

16	...	N-N3

16...P-Q5 would, of course, have been followed by 17 P-B4.

17	Q-B2	B×N
18	P×B	R-Q3

If 18...P-Q5 19 P-KB4 (19 P-QB4? N-N5) 19...P×P 20 P×P then the white pawns limit the action of Black's knights on both sides of the board.

19	P-KB4	KR-Q1
20	P-R3!	

Now the advance of the QP is out of the question. White has a clear plan: the knight goes to KB3, the

267

rooks double on the K-file and then, according to circumstances, the KBP or the Q-side pawns march up. Black tries to create some counterplay by advancing his KRP, but he does not succeed.

20	...	P-KR4
21	K-N2	P-R5
22	R-K2	N-B1
23	N-Q2	R-R3
24	N-B3	

What can Black do about his KRP? He cannot defend it, while if he advances it, it will be encirled. Exchanging it leads to the opening of lines, which is dangerous for Black.

24	...	P×P
25	P×P	N-Q2
26	QR-K1	K-B1

There does not seem to be any other way of defending the first rank. The white pawns now march ahead and completely disorganize the inter-action of Black's pieces.

27	P-KN4	Q-B2
28	P-N5	R-KR1
29	K-N3	N-B4
30	B-B5	P-KN3
31	P-N4!	

Before the bishop retreats the knight has to go from B4.

31	...	N-K5ch

31...P×B 32 P×N Q-Q2 33 R-R2 K-

N2 34 N-R4 is quite bad, as is 31...N-Q2 32 B×P P×B 33 Q×P, with an irresistible attack for White.

32	B×N	P×B
33	Q×P	K-N2
34	P-N5	N-R4
35	Q-K7!	

This forces a won ending, since 35...Q×QBP is bad because of 36 R-K3 Q-N7 37 R-K5.

35	...	Q×Q
36	R×Q	R-Q6
37	R-B7	N-N6
38	K-N4	R-KB1
39	R(K1)-K7	Resigns

There is no defence against the threatened 40 R×BPch R×R 41 R×Rch K×R 42 N-K5ch.

GAME 62

White: Karpov
Black: Uhlmann

Madrid 1973

1	P-K4	P-K3
2	P-Q4	P-Q4
3	N-Q2	P-QB4
4	P×QP	KP×P
5	KN-B3	N-QB3
6	B-N5	B-Q3
7	P×P	B×BP
8	O-O	N-K2
9	N-N3	B-Q3
10	B-N5	O-O

11	B-KR4	B-KN5
12	B-K2	B-R4

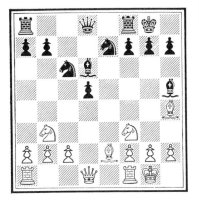

13	R-K1	Q-N3
14	N(B3)-Q4	B-N3
15	P-QB3	KR-K1
16	B-B1	B-K5
17	B-N3	B×B
18	RP×B	P-QR4

18...QR-Q1 is better.

19	P-R4!	N×N
20	N×N!	N-B3

20...Q×P loses to 21 N-N5 threatening the deadly 22 R-K2.

21	B-N5	R(K1)-Q1
22	P-KN4!	

An excellent manoeuvre, guaranteeing some endgame advantage.

22	...	N×N

It was more exact to play ...QR-B1 first.

23	Q×N	Q×Q
24	P×Q	QR-B1

White's position is stronger than it appears at first sight. For example, after 24...K-B1 25 R-K3 and 26 QR-K1 followed by P-B3, he has the advantage.

25	P-B3	B-N3
26	R-K7	P-N3
27	QR-K1	P-R3
28	R-N7	R-Q3

Or 28...R-B7 29 R(K1)-K7 K-B1 30 R(K7)-Q7! gives White a clear advantage.

29	R(K1)-K7	

There is now no defence against P-B4-B5.

29	...	P-R4

Or 29...R-B7 30 R-N8ch K-R2 31 R(K7)-K8 R-B8ch 32 K-R2 B-N8 33 R-K7.

30	P×P	B×P
31	P-KN4	B-N3
32	P-B4!	R-B8ch
33	K-B2	R-B7ch
34	K-K3	B-K5
35	R×BP	R-N3
36	P-N5	K-R2

36...R×QNP 37 R(B7)-K7 gives similar play.

37	R(B7)-K7	R×QNP
38	B-K8	R-N6ch
39	K-K2	R-N7ch
40	K-K1	R-Q3
41	R×KNPch	K-R1
42	R(KN7)-K7	Resigns

GAME 63

White: Kuzmin
Black: Uhlmann

Leningrad Interzonal 1973

Notes by Taimanov

1	P-K4	P-K3
2	P-Q4	P-Q4
3	N-Q2	P-QB4
4	KN-B3	QN-B3
5	P×QP	KP×P
6	B-N5	B-Q3
7	P×P	B×BP
8	O-O	N-K2
9	N-N3	B-Q3
10	B-N5	O-O
11	B-KR4	B-KN5

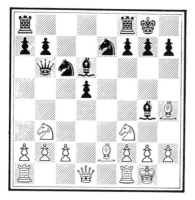

12	B-K2	Q-N3
13	B×N!	

This is what Kuzmin had in mind. The simplification begun by this surprising exchange, which reduces Black's chances of activating his pieces, leaves him with all his weaknesses and without any counter-chances. It is true that this positional advantage could prove insufficient for victory, but playing such an ending is a pleasure for White, whereas it is torture for Black.

13	...	N×B

It is curious that Uhlmann thought for one hour and twenty minutes over this natural move! It seems that Kuzmin's coup achieved its aim; Uhlmann was not keen on going into an ending without prospects, but there was no choice. If 13...B×B?! 14 Q×P QR-Q1 15 Q-B4 and Black does not get enough compensation for the pawn.

14	Q-Q4	Q×Q
15	N(B3)×Q	B-Q2

It was hardly worth wasting a tempo on this retreat. After 15...B×B 16 N×B QR-B1 Black has as good a chance of defending as in the game.

16	QR-Q1	KR-Q1
17	KR-K1	K-B1
18	P-QB3	

The position is unusual in that despite White's accumulation of small advantages, Black suffers from very few small disadvantages. It is only his QP which can cause him any worry at the moment, and for this reason Uhlmann should have been more patient and should have diligently parried threats as they appeared — particularly as he had quite a few useful moves of his own — ...P-KN3, ...QR-B1, ...P-QR3. The German Grandmaster, however, is of a different nature. He will not reconcile himself to the role of "passive sufferer", and with the following moves he tries to intervene actively in the struggle, but, alas, he makes things worse for himself.

18 ... P-QR4?

Uhlmann's "pseudo-activity" only leads to the creation of new weaknesses in his camp.

19 P-QR3 P-R5

In the same gambling style. 19...P-QN3 would have been a lesser evil.

20 N-R1!

It seems that Uhlmann has just given the white knight a push along its intended route: R1-B2-K3.

20 ... N-B1

Although Black's position is already not very good, perhaps it could have been held by stubborn defence. First of all, the knight

should have remained where it was, defending the weakness on Q4. Perhaps it would have been worth while considering regrouping by means of ...B-B4, ...B-K1 and ...R-Q3.

Uhlmann, however, puts all his hopes in counterplay and, in particular, in moving his knight to B5.

21	N(R1)-B2	N-N3
22	N-K3	B-B5
23	N(Q4)-B2	B-K3
24	R-Q4	

An instructive moment. These support points are now diving boards for reshuffling. White's manoeuvre underlines the disadvantages of the march of the black RP.

24 ... B×N

After this exchange the weaknesses on the black squares are vulnerable, but even with 24...B-K4 25 R-QN4 R-Q3 26 N-Q4 Black's position is pitiful.

25	N×B	N-B5
26	R(K1)-Q1!	

An excellent move, destroying all Black's illusions.

26 ... R(Q1)-QB1

It seems he has to part with the pawn. 26...N×NP is not good, because of 27 R(Q1)-Q2 and if 26...N×N 27 P×N then the pawns on

Q4 and on R4 are easy prey for White.

27 N×P

27 N×N P×N 28 B-B3 probably wins without placing too heavy a demand on White's technique, but Kuzmin prefers a more forcing method.

27	...	B×N
28	R×B	N×NP
29	R-N1	N-B5
30	R×P	

White has won a pawn and kept the initiative. The weakness of the pawns on R3 and B3 cannot be exploited because of the threats on the seventh rank.

30 ... N-R4

Otherwise 31 R(Q5)-Q7 is decisive.

31	R(N7)-N5	N-B5
32	R-Q7!	P-N3
33	P-KB4	

This move was unanimously deplored by all the commentators. Indeed, after the natural 33 R(N5)-Q7 N-K4 34 R-K7 R-K1 35 R×Rch R×R 36 P-KB4 N-B3 37 B-N5, White wins straight away. However, the move played does not do any harm. Victory (in spite of opinions to the contrary) is still firmly in hand.

33 ... R-R3(!)

The best chance. Black intends to put his rook on KB3, defending against the threat on the seventh.

34 R-N4(!)

The only way of keeping the advantage. Although White's attacking chances are bleak, he has not exhausted all possible methods of realizing his advantage.

34 ... R(R3)-QB3

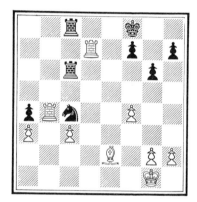

35 B-Q3

This manoeuvre, which was given an exclamation mark by Sakharov, deserves in my opinion at least one question mark. With the simple combination 35 B×N R×B 36 R-Q8ch White could have reduced to a won rook ending, but instead he gives up an important pawn.

Note that 35 R×RP is no good because of 35...N-N3.

35 ... K-N2?

Inexplicable! Having endured so much Uhlmann, as if not believing in his lucky star, lets a simple chance of salvation slip away. After the obvious 35...N×P 36 R×RP (36 R(N4)-N7 R-B3) 36...N-B5 37 R(R4)-R7 R-B3 Black is all right. Now, however, Black is in trouble.

| 36 | R(Q7)-Q4! | N×P |
| 37 | P-B4 | |

This is the whole point. The black knight is trapped.

| 37 | ... | R-R3 |
| 38 | K-B2 | |

The king in person sets out on the hunt.

38	...	R-R4
39	K-K3	R-B2
40	K-Q2	P-R4
41	R-K4!	

This was the sealed move. As the king cannot get near the knight (41 K-B3 N-N4ch), White sends the heavy artillery after him.

41	...	R-Q2
42	R-K1	R-QB4
43	R-QB1!	Resigns

There is no defence to 44 R-QB3.

GAME 64

White: Vogt
Black: Uhlmann

Potsdam 1974

1	P-K4	P-K3
2	P-Q4	P-Q4
3	N-Q2	P-QB4
4	P×QP	KP×P
5	KN-B3	N-QB3
6	B-N5	B-Q3
7	P×P	B×BP
8	O-O	N-K2
9	N-N3	B-Q3
10	B-N5	O-O
11	B-KR4	B-KN5
12	B-K2	R-K1
13	R-K1	Q-N3!
14	N(B3)-Q4	N-N3!
15	N×N	R×B

The most precise continuation.

| 16 | R×R | P×N |

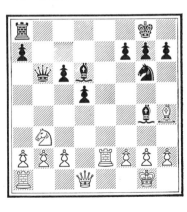

| 17 | B-N3 | B-K2! |

Black also has good play after 17...B×B 18 P×B N-B1 followed by 19...N-K3.

18	P-KR3	B×R
19	Q×B	P-QR4
20	P-B3	P-R4!

Gaining more space, as 21 Q×P P-R5 22 N-Q4 Q×P is very good for Black.

21	N-Q4	P-KR5
22	B-R2	B-B3
23	R-Q1	P-R5!
24	Q-B2	Q-B4
25	Q-Q3	R-K1
26	P-QN4!	P×Pe.p.
27	P×P	Q-N3
28	P-QN4	R-K5
29	B-Q6	

29 P-B3 is more exact.

| 29 | ... | B×N |
| 30 | P×B | Q-Q1! |

The sudden switch of the queen to the K-side brings the white king into danger.

31	B-B5	N-B5
32	Q-KB3	Q-N4
33	R-R1	K-R2
34	K-R2	R-K3!
35	Q-N4	

Passive defence by 35 R-KN1 is better, as the ending is now won for Black.

35	...	Q×Q
36	P×Q	R-K7
37	R-KB1	

After 37 K-N1 both 37...P-R6 and 37...N-Q6 are good for Black.

| 37 | ... | N-Q6! |
| 38 | P-B4 | |

Equally hopeless is 38 P-B3 N-B5 39 R-KN1 R-Q7 followed by ...N-K7.

| 38 | ... | N-B7! |

Or 38...N×B 39 QP×N R-N7 with a favourable rook ending.

| 39 | R-QR1 | N×Pch |

First 39...K-N3 would have been more exact.

40	K-R3	N-K6
41	R-R6	R×P
42	K×P	

Not of course 42 R×P R-N6ch 43 K-R2 N-N5ch 44 K-R1 P-R6 followed by ...N-B7ch and ...R-N7 mate.

42	...	R-N5ch
43	K-R3	R×P
44	R×P	P-N4

This pawn cannot be stopped without the loss of a piece.

| 45 | P-N5 | |

Or 45 B-Q6 P-N5ch 46 K-R2 (after

46 K-N3 or R4 then 46...R-B3 wins a piece) 46...R-B7ch 47 K-N1 P-N6 48 B×P R-KN7ch wins the bishop.

45	...	P-N5ch
46	K-R4	

Or 46 K-R2 R-B7ch 47 K-N3 R-B6ch 48 K-R4 P-B3 threatening ...R-R6 mate.

46	...	P-B3!
47	B-Q6	R-B6
48	B-N3	K-N3
49	Resigns	

GAME 65

White: Neukirch
Black: Uhlmann

Potsdam 1974

1	P-K4	P-K3
2	P-Q4	P-Q4
3	N-Q2	P-QB4
4	P×QP	KP×P
5	B-N5ch	N-B3
6	KN-B3	B-Q3
7	O-O	

The current preference is for 7 P×P.

7	...	P×P
8	N-N3	N-K2
9	N(N3)×P	O-O
10	B-N5	

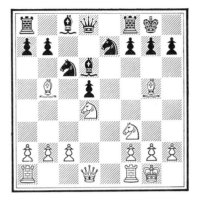

10	...	Q-B2

Against Geller (Amsterdam, 1970) I (Uhlmann) played 10...P-B3 but White can then simplify by 11 N×N P×N 12 B×QBP! B×Pch! 13 N×B N×B.

11	P-KR3	P-B3
12	B-K3	N-K4!

The idea behind 11...P-B3. Black's strong-point on K4 more than compensates for his isolated QP and weakness on K3.

13	P-QN3	P-QR3
14	B-K2	B-Q2
15	Q-Q2	P-QN4
16	QR-Q1	K-R1
17	N-K1	N(K4)-N3

The correct recipe, preparing to advance the KBP and to counter a similar idea by White. The latter's pieces are not well co-ordinated, as we shall soon see.

18	N-Q3	P-B4!
19	B-N5	

The best reply, as 19 P-KB4 gives Black a clear advantage after 19...N-N1! followed by ...N-B3-K5.

19	...	P-B5
20	B×N	B×B
21	B-N4	

21 B-B3 is a little better.

21	...	B-KB3
22	B×B	

Or 22 N-N4 B×B 23 P×B B×N 24 Q×B P-B6! 25 P-N3 QR-Q1 with the better position.

22	...	B×N
23	B-N4	B-B6
24	Q-K2	

It is essential to play 24 Q-B1.

24	...	P-B6!
25	Q-K3	

The BP is taboo, as White loses a piece after 25 B×P QR-K1.

25	...	QR-K1!
26	Q-B5	

This gives Black a won ending. 26 Q-N5 is the best defence.

26	...	Q×Q
27	N×Q	P×P
28	K×P	P-KR4!

The point, as now 29 B×P loses to 29...N-B5ch.

29	B-Q7	N-B5ch
30	K-N1	R-K2
31	Resigns	

There is no defence to the threats of ...B-N5 or ...B-Q5.

Part Four

Miscellaneous Systems

1	P-K4	P-K3

2	P-Q4	P-Q4
3	P-K5	

2	P-Q4	P-Q4
3	P×P	

and	2	P-Q3

Chapter 12

The Advance Variation

White: Alexander
Black: Uhlmann

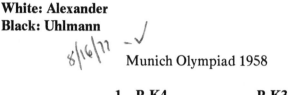

Munich Olympiad 1958

1	P-K4	P-K3
2	P-Q4	P-Q4
3	P-K5	

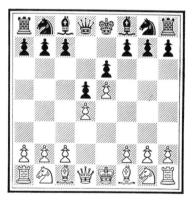

This variation, also named after Nimzovich, has waned in popularity of late. However, it is a perfectly valid method of play and could rapidly come back into fashion. White states his strategic intentions at once. He aims to blockade the black centre pawns, either by supporting his centre with P-QB3 or else by making the temporary sacrifice of a pawn on Q4, so that he can later occupy this square with a piece.

3 ...   P-QB4

The logical counter. If 3...P-KB3 4 B-Q3, and if 3...P-QN3 4 P-QB3 and Black must first play 4...Q-Q2 if he wants to continue with ...B-R3 (4...B-R3?? 5 B×B N×B 6 Q-R4ch winning a piece).

4 P-QB3

Let us have a quick look at the alternatives:

(a) **4 Q-N4 P×P 5 N-KB3 P-B4 6 Q-N3 N-QB3 7 B-Q3 B-Q2 8 O-O Q-B2 9 P-B3 O-O-O 10 B-KB4** Not 10 P×P N-N5! **10...KN-K2 11 P×P** Or 11 N-N5 P-KR3 12 N-B7 P-KN4! 13 B-B1 P-B5 14 Q-R3 B-N2 with advantage to Black. **11...N-N3 12 N-B3 N×B 13 Q×N P-KR3 14 P-KR4 P-KN4!** with good play for Black. Honfi-Portisch, Hungary 1964.

(b) **4 N-KB3 N-QB3 5 B-Q3 P×P 6 O-O P-B3** Or 6...KN-K2 7 B-KB4 N-N3 8 B-N3 B-K2 with complex play. **7 B-QN5** If 7 B-KB4? P-KN4! and 8...P-N5. **7...B-Q2 8 B×N P×B 9 Q×P Q-N3 10 Q-KB4 P-KB4** with unclear play.

(c) **4 P×P N-QB3 5 N-KB3 B×P 6 B-Q3 P-B3 7 Q-K2 P×P 8 N×P N-B3 9 B-KB4 O-O 10 O-O N-K5 11 N×N P×N 12 B-K3 B×B 13 Q×B N-B3 14 N-Q2 Q-N3** with equality. Becker-Maroczy, Carlsbad 1929.

4 ...   N-QB3

The plan of exchanging white-squared bishops was somewhat discredited by the game I. Zaitsev-Doda, USSR 1968: **4...Q-N3 5 N-B3 B-Q2 6 B-K2 B-N4 7 P-B4!** The old continuation 7 O-O gave Black equality after 7...B×B 8 Q×B Q-R3 9 Q-Q1 N-Q2 (not 9...N-QB3 10 P×P B×P 11 P-QN4 B-K2 12 N-R3 Q-N3 13 B-K3 Q-Q1 14 N-QN5 P-KR4 15 B-B5 and Black suffered from the weakness of his Q3 square in Ciocaltea-Portisch, Ploesti 1965) 10 R-K1 N-K2 11 N-R3, Mititelu-Barcza, Budapest 1960. An interesting alternative is 7 P×P B×P 8 P-QN4 B-B1 with an unclear position. **7...B×P 8 B×B P×B** If 8...Q-N5ch 9 QN-Q2 P×B 10 P-QR3 with the better game. **9 P-Q5! P×P 10 Q×P N-K2 11 Q-K4 N-Q2 12 O-O Q-QB3 13 Q×BP N-QN3 14 Q-K2** with a positional plus.

5 N-B3   Q-N3

The most exact move. After 5...KN-K2 White can play 6 N-R3 (if 6 B-Q3 P×P 7 P×P N-B4 8 B×N P×B 9 N-B3 B-K3 10 N-K2 B-K2 11 P-KR4 P-KR3 with equality) 6...N-B4 7 N-B2 B-Q2 8 B-Q3 with advantage to White.

6 P-QR3

A solid continuation usually leading to dour positional struggles.

Those with more aggressive tendencies would prefer the Milner-Barry Gambit, **6 B-Q3.** This move involves a pawn sacrifice which theory considers insufficient but which practice has shown to be not without danger: **6...P×P 7 P×P B-Q2 8 O-O N×QP 9 N×N Q×N 10 N-B3** The only way to obtain real attacking chances. After 10 Q-K2 N-K2 11 N-B3 N-B3 12 B-K3 (not 12 N-N5 Q×KP 13 Q×Q N×Q 14 N-B7ch K-Q1 15 N×R N×B with advantage to Black) 12...Q×P 13 P-B4 Q-Q3 14 N-N5 Q-N1 15 P-B5 P-K4 16 Q-R5 P-QR3 17 P-B6 P-KN3 18 B×P B-K3! with great advantage to Black. Sturm-Schmid, 1954. **10...P-QR3!** It is extremely risky to take the second pawn, as after 10...Q×KP 11 R-K1 Q-N1 (or 11...Q-Q3 12 N-N5 B×N [if 12...Q-N1 13 Q-B3 B-Q3 14 Q×QP B×Pch 15 K-R1 B-B3 16 Q-N5 with a clear advantage to White] 13 B×Bch K-Q1 14 Q-B3 with good play for the pawn, in view of his lead in development and the vulnerability of the black king) 12 N×P B-Q3 13 Q-N4 K-B1 14 B-Q2 White has a strong attack. **11 Q-K2 N-K2 12 K-R1** This move gives Black the greatest trouble. After 12 R-Q1 Black has 12...Q-KR5 13 P-B4 (13 P-KN3 Q-R6 gives White nothing) 13...N-B3 14 R-B1 B-B4ch 15 K-R1 O-O 16 P-B5 P×P 17 N×P Q-Q5! with advantage. Cornelis-Bouwmeester, Lugano Olympiad 1968. An alternative is 12...N-B3 13 B×QRP Q×KP 14 B×P! (not at once 14 Q×Q N×Q 15 B×P R-R2 16 B×P P×B 17 R-K1 P-B3 and Black is better) 14...Q×Q 15 N×Q R-QN1 16 B×N B×B and it is not clear whether White can exploit his two Q-side passed pawns.

For an examination of 12 K-R1 see Badestein-Uhlmann, East Germany 1973 (illustrative game 66).

Another interesting, but somewhat dubious move is **6 B-K2 P×P** There are great complications after 6...N-R3!? 7 B×N Q×P 8 B-QB1 Q×R 9 Q-B2 P×P 10 O-O B-Q2 11 KN-Q2 P×P! 12 N-N3 N-N5 13 N×Q N×Q 14 N×N P-QN4! and Black has an excellent game, as 15 N×P loses to 15...R-B1 and if 15 B-R3 P-QR4. For 6...P-B3 see Zhuravlev-Sacharov, USSR 1971 (illustrative game 67). **7 P×P N-R3** The best move. White stands better after 7...KN-K2 8 N-R3! N-B4 9 N-B2 B-N5ch 10 K-B1 B-K2 11 P-KN3 B-Q2 12 K-N2 P-KR4 13 P-KR3. Klaman-Chistiakov, USSR 1949. **8 N-B3** After 8 B×N Q×NP 9 QN-Q2 P×B White has hardly anything for the pawn. Black is also better after 8 P-QN3 N-B4 9 B-N2 B-N5ch 10 K-B1 P-KR4 11 N-B3 B×N 12 B×B B-Q2. Kholmov-Petrosian, USSR 1949. **8...N-B4 9 N-QR4 B-N5ch 10 B-Q2** Not 10 K-B1 Q-Q1 11 B-KN5 B-K2 12 B×B Q×B 13 Q-Q2 O-O 14 P-KN3 B-Q2 15 N-B3 P-B3 16 P-KN4 N(B4)×P! with a clear advantage to Black. Camilleri-Uhlmann, Raach 1969. **10...Q-R4 11 B-B3 P-QN4 12 P-QR3 B×Bch 13 N×B P-N5** with even chances.

6 ... P-B5

The best reply, as it prevents White's intended expansion on the Q-side. Weaker are:

(a) 6...B-Q2 7 P-QN4! The point of 6 P-QR3, gaining space on the Q-side **7...P×QP 8 P×P KN-K2** If 8...P-B3 9 B-Q3! **9 N-B3 N-B4 10 N-QR4!** Less good is 10 B-N2 N(B4)×P 11 N×N Q×N 12 Q×Q N×Q 13 N×P N-B7ch 14 K-Q1 R-B1. **10...Q-Q1 11 B-N2 N-R5 12 N×N Q×N 13 B-Q3 P-B4 14 O-O B-K2 15 P-B4 O-O 16 N-B5 B×N 17 QP×B** with advantage to White. Unzicker-Gligoric, Stockholm Interzonal 1952.

281

(b) 6...P-QR4 7 B-K2 P×P After 7...B-Q2 White can play 8 P-QN3 P×P 9 P×P KN-K2 10 O-O N-B4 11 B-K3 B-K2 12 N-B3 O-O 13 B-Q3 N×B 14 P×N P-B3 15 N-KN5! with advantage. Cortlever-Van Seters, Beverwijk 1958. **8 P×P KN-K2 9 N-B3 N-B4 10 N-QN5!** and according to Keres, White is better.

7 P-KN3

Allowing White the option of developing his KB on KN2 or KR3. For 7 QN-Q2 see Zinn-Hamann, Lugano Olympiad 1968 (illustrative game 68).

7 ...   P-B3

7...N-R4 is possible e.g. 8 QN-Q2 B-Q2 9 B-R3 P-B4?! (better is 9...N-K2) 10 P×P e.p. P×P 11 O-O O-O-O 12 R-K1 B-N2 13 R-N1 R-K1 14 P-N3 P×P 15 N×P N×N 16 R×N Q-R3 17 R-N2 with an edge for White. Prahov-Makarov, USSR 1962. Or here 9 B-N2 O-O-O 10 O-O P-KR3 11 R-K1 N-K2 12 N-B1 N-B4 13 N-K3 N×N 14 R×N B-K2 15 R-K1 Q-N6 16 Q-K2 B-QR5 17 B-K3 K-N1 18 QR-Q1 Q-B7! 19 R-Q2 Q-B4 and Black stands better. Clarke-Petrosian, Munich Olympiad 1958.

8	P×P	N×BP
9	B-N2	B-Q3
10	O-O	O-O
11	Q-K2	K-R1!?

It is possible to play 11...N-QR4 12 QN-Q2 B-Q2 and if now 13 N-K5 Black has 13...B-K1! etc.

12	N-K5	B×N?!

Better is first 12...N-QR4 13 N-Q2 and then 13...B×N.

13	P×B	N-Q2
14	B-K3	N-B4
15	N-Q2	Q-R4
16	P-B4	B-Q2
17	B×N?!	

After 17 N-B3! White stands better.

17	...	Q×Bch
18	Q-B2	Q×Qch
19	R×Q	P-KN4!
20	N-B1	R-B2
21	N-K3	P×P
22	P×P	R-KN1

Black has succeeded in weakening White's KBP but White can still defend himself.

23	QR-KB1	P-N4
24	P-R3	P-KR4

Preventing 25 N-N4.

25	N-B2	B-K1
26	N-N4	N-K2

Black should keep his knight for the control of the dark squares while White's knight is not stable on QN4.

27	K-R2	R(N1)-B1
28	K-N1	R-N2
29	N-B2	N-B4

| 30 | K-R2 | P-R5 |
| 31 | N-Q4 | N×N |

A new idea. By exchanging knights now, Black creates a pawn majority on the Q-side. White's task is to activate his bishop on the other wing.

32	P×N	B-N3
33	P-B5!	R×P
34	R×R	B×R
35	R-B4?	

After having found his best chance of salvation, White misses the best reply in 35 B×P. True, White will still recapture the pawn but he allows time for the decisive advance of Black's dangerous Q-side pawns.

35	...	R-KB2
36	R×Pch	K-N2
37	B-B3	P-R4
38	B-Q1	P-N5
39	R-B4	B-N3
40	R-N4	

In the bishop ending White loses a piece to the passed QBP.

| 40 | ... | R-B7ch |
| 41 | Resigns | |

GAME 66

White: Badestein
Black: Uhlmann

East Germany 1973

1	P-K4	P-K3
2	P-Q4	P-Q4
3	P-K5	P-QB4
4	P-QB3	N-QB3
5	N-B3	Q-N3
6	B-Q3	P×P
7	P×P	B-Q2
8	O-O	N×QP
9	N×N	Q×N
10	N-B3	P-QR3!
11	Q-K2	N-K2
12	K-R1	

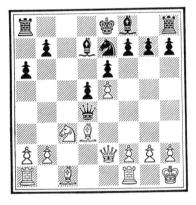

12	...	N-B3
13	P-B4	N-N5
14	R-Q1!	

Far better than 14 B-N1 Q-B5!
15 Q-B3 P-Q5 with advantage.

14	...	N×B

15	R×N	Q-B5

Or 15...Q-N3 is possible.

16	B-K3	B-N5
17	P-QN3	Q-B2
18	R-QB1	R-QB1!?

The prelude to a queen sacrifice.

19	N-R4	Q×Rch

The logical continuation, but both
19...B-B3 and 19...Q-Q1 were
possible.

20	B×Q	R×Bch
21	R-Q1	R×Rch
22	Q×R	O-O
23	N-N6	B-B3
24	Q-Q4	B-K2
25	P-KR3	P-B3!

Opening up the position for the
two bishops.

26	P-B5?	

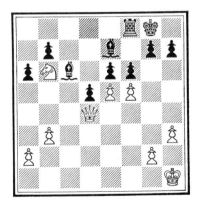

White overlooks a subtle manoeuvre by Black. 26 P-QR4 is better.

26	...	B-Q1!
27	P×KP	

Somewhat better is 27 P×BP R×P! (White has good counter-chances after the risky 27...P-K4 28 Q×KP! B×N 29 Q-K6ch K-R1 30 P-B7 B-B4 31 P-B6 etc.) 28 P×P B-B2! 29 P-KN3 (or 29 K-N1) 29...R×P and Black's pieces can develop their full power.

27	...	P×P
28	Q-B5	B×N!

The simplest way to exploit his advantage.

29	Q×B(N6)	R-K1
30	P-K7	R×P
31	Q-Q8ch	R-K1
32	Q-Q6	P-K5
33	K-N1	P-K6
34	K-B1	B-N4ch!
35	K-K1	R-KB1!
36	Q×QPch	K-R1
37	K-Q1	P-R3
38	Q-QB5	P-K7ch
39	K-Q2	R-Q1ch
40	Resigns	

GAME 67

White: Zhuravlev
Black: Sakharov

USSR 1971

Notes by Zhuravlev

1	P-K4	P-QB4
2	P-QB3	P-K3
3	P-Q4	P-Q4
4	P-K5	

Such transpositions should be well known to every Sicilian player if he is not to be tricked into an unfamiliar set-up.

4	...	Q-N3
5	N-KB3	N-QB3
6	B-K2	P-B3

This is a deviation from the known main line 6...P×P 7 P×P KN-K2 8 N-R3 N-B4 and so on. The idea of the move in the text is quite clear: Black undermines White's centre by exerting pressure on it with his pieces. Naturally, White immediately opposes this plan.

7	O-O	B-Q2
8	N-R3	P×KP
9	P×KP	N-R3

286

10 R-K1

In one of Lutikov's games White allowed his opponent dangerous counterplay after 10 B×N P×B. Two bishops and the open KB and KN files proved to be good compensation for the weaknesses of the pawn formation.

| 10 | ... | N-B2 |
| 11 | B-B1 | |

11 B-Q3 was more active: there is no need to be afraid of losing a tempo after ...P-QB5.

| 11 | ... | B-K2 |
| 12 | P-R4!? | |

A very unusual reaction! Such a weakening looks advantageous for Black, especially in view of the impending castling on opposite sides. However, it is not obvious how to prevent the straightforward advance ...P-KN4-N5 by Black.

| 12 | ... | P-KR3 |

12...P-N3 followed by ...P-KR3 and then ...P-KN4 is more accurate.

13	P-R5	O-O-O
14	R-N1	QR-B1
15	P-QN4	

Forced bravado! Black is ready for action, starting with ...N-N4, with numerous threats, so White decides to open fire first at the cost of a pawn.

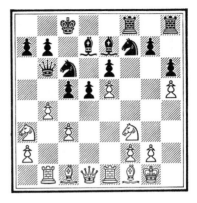

| 15 | ... | P×P |
| 16 | B-K3 | |

It would have been a mistake to play 16 P×P because of 16 ...N(B2)×KP!

| 16 | ... | Q-R4 |
| 17 | N-QN5 | P-R3 |

This allows White to create serious threats on the black squares. It seems that Black should have been satisfied with the variation 17...P×P 18 Q-N3 Q-N5! 19 N×Pch N×N 20 B×N Q×Q 21 R×Q with approximately equal chances.

| 18 | N-R7ch | N×N |

In view of the fact that after this exchange Black cannot take advantage of the position of the white bishop on QR2, 18...K-N1 looks safer.

| 19 | B×N | N-Q1 |

The best defensive chance. Not, of course, 19...P-QN3 if only because of 20 P×P B×P 21 R×B Q×R 22 B×RPch K-Q1 23 Q-Q3, with an irresistable attack.

| 20 | N-Q4! | Q×P? |

By playing 20...N-B3 21 N×N B×N 22 P×P B×P 23 R-K3 R-B5 24 R-KB3! R(R1)-B1 25 R×R R×R Black does not get out of his difficulties, but has a good chance of defending in practice. But now he can hardly save the game.

| 21 | R-K2 | Q-R5 |
| 22 | R-B2! | |

This is what the master from Rostov missed. Now the threat is 23 P×Pch B-QB3 24 R×Bch and so on.

22	...	P-N6
23	R×P	N-B3
24	Q-N1	N×B
25	R×P!	

Winning the queen by 25 R-R2 allows Black some chances of salvation after 25 ...Q×R 26 Q×Q N-B3!

25	...	N-B3
26	R×B	K×R
27	Q-N7ch	K-K1
28	N×N	Q-R6
29	B-Q3!	R-B4
30	B×R	P×B

| 31 | Q-B8ch | B-Q1 |
| 32 | P-K6 | |

Black lost on time. He can only aviod mate at the cost of a piece.

GAME 68

White: Zinn
Black: Hamann

Lugano Olympiad 1968

1	P-K4	P-K3
2	P-Q4	P-Q4
3	P-K5	P-QB4
4	P-QB3	N-QB3
5	N-B3	Q-N3
6	P-QR3	P-B5
7	QN-Q2	

7	...	B-Q2
8	B-K2	N-R4
9	O-O	N-K2
10	R-N1	

The attempt to seize the initiative

on the K-side with 10 N-N5 failed
after 10...P-KR3 11 N-R3 O-O-O 12
N-B4 P-N3 13 R-N1 K-N1. I. Zaitsev-
Petrosian, USSR Championship
1969.

10	...	O-O-O
11	P-QN4	P×P e.p.
12	B-N2	

Not 12 P-B4 B-R5 13 P-B5 Q-B2
14 B-N2 N(K2)-B3 15 R-K1 R-N1 16
B-Q3 P-KN4! and Black has a K-side
attack. Lebedev-Petrosian, USSR
1958.

| 12 | ... | P-KR3 |

A good prophylactic move preventing N-N5.

13	P-B4	B-R5
14	P-B5	Q-B2
15	R-B1	

More exact is 15 B-B3 N(K2)-B3
16 N-K1 P-QN3 17 N-Q3 with equal
chances.

| 15 | ... | K-N1 |

| 16 | R-B3 | N(K2)-B3 |
| 17 | Q-N1 | P-QN3! |

Not only opening up the QB-file,
but also releasing the power of the
KB.

18	P×P	Q×NP
19	B-Q1	K-R1
20	R-K1	B-K2
21	R(K1)-K3	R-QN1
22	P-R3	KR-QB1
23	N×P	N-B5!
24	R(K3)-Q3	N(B3)-R4

All Black's pieces are working
together at full power, and White has
no defence.

25	N×N	Q×N
26	B×B	Q×B
27	Q-QB1	R×B
28	Q×R	N×Q
29	R×Rch	K-N2
30	R(Q3)-B3	N-B5
31	R-KN8	P-N3
32	R-KR8	B×P
33	R×P	Q-Q8ch
34	K-R2	B-N7!
35	Resigns	

Chapter 13

The Exchange Variation

White: Seidman
Black: R. Byrne

USA 1962

1	P-K4	P-K3
2	P-Q4	P-Q4
3	P×P	

This exchange gives up the tension in the centre and usually leads to rapid equality. Because of this drawing tendency, the line of play has few adherents.

3	...	P×P

4	B-Q3

The usual move here. After 4 N-QB3 B-QN5 Black has transposed to a line of the Nimzovich (Winawer) Variation — see page 14.

4 ... N-QB3

More exact than 4...B-Q3 5 N-K2 (or 5 N-QB3 P-QB3 [perhaps 5...N-K2 is more exact] 6 P-KR3 N-K2 7 Q-R5 Q-N3 8 KN-K2 B-K3. Grob-Szabo, Hastings 1947/8, when White can introduce promising complications with 9 B-KB4) 5...N-K2 (After 5...Q-R5 6 QN-B3 P-QB3 7 B-K3 N-B3 8 Q-Q2 N-N5 9 P-KN3 Q-K2 [or 9...Q-R6 10 N-B4 B×N 11 B×B with advantage] 10 B-KB4 O-O 11 P-KR3, White is a little better.) 6 B-KB4 B-KB4 7 QN-B3 P-QB3, and this almost symmetrical position is equal.

5 P-QB3

After 5 N-K2 Black has 5...N-N5 6 O-O N×B 7 Q×N B-Q3 with equality.

5 ... B-Q3
6 N-K2

What can happen when White tries to play more sharply with 6 Q-B3 can be seen in Kovacs-Korchnoy, Sarajevo 1969 (illustrative game 69).

6 ... Q-R5
7 N-R3

Not 7 N-Q2 B-KN5 8 Q-B2 (or 8 Q-N3 O-O-O 9 Q×QP N-B3 followed by ...KR-K1 with a strong attack) 8...O-O-O 9 N-B1 P-KN3 10 B-K3 KN-K2 11 O-O-O B-KB4 12 N(B1)-N3 B×B 13 Q×B P-KR3 and Black has the edge. Winter-Alekhine, Nottingham 1936. White can, however, play 7 P-KN3 Q-R6 8 N-B4, or here 7...Q-R4 8 B-KB4 with equality.

7	...	P-QR3
8	Q-Q2	KN-K2
9	N-B2	B-KB4
10	B×B	N×B
11	Q-N5	Q×Q
12	B×Q	Drawn

GAME 69

White: Kovacs
Black: Korchnoy

Sarajevo 1969

1 P-K4	P-K3
2 P-Q4	P-Q4
3 P×P	P×P
4 B-Q3	N-QB3
5 P-QB3	B-Q3
6 Q-B3	

6 ...	QN-K2!?

Also possible is 6...B-K3 7 N-K2
Q-Q2 8 B-KB4 KN-K2 9 B×B Q×B
10 Q-N3 Q×Q 11 N×Q N-B1 with
equality.

7 B-KB4

Better is 7 N-K2 P-QB3 8 B-KB4
N-B3 9 B×B Q×B 10 Q-N3 with
equality. Damjanovic-Ivkov, Yugoslavia 1963.

7 ...	N-KB3

8 P-KR3

8 N-K2 is better.

8 ...	B×B
9 Q×B	O-O
10 N-K2	N-N3
11 Q-R2?	

It was essential to play 11 Q-B1.

11 ...	R-K1
12 O-O	B-B4!
13 B×B	

White misses his last chance of
survival by 13 N-B1. Black's rook
now penetrates to the seventh rank.

13 ...	R×N
14 P-QN3	Q-K2
15 B-Q3	R-N7
16 Q-N3	R-K1
17 Q-N5	N-K5
18 Q-B1	

Not 18 Q×P N×KBP.

18 ...	R×BP!

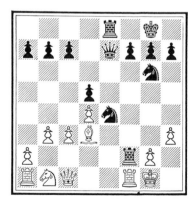

19	R×R	N×R
20	K×N	

If 20 B×N N×RPch 21 P×N BP×B
and White cannot prevent the entry
of Black's queen and rook into his
king's position. e.g. 22 N-Q2 Q-N4ch
23 K-B2 Q-R5ch winning; or 22 N-
R3 Q-Q3! 23 Q-N2 R-K6! 24 N-N5
R-N6ch 25 K-R2 Q-B5 26 R-KN1 R-
Q6ch winning.

20	...	Q-B3ch
21	K-N1	N-B5

22	B-B1	R-K7!!
23	N-Q2	N×RPch!
24	K-R2	N-B5!
25	K-N3	

If 25 N-B3 Q-KR3ch 26 K-N1
R×NPch! 27 B×R N-K7ch wins.

25	...	N-Q6
26	Resigns	

If 26 B×R Q-B5ch 27 K-R3 N-B7
mate.

Chapter 14

The King's Indian Attack

White: Savon
Black: Uhlmann

Skopje 1968

1	P-K4	P-K3
2	P-Q3	

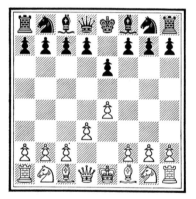

This move leads to a closed form of the Sicilian Defence or, more often, to the King's Indian Attack (sometimes called the Reversed King's Indian).

White's QP gives firm support to his outpost at K4. His plan is to increase his spatial control on the K-side and thereby to create serious threats on that flank. The idea is suggested by Black's very first move which does little to counter White's intentions. However, White's build-up is rather slow and Black might be able to develop counterplay on the opposite wing.

Tchigorin's move, **2 Q-K2,** can transpose to the King's Indian Attack (in which White's queen usually plays to K2) but by playing his moves in a different order Black can bypass the K.I.A. set-up and take a more aggressive stance. **2...P-QB4 3 P-Q3 N-QB3!** The point. White must prevent ...N-Q5 when Black gets a good form of the Closed Sicilian. **4 P-QB3 N-B3 5 P-KN3 P-Q4! 6 N-Q2 B-K2 7 P-KB4 O-O 8 B-N2 P-QN4!** with a good game for Black. Bellon-Uhlmann, Madrid 1973 (illustrative game 70).

2 ...   P-Q4

After 2...P-QB4 3 N-Q2 N-QB3 4 P-KN3 P-KN3 5 B-N2 B-N2 6 KN-B3 KN-K2 7 O-O O-O 8 P-B3 P-Q3 9 P-QR4 Q-B2 10 R-K1 B-Q2 the position is similar to one arising from the Sicilian Defence.

3 N-Q2   N-KB3
4 KN-B3

4 P-KN3 is sometimes played first. e.g.: **4..P×P** For 4..P-QN3!? see Sax-Larsen, Teesside 1972 (illustrative game 71). **5 P×P B-B4 6 B-N2 N-B3 7 KN-B3 P-K4! 8 Q-K2** Better is 8 O-O O-O 9 P-B3 P-QR4 10 Q-B2 B-K3 11 N-N5 B-Q2 with equality. Csom-Fuchs, Berlin 1968. **8...O-O 9 O-O P-QR4 10 P-QR4?!** 10 N-B4 Q-K2 11 P-B3 is better. **10...P-QN3 11 P-B3 B-R3 12 N-B4 Q-Q2** and Black stands better. Jansa-Hübner, Athens 1969.

4 ...   P-B4

The usual move, popularized by Uhlmann.

Also possible is **4...P-QN3 5 P-K5** Or 5 Q-K2 B-K2 6 P-KN3 P-B4 7 B-N2 N-B3 8 O-O O-O 9 P-K5 N-K1 10 R-K1 P-B4 11 P×P e.p. B×P with equality. Pachman-Schmid, Helsinki Olympiad 1952. **5...KN-Q2 6 P-KN3** Another possibility is 6 P-Q4 P-QB4 7 P-B3 P-B3 8 P×KBP Q×P 9 N-N3 B-N2 (9...B-Q3 seems more exact) 10 B-KN5 Q-B2 11 B-N5 B-B3 with even chances. Vasyukov-Bagirov, USSR Championship 1967. **6...P-QB4 7 B-N2 N-QB3 8 Q-K2 Q-B2 9 O-O B-K2** Not 9...N(Q2)×P 10 N×N Q×N 11 Q×Q N×Q 12 R-K1 N-Q2 13 B×P etc. **10 R-K1 B-R3 11 P-B3 P-KN4! 12 P-KR3 P-KR4 13 P-KN4 P×P 14 P×P O-O-O** and Black's attack is stronger than White's.

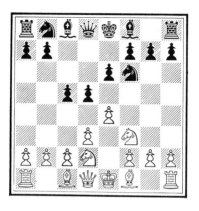

5	**P-KN3**	**N-B3**
6	**B-N2**	**B-K2**
7	**O-O**	**O-O**
8	**P-K5**	**N-Q2**
9	**R-K1**	**P-QN4**

Better than 9...Q-B2 where the queen is badly placed after White's intended Q-K2, N-B1, B-B4, N-K3 with the sacrifice N×QP in the air.

10	**N-B1**	**P-QR4**
11	**P-KR4**	**P-N5**
12	**B-B4**	

A frequently played alternative is 12 P-R5 e.g. 12...B-R3 13 P-R6 P-N3 14 N(B1)-R2 P-R5 15 B-B4 B-QN4 16 N-N4 N-Q5 with unclear play. Rubinetti-Uhlmann, Mar del Plata 1966.

12	**...**	**B-R3**

Nor 12...P-R5 13 P-R3 P×P 14 P×P B-R3 15 N-K3 N-Q5 16 P-B4 with a clear advantage for White. Gheorghiu-Uhlmann, Sofia 1967.

13 N-K3

For 13 N-N5!? see Browne-Uhlmann, Amsterdam 1973 (illustrative game 72).

| 13 | ... | **P-R5** |
| 14 | **P-B4** | |

This opening of lines on the Q-side only favours Black.

| 14 | ... | **P×P e.p.** |
| 15 | **P×P** | **P-Q5!** |

In order to put pressure on White's QP, Black makes the difficult decision of opening up the long diagonal for White's KB and giving him the use of his K4 square.

16	**P×P**	**P×P**
17	**N-B4**	**N-B4**
18	**N-N5**	**N-N5!**

The point of 15...P-Q5. If White now tries to attack the king by 19 Q-R5 P-R3 20 N-K4 he loses a piece after 20...N(B4)×P 21 B×P P-N3! 22 Q-N4 B×N.

| 19 | **B×R** | **Q×B** |
| 20 | **Q-R5** | **B(K2)×N** |

20...P-R3 was also possible.

| 21 | **B×B** | **N(N5)×QP** |
| 22 | **B-B6!** | |

White's only salvation lies in the following complications. Black now does best to capture the bishop, as 22...N×R 23 R×N N-K5 24 Q-N4! is risky for him.

22	...	**P×B**
23	**P×P**	**K-R1**
24	**N-Q6?**	

In this complex position White could draw by 24 R-K5!! N×R 25 N×N Q-K1 26 Q-R6 R-N1 27 Q-R5 R-B1 with a draw by repetition.

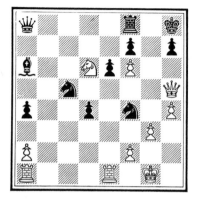

There is no defence.

25 N×Pch

After 25 P×N R-KN1ch wins the queen.

25	...	R×N
26	P×N	R×P
27	Q-K5	N-Q2
28	Q×QP	Q-KN1ch
29	K-R2	Q-N5
30	R-K3	

Or 30 Q×N Q×RPch 31 K-N2 Q-N5ch and 32...R-R3 mate.

| 30 | ... | P-K4! |
| 31 | Resigns | |

GAME 70

White: Bellon
Black: Uhlmann

Madrid 1973

1	**P-K4**	**P-K3**
2	**Q-K2**	**P-QB4**
3	**P-Q3**	**N-QB3**
4	**P-QB3**	**N-B3**
5	**P-KN3**	**P-Q4!**
6	**N-Q2**	**B-K2**
7	**P-KB4**	**0-0**
8	**B-N2**	**P-QN4**

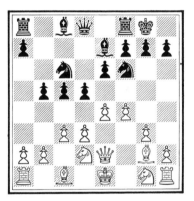

Rapid play on the Q-side is the correct strategy here.

9	**KN-B3**	**P-B5!**
10	**P-K5?**	

After this move White is already in serious difficulties. He had to play 10 P-Q4 N×KP 11 N×N P×N 12 Q×KP B-N2 with a comfortable game for Black. If 10 P×BP NP×P 11 P×P P×P

12 N-K5 N×N 13 P×N B-KN5 14 B-B3 (not 14 Q-K3 N-Q2 15 B×P B-QB4 16 Q-B4 N×P winning) 14 ...B×B 15 Q×B N-K1 with some advantage to Black.

10	...	**P×P**

This opens up the Q-side, providing good squares for Black's pieces.

11	**Q×P**	**N-Q2!**
12	**N-N3**	

White can hardly take the pawn as Black has a devastating attack after 12 Q×NP N-B4!! 13 Q-B1 (what else? 13 Q×N(6) B-Q2 wins the queen, or 13 P-QN4 R-N1 14 Q-B1 B-R3 etc.) 13 ...B-R3 14 Q-N1 N-Q6ch 15 K-Q1 B-B4 etc.

12	...	**P-N5**
13	**N(N3)-Q4**	**N-R4!**
14	**0-0**	**P×P**
15	**P-N3**	

Whatever White plays, he is in trouble. If 15 Q×BP B-R3 and if 15 P×P N-B4. Nor is 15 P-QN4 any good after 15...B×P 16 N-KN5 P-N3 17 N(N5)×KP P×N 18 N×P N-B4 and the attack is beaten off.

15	...	**N-B4**
16	**Q-B2**	

He had to capture the dangerous pawn, although Black's advantage is still great after 16 Q×BP N-K5 17 Q-N2 B-R3.

16	...	N-K5
17	N-KN5	N×N
18	P×N	B-R3
19	R-B4	R-B1
20	B-KR3	N-B3!

The simplest.

21 R-R4

The piece sacrifice 21 N×P fails to 21...Q-N3ch 22 K-R1 N-N5 with a winning endgame.

21	...	P-N3
22	N-B3	Q-N3ch
23	K-R1	N-N5
24	Q-KN2	N-Q6
25	R-Q4	N×P
26	B-K3	B-B4
27	N×N	B×R
28	N-Q7	B×B!

The final point.

29	N×Q	P×N
30	Q-B3	P-Q5
31	Q-KB6	

and **White Resigned** as the pawns cannot be stopped.

GAME 71

White: Sax
Black: Larsen

Teesside 1972

1	P-K4	P-K3
2	P-Q3	P-Q4
3	N-Q2	N-KB3
4	P-KN3	P-QN3!?

5	B-N2	B-N2
6	P-K5	

After 6 KN-B3 P×P 7 N-N5 QN-Q2 (or 7...N-B3) 8 N(N5)×P(K4) N×N 9 N×N N-B4 the game is equal. Browne-Rajkovic, Hastings 1972/3.

6	...	N-N1!?

An original manoeuvre, but the obvious 6...KN-Q2 7 P-KB4 P-QB4 is probably better.

7	KN-B3	N-K2
8	O-O	

8 P-KR4 is worthy of consideration.

8	...	P-QB4
9	R-K1	QN-B3
10	P-B3	N-B4

11	P-QR3	B-K2
12	N-B1	

If 12 P-QN4 then 12...P-Q5 is strong.

12	...	P-KR3

Black must be careful e.g. 12...Q-Q2 13 P-KN4 N-R5 14 N×N B×N 15 P-N5 and Black's KB has difficulty getting back into the game.

13	N-K3	N×N
14	B×N	Q-Q2
15	P-Q4	P-B5
16	N-Q2	N-R4
17	P-B4	P-R4
18	P-B5?!	

This pawn sacrifice is over-optimistic.

18	...	P×P
19	N-B3	N-B3!
20	P-N3	P×P
21	P-B4?!	

The philosophy of "attack at all costs" is not always justified. Black can pick up the offered pawns, then later sacrifice a piece in comfort, letting his pawn mass do the rest.

21	...	P×P
22	P-Q5	O-O-O!
23	P×N	Q×P
24	Q-K2	R-Q6!
25	N-R4	

The threat was 25...R×B 26 Q×R B-B4 winning the queen.

25	...	Q-K3
26	B×Bch	K×B
27	Q-B3ch	K-R3!
28	N×P	B-B4
29	Q-K4	P-N3
30	N-N7	

If 30 N-Q4 Q-N5!

30	...	R×B
31	R×R	Q-N5
32	K-N2	R-Q1!?

The simplest is 32...Q×Q 33 R×Q P-B6.

33	P-K6	R-Q7ch
34	K-R1	Q×Qch
35	R×Q	P-B6!
36	P×P	

If 36 P-K7 B×KP 37 R×B P-B7 wins.

36	...	P-N7
37	R-KB1	P-B7
38	R(K4)-K1	R-B7!!
39	N-K6	

A pretty mate occurs after 39 R×R P-N8=Q 40 R(B2)-B1 P-B8=Q 41 R×Q Q-K5ch.

39	...	R×Rch
40	R×R	B×P
41	Resigns	

GAME 72

White: Browne
Black: Uhlmann

Amsterdam 1973

1	P-K4	P-K3
2	P-Q3	P-Q4
3	N-Q2	N-KB3
4	KN-B3	P-B4
5	P-KN3	N-B3
6	B-N2	B-K2
7	O-O	O-O
8	P-K5	N-Q2
9	R-K1	P-QN4
10	N-B1	P-QR4
11	P-KR4	P-N5
12	B-B4	B-R3

13   N-N5!?

This move was played for the first time in the game Bronstein-Uhlmann, Moscow 1971, when White won easily after 13...Q-K1 14 Q-N4 P-R5?? 15 N×KP.

13	...	Q-K1
14	Q-R5	B×N!
15	Q×B	

If 15 P×B P-B4 with good play for Black.

15	...	P-R5
16	N-K3	K-R1
17	QR-Q1	P-R3
18	Q-R5	P-B4!
19	Q×Q	QR×Q
20	N-B4	

This tactical method of solving the weakness of the KP fails to a counter-combination.

20	...	N-Q5!
21	N-Q6	N×BP!
22	N×R	R×N!

This exchange sacrifice cripples White's position, whereas 22...N×R 23 N-B7 N×B 24 K×N B-N2 gives unclear play.

23	R-K2	P-N6!

By guarding the knight Black restricts the activity of the white rooks.

24	P×P	P×P
25	R(K2)-Q2	B-N4
26	R-QB1	R-R1
27	B-B3	R-R7
28	B-Q1	B-R5!
29	R-N1	

If White gives back the exchange

302

by 29 B×N P×B 30 R(B1)×P B×R 31 R×B then 31 ... K-N1! gives Black an advantage.

29	...	K-N1
30	P-N4	P×P
31	B×NP	K-B2
32	K-N2	B-N4!
33	B-N3	

33 B-Q1 fails to 33 ... B×P 34 R×B N-K8ch.

33	...	N-N3
34	B-Q1	B×P!
35	R×B	N-K8ch
36	K-B1	N×R
37	B×P	R×P
38	R×R	N×R
39	K-K2	P-B5
40	B-B2	P-Q5
41	B-K4	P-Q6ch
42	K-Q2	N(N3)-R5
43	K-K3	N-B4!
44	B-B3	N-N6
45	Resigns	

Index to Variations

Part Two — Other Systems with 3 N-QB3
1 P-K4 P-K3 2 P-Q4 P-Q4 3 N-QB3 (135-185)

The Classical Variation: Chapter 5 (136-144)

3 N-QB3 N-KB3 4 B-KN5 (4 P-K5, 137) **4...B-K2 5 P-K5** (5 B×N, 137) **5...KN-Q2** (5...N-K5, 138; 5...N-N1, 139) **6 B×B Q×Q 7 P-B4!** (7 Q-Q2, 141; 7 N-N5, 141; 7 B-Q3, 141; 7 N-B3, 141; 7 Q-N4, 141) **7...O-O** (7...P-QB4, 141; 7...P-QR3, 141) **8 N-B3 P-QB4 9 P×P** The main continuation, 141-144. (9 B-Q3, 141)

The Albin/Chatard/Alekhine Attack: Chapter 6 (145-152)

3 N-QB3 N-KB3 4 B-KN5 B-K2 5 P-K5 KN-Q2 6 P-KR4 P-QB4 (6...P-QR3, 146; 6...P-B3, 146; 6...P-KR3, 146; 6...B×B, 146) **7 B×B** (7 Q-N4, 147; 7 N-N5, 147) **7...K×B** The main continuation, 148-150. (7...Q×B, 148)

The MacCutcheon Variation: Chapter 7 (153-160)

3 N-QB3 N-KB3 4 B-KN5 B-N5 5 P-K5 (5 P×P, 154) **5...P-KR3 6 B-Q2!** (6 P×N, 154; 6 B×N, 154; 6 B-K3, 154; 6 B-R4, 154) **6...B×N 7 P×B** (7 B×B, 154) **7...N-K5 8 Q-N4! P-KN3** (8...K-B1, 155) **9 B-Q3** The main continuation, 156-159. (9 B-B1, 156)

The Rubinstein and Burn Variations: Chapter 8 (161-185)

3 N-QB3 P×P (3...N-QB3, 161; 3...N-KB3 4 B-KN5 P×P, 161) **4 N×P N-Q2** (4...N-KB3, 163; 4...B-Q2, 163; 4...B-K2, 163) **5 N-KB3** (5 P-KN3, 163) **5...KN-B3 6 B-KN5** The main continuation, 163-167. (6 N×Nch, 163)

Part Three — The Tarrasch Variation
1 P-K4 P-K3 2 P-Q4 P-Q4 3 N-Q2 (186-276)

3...N-KB3: Chapter 9 (187-218)

3...N-KB3 4 P-K5 KN-Q2 5 B-Q3 (5 P-KB4, 188) **5...P-QB4** (5...P-QN3, 192) **6 P-QB3** (6 KN-B3, 192) **6...N-QB3** (6...P-QN3, 192) **7 N-K2** (7 KN-B3, 193) **7...Q-N3** (7...P-B3, 194; 7...P×P, 194) **8 N-B3 P×P 9 P×P P-B3!** (9...Q-N5ch, 197; 9...B-N5ch, 197) **10 P×P** (10 N-B4, 198) **10...N×BP 11 O-O B-Q3** (11...B-Q2, 198) **12 N-B3** The main continuation, 199-202. (12 N-N3, 199; 12 P-QR3, 199; 12 P-QN3, 199; 12 R-N1, 199; 12 B-Q2, 199; 12 Q-Q2?!, 199; 12 B-KB4, 199; 12 N-B4, 200)

3...N-QB3: Chapter 10 (219-228)

3...N-QB3 4 KN-B3 N-B3 5 P-K5 N-Q2 (5...N-K5, 220) **6 N-N3!** (6 P-KN3, 220; 6 P-QN3, 220; 6 P-B4, 220; 6 B-N5, 220; 6 B-K2, 220; 6 P-B3, 220) **6...B-K2** The main continuation, 221-223. (6...P-B3, 221)

3...P-QB4: Chapter 11 (229-276)

3...P-QB4 4 P×QP (4 P×BP, 230; 4 KN-B3, 230) **4...KP×P** (4...Q×P, 232) **5 KN-B3** (5 B-N5ch, 234) **5...N-QB3** (5...N-KB3, 237; 5...P-QR3, 237; 5...P-B5, 238) **6 B-N5**(6 P×P, 238) **6...B-Q3** (6...P-B5, 238; 6...P-QR3, 239; 6...Q-K2ch, 239) **7 P×P** (7 O-O, 239) **7...B×BP** (7...Q-K2ch, 240) **8 O-O KN-K2 9 N-N3** (9 P-B4, 240) **9...B-Q3!** (9...B-N3, 240) **10 N(N3)-Q4** (10 B-N5, 242; 10 N(B3)-Q4, 246; 10 B×Nch, 246; 10 B-K3, 246; 10 B-Q2, 246; 10 P-B3 will transpose to the main line) **10...O-O 11 P-B3** (11 B-K3, 247; 11 B-N5, 248; 11 P-KR3, 248; 11 B-Q3, 249; 11 P-QN3, 249) **11...B-KN5** (11...Q-Q2, 250) **12 Q-R4** (12 B-K2, 250) **12...B-R4 13 R-K1** The main continuation, 250-254. (13 B×N, 250; 13 B-K3, 251; 13 B-Q3, 251)

Part Four — Miscellaneous Systems
The Advance Variation (278-289)
The Exchange Variation (290-293)
The King's Indian Attack (294-303)

The Advance Variation: Chapter 12 (278-289)

3 P-K5 P-QB4 (3...P-KB3, 279; 3...P-QN3, 279) **4 P-QB3** (4 Q-N4, 279; 4 N-KB3, 279; 4 P×P, 279) **4...N-QB3** (4...Q-N3, 279) **5 N-B3 Q-N3** (5...KN-K2, 280) **6 P-QR3** (6 B-Q3, 280; 6 B-K2, 281) **6...P-B5** (6...B-Q2, 281; 6...P-QR4, 282) **7 P-KN3** The main continuation, 282-284. (7 QN-Q2, 282)

The Exchange Variation: Chapter 13 (290-293)

3 P×P P×P 4 B-Q3 (4 N-QB3, 291) **4...N-QB3** (4...B-Q3, 291) **5 P-QB3** The main continuation, 291. (5 N-K2, 291)

The King's Indian Attack: Chapter 14 (294-303)

2 P-Q3 (2 Q-K2, 295) **2...P-Q4** (2...P-QB4, 295) **3 N-Q2 N-KB3 4 KN-B3** (4 P-KN3, 295) **4...P-B4** The main continuation, 295-298. (4...P-QN3, 295)

Index to Complete Games

This index includes all annotated, illustrative games as well as the main game of each chapter, but unannotated games given in full in the text have been omitted. The numbers refer to pages and where a number is given in **bold type** the first named player had the white pieces. Where no annotator is named in the heading to a game, the notes to that game are by Gligoric and/or Uhlmann.

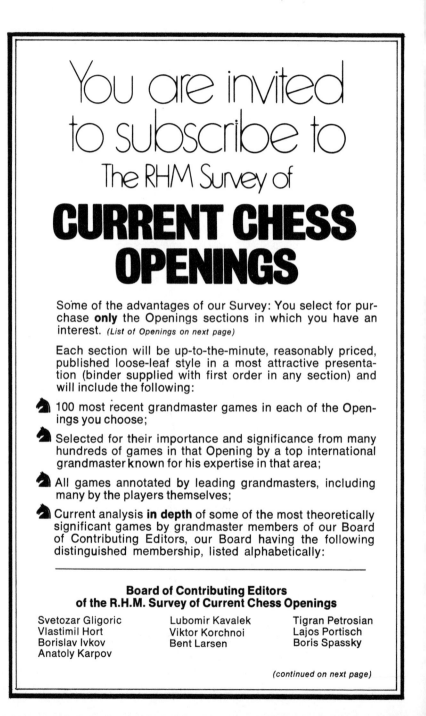

List of Openings

(Covering all Important Variations in each Opening)

Sicilian	Pirc	Dutch
King's Indian	Alekhine	Larsen's
Grünfeld	Ruy Lopez	Queen's Gambit
Nimzo-Indian	Benoni	King's Gambit
English	French	Queen's Indian
Reti	Caro-Kann	Benko Gambit
	(additions will be made)	

All "Chess Opening" theory is in a perpetual stage of change, some lines being successfully challenged and discarded, other lines improved, new and promising lines being continually discovered as thousands of games are played in current grandmaster tournaments.

Not only can your own game in your favorite Openings be greatly improved by study of the 100 current games in the Openings section selected by you, but you will gain new and valuable insights into the middle game play and end game play flowing naturally from each line through the individual game annotation and analysis-in-depth by the many world-famed grandmasters who will be serving on our Board of Contributing Editors.

The average cost of each full-size section containing all we have just described should be modest, but **send no money**— only your name and address on a postcard—so that you will be entered as a subscriber to receive announcements and full descriptions of each Openings section as they become ready for shipment. There is no charge for entering this subscription, and it puts you under no obligation. You later order only what you wish to order.

But you can help us (and yourself) by listing on the postcard the **5 top choices of Openings** you would like to see covered. This informal "straw poll" will guide us in the order of publication of individual Openings sections.

We are now preparing publication of sections covering some of the most popular Openings and commencing work on all the rest, and to receive announcements of each section as it becomes available, merely send your full name and address on a postcard to:

Dept. 13

R.H.M. SURVEY OF CURRENT CHESS OPENINGS

840 Willis Avenue, Albertson, New York 11507

In Europe write to R•H•M PRESS LTD. • P.O. Box 55 London N13, England 5BE

8 of the 10
Top-Rated Chess Grandmasters in the world are on the Board of Contributing Editors of the Chess division of R·H·M Press

including the
new world champion,
Anatoly Karpov
and two previous
world chess champions,
Boris Spassky and Tigran Petrosian.